Rule of Law Reform and Development

Rule of Law Reform and Development

Charting the Fragile Path of Progress

Michael J. Trebilcock

Professor of Law and Economics, Faculty of Law, University of Toronto, Canada

and

Ronald J. Daniels

Provost, University of Pennsylvania, USA

Edward Elgar
Cheltenham, UK • Northampton, MA, USA

Published by
Edward Elgar Publishing Limited
Glensanda House
Montpellier Parade
Cheltenham
Glos GL50 1UA
UK

Edward Elgar Publishing, Inc.
William Pratt House
9 Dewey Court
Northampton
Massachusetts 01060
USA

A catalogue record for this book
is available from the British Library

Library of Congress Control Number: 2008927702

ISBN 978 1 84720 754 8 (cased)

Typeset by Manton Typesetters, Louth, Lincolnshire, UK
Printed and bound in Great Britain by MPG Books Ltd, Bodmin, Cornwall

Contents

List of tables   vii
List of research assistants   viii

1 The relationship of the rule of law to development   1
   I.   The rule of law and development   1
   II.   Defining the rule of law   12
   III.   The elements of a procedural definition of the rule of law   29
   IV.   Impediments to rule of law reform   37

2 The judiciary   58
   I.   Normative benchmarks   58
   II.   Experience with judicial reforms   66
   III.   Conclusion   104

3 Police   107
   I.   Normative benchmarks   107
   II.   Experience with police reforms in developing countries   119
   III.   Conclusion   143

4 Prosecution   145
   I.   Normative benchmarks   145
   II.   Experience with prosecutorial reforms   156
   III.   Conclusion   169

5 Correctional institutions   170
   I.   Normative benchmarks   170
   II.   Experience with corrections reform   175
   III.   Conclusion   196

6 Tax administration   200
   I.   Normative benchmarks   200
   II.   Experience with tax administration reforms   215
   III.   Conclusion   234

7 Access to justice   236
   I.   Normative framework   236

   II.   Experience with access to justice reforms in developing
         countries   252
   III. Conclusion   276

8 Legal education   279
   I.   Normative benchmarks   279
   II.   Experience with legal education reforms in developing
         countries   289
   III. Conclusion   304

9 Professional regulation   307
   I.   Normative benchmarks   307
   II.   Experience with professional regulation reforms in
         developing countries   318
   III. Conclusion   330

10 Rethinking rule of law reform strategies   332
   I.   Introduction   332
   II.   Review of empirical evidence   333
   III. Stylized political formations   339
   IV.   Options for the international community   341
   V.   Reform strategies in political context   352

Index   357

Tables

1A.1   World Bank: rule of law indicators for selected countries, 1996
       and 2002   42
1A.2   Freedom House: freedom ratings, 2004   48
1A.3   Transparency International: corruption perceptions index, 2004   53

List of research assistants

Elizabeth Acorn
Nicholas Daube
Tracey Epps
Salman Haq
Sarah Horan
Marina Mandal
Graham Mayeda
Thomas Ringer
Josh Rosensweig
Emma Ruby-Sachs
Adam Samarillo
Vasuda Sinha
Matthew Sudak

1. The relationship of the rule of law to development

I. THE RULE OF LAW AND DEVELOPMENT

According to Thomas Carothers,

> One cannot get through a foreign policy debate these days without someone proposing the rule of law as a solution to the world's troubles. The concept is suddenly everywhere – a venerable part of western political philosophy enjoying a new run as a rising imperative of the era of globalization. Unquestionably, it is important to life in peaceful, free, and prosperous societies. Yet its sudden elevation as a panacea for the ills of countries in transition from dictatorships or statist economies should make both patients and prescribers wary. The rule of law promises to move countries past the first, relatively easy phase of political and economic liberalization to a deeper level of reform. But that promise is proving difficult to fulfill.[1]

In a similar vein, Yves Dezalay and Bryant Garth claim that "the rule of law has become a new rallying cry for global missionaries. Money doctors selling competing economic expertises continue to be very active on the global plain but the 1990s also witnessed a tremendous growth in rule doctors armed with their own competing prescriptions for legal reforms and new legal institutions at the national and transnational level … So far the rule of law industry cannot claim too many successes in the latest campaign."[2]

According to Brian Tamanaha,

Brian Tamanaha

> For all but the most sanguine observers, the triumphalist confidence of the 1990s has dissolved … Amidst this host of new uncertainties there appears to be widespread agreement, traversing all fault lines, on one point, and one point only: that the "rule of law" is good for everyone … This apparent unanimity in support of the rule of law is a feat unparalleled in history. No other single political ideal has ever achieved global endorsement … Notwithstanding its quick and remarkable ascendance as a global ideal, however, the rule of law is an exceedingly elusive notion …

---

[1]   Thomas Carothers, "The Rule of Law Revival" (1998) 77 *Foreign Affairs* 95.

[2]   Yves Dezalay and Bryant Garth (eds), *Global Prescriptions: The Production, Exportation and Importation of a New Legal Orthodoxy* (Ann Arbor, MI: University of Michigan Press, 2002) Introduction.

If it is not already firmly in place, the rule of law appears mysteriously difficult to establish.[3]

Reflecting this new orthodoxy, in the 1990s there was a massive surge in development assistance for law reform projects in developing and transition economies involving investments of many billions of dollars. The World Bank alone reports that it has supported 330 "rule of law" projects and spent \$2.9 billion on this sector since 1990.[4]

This book addresses a number of key issues regarding the relationship between the rule of law and development. First, whom do we include in our universe of developing countries? The World Bank classifies countries as low income, lower-middle income, upper-middle income, and high income countries by reference to per capital gross national income. More than 100 countries with populations in excess of 30,000 fall into the first three categories. Other classifications are obviously possible. For example, beginning in 1990 the United Nations Development Program (UNDP) has published an annual Human Development Index (HDI) that classifies countries according to their level of human development, which includes variables relating to per capita income, health, and educational status, and in many cases yields significantly different ratings or rankings than classification systems that focus exclusively on per capita gross national income.[5]

Todaro and Smith, in a widely respected economic development treatise (now in its ninth edition),[6] rightly caution against over-generalizations in assuming a common set of characteristics of developing countries, noting that developing countries exhibit marked diversity along at least the following dimensions:

1. the size of the country (geographic area, population, and national income)
2. its historical and colonial background
3. its endowment of physical and human resources
4. its ethnic and religious composition
5. the relative importance of its public and private sectors (and informal sectors)

---

[3]   Brian Z. Tamanaha, *On the Rule of Law: History, Politics, Theory* (Cambridge and New York: Cambridge University Press, 2004) at 1, 3, 4.

[4]   See David Trubek, "The Rule of Law in Development Assistance: Past, Present and Future," in David Trubek and Alvaro Santos (eds), *The New Law and Economic Development: A Critical Appraisal* (Cambridge and New York: Cambridge University Press, 2006) at 74.

[5]   See Michael Todaro and Stephen Smith, *Economic Development* (Boston, MA and Toronto: Addison Wesley, 9th edn, 2006) at 57–63.

[6]   *Op. cit.* at 37–46.

6. the nature of its industrial structure
7. its degree of dependence on external economic and political forces
8. the distribution of power in the institutional and political structure within the nation.

While recognizing the importance of this caveat against over-generalization, again drawing principally on Todaro and Smith,[7] certain characteristics are common to many developing countries. First, for many developing countries, very low income levels and high levels of absolute poverty are often common. Over 80% of the world's total income is produced in the economically developed countries by about 15% of the world's people. The collective per capita incomes of the low and middle-income countries average less than one-twentieth of per capita incomes of rich nations. The average income in the richest 20 countries is 37 times the average of the poorest 20 – a gap that has doubled in the past 40 years.[8] Of the world's 6 billion people, 2.8 billion – almost half – live on less than two dollars a day, and 1.2 billion – a fifth – live on less than one dollar a day. While the proportion of the population in developing countries living in absolute poverty has declined significantly in recent years, population growth has meant that the estimated number of absolutely poor people has remained largely unchanged. With respect to health, life expectancy for the least developed countries at the end of the 1990s, despite improvements, still averages only 48 years compared to 63 years in other developing countries, and 75 years in developed countries. Infant mortality rates (the number of children who die before their first birthday out of 1,000 live births) average about 96 in the least developed countries, compared to approximately 64 in other developing countries, and eight in developed countries. Specific health problems have also had a dramatically disproportionate impact on developing countries. For example, with respect to HIV/AIDS, of the 36 million who have contracted HIV/AIDS, 90% live in developing countries, almost 20 million in sub-Saharan Africa. With respect to education, among the least developed countries, literacy rates average only 45% of the population compared to 64% in other developing countries and 99% in developed countries. The vast majority of people in most developing countries live and work in rural areas. Sixty-two percent of the labour force in developing countries is engaged in agriculture compared to only 7% in developed countries. While since 1972 the number of (nominal) democracies in the world has increased from about 40 to over 100, a number of these are fragile, shallow or corrupt: Carothers

---

[7] Todaro and Smith, *op. cit.*, 46–57.
[8] See World Bank, *Attacking Poverty*, World Development Report 2001, at p. 3.

judges that fewer than 20 of these countries are clearly en route to becoming successful, well-functioning democracies.[9]

These highly selective statistics are sufficient to provide a sense of the challenges facing individuals, communities, public and private sector institutions (for profit and non-profit), and the international community in mitigating the devastating economic and social consequences of these disparities in human well-being.

Second, what do we mean by "development"? In the early post-war decades, international economic institutions such as the World Bank and the International Monetary Fund, and many bilateral aid agencies, tended to focus exclusively or predominantly on economic measures of development such as GDP per capita and growth thereof. These measures of development have attracted increasing criticism from many quarters. For example, Amartya Sen, in his book, *Development as Freedom*,[10] argues that a full conception of development embraces a wide range of dimensions of human well-being that bear on the capabilities of individuals to live lives they have reason to value, including (1) political freedoms; (2) economic facilities; (3) social opportunities; (4) transparency guarantees; and (5) protective security. The United Nations Human Development Index, noted above, has attempted to address some of these criticisms by developing an index that includes not only economic measures of development but measures of health and educational status. More recently (1999), the former President of the World Bank, James Wolfensohn, proposed a Comprehensive Development Framework that incorporated a wide range of economic and social indicators of human well-being.

Third, what is the role of the rule of law in development? As we elaborate in the next section of this chapter, the claim that the robustness of a country's commitment to the rule of law is an important determinant of its development trajectory rests upon both instrumental foundations and on intrinsic or deontological foundations.[11] The instrumental perspective is strongly represented in the writings and research of economists associated with the school of so-called New Institutional Economics, which emphasizes that the protection of private property rights and the facilitation and enforcement of long-term contracts are essential to raising levels of investment and rates of economic growth.[12] In the end, this is an empirical claim, which is not uncontentious, with skeptics point-

---

[9]   Thomas Carothers, "The End of the Transition Paradigm," (2002) 13 *Journal of Democracy* 5–21.

[10]   Amartya Sen, *Development as Freedom* (New York: Knopf, 1999).

[11]   See Alvaro Santos, "The World Bank's Uses of the 'Rule of Law' Promise in Economic Development," in Trubek and Santos (eds), *op. cit.* at 256–66.

[12]   See e.g. Douglass North, *Institutions, Institutional Change and Economic Performance* (Cambridge University Press, 1992); Kenneth Dam, *The Law-Growth Nexus:*

ing to the economic success of China and other high-performing Asian economies with weak rule of law traditions.[13] However, it needs to be added that protection of private property and contractual and tortious rights can also be supported on deontological, e.g., corrective justice, grounds.[14] From a deontological perspective, such as that adopted by Sen, where freedom, in its various dimensions, is both the end and means of development, various freedoms, such as freedom from torture and other abuses of civil liberties by tyrannical rulers, freedom of expression, freedom of political association, freedom of political opposition and dissent, are defining normative characteristics of development; the rule of law, to the extent that it guarantees these freedoms, has an intrinsic value, independent of its effect on various other measures of development and does not need to be justified solely in instrumental terms, although a commitment to protecting these freedoms may also coincidentally serve important instrumental functions.[15]

Just as the normative conception of development has evolved from narrow economic measures of development to embrace a wide range of economic and social indicators of human well-being, a parallel process of evolution has occurred in many development circles as to effective development strategies and the role of institutions, both domestic and international, in the formulation and effectuation of these strategies.[16] Early post-war development strategies emphasized the importance of the capital investment process in promoting development and often assumed a catalytic role for the state in developing countries in facilitating or even undertaking in many circumstances the capital investment function. As Pranah Bardhan remarks, in these theories of development "the state was often left floating in a behavioural and institutional

---

The Rule of Law and Economic Development (Boston: Brookings Institution Press, 2006).

[13] See e.g. Tom Ginsburg, "Does Law Matter for Economic Development? Evidence from East Asia" (2000) 34 *Law and Society Review* 829; Graham Mayeda, "Appreciate the Difference: Different Domestic Norms in Law and Development Reform: Lessons from China and Japan" (2006) 51 *McGill Law Journal* 547; Randall Peerenboom (ed.), *Asian Discourses of Rule of Law* (London: Routledge, 2004); Michael Trebilcock and Jing Leng, "The Role of Formal Contract Law and Enforcement in Economic Development" (2006) *Virginia Law Review* 1517.

[14] See Ernest Weinrib, "The Intelligibility of the Rule of Law," in Allan Hutchinson and Patrick Monahan (eds), *The Rule of Law: Ideal or Ideology* (Toronto: Carswell, 1986).

[15] See Amartya Sen, "What is the Role of Legal and Judicial Reform in the World Development Process?," World Bank Legal Conference, Washington, DC, June 5, 2000.

[16] Todaro and Smith, *op. cit.*, chap. 4; William Easterly, *The Elusive Quest for Growth: Economists' Adventures and Misadventures in the Tropics* (Cambridge, MA: MIT Press, 2001).

vacuum."[17] A sharply divergent perspective on development strategies was adopted in some developing countries in response to the disappointments and failures of immediate post-war development strategies, loosely grouped under the rubric of dependency theories, which assigned an even more prominent, indeed even more heroic, role to the state than did early development theories, and in many cases adopted socialist forms of central planning, a heavy reliance on state ownership and state regulation of the economy, and relative insulation from the international economy through import substitution policies and extensive restrictions on foreign investment. Partly in reaction to the disappointments or failures of state-led growth development strategies, in the 1980s official development circles embraced a much more limited role for the state, reflecting economic liberalization policies then enjoying wide currency in many developed countries. On this perspective, the state, in many developing countries, was not the solution to the challenges of development, but in many respects the problem. Hence, an emphasis on prudent macroeconomic policies, domestic deregulation, and international economic liberalization with respect to trade and foreign investment policies (the so-called Washington Consensus).

Beginning in the early 1990s, the focus on development strategies has shifted, in important respects, to issues of domestic governance. Implicitly rejecting both the expansive role for the state in development propounded by early development theorists and the minimalist role for the state in development espoused by many proponents of the so-called Washington Consensus, proponents of the relationship between governance and development accept that in developing countries (as in developed countries) even on a limited view of the role of the state, the state is indispensable in formulating and implementing a wide range of economic and social policies that bear on human well-being, and that failures of governance in many developing countries are an important explanation for many of the characteristics of low levels of development cited above.[18]

The overall tenor of this perspective can be captured by examining one particularly influential study entitled, "Governance Matters." This study was undertaken by Kaufmann, Kraay, and Zoido-Lobatón, all of whom are affiliated with the World Bank, as part of the World Bank's ongoing research on governance, which has been updated on a regular basis.[19] The World Bank's Governance

---

[17]   Pranah Bardhan, "Introduction to the Symposium Issue of the State and Economic Development" (1990) 4 *Journal of Economic Perspectives* 3.

[18]   For historical perspectives on the role of the state in development, see contributions by David Trubek and David Kennedy in David Trubek and Alvaro Santos (eds), *op. cit.*

[19]   Daniel Kaufmann, Aart Kraay, and Pablo Zoido-Lobatón, "Governance Matters" (1999) *World Bank Policy Research Working Papers No. 2196* (available for download

project involves compiling a large number of subjective measures of institutional quality – meaning data obtained from either polls of country experts or surveys of residents – and grouping them into six clusters: "voice and accountability," "political stability," "government effectiveness," "regulatory quality," "rule of law," and "control of corruption." They describe these clusters as follows:

Gov. Matters

- *Voice and accountability*: Measures the extent to which citizens of a country are able to participate in the selection of governments and combines indicators measuring "various aspects of the political process, civil liberties, political rights" and "the independence of the media."
- *Political stability*: Measures "perceptions of the likelihood that the government in power will be destabilized or overthrown by possibly unconstitutional and/or violent means."
- *Government effectiveness*: Measures the inputs required for the government to be able to produce and implement good policies. Combines "perceptions of the quality of public service provision, the quality of the bureaucracy, the competence of civil servants, the independence of the civil service from political pressures, and the credibility of the government's commitment to policies."
- *Regulatory quality*: Includes "measures of the incidence of market-unfriendly policies such as price controls or inadequate bank supervision as well as perceptions of the burdens imposed by excessive regulation in areas such as foreign trade and business development."
- *Rule of law*: Includes measures of "the extent to which agents have confidence in and abide by the rules of society. These include perceptions of the incidence of both violent and non-violent crime, the effectiveness and predictability of the judiciary, and the enforceability of contracts."
- *Control of corruption*: Measures perceptions of corruption, ranging from the frequency of "additional payments to get things done" to the effects of corruption on the business environment. Corruption is defined as "the exercise of public power for private gain."

The authors of "Governance Matters" created indexes that measure institutional quality along each of these six dimensions as well as a composite

on http://www.worldbank.org/research); "Rethinking Governance: Empirical Lessons Challenge Orthodoxy," World Bank, Discussion Draft, March 11, 2002, see also Kaufmann, Kraay, and Massimo Mastruzzi, "Governance Matters IV: Governance Indicators for 1996–2004" (World Bank, May 2005); "Governance Redux: The Empirical Challenge," in Xavier Sala-i-Martin et al. (eds) *The Global Competitiveness Report 2003–2004, World Economic Forum & Harvard University* (New York: Oxford University Press, 2004); "Governance Indicators for 1996–2006" (World Bank, May 2007).

"governance" index designed to measure the overall quality of governance in a society. They then regressed these three measures of development: per capita GDP, infant mortality and adult literacy on these indices. They found strong correlations and indeed causation between each of their sub-indices of institutional quality, including the rule of law index, as well as a composite governance index, and their measures of development; hence their conclusion that "Governance Matters." In a more recent iteration of this work, Kaufmann reports:

> The effects of improved governance on income in the long run are found to be very large, with an estimated 400 percent improvement in per capita income associated with an improvement in governance by one standard deviation, and similar improvements in reducing child mortality and illiteracy. To illustrate, an improvement in rule of law by one standard deviation from the current levels in Ukraine to those "middling" levels prevailing in South Africa would lead to a fourfold increase in per capita income in the long run. A larger increase in the quality of the rule of law (by two standard deviations) in Ukraine (or in other countries in the former Soviet Union), to the much higher level in Slovenia or Spain, would further multiply this income per capita increase. Similar results emerge from other governance dimensions: a mere one standard deviation improvement in voice and accountability from the low level of Venezuela to that of South Korea, or in control of corruption from the low level of Indonesia to the middling level of Mexico, or from the level of Mexico to that of Costa Rica, would also be associated with an estimated fourfold increase in per capita incomes, as well as similar improvements in reducing child mortality by 75 percent and major gains in literacy.[20]

Drawing on the Kaufmann *et al.* data, Rodrik, Subramanian and Trebbi, in a recent paper, "Institutions Rule: The Primacy of Institutions over Geography and Integration in Economic Development,"[21] estimate the respective contributions of institutions, geography, and international trade in determining income levels around the world. The authors find that the quality of institutions "trumps" everything else. Once institutions are controlled for, conventional measures of geography have at best weak direct effects on income, although they have a strong indirect effect by influencing the quality of institutions. Similarly, once institutions are controlled for, trade is almost always insignificant except for indirect effects on institutions. In their study, the authors use a number of elements that capture the protection afforded to property rights as well as the strength of the rule of law. To convey a flavour of the striking nature of their

---

[20]   Daniel Kaufmann, "Governance Redux: The Empirical Challenge" (Washington DC: World Bank, 2004) at 14.
[21]   Dani Rodrik, Arvind Subramanian, and Francesco Trebbi, "Institutions Rule: The Primacy of Institutions Over Geography and Integration in Economic Development" (2004) 9 *Journal of Economic Growth* 131.

findings, the authors find that an increase in institutional quality of one standard deviation, corresponding roughly to the difference between measured institutional quality in Bolivia and South Korea, produces a two log points rise in per capita incomes, or a 6.4-fold difference – which, not coincidentally, is also roughly the income difference between the two countries.

In another recent paper,[22] Fukuyama, in a brief review of some of the empirical literature on determinants of economic development, concludes: "I believe that the institutionalists have won this argument hands down."

However, this said, there are several reasons why these cross-country statistical analyses should be interpreted with some caution. To begin with, even taking their results at face value, these studies reveal only imperfect correlations between legal and development-related variables. Even studies that find strong and statistically significant correlations between the rule of law and measures of development typically find that there are a number of countries whose level of development lies quite some distance – in either direction – away from the level that would be predicted by its rule of law score. The amount of unexplained variation in these studies leaves one to wonder about the importance of legal variables as opposed to other explanatory variables. It is also worth noting that many of these cross-country studies adopt narrow readily quantified measures of development, leaving themselves open to charges of placing undue emphasis upon economic conceptions of development as opposed, for example, to conceptions that place more emphasis upon factors such as freedom or environmental quality.

There are also reasons not to take the results of these studies at face value. Serious concerns have been raised about the reliability of the legal data upon which these studies rely, especially since it typically consists of subjective assessments, by either experts or selected members of society, of the quality of legal systems. One potential problem with these assessments is that they may be tainted by the assessors' knowledge of the development performance of the surrounding society. This raises the distinct possibility that positive perceptions of legal systems may be the consequence rather than the cause of development. There is also concern that subjective assessments may be unreliable in the sense of failing to have a consistent meaning across countries and over time. This sort of reliability is difficult to ensure when one relies upon surveys of people who have information on only one legal system at a particular point in time. Relying upon assessments by experts charged with evaluating a number of legal systems over time may be a way of avoiding this concern, but this approach raises concerns about the quality of the information possessed by the experts.

---

[22]　Francis Fukuyama, "Development and the Limits of Institutional Design," Global Development Network, St Petersburg, Russia, January 20, 2006 at 3.

Perhaps even more important than the question of reliability, however, is the question of the *validity* of the legal data being used in these cross-country studies. There is reason to doubt whether the data being used in many of these studies measures the characteristics of legal rather than non-legal features of the societies in question. Take, for example, the rule of law variables that many studies have found to be positively correlated with various indicia of development. The typical inference is that the quality of legal institutions causally influences development by determining the degree of respect for the rule of law. But what exactly does the rule of law variable measure? In most studies the rule of law appears to be measured in part by reference to the characteristics of legal institutions and in part by reference to the extent of compliance with the law. Ideally, however, these measures would be distinguished because levels of compliance with the law in any given society need not be connected to characteristics of the society's legal system. Widespread compliance with the law might signify that a society possesses potent legal norms, but it might also signify that the society possesses potent informal mechanisms that facilitate the enforcement of legal norms or potent non-legal norms whose content happens to overlap with that of legal norms or the absence of social or economic factors that tend to induce lawbreaking. For example, low rates of violent crime in a given society might reflect the existence of harsh criminal laws; or a large police force; or a population that is particularly willing to report crimes, appear as witnesses in legal proceedings or shun offenders; or an unusually dedicated police force; or, the fact that a large proportion of the population has deep ethical commitments to non-violence; or, the absence of economic inequality; or geographical circumstances that are unfavourable to the production or transshipment of illegal narcotics. As it stands, therefore, countries that score well on rule of law indices that are based at least in part upon rates of compliance with the law may be scoring highly for reasons that have little to do with the "strength" of their legal system.

Moreover, the coarse-grained nature of the data employed in these cross-country statistical studies provides very little traction on which design features of given classes of institutions that are causally related to particular development outcomes are of particular importance. For example, Fukuyama, in the paper noted above, where he concludes that institutionalists have won the argument hands down with non-institutionalists on determinant of developments, also notes that public administration is not a science susceptible to formalization under a set of universal rules and principles[23] and that macro-political institutions also are not susceptible to characterization in terms of optimal formal

---

[23]   See also Francis Fukuyama, *State-Building: Governance and World Order in the 21st Century* (Ithaca, NY: Cornell University Press, 2004).

political arrangements. Rather, the full specification of a good set of institutions will be highly context-dependent, will change over time, and will interact with the informal norms, values and traditions of the society in which they are embedded.

Similarly, Rodrik, Subramanian and Trebbi, in the paper cited above, despite its perhaps triumphalist title, actually reach rather salutary, perhaps even sobering, conclusions:[24]

> How much guidance do our results provide the policy-makers who want to improve the performance of their economies? Not much at all. Sure, it is helpful to know that geography is not destiny, or that focusing on increasing the economy's links with world markets is unlikely to yield convergence. But the operational guidance that our central result on the primacy of institutional quality yields is extremely meager ...
>
> We illustrate the difficulty of extracting policy – relevant information from our findings – using the example of property rights. Obviously, the presence of clear property rights for investors is a key, if not *the* key, element in the institutional environment that shapes economic performance. Our findings indicate that when investors believe their property rights are protected, the economy ends up richer. But nothing is implied about the actual form that property rights should take. We cannot even necessarily deduce that enacting a private property rights regime would produce superior results compared to alternative forms of property rights ...
>
> There is growing evidence that desirable institutional arrangements have a large element of context specificity, arising from differences in historical trajectories, geography, political economy, or other initial conditions ... This could help explain why successful developing countries – China, South Korea, and Taiwan among others – have almost always combined unorthodox elements with orthodox policies. It could also account for why important institutional differences persist among the advanced countries of North America, Western Europe and Japan – the role of the public sector, the nature of the legal systems, corporate governance, financial markets, labour markets, and social insurance mechanisms among others ...
>
> Consequently, there is much to be learned about what improving institutional quality means on the ground. This, we would like to suggest, is a wide open area of research. Cross-national studies are at present just a beginning that point us in the right direction.

Finally, in a similar vein, in a recent paper, "Institutions and Development: A View from Below,"[25] Rohini Pande and Christopher Udry state:

> Recent years have seen a remarkable and exciting revival of interest in the empirical analysis of how a broad set of institutions affects growth. The focus of the recent

---

[24]   Rodrik *et al.*, *supra* note 21 at 157–8.

[25]   Rohini Pande and Christopher Udry, "Institutions and Development: A View from Below," Economic Growth Center, Yale University, November 18, 2005 at 1–3, available at http://ssrn.com/abstract=864044.

outpouring of research is on exploiting cross-country variation in "institutional quality" to identify whether a causal effect runs from institutions to growth. These papers
conclude that institutional quality is a significant determinant of a country's growth
performance.

   These findings are of fundamental importance for development economists and
policy practitioners in that they suggest that institutional quality may cause poor
countries and people to stay poor. However, the economic interpretation and policy
implications of these findings depend on understanding the specific channels through
which institutions affect growth, and the reasons for institutional change or the lack
thereof ... However, we argue that this literature has served its purpose and is essentially complete. The number of variables available as instrumental variables is limited,
and their coarseness prevents close analysis of particular causal mechanisms from
institutions to growth ... This suggests that the research agenda identified by the institutions and growth literature is best furthered by the analysis of much more
micro-data than has typically been the norm in this literature.

The authors go on to illustrate the importance of this micro-perspective by
describing property rights in land in four African countries (Gambia, the Democratic Republic of Congo, Ghana and Côte d'Ivoire), emphasizing the importance of the distinction between *de jure* and *de facto* land rights, the importance of customary law, the heterogeneity of land rights even within
countries, and the intertwining of political and contractual institutions.

Thus, while empirically there appears to be an increasingly firm consensus
that institutions, including legal institutions, are an important determinant of
economic development (and probably other aspects of development), there is
much less consensus on what an optimal set of institutions might look like.
Optimal institutions generally, including legal institutions in particular, will
often be importantly shaped by factors specific to given societies, including
history, culture, political traditions and institutional culture. This in turn implies
some degree of modesty on the part of the external community in promoting
rule of law or other legal reforms in developing countries and correspondingly
a larger role for "insiders" with detailed local knowledge.[26]

II.   DEFINING THE RULE OF LAW

Even if the rule of law is a key factor in development, a key threshold question
must be addressed: what is it that we mean by "rule of law"? In the development context, even those writers who purport to find near universal support for
the "rule of law," acknowledge great uncertainty about what it is, precisely,

---

[26]   For an eloquent and persuasive articulation of the importance of local knowledge,
see James C. Scott, *Seeing like a State* (New Haven, CT: Yale University Press, 2002).

that is universally supported.[27] For example, Rachel Kleinfeld, in a recent essay,[28] states: "Read any set of articles discussing the rule of law, and the concept emerges looking like the proverbial blind man's elephant – a trunk to one person, a tail to another. In fact, the phrase is commonly used today to imply at least five separate meanings or end goals." She identifies these as: (1) Government bound by law; (2) Equality before the law; (3) Law and order; (4) Predictable efficient justice; (5) Lack of state violation of human rights. She goes on to argue that conceptual confusion has further arisen because practitioners working to build the rule of law abroad have developed an entirely different way of looking at the concept, based not on end goals but on institutions to be reformed.

Matthew Stephenson, in an essay in the same volume, on the rule of law in China,[29] notes that one academic China law expert put the point bluntly: "'Rule of law has no meaning. Everyone uses the phrase because everyone can get behind it and it might make it easier to get funding.' Another scholar states: 'The rule of law means whatever one wants it to mean. It is an empty vessel that everyone can fill up with their own vision.' This ambiguity serves a very clear political purpose, stated explicitly by one State Department official: 'The beauty of the rule of law is that it's neutral. No one – the human rights community, the business community, the Chinese leadership – objects to it.'"[30]

According to Tamanaha, in a recent insightful intellectual history of the rule of law:

> Some believe that the rule of law includes protection of individual rights. Some believe that democracy is part of the rule of law. Some believe that the rule of law is purely formal in nature requiring only that laws be set out in advance in general, clear terms, and be applied equally to all. Others assert that the rule of law encompasses "the social, economic, educational, and cultural conditions under which man's legitimate aspirations and dignity may be realized" ... "There are almost as many conceptions of the rule of law as there are people defending it."[31]

---

27   Adam Bouloukos and Brett Dakin, "Toward a Universal Declaration of the Rule of Law: Implications for Criminal Justice and Sustainable Development" (2001) 42 *International Journal of Comparative Sociology* 145 at 157–8, 146. See also Richard H. Fallon Jr., "The Rule of Law as a Concept in Constitutional Discourse" (1997) 97 *Columbia Law Review* 1–56.
28   Rachel Kleinfeld, "Competing Definitions of the Rule of Law," in Thomas Carothers (ed.), *Promoting the Rule of Law: In Search of Knowledge* (Carnegie Endowment for International Peace, 2006) at 32.
29   Matthew Stephenson, "A Trojan Horse in China," in Carothers (ed.), *op. cit.* at 196.
30   See also Randall Peerenboom, "Varieties of Rule of Law," in Peerenboom (ed.), *Asian Discourses of Rule of Law* (London: Routledge, 2004).
31   Tamanaha, *On the Rule of Law*, *supra* note 3, at p. 3.

In this book, we employ and defend what we have termed a *procedural defini-tion* of the rule of law in terms of optimal institutional arrangements. In order to understand what is distinctive about this definition, it is helpful to begin by situating it in the broader literature on the rule of law, and by contrasting our definition with other plausible alternatives that have been proposed. We will begin with a brief discussion of the emergence of the rule of law as a discrete subject of political thought. We will then identify, and critique, what we will call the "thick" and "thin" approaches to theorizing the rule of law. These cri-tiques will serve to inaugurate a defence of a "thinner" (though not merely "thin") approach to the rule of law from a modern liberal perspective, and pre-figure the elaboration of our "procedural" definition in greater detail.

A.   The Rule of Law as a Subject of Political Thought

As Raz suggests, the idiom of the "rule of law" itself is a simple one, meaning precisely what it says: "that people should obey the law and be ruled by it."[32] As he goes on to point out, "in political and legal theory it has come to be read in a narrower sense, that the government shall be ruled by the law and subject to it. ... Actions not authorized by law cannot be the actions of the government as a government."[33]

It is interesting, however, to note that the political philosophers of the French and English Enlightenments did not treat the rule of law and the nature of gov-ernment as discrete issues. In Hobbes's *Leviathan*, for instance, the law is nothing less than the very embodiment of the will of the Sovereign – and hence inseparable from questions of government. According to Locke, law is both those rules to which we bind ourselves through the social contract and those rules formulated by the sovereign in accordance with that contract. The origin of the law and the origin of the state are one and the same. For Montesquieu, the law is a vast and protean category, comprising not only the positive law but also the principle of justice preceding man-made law, as well as natural laws governing the relations between human beings and states. His theory does not sensibly distinguish between principles of government and principles of law. While it is customary to speak of these theorists' conceptions of the "rule of law," this is largely a term of art, applied retrospectively. In fact, many, if not most, of the most influential figures in political thought from Machiavelli to Burke held legal theory inseparable from personal and political ethics, as well as from the rules of skilled statecraft.

---

[32]   Joseph Raz, *The Authority of Law, Essays on Law and Morality* "The Rule of Law and its Virtue," (Clarendon Press: Oxford, 1979) p. 212.

[33]   *Id.*

One of the first and most influential theorists to contest the omnipotence of the Sovereign was <u>Rousseau</u>, who assumed, as basic to a good political system, the abolition of the monarchy and its replacement with a populist parliamentary system of government.[34] Essential to this system was a set of overriding conventions for the translation of legislative pronouncements into executive action: laws binding on parliamentary government, or what we might latterly call a constitution. Rousseau asserted that only the "legal state,"[35] one predicated on the supremacy of made law, could assure justice and liberty in the context of delegated authority. Henceforth, populist democracy became closely associated with the stipulation that made law have a certain irrevocable authority ("rule") over government, an association seized upon by Payne, Hamilton and Madison and enshrined in the constitutions of post-revolutionary America and France. As Posner points out, the sense of the rule of law important to "the struggle of the English and later the Americans against royal tyranny, is that the officials in a society, the 'rulers,' are subject to law, rather than having unfettered discretionary power."[36]

The phrase "rule of law" itself is attributable to the British jurist Albert Venn Dicey, whose 1885 *Introduction to the Study of the Law of the Constitution* describes the rule of law as a "feature" of the political institutions of England, apprehensible in two different ways: "[T]hat no man is punishable or can be lawfully made to suffer in body or goods except for a distinct breach of law established in the ordinary legal manner before ordinary courts of the land;"[37] and "that ... every man, whatever his rank or condition, is subject to the ordinary law of the realm and amenable to the jurisdiction of the ordinary tribunals."[38] Though Dicey's definition of the rule of law is principally an attempt to describe certain actual characteristics of the British political system, it has provoked grand speculation about the prospects of the rule of law as a universal value.

---

[34] Bob Fine, *Democracy and the Rule of Law* (Caldwell, NJ: Blackburn Press 2002) p. 10. Fine describes the emergence of the study of law as a subject in its own right as the consequence of a complex series of philosophical transformations taking place towards the end of the nineteenth century.

[35] *Id.*, p. 32

[36] Richard Posner, "Constitutional Law From a Pragmatic Perspective" (2005) 55 *University of Toronto Law Journal* 299.

[37] Albert Venn Dicey, *Introduction to the Study of the Law of the Constitution*, 10th edn (London: Macmillan, 1960) p. 187.

[38] *Id.*

B.   "Thick" Conceptions of the Rule of Law

Liberals, inspired by the egalitarian and anti-authoritarian properties of the rule of law as articulated by Rousseau, Dicey and others, have been among its most enthusiastic exponents. The association of the rule of law with democracy and liberty has been given radical interpretations by some, often stretching the concept far beyond Dicey's descriptive account and out into strongly prescriptive territory.

Hayek, for instance, favours a "thick" conception comprising certain "universal moral principles,"[39] inherently liberal in character. He links the rule of law to freedom, stating (with little in the way of further argumentation) that "it will readily be seen that whatever form it takes, any ... recognized limitations on the powers of legislation imply the recognition of the inalienable right of the individual, inviolable rights of man."[40] His *The Constitution of Liberty* associates the rule of law not only with America's greatness as one of the first constitutional democracies but, indeed, with freedom itself:

> [W]hen we obey laws, in the sense of general abstract rules laid down irrespective of their application to us, we are not subject to another man's will and are therefore free. ... Because the rule is laid down in ignorance of the particular case and no man's will decides the coercion used to enforce it, the law is not arbitrary.[41]

Even equality, he considers, owes tribute to the rule of law:

> The true contrast to a reign of status is the reign of general and equal laws, of the rules which are the same for all, or, we might say, of the rule of *leges* in the original meaning of the Latin word for laws – *leges*, that is, as opposed to the *privi-leges*.[42]

Of more recent vintage, Sunstein's conception of the rule of law tends towards thickness by advocating the inextricability of the rule of a particular kind of constitutional law from deliberative democracy. On Sunstein's view, not only is the rule of law an inseparable part of the internal morality of deliberative democracy, but this internal morality actually spells out much of the necessary content of the law properly so-called: "constitutional protection of many individual rights, including the right of free expression, the right to vote, the right to political equality, and even the right to private property, for people cannot be

---

[39]   Michael Neumann, *The Rule of Law* (Burlington, VT: Ashgate, 2002) p. 3.

[40]   Friedrich Hayek, *The Road to Serfdom* (London: Routledge and Kegan Paul, 1944) p. 63.

[41]   Friedrich Hayek, *The Constitution of Liberty* (Chicago: University of Chicago Press, 1960) p. 153.

[42]   *Id.*, p. 154.

independent citizens if their holdings are subject to unlimited government readjustment."[43]

Even thicker still is Sunstein's stipulation that a democratic constitution must be hostile towards "traditions *as such* ... A democratic constitution makes it more likely that people will look behind traditions in order to see what can be said on their behalf."[44] In such statements, it seems that the rule of law-*qua*-constitution is relied upon to produce not only limited government and a positive program of democratic rights, but also to inure its citizens with one of the tenets of what Barry has called "the liberal outlook;" *viz.*, "the belief that every doctrine should be open to critical scrutiny and that no view should be held unless it has in fact withstood critical scrutiny."[45]

Many contemporary theorists, however, are highly critical of what Raz calls "the promiscuous use made in recent years of the expression 'the rule of law'"[46] to mean, as Hayek, Sunstein and others do, a comprehensive political morality. Shklar, for instance, decries the scourge of "legalism," by which she means "the ethical attitude that holds moral conduct to be a matter of rule following, and moral relationships to consist of duties and rights determined by rules."[47] Shklar is critical of legalism's treatment by the legal profession as "the only morality among men,"[48] and its transformation into what she calls a "grand or total ideolog[y]."[49]

There is a danger, Shklar argues, in investing legalism – the rule of law – with responsibility for democratic liberalism's other moral values, such as equality and a regime of rights.[50] There is no reason, she maintains, to expect that the rule of law alone will promote "the rule of reason throughout society, or even the legal rule of rights."[51] It is not that the rule of law does not have a place in securing rights and equality. At its very best, its structural solidity makes it a good bulwark against the violation of substantive rights; at the least, it is "quite

---

[43] Cass Sunstein, *Democracy's Constitution* (New York: Oxford University Press, 2001) p. 7.

[44] *Id.*

[45] Brian Barry, "How Not to Defend Liberal Institutions," in *Liberty and Justice: Essays in Political Theory 2* (Oxford: Clarendon Press, 1991) p. 24.

[46] Raz, *supra* note 32, p. 211.

[47] Judith Shklar, *Legalism* (Cambridge, MA: Harvard University Press, 1964) p. 1.

[48] *Id.*, p. 2.

[49] *Id.*, p. 4.

[50] For a further discussion of Raz and Shklar on the rule of law in relation to liberalism, see Thom Ringer, "Legalism and its Virtue" (http://users.ox.ac.uk/~ball1843/legalism.pdf).

[51] Judith Shklar, "Political Theory and the Rule of Law," in A. Hutchinson and P. Monahan (eds), *The Rule of Law: Ideal or Ideology?* (Toronto: Carswell, 1987) p. 16.

Judith Shklar

compatible with a strong theory of individual rights."[52] It is, however, misguided to view the law as the source of these values, or as inherently more hospitable to them than to terror and oppression.

Raz frames his critique in similar terms:

> The rule of law is a political ideal which a legal system may lack or may possess to a greater or lesser degree. That much is common ground. It is also to be insisted that the rule of law is just one of the virtues which a legal system may possess and by which it is to be judged. It is not to be confused with democracy, justice, equality (before the law or otherwise), human rights of any kind or respect for persons or for the dignity of man. A non-democratic legal system, based on the denial of human rights, on extensive poverty, on racial segregation, sexual inequalities, and religious persecution may, in principle, conform to the requirements of the rule of law better than any of the legal systems of the more enlightened Western democracies. This does not mean that it will be better than those Western democracies. It will be an immeasurably worse legal system, but it will excel in one respect: in its conformity to the rule of law.[53]

As Raz elaborates:

> If the rule of law is the rule of good law, then to explain its nature is to propound a complete social philosophy. But if so, the term lacks any social function. We have no need to be converted to the rule of law just in order to discover that to believe in it is to believe that good should triumph.[54]

At bottom, as Craig notes, the most persuasive claim in Raz's critique is that "the adoption of a fully substantive conception of the rule of law has the consequence of robbing the concept of any function which is independent of the theory of justice which imbues such an account of law."[55] In other words, in claiming that the rule of law consists in the rule of *just* law, the theoretical burden of explaining what is worthwhile about the rule of law is simply shifted from the clause "rule of law" to the qualifier "just;" that is, to the concept of justice.

The dangers of vesting the rule of law with a substantive conception of justice have been considered by numerous commentators. Critics of liberal neutrality, like Barry and Sandel, have noted that it is difficult not to assume too much about what "justice" requires, and even more difficult to resist the surreptitious

---

[52]   *Id.*, p. 5.

[53]   Raz, *supra* note 32, at p. 211.

[54]   Joseph Raz, "The Rule of Law and its Virtue" (1977) 93 *Law Quarterly Review* 195 at 195–6.

[55]   Paul Craig, "Formal and Substantive Conceptions of the Rule of Law: An Analytical Framework" (1997) 16 *Public Law* 16, 487.

insertion of moral content under the guise of the neutral-sounding guise of "justice."[56] As Miller further points out, justice is a radically subjective concept, and amenable to manifold idiosyncratic and sometimes arbitrary interpretations.[57] Thus, by treating any particular conception of justice as universal and self-evident, one may actually be doing violence to democracy.

Waldron has still other reasons for resisting the "thick" conception of the rule of law. He is sceptical of the tendency of the "thick" model's proponents to treat the courts as the best (and sometimes the only) forum for settling highly divisive questions of principle and moral importance. As Sunstein's account shows, "thick" legalism is often embedded in a particular view of the role of the constitution, and the courts charged with protecting it, as "backstops" on, or borders for, democratic debate. In a vein characteristic of this attitude, Dworkin argues that "[t]here would be no point in the boast that we respect individual rights unless that involved some sacrifice, and the sacrifice in question must be that we give up whatever marginal benefits our country would receive from overriding these rights when they prove inconvenient."[58]

For both Dworkin and Sunstein, this "sacrifice" seems to mandate a bill of positive rights, defended by an able and empowered judiciary, and limitative of the scope and depth of democratic debate, effectively blocking certain majoritarian decisions from the outset. Indeed, for Sunstein, it seems that "designing democracy" is in large part a question of constitutional draftsmanship. For Beatty, judicial review under an entrenched bill of rights is designed to constrain majoritarian encroachments on minority rights through the application of a principle of proportionality designed to ensure minimal impairment of these rights.[59] Yet Waldron warns that this reliance on constitutional backstops and judicial review is not without noxious consequences for democratic deliberation:

> [W]e allow majority voting by judges without regard to their comparative wisdom. What is the justification for denying the benefit of a similar decision procedure to the mass of others who may have thought as honestly and as high-mindedly about the issues as the judges have? … A concern for the fairness and integrity of the process

---

[56] Michael Sandel, *Liberalism and the Limits of Justice* (Cambridge and New York: Cambridge University Press, 1998); Barry, *supra* note 45; see also S. Mulhall and A. Swift, "Political Liberalism: For and Against," in *Liberals and Communitarians* (Oxford: Blackwell, 1992).

[57] David Miller, *Principles of Social Justice* (Cambridge, MA: Harvard University Press 1999).

[58] Ronald Dworkin, "Taking Rights Seriously," *Taking Rights Seriously* (London: Duckworth, 1977).

[59] David Beatty, *The Ultimate Rule of Law* (Oxford: Oxford University Press, 2004).

[of democratic deliberation] is something that [the free, self-aware but other-respecting] citizen will exhibit along with everything else. He does not need a judge to do it for him.[60]

It need not be assumed, Waldron claims, that justice is a matter for the courts alone. Though this seems a basic assumption of the "rule of law as the rule of *just* law" school, it is not uncontroversial.

C. "Thin" Conceptions of the Rule of Law

As against the "thick" conception of the rule of law problematized above, a number of theorists have retreated to a formalistic definition of the rule of law limited to those few spare features common to most, though not all, legal systems. On Rawls's view, for instance, the rule of law is, as Neumann puts it, "simply the conception of formal justice applied to a legal order or system."[61] Formal justice, in turn, is a thin, non-moral principle of reason "addressed to rational persons for the purpose of regulating their conduct and providing the framework for their cooperation."[62] Thus, Rawls concludes, "because these precepts guarantee only the impartial and regular administration of rules, whatever these are, they are compatible with injustice."[63]

The rule of law, in Rawls's view, stands merely for the principle that rational people need a predictable system to guide their behaviour and organize their lives in a way that minimizes unproductive conflict with other agents. If that system be predictable but brutal ("Yield to merging traffic or you will be tortured") or predictable but otherwise unfair ("All red-haired persons shall be consigned to a life of hard labour"), so be it. These matters are not germane to the question of whether or not such a system is a legal system properly so called. For Rawls, the rule of law means, and only means, the rule of a system of rationally comprehensible rules bearing some instrumental relationship to the function of social coordination.

Raz, like Rawls, invokes the social coordinative function of the law as the basis for his minimalist conception:

This is the basic intuition from which the doctrine of the rule of law derives: the law must be capable of guiding the behaviour of its subjects. It is evident that this conception of the law is a formal one. It says nothing about how the law is to be made: by

---

[60]   Jeremy Waldron, "Rights and majorities: Rousseau Revisited," *Liberal Rights* (New York: Cambridge University Press, 1993) pp. 417–18.

[61]   Neumann, *supra* note 39.

[62]   John Rawls, *A Theory of Justice* (Cambridge, MA: Belknap Press, 1971) p. 235.

[63]   *Id.*

tyrants, democratic majorities, or any other way. It says nothing about fundamental rights, about equality, or justice ... Racial, religious, and all manner of discrimination are not only compatible [*sic*] but often institutionalized by general rules.[64]

Raz then goes on to suggest an itemized outline of the concept of the rule of law, each item of which correlates to the law's coordinative function:

(1) All laws should be prospective, open, and clear.
(2) Laws should be relatively stable.
(3) The making of particular laws (particular legal orders) should be guided by open, stable, clear and general rules.
(4) The independence of the judiciary must be guaranteed.
(5) The principles of natural justice must be observed.
(6) The courts should have review powers over the implementation of the other principles.
(7) The courts should be easily accessible.
(8) The discretion of the crime-preventing agencies should not be allowed to pervert the law.[65]

Thus, Raz attempts to distill a definition of the rule of law abstracted from any positive moral content and hence normatively unobjectionable.

In similar vein, in one of his most famous works, first published in 1963, Fuller identified eight distinct desiderata in the design of a legal system. Stated in summary form those desiderata were that laws should: (1) be of general application, (2) be publicized or at least made available to affected parties beforehand, (3) be prospective in application, (4) be understandable, (5) be coherent (i.e. not contradictory), (6) not require conduct beyond the powers of the affected party, (7) not be subject to frequent changes, and (8) reflect congruence between rules as announced and their actual administration. Somewhat controversially, Fuller argued that a legal system that failed to satisfy these desiderata would not merely be bad, but could not properly be called a legal system at all.[66] He seemed to take the position that a legal system that failed along some or all of these dimensions would not be capable of serving any useful social purpose (partly because it would be unlikely to elicit citizens' voluntary cooperation) and that the social purposes performed by law are crucial.[67]

Again, William Whitford in a review of alternative conceptions of the rule of law argues for what he calls a minimalist conception of the rule of law: "The accountability of transparent government decisions (including judicial responses

---

[64] Raz, *supra* note 32, pp. 211–14.
[65] Raz elaborates on his suggested items in *ibid.*, at 214–18.
[66] See *e.g.* Lon L. Fuller, *The Morality of Law*, rev. edn (New Haven: Yale University Press, 1969) at 39.
[67] *Ibid.*, especially at 200–24.

to private laws) to predetermined standards applied by an independent body, probably a court, through a procedure that can be practically utilized by the aggrieved."[68]

Neumann, however, is sceptical of the claim of Raz, Rawls, Fuller and other rule of law "minimalists" that they manage to divest the concept of law of all but its most minimal moral content, suggesting rather that both end up "thickening" their definitions by smuggling in quasi-moral principles. As he points out, for instance, there is nothing about the social coordinative function of the law that requires it to be "fair." That is, while both Rawls and Raz justify the minimum stipulation of an independent, non-bribable judiciary in relation to the minimalist virtue of predictability, "there is really no reason to suppose that fairness and independence add more predictability to the legal system than quite a wide range of unfair and dependent alternatives."[69] In fact, he adds, "even fair trials can be unpredictable in the extreme ... because fair procedure may nevertheless allow for a wide range of interpretative strategies."[70] Much as "thickeners" come under criticism for investing "justice" with dense moral content in their conception of "rule of law as the rule of *just* law," Rawls and Raz can plausibly be accused of doing the same thing with "fairness" when they give their approval to the rule of law as the rule of *fairly implemented* law.

To make his point, Neumann takes the "thin" conception to a radical extreme, construing law as, and merely as, social coordination. His conclusion is that without a background of normative expectations, there is nothing to make tractable our expectation that the law be fair, even when fairness is construed, rather uncontroversially, in terms of basic axioms like "equality before the law" or "the like treatment of like cases:"

> It is not against the rule of law if a nobleman's testimony counts twice as much as a peasant's. These inequalities will be factored into citizen's (*sic*) assessment of their chances at breaking the law just as equalities are factored in, or "acceptable" inequalities like giving less weight to the testimony of children or more to the testimony of likeable college professors. We know that life is not fair and we plan our lives accordingly. From the standpoint of the rule of law, it matters not at all whether this unfairness is found inside or outside the courtroom, so long as it is predictable unfairness.
>
> ...
>
> "Like" cases need not be universal; not *all* cases of murder by *anyone* need get the same sort of treatment. As far as the demands of predictability are concerned, it is quite all right if the law treats cases of murder by nobles differently from cases of murder by peasants: if each *type* of case is treated consistently, if peasant murderers

---

[68]   William Whitford, "The Rule of Law" (2000) *Wisconsin Law Review* 723 at 726.
[69]   *Id.*, p. 11.
[70]   *Id.*

and noble murderers both know what to expect, we will all know our places and can all get on with our lives accordingly. Things will go as they are expected to go, things will be according to the bad and unfair laws of our land, and that is all the rule of law requires, at least in its narrowest conception.[71]

Neumann's critique serves to show that a concept of the rule of law justified only in terms of its relationship to predictable social coordination may not contain even core values such as equality before the law and the like treatment of like cases. Indeed, Neumann himself thinks that his exploration of the margins of rule of law minimalism is among the best arguments *in favour* of a normatively invested definition of the rule of law.

D. Towards a "Thinner" Conception of the Rule of Law

The foregoing discussions of "thick" and "thin" conceptions of the rule of law manage to identify some problematic tendencies characteristic of such theories in general. Thick conceptions are apt to mistake the rule of law *simpliciter* with the rule of just law; to mistake the rule of law with respect for individual rights and freedoms; to invest laws and legal institutions with responsibility for the creation and maintenance of a just society; and to charge the courts with settling principled debates in which ordinary citizens might be thought to have a crucial deliberative stake.

For their part, as we have just seen, "thin" conceptions are susceptible to two compelling criticisms. The first, and most obvious, is that they are not so thin after all, hiding a thicker mantle of moral content under the cover of a less controversial concept such as "fairness." The second, and more subtle, is that, in retreating to the boundary line of minimalism, and accepting only that which is logically (as opposed to morally) necessary to a functional definition of the law, they may end up surrendering crucial territory – even much of what makes the rule of law an appealing ideal in the first place, such as equality before the law and the like treatment of like cases.

Consequently, neither a totally "thin" nor "thick" conception is appealing. Instead, we favour what might be called a "thinner" conception of the rule of law, a nomenclature intended to demarcate our model from both alternative extremes of "thick" and "thin."

A "thinner" model should see the rule of law as both a set of ideals and an institutional framework. Our model will thus comprise elements of both of what Summers calls "formal" and "substantive" theories of the rule of law.[72] It is

---

[71] *Id.*, pp. 45–9.
[72] Robert S. Summers, "A Formal Theory of the Rule of Law" (July 1993) 6 *Ratio Juris* 2, p. 127.

formal to the extent that it is preoccupied with conceptual, institutional and axiological components. That is, it is concerned first and foremost with both the conceptual soundness and institutional protection of "rules, … interpretive and applicational methodologies, and … processes of judicial and other enforcement,"[73] with the axiological purpose of providing such functions as social and economic coordination, "certainty and predictability of governmental action; private autonomy [and] actual equality of legal treatment at the hands of the government."[74]

Indeed, initiating a discussion of "rule of law *reform*," as we have set out to do in this book, implies the existence of a background of normative expectations, *viz.*, some standard by which "reform" is to be evaluated, and to which reform efforts should aspire. Moreover, we are seeking a definition of the rule of law which coheres with the goals of development, a normatively driven project *par excellence*. A definition of the rule of law *for* development can scarcely be indifferent towards the values inherent *in* development.

Summers objects to a model imbued with even this level of substantive content, preferring a purely formal system on the basis of the popular legitimacy he believes it is more likely to enjoy:

> The more the theory of the rule of law is "de-substantivized" to embrace only those institutional forms that as such serve values associated with a formal rule of law, the more likely it is that the formal rule of law will receive its due. On such a politically neutral conception, far more people from all segments of the political spectrum can be enlisted to support the rule of law and to criticize departures from it.
>
> On the other hand, if the rule of law is taken in general discourse within the society to mean not just governance through rules (and facilitative institutional features) but also capitalism (or socialism), a Bill of Rights (or no Bill of Rights), general democracy (or limited democracy), etc., then the formal rule of law is not so likely to command the range of *neutral* support it merits (and requires), for then the rule of law cannot be so readily seen to be a set of institutionalized forms and values worthy of the support of all officials and citizens, regardless of political allegiances.[75]

Though sensitive to his argument, we do not share Summers's skepticism about the prospects of a limited substantive conception of the rule of law for broad popular support. Nor do we agree with Summers's purely speculative counterfactual, *viz.*, that in politically pluralistic contexts (e.g., those found in many developed and developing nations), a completely formal, minimalist theory is any less likely to be polarizing and controversial. Brooks, for instance, considers that there is "little evidence" for the assumption that the establishment

---

73   *Id.*, p. 129.
74   *Id.*, p. 131.
75   *Id.*, p. 137.

of the formal dimensions of the rule of law "will lead reliably and predictably to the emergence of a robust societal commitment to the more substantive aspects of the rule of law."[76] If nothing else, it seems plausible that interested parties are at least as likely to be aggrieved by what is *left out* by a formalistic approach as by what is *brought in* by a more substantive one.

While imperfect, and outlined only in a tentative way here, we believe that a procedural approach to the rule of law stands a good chance of yielding institutions that are both strong and worthy of popular legitimacy, and conducive to the broader goals of development. Our procedural definition of the rule of law consists in an enumeration (by no means comprehensive) of normative benchmarks for key legal institutions, running the gamut from the judiciary to the legal education system. These normative benchmarks, in turn, are to be justified in terms of the contribution they make to human development. It will become apparent that these normative benchmarks, if taken seriously, correlate with a minimal constellation of civil and political rights, and a basic arrangement of economic facilities related to the protection of property and contractual rights. Simply put, *our definition focuses on what is necessary,* in each of these sets of institutions and in a legal state more generally, *to assure maximum compatibility with the most widely acceptable, minimal goals of development.*

The capability-building approach to development propounded by Sen identifies the expansion of freedom as both "(1) the *primary end* and (2) the *principal means* of development."[77] "Capability," in turn, is a type of freedom, *viz.*, "the freedom to achieve various lifestyles"[78] which a person may have reason to value. A person's capabilities may be understood as either her realized functions (what she is actually able to do) or as the set of alternatives she has (her "real opportunities"[79]). The "capability" view of freedom emphasizes that freedom consists in both pursuing what one has chosen, as well as in the simple fact of having a choice to do or not do a number of things, and from those choices, to construct one's way of life. By taking a capability view, as Sen points out, "[i]t is possible to attach importance to having opportunities that are not taken up,"[80] and hence to take a more holistic view of freedom.

One of the attractions of a capability perspective (as contrasted with utilitarian, libertarian or Rawlsian "primary goods"-based evaluative systems) is its intrinsic pluralism. By emphasizing freedom as opposed to the adduction of specific qualities (wealth; education; health) as the goal of development, the

---

[76] Rosa Ehrenreich Brooks, "The New Imperialism: Violence, Norms, and the Rule of Law" (2003) 101 *Michigan Law Review* 2275 at 2284.

[77] Sen, *supra* note 10, at p. 36 (emphasis in original).

[78] *Id.*, p. 75.

[79] *Id.*

[80] *Id.*, p. 76.

capability perspective is able to circumvent disagreements about particular qualities and their contestable normative valuations and act as a neutral basis for collaboration. The principle is disarmingly simple: as long as it can be agreed upon that freedom matters to any conception of the good life, we might be persuaded to at least assent to a program of development that takes the maximization of freedom as its principal end. Moreover, the capability perspective's pluralism extends to means as well as *ends*. Since there are many ways of expanding freedom, and since freedom must be, to a certain extent, understood contextually, no one set of limited instruments will be suitable to its maximization.

What does such a vision of freedom require of legal institutions? At a minimum, Sen suggests, "the general preeminence of basic political and liberal rights."[81] Political and liberal rights correlate to development as capability building in three different ways, in terms of:

1) their *direct* importance in human living associated with basic capabilities (including that of political and social participation)
2) their *instrumental* role in enhancing the hearing that people get in expressing and supporting their claims to political attention …
3) their *constructive* role in the conceptualization of "needs" (including the understanding of "economic needs" in a social context)[82]

The basic function of a legal system suggested by the capability approach is to secure those elementary civil and political rights conducive to basic capabilities, and even to their economic preconditions. The capabilities approach rejects the view of rights as, in Ignatieff's turn of phrase, "lapidary bourgeois luxur[ies]"[83] secondary to economic development, and emphasizes instead the interconnectedness of rights and prosperity as different facets of freedom.

It is important at this juncture to emphasize that Sen's vision of development presupposes no particular legal system. Whilst preoccupied with the veneration of certain rights, nowhere does Sen argue, for instance, that these rights must take the form of a constitutionally enshrined bill of rights under the purview of a supreme court, as is the case in many extant and emerging democracies. He does, however, accord civil and political rights a high degree of importance and priority over other principles of government. Though we are extrapolating here from Sen, it seems that legal arrangements unconstrained by consideration for civil and political rights are a serious detriment to the project of capability building.

---

[81]   *Id.*, p. 148.
[82]   *Id.*
[83]   Michael Ignatieff, *Human Rights as Idolatry, Human Rights as Politics and Idolatry* (Princeton, NJ: University Press, 2001) p. 90.

Thus, at a minimum, a conception of the rule of law compatible with the capability approach to development as advocated by Sen must accord intrinsic respect to at least the most basic "instrumental freedoms:" (1) political freedoms ("opportunities of political dialogue, dissent and critique as well as voting rights and participatory selection of legislators and executives"[84]); (2) economic facilities ("the opportunities that individuals respectively enjoy to utilize economic resources for the purpose of consumption, or production, or exchange;"[85] in other words, some measure of market freedom); and (3) transparency guarantees ("the freedom to deal with one another under guarantees of disclosure and lucidity"[86]). The precise ways in which these instrumental freedoms are vindicated will vary by context. However, it would seem that a rule of law framework which does not, in most of its institutional structures, accord these freedoms at least *prima facie* consideration, will not be compatible with the capability approach to development. Though merely a tentative surmise from Sen's work, which does not itself specifically address legal reform in relation to development, we consider it a modest one. We note here that an emphasis on civil and political rights, rather than on economic and social rights (as defined by the International Covenant on Civil and Political Rights and the International Covenant on Economic, Social and Cultural Rights) – and on civil more than political rights – is most compatible with a procedural rather than substantive conception of the rule of law.

In contrast to the capabilities approach, the New Institutional Economists construe development in economic terms. They argue that the hallmarks of developed modern economies (e.g., "formal contracts, bonding of participants, guarantees, brand names, elaborate monitoring systems, and effective enforcement mechanisms"[87]) are in fact corollaries of "well-specified and well-enforced property rights,"[88] rights which many developing economies lack. The establishment and entrenchment of such a set of rights, argues Douglass North, are "only possible as the result, first, of the development of a third party to exchanges, namely government, which specifies property rights and enforces contracts; and second of the existence of norms of behavior to constrain the parties in interaction."[89]

The expansion of government, however, can mean "unequal distribution of coercive power,"[90] as individuals of superior power tend to gain the ability to

---

[84]   Sen, *supra* note 10, at p. 38.
[85]   *Id.*, pp. 38–9.
[86]   *Id.*, p. 39.
[87]   Douglass C. North, "Institutions and Economic Growth: An Historical Introduction" (1989) 17 *World Development* 9, p. 1320.
[88]   *Id.*
[89]   *Id.*
[90]   *Id.*, p. 1321.

"enforce the rules to their advantage, regardless of their effects on efficiency,"[91] thus reducing the extent to which everyone benefits from economic growth and the complex interdependence facilitated by a structure of property rights in the first place. Poorly designed and monitored institutions can lead to economic stagnation and decline, as selective enforcement and other forms of corruption reduce investor confidence, raise the transaction costs of conducting trade, and discourage people from engaging in the forms of bargaining which are constitutive of commerce. As Nabli and Nugent summarize:

> [B]y affecting transaction costs and coordination possibilities, institutions can have the effect of either facilitating or retarding economic growth. The choice of appropriate political institutions, rules and policies enhances economic growth. Moreover, by affecting resource mobility and the incentives for innovation and accumulation, institutions may induce or hinder economic efficiency in the allocation of resources and growth. Institutions affect growth also through their effects on expectations, social norms and preferences.[92]

On a New Institutional Economics (NIE) view, the function of the rule of law is to craft optimal institutions for the clarification and enforcement of property and contract rights. However, this largely abstracts from substantive issues of how such rights should be defined and in the case of property rights distributed, and what institutional arrangements (formal and informal) in particular contexts best fulfil these functions.[93] Cognizant that the institutional needs of economies change as different norms become habituated and the appearance of new transactional behaviours necessitates new mechanisms of enforcement, NIE's proponents emphasize the importance of managed change. "[S]ince a basic and valuable characteristic of institutions is predictability and the preservation of expectations," argue Nabli and Nugent, "if such transitions are either too rapid or too frequent, they can undermine predictability and thereby impose social losses."[94]

Extrapolating from the conclusions of NIE, there are some helpful abstractions about the rule of law. In particular, NIE underscores the social coordinative function of institutions, including legal ones, flowing from their ability to create

---

[91]   *Id.*

[92]   Mustapha K. Nabli, and Jeffrey B. Nugent, "The New Institutional Economics and its Applicability to Development" (1989) 17 *World Development* 9, p. 1342.

[93]   See *e.g.* Rodrik *et al.*, *supra* note 21, "Institutions Rule: The Primacy of Institutions Over Geography and Integration in Economic Development" (2004) *J. of Economic Growth* at p. 157; Rohini Pande and Christopher Udry, "Institutions and Development: A View from Below" (Yale University Economic Growth Center, Discussion Paper No. 928, 2005); Trebilcock and Leng, *op. cit.*

[94]   *Op. cit.* at p. 1343.

and manage expectations and the conditions of predictability. The rule of law over institutions, on an NIE view, *should consist in norms of rule-making and rule-implementation subordinate to the principle of stabilized change,* thus avoiding abrupt institutional changes which threaten to disrupt social coordination, and the predictability on which it depends. In this emphasis on social coordination, the NIE-based conception of the rule of law hearkens back to the "thin" tradition discussed earlier. However, its emphasis primarily on property rights and contract enforcement is too thin a conception of the rule of law. To focus most rule of law reform efforts on property rights and contract enforcement (as Richard Posner advocates)[95] is to engage a very narrow political constituency as proponents of reform and to forego the support of the much larger potential political constituencies to whom formal property rights and formal contract enforcement are of little immediate salience (and in some cases a source of potential antipathy), but to whom protection against abuses of basic civil and political rights is of general concern. In these respects, private and public law should be seen as necessary functional and political complements.[96]

III. THE ELEMENTS OF A PROCEDURAL DEFINITION OF THE RULE OF LAW

We do not wish to endorse any particular conception of development theory. Rather, in selecting for our analysis two divergent theories of development, we seek to extrapolate a cluster of features which a definition of the rule of law, *minimally* compatible with at least both theories, must to a certain extent reflect. That is, given the different *teleogical* (ends-oriented) objectives of these conceptions of development, we wish to discern what conception of the rule of law might be minimally compatible with the *means* allowable to both conceptions of development. The cluster of features we enumerate as follows:

A. Process Values

A procedurally oriented conception of the rule of law would in part focus on process characteristics of the legal system such as (a) *Transparency* in lawmaking and adjudicative functions. By transparency we mean that law, decrees,

---

[95]   See Richard A. Posner, "Creating a Legal Framework for Economic Development," (1998) 13 *World Bank Research Observer* 1, 1.

[96]   See Daniel A. Farber, "Rights as Signals," (2002) 31 *Journal of Legal Studies* 83, 84–5; Amartya Sen, "What is the Role of Legal and Judicial Reform in the Development Process?," Address Before the World Bank Legal Conference 1–2 (June 5, 2000), available at http://ww1.worldbank.org/publicsector/legal/legalandjudicial.pdf.

ordinances, and regulations, once made, are publicly promulgated and widely accessible to the citizenry at large. By transparency, we also mean that the law-making process at these various levels of government is non-secretive and open to public scrutiny and participation in that affected citizens receive notice of lawmaking initiatives and opportunities for involvement in consultative or de-liberative processes before these initiatives result in binding laws. Transparency for us would include open court proceedings and publicly accessible reasons for ensuing decisions; (b) *Predictability*, by which we mean that laws, once enacted or adopted, will be enforced in a predictable and consistent way, rela-tively free from the exercise of arbitrary discretion influenced by factors extraneous to the ostensible objectives of the law, such as corruption, cronyism, patronage, or discrimination related to ascriptive factors such as race, religion or gender; (c) *Stability*, by which we mean that laws that are intended or are likely to induce major reliance interests are not subject to frequent, convulsive, and sudden changes; and (d) *Enforceability*, by which we mean that laws that are adopted are effectively enforced by government and/or are effectively en-forceable through the courts or other agencies of the state by private parties. We believe that these normative characteristics of a formal legal system (largely "due process" or "natural justice" values as Western constitutional and admin-istrative lawyers might characterize them) are likely to be widely endorsed in most societies, for without them it is difficult to think of social purposes that a formal legal system could usefully serve as distinct from private purposes that the absence of one or more of these features might advance. While undoubtedly they do not capture all elements of a just legal system on a thick conception of the rule of law, they are surely a necessary, albeit not sufficient condition for the realization of almost any defensible conception of the rule of law.

B.   Institutional Values

Many of the major classes of the legal institutions that we review in subsequent chapters, such as the judiciary, prosecutors, the police, the penal system, special-ized law enforcement or administrative agencies (such as tax administration), legal aid agencies, and legal education institutions, raise complex issues of in-dependence and accountability – two critically important dyadic institutional values that require difficult balances to be struck with respect to each class of institution. Neither "independence" nor "accountability" are straightforward concepts, and indeed each is highly contested terrain in both the theoretical lit-erature and jurisdiction-specific experience. "Independence" poses the question: Independent from whom, with respect to what? Likewise, "accountability" poses the question: Accountable to whom, with respect to what? Absolute independ-ence is a chimera and it is neither attainable nor desirable and would entail unaccountable mini autocracies. Equally, unconstrained forms of political accountability, however, may fundamentally undermine neutral and objective administration of the law, especially when the government or its officials or supporters have interests directly at stake.

With respect to "independence," it is easier to describe the characteristics of independent decision-making, or its correlate dependent decision-making, than to prescribe institutional safeguards for independent decision-making, where conventions vary widely from one country to another, even amongst those countries who are regarded as having strong rule of law traditions. For example, in the case of the judiciary, we would view judicial decisions as "independent" if they are reached on the factual and legal merits of the issues before the court, uninfluenced by considerations that are extraneous to those merits, such as personal relations between the judge and one of the parties, corruption, cronyism, political interference or coercion in particular decisions, especially those affecting the government of the day or its officials. Yet mechanisms to ensure judicial independence vary widely. For example, in the US, most state court judges are directly elected, and promotions to higher levels of the state court system are also often subject to direct election. With respect to federal court appointees, including the US Supreme Court, judicial appointees are nominated by the President, but are subject to a Senate confirmation process. The US also widely uses juries in both criminal and civil proceedings, where jury selection is determined in part by a random process (in effect, by lottery), subject to various grounds for challenge. In other jurisdictions, with a strong rule of law tradition, judicial appointments are typically made by the executive arm of government (sometimes pursuant to a specifically designed judicial training and career-track), rather than by direct election, and without a legislative confirmation process, and juries play a much more limited role.

In the case of law enforcement officials, such as prosecutors and the police, in some US states, district attorneys and police commissioners run for political office through direct election. In most other jurisdictions with strong rule of law traditions, these officials are appointed pursuant to more general public service appointment processes and are not overtly subject to a directly political validation process. Officials administering specialized law enforcement agencies or the penal system are typically subject to similar appointment processes.

In order to protect professional independence, in many jurisdictions bar associations are delegated extensive self-regulatory authority over criteria for admission to the legal profession and compliance therewith, as well as disciplinary powers over members, while in other jurisdictions with strong rule of law traditions the legal profession is often supervised directly by the courts of the jurisdiction.

With respect to legal education institutions, to the extent that they are part of a university system, they will claim a high measure of independence in setting curricula, and allowing faculty and students broad academic freedom in terms of what is taught, learned, and researched, but again practices vary widely even in developed countries on both the relative roles of public and private legal education institutions and the role of the state in financing and regulating them.

With respect to the correlative value of "accountability", while a high degree of independence in decision-making by personnel in these legal institutions may be valued, it is equally true that some mechanisms of accountability are typically required.[97] For example, decisions of judges in lower courts are typically subject to a judicial appeal process to higher courts. Gross dereliction of duty, abuse of office, and other flagrant forms of judicial misconduct are typically subject to some form of judicial disciplinary process, which may be administered by the courts themselves or by a semi-independent body representing a diverse range of relevant stakeholders. Operational accountability in the efficient and appropriate expenditure of public monies is often ensured through various budgetary allocation processes and public audit mechanisms, although mechanisms for management of the court system vary widely.

With respect to law enforcement officials, such as prosecutors and the police, in some cases quasi-independent oversight bodies are constituted to receive and evaluate citizens' complaints relating to abuse of office or other forms of misconduct. For officials involved in other law enforcement activities, such as specialized law enforcement agencies or the penal system, in some jurisdictions special complaints mechanisms are constituted, or to the extent that these officials are part of a broader public service regime they are subject to disciplinary mechanisms that pertain to public servants more generally.

With respect to bar associations exercising delegated, self-regulatory powers over members of the legal profession, many of their decisions may be subject to judicial review, and regulation-making powers pertaining to, e.g., admission standards or codes of professional conduct may be subject to some form of political oversight, in part as a safeguard against professional protectionism.

With respect to legal education institutions, bar associations may be delegated some degree of authority to regulate curricula offerings, through accreditation requirements, while other aspects of the academic programs undertaken by these institutions are typically subject to internal governance mechanisms relating to law school and university administration involving representation by affected stakeholders. Fiscal accountability for the prudent expenditure of public monies

---

97   See Dennis Galligan, "Principal Institutions and Mechanisms of Accountability," in Rudolph van Puymbroeck (ed.), *Comprehensive Legal and Judicial Developments: Toward an Agenda for a Just and Equitable Society* (Washington, DC: World Bank, 2001).

may in part be ensured through these internal accountability mechanisms, but may also be subject to external scrutiny through budget allocation and public audit processes.

In succeeding chapters, we review, with respect to each major class of legal institution, mechanisms for striking an appropriate balance between "independence" and "accountability" in more detail. It is sufficient, for the moment, to emphasize that there is no single agreed blueprint, even amongst countries with strong rule of law traditions, on how this balance should be struck with respect to any of these classes of institutions, underscoring the importance of sensitivity to local historical, social, and political variables. That is to say, even amongst developed countries with strong rule of law traditions, there are obviously many different institutional routes to promoting the relevant institutional values of "independence" and "accountability," and it should not be assumed that amongst developing countries with a commitment to strong rule of law values such diversity of instrumental approaches will be any less marked.

C. Legitimacy Values

The concept of legitimacy is as much contested terrain as the concepts of independence and accountability. Toharia calls "social" legitimacy "the level of *auctoritas* enjoyed by ... institutions; that is, their capacity to engender the belief that they deserve obedience and respect."[98] Danner views legitimacy as the "justification for the exercise of authority."[99] Lindseth describes it as "a broad,

---

[98]   Jose Juan Toharia, "Evaluating Systems of Justice Through Public Opinion: Why, What, Who, How, and What For?," in Erik G. Jensen and Thomas C. Heller (eds), *Beyond Common Knowledge: Empirical Approaches to the Rule of Law* (Stanford, CA: Stanford University Press, 2003) at 24. There are many subtle variations of the term "legitimacy" in the literature, which we will discuss in greater depth below. Toharia views social legitimacy as "a purely sociological phenomenon, a state of the collective mind that is not tied to legal and political technicalities: it is – or is not – granted by the public and, as such, can vary substantially over time" (p. 55). Our own view of legitimacy is more closely tied to the design of the institution itself and its capacity to both deliver justice in an effective, efficient, and impartial manner while inspiring and maintaining moral authority with the public on which legal institutions often ultimately depend for their long-term viability. See also Barry R. Weingast, "The Political Foundations of Democracy and the Rule of Law" (June 1997) 91 *The American Political Science Review* 2, 262. Weingast notes that "[t]o survive, the rule of law requires that limits on political officials be self-enforcing ... [S]elf-enforcement of limits depends on the complementary combinations of attitudes and reactions of citizens *as well as* institutional restrictions."

[99]   Allison Marston Danner, "Enhancing the Legitimacy and Accountability of Prosecutorial Discretion at the International Criminal Court" (July, 2003) 97 *American Journal of International Law* 510, 535.

empirically determined societal acceptance of the system."[100] According to Huntington,[101] "legitimacy is a mushy concept that political analysts do well to avoid." He notes that in the past, tradition, religion, the divine right of kings, and social deference provided legitimation for non-democratic rule and in modern times authoritarianism has been justified by nationalism and by ideology. In the case of democratic regimes, laws and policies promulgated by these regimes typically derive their legitimacy from notions of direct or delegated consent by members of the polity.[102]

While evidence suggests that in many societies appropriate attention to procedural values and to institutional values that strike an appropriate balance between independence and accountability may ensure high levels of social legitimacy for legal institutions,[103] this will not invariably be the case. For example, even a relatively thin conception of the rule of law may rule out certain social norms or practices that are deeply entrenched in the community, for example, denial of basic human rights on the basis of gender or ethnicity. Similarly, even legal institutions that conform to a relatively thin conception of the rule of law may still be in tension with traditional religious or community-based forms of dispute resolution, which may not conform well with even procedural rule of law norms. The avoidance of a thick substantive conception of the rule of law can mitigate these tensions, but not eliminate them.

A number of scholars have critiqued the legitimacy of even limited conceptions of the rule of law as applied to developing countries on the grounds of inconsistency with prevailing and deeply entrenched social norms. For example, Trubek and Galanter, in a widely cited paper,[104] critique what they call the model of liberal legalism on these grounds:

> The ethnocentric quality of liberal legalism's model of law in society is apparent. Empirically, the model assumes social and political pluralism, while in most of the Third World we find social stratification and class cleavage juxtaposed with authoritarian or totalitarian political systems. The model assumes that state institutions are the primary locus of social control, while in much of the Third World the grip of tribe, clan, and local community is far stronger than that of the nation-state. The

---

[100]   Peter L. Lindseth, "Democratic Legitimacy and the Administrative Character of Supranationalism: The Example of the European Union" (April 1999) 99 *Columbia Law Review* 628, 645.

[101]   Samuel P. Huntington, *The Third Wave: Democratization in the Late 20th Century* (Norman, OK: University of Oklahoma Press, 1991).

[102]   *Op. cit.*, p. 46.

[103]   See Tom Tyler, *Why People Obey the Law* (New Haven, CT: Yale University Press, 1990).

[104]   David Trubek and Marc Galanter, "Scholars in Self Estrangement: Some Reflections on the Crisis in Law and Development Studies in the United States" (1974) 4 *Wisconsin Law Review* 1062.

model assumes that rules both reflect the interests of the vast majority of citizens and are normally internalized by them, while in many developing countries rules are imposed on the many by the few and are frequently honoured more in the breach than in the observance. The model assumes that courts are central actors in social control, and that they are relatively autonomous from political, tribal, religious, or class interests. Yet in many nations courts are neither very independent nor very important.[105]

Similarly, in a more recent paper, in part drawing on recent experience in Kosovo, Brooks argues that the rule of law model has failed in many developing countries[106] Brooks writes:

> In his recent book, *Aiding Democracy Abroad* Tom Carothers of the U.S. Institute for Peace even offers (by no means uncritically) what he refers to as the "Rule of Law Assistance Standard Menu." It includes "reforming institutions" (judicial reform, strengthening legislatures, police and prison reform, etc.), "[r]ewriting laws" (modernizing criminal, civil, and commercial laws), "[u]pgrading the legal profession through support for stronger bar associations and law schools," and "[i]ncreasing legal access and advocacy" through the support of legal-advocacy NGOs, law-school clinics, and so on.
>
> This model simply does not work. What this type of formalistic approach fails fully to recognize or acknowledge is that creating the rule of law is most fundamentally an issue of norm creation. The rule of law is not something that exists "beyond culture" and that can be somehow added to an existing culture by the simple expedient of creating formal structures and rewriting constitutions and statutes. In its substantive sense, the rule of law *is* a culture, yet the human-rights-law and foreign-policy communities know very little – and manifest little curiosity – about the complex processes by which cultures are created and changed.[107]

In another recent paper, Berkowitz, Pistor, and Richard argue that the way a law was initially transplanted and received in a country is an important determinant of effective legal institutions (legality), measuring legality in terms of survey data on the effectiveness of the judiciary, rule of law, the absence of corruption, low risk of contract repudiation and low risk of government expropriation.[108] Using data from 49 countries, they show that countries that have developed legal orders internally, adapted the transplanted law and/or had a population that was already familiar with basic principles of the transplanted

---

[105]   *Op. cit.* at 1080, 1081.
[106]   Brooks, *supra* note 76, at p. 2275.
[107]   *Op. cit.* at 2284, 2285.
[108]   Daniel Berkowitz, Katharina Pistor and Jean-Francois Richard, "Economic Development, Legality, and the Transplant Effect" (2003) 47 *European Economic Review* 165–95; see also Robert Seidman, "Administrative Law and Legitimacy in Anglophonic Africa: A Problem in the Reception of Foreign Law" (1970) 5 *Law and Society Review* 161–204.

law had more effective legality than countries that received foreign law without any similar predispositions.

This line of critique of the relevance of even a relatively thin conception of the rule of law to many developing countries has in turn attracted criticism. For example, Tamanaha,[109] in a critique (*inter alia*) of the paper by Trubek and Galanter points out:

> One of the major sources of oppression and rapaciousness in developing countries today is authoritarian governments. The central premise of the liberal rule-of-law system is the protection of individuals from the tyranny of the government. Law-and-development theorists should be striving to devise ways in which the rule-of-law model can be adapted to local circumstances and nurtured into maturity, rather than expending the bulk of their efforts in tearing this model down.
>
> Informative though it was, the legal liberal paradigm elucidated by Trubek and Galanter was seriously misleading insofar as it implied that all the elements described were prerequisite to a rule-of-law system. Even the United States, as they observed, did not satisfy the description. Operating around the world today are many variations of the rule of law, coexisting with individualist-oriented as well as with communitarian-oriented cultures. It has always consisted more of a bundle of ideals than a specific or necessary set of institutional arrangements.
>
> A minimalist account of the rule of law would require only that the government abide by the rules promulgated by the political authority and treat its citizens with basic human dignity, and that there be access to a fair and neutral (to the extent achievable) decision maker or judiciary to hear claims or resolve disputes. These basic elements are compatible with many social-cultural arrangements and, notwithstanding the potential conflicts, they have much to offer to developing countries.[110]

Tamanaha also points out that the critique of liberal legalism developed by Trubek and Galanter (and other scholars) often leads to a "state law bad, folk law good" attitude, when in fact often "folk law is the culprit" in sanctifying various basic human rights abuses of, e.g., women and ethnic or religious minorities.[111] In this respect, it is worth noting that in recent work on the relationship between formal law and informal social norms, scholars such as McAdams have argued that formal law and legal institutions have the potential to shape and modify social norms over time.[112] That is to say, social or cultural norms and practices should not necessarily be viewed as a timeless given.

---

[109]   Brian Tamanaha, "The Lessons of Law and Development Studies" (1995) 89 *Journal of International Law* 470–86.

[110]   *Op. cit.* at 476.

[111]   *Op. cit.* at 481, 484.

[112]   See Richard McAdams, "The Origin, Development and Regulation of Norms" (1997) 96 *Michigan Law Review* 338; McAdams, "The Legal Construction of Norms: A Focal Point Theory of Expressive Law" (2000) 86 *Virginia Law Review* 1649.

In similar spirit to Tamanaha, Holmes, in a discussion of concepts of legitimacy in France after the Revolution[113] concludes: *legality vs. legitimacy*

> The relation between legality and legitimacy is an extremely difficult one to sort out. We normally assume, at any rate, that it is quite meaningful and not at all redundant to ask about the legitimacy of laws. That is to say, most of us would agree that we cannot reasonably answer the question, "Why obey these laws?" with a simple reaffirmation that they *are* laws. Something else is needed and this something else is a claim about the legitimacy of the laws in question. Thus, although legitimacy and legality may be closely affiliated with one another, they cannot be identified, even by liberals.
>
> To this sort of objection, if it is an objection, I would respond in two ways. First I would reiterate that a government which obeys its own laws is something and not nothing. Governments which approach this standard of purely formal legality are historically rare, and valuable at the very least because they allow individuals to make plans despite the contingency of the future. While I believe this answer is relevant to the objection, I also admit that it is somewhat evasive. It skirts the questions: What sort of laws do you mean? What if a country had atrocious laws and obeyed them to the letter?
>
> At this point I would take a second, slightly different tack, a quite predictable one given the basic argument of this article. I would retreat to a distinction between two incongruous ways of conceiving the obligation to obey the law. On the one hand, we can call a regime or legal system legitimate only if it corresponds to an official or orthodox view of the human good; on the other hand, we can attribute legitimacy to a regime simply because it provides the necessary conditions for a variety of heterodox and nonofficial conceptions of the good to be lived out side by side. In the first case, society is regimented according to the principles of a political regime. In the second case, the government adapts itself to a plurality of institutions and beliefs already existing in society.[114]

IV. IMPEDIMENTS TO RULE OF LAW REFORM

Despite the claimed instrumental and intrinsic importance of the rule of law to development, and despite the fact that over the past 20 years external donors have invested billions of dollars in rule of law reform initiatives in many developing countries, rule of law deficiencies in many developing countries are both serious and persistent. According to the World Bank's Governance data on the status of the rule of law in many countries throughout the world (reproduced in Table 1A.1 in the Appendix to this chapter), only three out of 18 Latin American countries had positive rule of law ratings in 2002 (Chile, Costa Rica and Uruguay), and between 1996 and 2002 in many cases ratings deteriorated. In

---

[113] Stephen Holmes, "Two Concepts of Legitimacy: France After the Revolution" (1982) 10 *Political Theory* 165–83.

[114] *Op. cit.* at 181, 182.

sub-Saharan Africa, only six out of 47 countries had positive rule of law ratings in 2002 (Botswana, Cape Verde, Mauritius, Namibia, Seychelles and South Africa), and many ratings again deteriorated between 1996 and 2002. In all 12 countries of the former Soviet Union, ratings were negative in both years. The countries of Eastern Europe present a far more positive picture. Asia, with its huge diversity of countries, varying enormously in size, colonial history, legal heritage, political ideology and religious complexion, presents a much more mixed picture, defying ready generalizations, although rule of law ratings are generally low, with notable exceptions such as Singapore and Hong Kong. While we accept that the rule of law measures used by the World Bank in its Governance data base are susceptible to various methodological criticisms,[115] we doubt that any defensible recasting of the variables is likely to seriously undermine the general conclusion that many developing countries face serious and persistent deficits in the quality of their rule of law institutions and processes. On a conception of the rule of law as encompassing the protection of various civil and political rights (as Sen's conception of development as freedom would encompass), many developing countries perform poorly, as reflected in Table 1A.2 from Freedom House appended to this chapter; similarly, in the case of corruption, defined as the abuse of public office (often legal offices) for private gain (Table 1A.3). As will be evident, ratings on the rule of law, freedom, and corruption indices are often highly correlated.

The central puzzle posed by the serious and persistent deficiencies in the rule of law in many developing countries, as reflected in these data, is as follows: if a strong commitment to the rule of law is an unequivocally important instrumental and intrinsic dimension of development, why is it that so many developing countries are either unwilling or unable to adopt strong rule of law institutions and processes or, in Mancur Olson's terms, why do these countries persistently leave big bills on the sidewalk?[116]

We hypothesize that the potential impediments that countries may encounter in implementing even a limited, procedural conception of the rule of law fall into three crude (and often overlapping) categories. First, these impediments may be what one might broadly describe as of a technical or resource-related character, where despite the political will on the part of their leadership and citizens poor countries simply lack the financial, technological, or specialized human capital resources to implement good institutions generally, including legal institutions, thus impairing their development prospects (whatever one's

---

[115]   See Kevin Davis, "What Can the Rule of Law Variables Tell Us About Rule of Law Reforms?" (2004) 26 *Michigan Journal of International Law* 141.

[116]   Mancur Olson, "Big Bills Left on the Sidewalk: Why Some Nations are Rich and Others Poor" (1996) 10 *Journal of Economic Perspectives* 3–24.

conception of development), in turn making them poorer (in some relevant normative sense) and in turn further diminishing their ability to implement good institutions, hence a vicious downward spiral. With respect to impediments to rule of law reform of this character, presumably the general orientation of reform prescriptions entails either more effective or efficient deployment of existing resources devoted to a country's legal system, a re-ordering of a country's domestic priorities and reallocation of resources from other areas of expenditure to the legal system, or the infusion of resources from external donors (in the form of financial assistance, technological assistance, or technical advice and training, etc.). Indeed, on the narrowly instrumental economic rationale for rule of law reform, governments lacking the necessary resources should be prepared to borrow the money required to finance rule of law reforms and finance borrowing costs from future economic growth and increased tax revenues.

Another category of explanation for impediments faced by developing countries to rule of law reform relates to a variety of factors that might loosely be placed under the rubric of social-cultural-historical factors that have yielded a set of social values, norms, attitudes, or practices that are inhospitable to even a limited procedural conception of the rule of law.[117] While, as we and others have noted, deeply entrenched social values, attitudes, and practices are presumably not immutable,[118] the policy prescriptions entailed in overcoming this class of impediment are not nearly as obvious as in the case of technical or resource-related impediments nor is any impact likely to be immediate or dramatic.

A third class of potential impediments to effective implementation of even a limited conception of the rule of law might be loosely characterized as political economy-based impediments, where lack of effective political demand for reforms, on the one hand, and vested supply-side interests, on the other, render these reforms politically difficult to realize even if (by assumption) they would render most citizens better off in terms of their own values. On the demand side, because a procedurally-oriented conception of the rule of law has many of the attributes of a public good, diffuse citizen commitment to the rule of law is unlikely to translate into effective political mobilization for reforms. Instead, more particularized citizen grievances are likely to be channeled directly into the legislative or executive decision-making process. As well, one should not naively assume that all external constituencies are likely to benefit from rule of law reform. Indeed, those who derive benefits from corruption, cronyism, favouritism, etc., in existing institutional arrangements and legal processes are

---

[117] See Rosa Ehrenreich Brooks, *supra* note 76.
[118] See various contributions in Lawrence Harrison and Samuel Huntington (eds), *Culture Matters* (New York: Basic Books, 2000).

likely to resist such reforms.[119] On the supply side, vested or incumbent interests in institutions or processes that do not comport even with a minimalist, procedurally-oriented conception of the rule of law, e.g., a corrupt or incompetent judiciary, public prosecution, police, correctional system, tax administration or other specialized law enforcement, administrative or regulatory agencies, members of the private bar and legal education institutions, are likely to resist such reforms.

The critical relationship between the rule of law and issues of political economy (which we emphasize throughout this book) is insightfully articulated by Maravall and Przeworski:[120]

> To develop a positive conception of the rule of law one must start with political forces, their goals, their organization and their context. It is not stability that distinguishes the rule of law but the distribution of power. When power is monopolized, the law is at most an instrument of the rule of someone. Only if conflicting political actors seek to resolve their conflicts by recourse to law does law rule. Rule of law emerges when self-interested rulers willingly restrain themselves and make their behaviour predictable in order to obtain sustained, voluntary cooperation of well-organized groups commanding valuable resources. In exchange for such cooperation, rulers will protect the interests of these groups by legal means ...
>
> The difference between rule by law and rule of law lies in the distribution of power, the dispersion of material resources, the multiplication of organized interests; in societies that approximate the rule of law, no group becomes so strong as to dominate the others, and law, rather than reflect the interests of a single group, is used by the many. The rule of law is conceivable only if institutions tame or transform brute power. As organized interests multiply, a society will come closer to the rule of law: power will not be monopolized, and the law will not be used by the few against the many.

Holmes similarly argues:

> Why do people with power accept limits to their power? An even more pointed formulation is: why do people with guns obey people without guns? An economic twist is: why would the rich even voluntarily part with a portion of their wealth? In legal theory, the parallel question runs: why do politicians sometimes hand power to judges? Why do politicians allow judges, who control neither purse nor sword, to overturn and obstruct their decisions and sometimes even to send office-holders to

---

[119]   See Daniel Kaufmann, "Rethinking Governance," The World Bank, discussion draft, March 2003; Joel Hellman and Daniel Kaufmann, "The Inequality of Influence," The World Bank Institute: preliminary draft, December 2002; Karla Hoff and Joseph Stiglitz, "After the Big Bang? Obstacles to the Emergence of the Rule of Law in Post-Communist Societies" (2004) 94 *American Economic Review* 753–63.

[120]   José María Maravall and Adam Przeworski (eds), *Democracy and the Rule of Law* (Cambridge and New York: Cambridge University Press, 2003), Introduction at 2–4.

jail? ... Societies may approximate the rule of law if they consist of a large number of power-wielding groups, comprising a majority of the population, and if none of them become so strong as to be able thoroughly to dominate the others. We may be able to loosen the grip of a few organized interests on power by forcing them to share political leverage with a variety of other groups. This is polyarchy; it is also rough justice, the only kind human beings will ever experience. Formulated differently, the balancing of many partialities is the closest we can come to impartiality. This may not sound particularly ideal, but it is nevertheless historically quite rare and very difficult to achieve.[121]

In the following eight chapters, we specify the characteristics associated with a procedural conception of the rule of law more precisely with respect to various classes of legal institutions: the judiciary, prosecutors, police, penal systems, specialized law enforcement agencies, legal aid, bar associations, and legal education, drawing whenever possible on benchmarks reflected in international covenants, codes, agreements and guidelines that have attracted broad consensus amongst both developed and developing countries so as to minimize concerns over ethnocentric or normative imperialism, and against these benchmarks review selective recent rule of law reform experiences in Latin America, Africa, Central and Eastern Europe, and Asia. Our choice of countries and examples of rule of law reform initiatives are largely governed by pragmatic considerations of publicly available information on such initiatives. Where similar initiatives have been undertaken by several countries in a region, we typically only describe one such representative initiative in detail. We conclude each chapter with a brief assessment of the relevance of each of our three hypothesized impediments to rule of law reform to the experience reviewed. In the light of these impediments to rule of law reform in developing countries, Chapter 10 concludes the book by drawing from these empirical reviews the central implications for the role of the international community in promoting or supporting future rule of law reform efforts in developing countries.

In adopting this institutional focus, we largely reject the position of Kleinfeld[122] who argues that in much of the contemporary promotion of the rule of law abroad, institutions have been transmuted from means to ends in themselves. She argues that reforms to single institutions do not necessarily achieve any rule of law ends because each requires reforms across multiple institutions. According to Kleinfeld, defining the rule of law by its institutions also slants practitioners towards overly technocratic models of reform. The rule of law is as much a cultural and political model as a technocratic or even legal institution. An institutional attributes-type of definition also fails to ask why institutions

---

[121]   Stephen Holmes, "Lineages of the Rule of Law," in Maravall and Przeworski (eds), *id*.

[122]   Kleinfeld, *op. cit.*

are so bad – and whose interests are served through weak rule of law institutions. Another problem that arises from such institutional modeling is that reformers tend to waste time and scarce legal resources within developing countries in efforts to make laws and institutions look like those in their own systems.

However, in our view, Kleinfeld's preferred focus on ends-based conceptions of the rule of law conduces to largely sterile debates over normative abstractions, detached from their institutional instantiations, which, at the end of the day, is what is likely to matter most to a country's citizens. Moreover, eschewing extended abstract debates and focusing instead on what concrete procedural and institutional arrangements are likely to meet a given society's minimum conception of the rule of law reduces the risks of perfectionism. That is to say, while the characteristics of perfect procedural and institutional arrangements may be difficult to specify and defend from a rule of law perspective, either in the abstract or in particular contexts, it may be much easier to forge a social consensus around seriously dysfunctional characteristics that are broadly unacceptable. That is to say, it may be much easier to agree on what is ruled out, rather than what is ruled in.

APPENDIX

Table 1A.1   World Bank: rule of law indicators for selected countries, 1996 and 2002

	1996		2002	
Country/Territory	Point Estimate	Percentile Rank	Point Estimate	Percentile Rank
Latin America				
Argentina	0.27	65.7	–0.73	27.8
Bolivia	–0.62	29.5	–0.60	32.5
Brazil	–0.24	46.4	–0.30	50
Chile	1.19	86.7	1.30	87.1
Columbia	–0.44	36.1	–0.75	26.8
Costa Rica	0.61	74.1	0.67	72.2
Dominican Republic	–0.49	33.7	–0.43	42.8
Ecuador	–0.38	38.6	–0.60	33
El Salvador	–0.45	35.5	–0.46	39.7
Guatemala	–0.61	30.1	–0.84	21.6
Honduras	–0.81	18.7	–0.79	23.7
Mexico	–0.11	55.4	–0.22	52.1

Table 1A.1   continued

| Country/Territory | 1996 | | 2002 | |
	Point Estimate	Percentile Rank	Point Estimate	Percentile Rank
Nicaragua	−0.66	25.9	−0.63	32
Panama	0.25	65.1	0.00	55.7
Paraguay	−0.48	34.3	−1.12	11.9
Peru	−0.33	40.4	−0.44	40.7
Uruguay	0.49	72.3	0.56	69.1
Venezuela	−0.62	28.9	−1.04	13.4
Sub-Saharan Africa				
Angola	−1.36	3.6	−1.56	3.1
Benin	−0.01	57.2	−0.42	43.3
Botswana	0.76	81.3	0.72	72.7
Burkina Faso	−0.71	23.5	−0.55	34
Burundi	−0.18	49.4	−1.49	3.6
Cameroon	−1.12	12	−1.28	6.2
Cape Verde	0.08	60.2	0.19	60.3
Central African Republic	−0.18	49.4	−0.88	19.6
Chad	−0.18	49.4	−0.93	17
Comoros	N/A	N/A	−0.84	20.6
Congo	−1.20	6	−1.22	8.2
Congo, Dem. Rep.	−1.73	0.6	−1.79	0.5
Côte d'Ivoire	−0.65	27.1	−1.21	8.8
Equatorial Guinea	N/A	N/A	−1.19	9.3
Eritrea	−0.18	49.4	−0.51	36.1
Ethiopia	−0.26	45.8	−0.44	41.2
Gabon	−0.29	42.8	−0.27	50.5
Gambia	0.23	64.5	−0.50	37.1
Ghana	−0.11	54.2	−0.15	53.6
Guinea	−1.02	12.7	−0.75	27.3
Guinea-Bissau	−1.50	1.8	−1.00	15.5
Kenya	−0.73	22.9	−1.04	13.9
Lesotho	−0.29	43.4	−0.01	54.6
Liberia	−2.04	0	−1.42	4.1
Madagascar	−0.80	19.3	−0.19	53.1
Malawi	−0.19	48.2	−0.34	46.4
Mali	−0.73	22.3	−0.54	34.5

Table 1A.1   continued

Country/Territory	1996		2002	
	Point Estimate	Percentile Rank	Point Estimate	Percentile Rank
Mauritania	–0.58	31.3	–0.33	47.4
Mauritius	0.68	77.1	0.89	78.4
Mozambique	–1.17	7.2	–0.65	29.9
Namibia	0.34	68.7	0.45	67
Niger	–1.19	6.6	–0.78	25.8
Nigeria	–1.14	9	–1.35	5.2
Rwanda	–0.18	49.4	–1.01	14.4
São Tomé and Príncipe	N/A	N/A	–0.45	40.2
Senegal	–0.16	53	–0.20	52.6
Seychelles	N/A	N/A	0.52	68.6
Sierra Leone	–0.97	15.1	–1.25	7.2
Somalia	–1.60	1.2	–2.05	0
South Africa	0.34	67.5	0.19	59.8
Sudan	–1.38	3	–1.36	4.6
Swaziland	0.38	69.3	–0.67	29.4
Tanzania	–0.66	25.3	–0.49	38.7
Togo	–1.17	7.8	–0.67	28.9
Uganda	–0.83	17.5	–0.84	21.1
Zambia	–0.33	41	–0.52	35.6
Zimbabwe	–0.22	47	–1.33	5.7
Former Soviet Union				
Armenia	–0.44	36.7	–0.44	41.8
Azerbaijan	–0.81	18.1	–0.79	24.2
Belarus	–0.96	15.7	–1.12	11.3
Georgia	–0.80	20.5	–1.17	9.8
Kazakhstan	–0.69	24.7	–0.90	18.6
Kyrgyz Republic	–0.65	26.5	–0.83	22.2
Moldova	–0.19	48.8	–0.49	39.2
Russia	–0.80	19.9	–0.78	25.3
Tajikistan	–1.34	4.2	–1.27	6.7
Turkmenistan	–1.13	10.2	–1.16	10.8
Ukraine	–0.64	28.3	–0.79	24.7
Uzbekistan	–0.97	14.5	–1.16	10.3

Table 1A.1   continued

Country/Territory	1996		2002	
	Point Estimate	Percentile Rank	Point Estimate	Percentile Rank
Eastern Europe				
Albania	−0.30	42.2	−0.92	17.5
Bosnia-Herzegovina	−0.18	49.4	−0.88	19.1
Bulgaria	−0.09	56	0.05	56.7
Croatia	−0.50	33.1	0.11	58.8
Czech Republic	0.61	73.5	0.74	73.2
Estonia	0.33	66.9	0.80	74.7
Hungary	0.62	75.3	0.90	78.9
Latvia	0.18	62	0.46	67.5
Lithuania	−0.14	53.6	0.48	68
Macedonia	−0.53	31.9	−0.41	44.3
Poland	0.44	69.9	0.65	70.6
Romania	−0.27	44	−0.12	54.1
Slovak Republic	0.11	61.4	0.40	65.5
Slovenia	0.49	71.7	1.09	83.5
Turkey	0.02	58.4	0.00	55.2
Yugoslavia	−1.14	9.6	−0.95	16
East and Southeast Asia				
Brunei	0.67	76.5	0.64	70.1
Cambodia	−0.86	16.9	−0.86	20.1
China	−0.43	37.3	−0.22	51.5
Fiji	0.09	60.8	−0.39	45.4
Hong Kong	1.62	90.4	1.30	86.6
Indonesia	−0.34	39.8	−0.80	23.2
Kiribati	N/A	N/A	−0.32	47.9
Korea, North	−0.98	13.9	−1.00	14.9
Korea, South	0.77	81.9	0.88	77.8
Laos	−1.29	4.8	−1.05	12.9
Macao	N/A	N/A	0.75	73.7
Malaysia	0.80	82.5	0.58	69.6
Marshall Islands	N/A	N/A	−0.32	47.9
Micronesia	N/A	N/A	−0.64	30.4
Mongolia	0.45	70.5	0.36	64.9
Myanmar	−1.25	5.4	−1.62	2.1

Table 1A.1   continued

Country/Territory	1996		2002	
	Point Estimate	Percentile Rank	Point Estimate	Percentile Rank
Nauru	N/A	N/A	N/A	N/A
Papua New Guinea	−0.32	41.6	−0.82	22.7
Philippines	−0.11	54.8	−0.50	38.1
Samoa	N/A	N/A	0.94	79.9
Singapore	2.01	99.4	1.75	93.3
Solomon Islands	N/A	N/A	−0.64	30.4
Taiwan	0.96	84.3	0.95	80.9
Thailand	0.46	71.1	0.30	62.4
Timor, East	N/A	N/A	−1.11	12.4
Tonga	N/A	N/A	−0.64	30.4
Tuvalu	N/A	N/A	N/A	N/A
Vanuatu	N/A	N/A	−0.32	47.9
Vietnam	−0.47	34.9	−0.39	44.8
South Asia				
Afghanistan	−1.13	10.8	−1.61	2.6
Bangladesh	−0.65	27.7	−0.78	26.3
Bhutan	−1.13	10.8	0.10	58.2
India	−0.01	56.6	0.07	57.2
Maldives	N/A	N/A	0.44	66
Nepal	−0.34	39.2	−0.50	37.6
Pakistan	−0.41	38	−0.70	28.4
Sri Lanka	0.27	66.3	0.23	60.8
OECD				
Andorra	N/A	N/A	1.55	90.2
Australia	1.79	93.4	1.85	95.4
Austria	1.88	95.8	1.91	95.9
Belgium	1.57	89.2	1.45	89.7
Canada	1.77	92.8	1.79	93.8
Cyprus	0.58	72.9	0.83	76.8
Denmark	1.92	97	1.97	97.9
Finland	1.97	97.6	1.99	98.5
France	1.56	88.6	1.33	87.6
Germany	1.79	94	1.73	92.8
Greece	0.74	79.5	0.79	74.2

Table 1A.1   concluded

Country/Territory	1996		2002	
	Point Estimate	Percentile Rank	Point Estimate	Percentile Rank
Iceland	1.61	89.8	2.00	99.5
Ireland	1.67	91	1.72	92.3
Italy	0.84	83.1	0.82	75.8
Japan	1.51	88	1.41	88.7
Liechtenstein	N/A	N/A	1.55	90.2
Luxembourg	1.69	91.6	2.00	99
Monaco	N/A	N/A	N/A	N/A
Netherlands	1.84	95.2	1.83	94.8
New Zealand	1.97	98.2	1.91	96.4
Norway	1.99	98.8	1.96	97.4
Portugal	1.28	87.3	1.30	86.1
San Marino	N/A	N/A	N/A	N/A
Spain	1.16	86.1	1.15	84.5
Sweden	1.92	96.4	1.92	96.9
Switzerland	2.05	100	2.03	100
United Kingdom	1.84	94.6	1.81	94.3
United States	1.70	92.2	1.70	91.8

Notes:
1. The sources of this table are Daniel Kaufmann, Aart Kraay and Massimo Mastruzzi, "Govern-ance Matters III: Governance Indicators for 1996–2002," World Bank Discussion Draft, June 30, 2003 (available at http://www.worldbank.org/wbi/governance/pdf/govmatters3.pdf); World Bank, GRICS: Governance Research Indicator Country Snapshot (available at http://info.worldbank.org/governance/kkz2002/mc_region.asp). Only the data for 1996 and 2002 are se-lected in this table for the purpose of this chapter.
2. According to the compilers of the World Bank governance data, which is constructed on the basis of a number of polls of country experts and surveys of residents, the primary aggregate indicator for rule of law is countries' point estimates ranging from –2.5 to +2.5. Countries' percentile ranks ranging from 0 to 100 are also provided at the World Bank GRICS website and included in this table. Because countries' relative positions on the aggregate indicators are subject to margins of error, precise country rankings cannot be inferred from the World Bank data. It is indicated that the average standard error of the rule of law indicator is 0.26 for 1996 and 0.19 for 2002 (Kaufmann *et al.*, "Governance Matters III: Governance Indicators for 1996–2002," World Bank Discussion Draft, June 30, 2003).
3. For the purpose of this chapter, countries and territories in five regions/categories are included in this table: Latin America, sub-Saharan Africa, the former Soviet Union and Eastern Europe, Asia (minus Japan and the former Soviet Union republics in Central Asia), and OECD. Fol-lowing the world classification by the compilers of the World Bank governance indicators, Australia and New Zealand are listed under OECD in this table.
4. N/A in this table stands for "not available."

Table 1A.2   Freedom House: freedom ratings, 2004

Trend Arrow	Country	PR	CL	Freedom Rating
	Afghanistan	6	6	Not Free
	Albania	3	3	Partly Free
	Algeria	6	5	Not Free
	Andorra	1	1	Free
	Angola	6	5	Not Free
	Antigua and Barbuda	4	2	Partly Free
	Argentina	2 ▲	2 ▲	Free
↓	Armenia	4	4	Partly Free
	Australia	1	1	Free
	Austria	1	1	Free
	Azerbaijan	6	5	Not Free
	Bahamas	1	1	Free
	Bahrain	5	5	Partly Free
	Bangladesh	4	4	Partly Free
	Barbados	1	1	Free
↓	Belarus	6	6	Not Free
	Belgium	1	1	Free
	Belize	1	2	Free
	Benin	2 ▲	2	Free
	Bhutan	6	5	Not Free
	Bolivia	3 ▼	3	Partly Free
↑	Bosnia-Herzegovina	4	4	Partly Free
	Botswana	2	2	Free
	Brazil	2	3	Free
	Brunei	6	5	Not Free
	Bulgaria	1	2	Free
	Burkina Faso	4	4	Partly Free
	Burma	7	7	Not Free
	Burundi	5 ▲	5	Partly Free
	Cambodia	6	5	Not Free
↓	Cameroon	6	6	Not Free
	Canada	1	1	Free
	Cape Verde	1	1 ▲	Free
	Central African Republic	7 ▼	5	Not Free
	Chad	6	5	Not Free
	Chile	1 ▲	1	Free
	China (PRC)	7	6	Not Free

Table 1A.2   continued

Trend Arrow	Country	PR	CL	Freedom Rating
	Colombia	4	4	Partly Free
	Comoros	5	4	Partly Free
	Congo (Brazzaville)	5 ▲	4	Partly Free
↑	Congo (Kinshasa)	6	6	Not Free
	Costa Rica	1	2	Free
	Côte d'Ivoire	6	5 ▲	Not Free
	Croatia	2	2	Free
	Cuba	7	7	Not Free
	Cyprus (G)	1	1	Free
	Czech Republic	1	2	Free
	Denmark	1	1	Free
	Djibouti	5 ▼	5	Partly Free
	Dominica	1	1	Free
	Dominican Republic	3 ▼	2	Free
	East Timor	3	3	Partly Free
↑	Ecuador	3	3	Partly Free
	Egypt	6	6	Not Free
↓	El Salvador	2	3	Free
	Equatorial Guinea	7	6	Not Free
	Eritrea	7	6	Not Free
	Estonia	1	2	Free
	Ethiopia	5	5	Partly Free
↓	Fiji	4	3	Partly Free
	Finland	1	1	Free
	France	1	1	Free
↓	Gabon	5	4	Partly Free
	The Gambia	4	4	Partly Free
	Georgia	4	4	Partly Free
	Germany	1	1	Free
	Ghana	2	2 ▲	Free
	Greece	1	2	Free
	Grenada	1	2	Free
↓	Guatemala	4	4	Partly Free
	Guinea	6	5	Not Free
	Guinea-Bissau	6 ▼	4 ▲	Partly Free
	Guyana	2	2	Free
↓	Haiti	6	6	Not Free

Table 1A.2   continued

Trend Arrow	Country	PR	CL	Freedom Rating
↓	Honduras	3	3	Partly Free
	Hungary	1	2	Free
	Iceland	1	1	Free
	India	2	3	Free
	Indonesia	3	4	Partly Free
	Iran	6	6	Not Free
	Iraq	7	5 ▲	Not Free
	Ireland	1	1	Free
	Israel	1	3	Free
	Italy	1	1	Free
↓	Jamaica	2	3	Free
	Japan	1	2	Free
	Jordan	5 ▲	5	Partly Free
	Kazakhstan	6	5	Not Free
	Kenya	3 ▲	3 ▲	Partly Free
	Kiribati	1	1	Free
	Kuwait	4	5	Partly Free
	Kyrgyzstan	6	5	Not Free
	Laos	7	6	Not Free
	Latvia	1	2	Free
	Lebanon	6	5	Not Free
	Lesotho	2	3	Free
↑	Liberia	6	6	Not Free
	Libya	7	7	Not Free
	Liechtenstein	1	1	Free
	Lithuania	1	2	Free
	Luxembourg	1	1	Free
↑	Macedonia	3	3	Partly Free
	Madagascar	3	3 ▲	Partly Free
	Malawi	3 ▲	4	Partly Free
	Malaysia	5	4 ▲	Partly Free
	Maldives	6	5	Not Free
	Mali	2	2 ▲	Free
	Malta	1	1	Free
	Marshall Islands	1	1	Free
	Mauritania	6 ▼	5	Not Free
	Mauritius	1	2	Free

Table 1A.2 continued

Trend Arrow	Country	PR	CL	Freedom Rating
	Mexico	2	2	Free
	Micronesia	1	1 ▲	Free
	Moldova	3	4	Partly Free
	Monaco	2	1	Free
	Mongolia	2	2	Free
	Morocco	5	5	Partly Free
	Mozambique	3	4	Partly Free
	Namibia	2	3	Free
	Nauru	1	1 ▲	Free
	Nepal	5 ▼	4	Partly Free
	Netherlands	1	1	Free
	New Zealand	1	1	Free
↓	Nicaragua	3	3	Partly Free
	Niger	4	4	Partly Free
	Nigeria	4	4 ▲	Partly Free
	North Korea	7	7	Not Free
	Norway	1	1	Free
	Oman	6	5	Not Free
	Pakistan	6	5	Not Free
	Palau	1	1 ▲	Free
	Panama	1	2	Free
	Papua New Guinea	3 ▼	3	Partly Free
	Paraguay	3 ▲	3	Partly Free
	Peru	2	3	Free
	Philippines	2	3	Free
	Poland	1	2	Free
	Portugal	1	1	Free
↑	Qatar	6	6	Not Free
	Romania	2	2	Free
↓	Russia	5	5	Partly Free
	Rwanda	6 ▲	5	Not Free
	Saint Kitts and Nevis	1	2	Free
	Saint Lucia	1	2	Free
	Saint Vincent and the Grenadines	2	1	Free
	Samoa	2	2	Free
	San Marino	1	1	Free

Table 1A.2   continued

Trend Arrow	Country	PR	CL	Freedom Rating
	São Tomé and Príncipe	2 ▼	2	Free
	Saudi Arabia	7	7	Not Free
	Senegal	2	3	Free
↓	Serbia and Montenegro	3	2	Free
	Seychelles	3	3	Partly Free
	Sierra Leone	4	3 ▲	Partly Free
	Singapore	5	4	Partly Free
	Slovakia	1	2	Free
	Slovenia	1	1	Free
	Solomon Islands	3	3	Partly Free
	Somalia	6	7	Not Free
	South Africa	1	2	Free
	South Korea	2	2	Free
	Spain	1	1	Free
	Sri Lanka	3	3 ▲	Partly Free
	Sudan	7	7	Not Free
	Suriname	1	2	Free
	Swaziland	7 ▼	5	Not Free
	Sweden	1	1	Free
	Switzerland	1	1	Free
	Syria	7	7	Not Free
	Taiwan (Rep. of China)	2	2	Free
	Tajikistan	6	5	Not Free
	Tanzania	4	3	Partly Free
	Thailand	2	3	Free
	Togo	6	5	Not Free
↓	Tonga	5	3	Partly Free
	Trinidad and Tobago	3	3	Partly Free
	Tunisia	6	5	Not Free
	Turkey	3	4	Partly Free
	Turkmenistan	7	7	Not Free
	Tuvalu	1	1	Free
	Uganda	5 ▲	4	Partly Free
	Ukraine	4	4	Partly Free
	United Arab Emirates	6	6 ▼	Not Free
	United Kingdom†	1	1	Free
	United States	1	1	Free

Table 1A.2   concluded

Trend Arrow	Country	PR	CL	Freedom Rating
	Uruguay	1	1	Free
	Uzbekistan	7	6	Not Free
	Vanuatu	2 ▼	2	Free
↓	Venezuela	3	4	Partly Free
	Vietnam	7	6	Not Free
	Yemen	5 ▲	5	Partly Free
↑	Zambia	4	4	Partly Free
↓	Zimbabwe	6	6	Not Free

Notes:
The ratings in this table reflect global events from January 1, 2003, through November 30, 2003.
PR and CL stand for Political Rights and Civil Liberties.
1 represents the most free and 7 the least free rating.
↑↓ up or down indicates a general trend in freedom.
▲▼ up or down indicates a change in Political Rights or Civil Liberties since the last survey.
† excluding Northern Ireland.
The freedom ratings reflect an overall judgment based on survey results.

Source: Freedom House, *Freedom in the World 2004: The Annual Survey of Political Rights and Civil Liberties* (Lanham, MD: Rowman and Littlefield, 2004).

Table 1A.3   Transparency International: corruption perceptions index, 2004

Country rank	Country	2004 CPI Score*	Confidence Range**	Surveys Used***
1	Finland	9.7	9.5–9.8	9
2	New Zealand	9.6	9.4–9.6	9
3	Denmark	9.5	9.3–9.7	10
	Iceland	9.5	9.4–9.7	8
5	Singapore	9.3	9.2–9.4	13
6	Sweden	9.2	9.1–9.3	11
7	Switzerland	9.1	8.9–9.2	10
8	Norway	8.9	8.6–9.1	9
9	Australia	8.8	8.4–9.1	15
10	Netherlands	8.7	8.5–8.9	10
11	United Kingdom	8.6	8.4–8.8	12
12	Canada	8.5	8.1–8.9	12
13	Austria	8.4	8.1–8.8	10

Table 1A.3   continued

Country rank	Country	2004 CPI Score*	Confidence Range**	Surveys Used***
	Luxembourg	8.4	8.0–8.9	7
15	Germany	8.2	8.0–8.5	11
16	Hong Kong	8.0	7.1–8.5	13
17	Belgium	7.5	7.1–8.0	10
	Ireland	7.5	7.2–7.9	10
	USA	7.5	6.9–8.0	14
20	Chile	7.4	7.0–7.8	11
21	Barbados	7.3	6.6–7.6	3
22	France	7.1	6.6–7.6	12
23	Spain	7.1	6.7–7.4	11
24	Japan	6.9	6.2–7.4	15
25	Malta	6.8	5.3–8.2	4
26	Israel	6.4	5.6–7.1	10
27	Portugal	6.3	5.8–6.8	9
28	Uruguay	6.2	5.9–6.7	6
29	Oman	6.1	5.1–6.8	5
	United Arab Emirates	6.1	5.1–7.1	5
31	Botswana	6.0	5.3–6.8	7
	Estonia	6.0	5.6–6.7	12
	Slovenia	6.0	5.6–6.6	12
34	Bahrain	5.8	5.5–6.2	5
35	Taiwan	5.6	5.2–6.1	15
36	Cyprus	5.4	5.0–5.8	4
37	Jordan	5.3	4.6–5.9	9
38	Qatar	5.2	4.6–5.6	4
39	Malaysia	5.0	4.5–5.6	15
40	Tunisia	5.0	4.5–5.6	7
41	Costa Rica	4.9	4.2–5.8	8
42	Hungary	4.8	4.6–5.0	12
	Italy	4.8	4.4–5.1	10
44	Kuwait	4.6	3.8–5.3	5
	Lithuania	4.6	4.0–5.4	9
	South Africa	4.6	4.2–5.0	11
47	South Korea	4.5	4.0–4.9	14
48	Seychelles	4.4	3.7–5.0	3
49	Greece	4.3	4.0–4.8	9
	Suriname	4.3	2.1–5.8	3

Table 1A.3   continued

Country rank	Country	2004 CPI Score*	Confidence Range**	Surveys Used***
51	Czech Republic	4.2	3.7–4.9	11
	El Salvador	4.2	3.3–5.1	7
	Trinidad/Tobago	4.2	3.6–5.2	6
54	Bulgaria	4.1	3.7–4.6	10
	Mauritius	4.1	3.2–4.8	5
	Namibia	4.1	3.5–4.6	7
57	Latvia	4.0	3.8–4.3	8
	Slovakia	4.0	3.6–4.5	11
59	Brazil	3.9	3.7–4.1	11
60	Belize	3.8	3.4–4.1	3
	Colombia	3.8	3.4–4.1	10
62	Cuba	3.7	2.2–4.7	4
	Panama	3.7	3.4–4.2	7
64	Ghana	3.6	3.1–4.1	7
	Mexico	3.6	3.3–3.8	11
	Thailand	3.6	3.3–3.9	14
67	Croatia	3.5	3.3–3.8	9
	Peru	3.5	3.3–3.7	8
	Poland	3.5	3.1–3.9	13
	Sri Lanka	3.5	3.1–3.9	8
71	China	3.4	3.0–3.8	16
	Saudi Arabia	3.4	2.7–4.0	5
	Syria	3.4	2.8–4.1	5
74	Belarus	3.3	1.9–4.8	5
	Gabon	3.3	2.1–3.7	3
	Jamaica	3.3	2.8–3.7	6
77	Benin	3.2	2.0–4.3	3
	Egypt	3.2	2.7–3.8	8
	Mali	3.2	2.2–4.2	5
	Morocco	3.2	2.9–3.5	7
	Turkey	3.2	2.8–3.7	13
82	Armenia	3.1	2.4–3.7	5
	Bosnia and Herzegovina	3.1	2.7–3.5	7
	Madagascar	3.1	1.8–4.4	4
85	Mongolia	3.0	2.6–3.2	3
	Senegal	3.0	2.5–3.5	6
87	Dominican Republic	2.9	2.4–3.3	6

Table 1A.3   continued

Country rank	Country	2004 CPI Score*	Confidence Range**	Surveys Used***
	Iran	2.9	2.2–3.4	5
	Romania	2.9	2.5–3.4	12
90	Gambia	2.8	2.2–3.4	5
	India	2.8	2.6–3.0	15
	Malawi	2.8	2.2–3.7	5
	Mozambique	2.8	2.4–3.1	7
	Nepal	2.8	1.6–3.4	3
	Russia	2.8	2.5–3.1	15
	Tanzania	2.8	2.4–3.2	7
97	Algeria	2.7	2.3–3.0	6
	Lebanon	2.7	2.1–3.2	5
	Macedonia	2.7	2.3–3.2	7
	Nicaragua	2.7	2.5–3.0	7
	Serbia and Montenegro	2.7	2.3–3.0	7
102	Eritrea	2.6	1.6–3.4	3
	Papua New Guinea	2.6	1.9–3.4	4
	Philippines	2.6	2.4–2.9	14
	Uganda	2.6	2.1–3.1	7
	Vietnam	2.6	2.3–2.9	11
	Zambia	2.6	2.3–2.9	6
108	Albania	2.5	2.0–3.0	4
	Argentina	2.5	2.2–2.8	11
	Libya	2.5	1.9–3.0	4
	Palestinian Authority	2.5	2.0–2.7	3
112	Ecuador	2.4	2.3–2.5	7
	Yemen	2.4	1.9–2.9	5
114	Congo, Republic of	2.3	2.0–2.7	4
	Ethiopia	2.3	1.9–2.9	6
	Honduras	2.3	2.0–2.6	7
	Moldova	2.3	2.0–2.8	5
	Sierra Leone	2.3	2.0–2.7	3
	Uzbekistan	2.3	2.1–2.4	6
	Venezuela	2.3	2.2–2.5	11
	Zimbabwe	2.3	1.9–2.7	7
122	Bolivia	2.2	2.1–2.3	6
	Guatemala	2.2	2.0–2.4	7
	Kazakhstan	2.2	1.8–2.7	7

Table 1A.3   concluded

Country rank	Country	2004 CPI Score*	Confidence Range**	Surveys Used***
	Kyrgyzstan	2.2	2.0–2.5	5
	Niger	2.2	2.0–2.5	3
	Sudan	2.2	2.0–2.3	5
	Ukraine	2.2	2.0–2.4	10
	Cameroon	2.1	1.9–2.3	5
129	Iraq	2.1	1.3–2.8	4
	Kenya	2.1	1.9–2.4	7
	Pakistan	2.1	1.6–2.6	7
133	Angola	2.0	1.7–2.1	5
	Congo, Democratic Rep.	2.0	1.5–2.2	3
	Côte d'Ivoire	2.0	1.7–2.2	5
	Georgia	2.0	1.6–2.3	7
	Indonesia	2.0	1.7–2.2	14
	Tajikistan	2.0	1.7–2.4	4
	Turkmenistan	2.0	1.6–2.3	3
140	Azerbaijan	1.9	1.8–2.0	7
	Paraguay	1.9	1.7–2.2	7
142	Chad	1.7	1.1–2.3	4
	Myanmar	1.7	1.5–2.0	4
144	Nigeria	1.6	1.4–1.8	9
145	Bangladesh	1.5	1.1–1.9	8
	Haiti	1.5	1.2–1.9	5

Notes:
This table was compiled at the University of Passau on behalf of Transparency International. For information on data and methodology, please consult the frequently asked questions and framework document at http://www.transparency/org/surveys/#cpi.

*   CPI Score relates to perceptions of the degree of corruption as seen by business people and country analysts and ranges between 10 (highly clean) and 0 (highly corrupt).

**   Confidence range provides a range of possible values of the CPI score. This reflects how a country's score may vary, depending on measurement precision. Normally, with 5% probability the score is above this range and with another 5% it is below. However, particularly when only few sources (n) are available an unbiased estimate of the mean coverage probability is lower than the nominal value of 90%.

***   Surveys used refers to the number of surveys that assessed a country's performance. Eighteen surveys and expert assessments were used and at least three were required for a country to be included in the CPI.

Source: http://www.transparency.org/cpi/2004/cpi2004.en.html.

2. The judiciary

I. NORMATIVE BENCHMARKS

A. Introduction

Any attempt to elaborate an institutional approach to reform specific to the judiciary faces a tension between the importance of reform on the one hand, and the plurality of approaches to judging on the other. That judicial reform is a necessary part of the rule of law reform has been emphasized by leading development theorists[1] and is reflected prominently in international consensus.[2] However, it remains difficult, if not impossible, to identify an accepted gold standard of the judiciary.[3] A multitude of theories conceptualizing the judicial function has led to an "eclectic" approach to the judicial role that belies any attempt to identify one dominant and all-encompassing theory of the judiciary.[4] In the face of claims about the "judicialization of politics," it is difficult even to demarcate the boundaries of the judiciary in relation to the politicians that it is in part intended to monitor.[5] Therefore, while we stress the importance of judi-

---

[1]   Amartya Sen, "What is the Role of Legal and Judicial Reform in the Development Process?" (World Bank Legal Conference, Washington, DC, June 5, 2000) at 22.

[2]   United Nations Basic Principles on the Independence of the Judiciary were adopted by the 7th Congress on the Prevention of Crime and Torture in Milan, Italy in September 1985 and were endorsed by the General Assembly later that year. See G.A. Res. 40/32, U.N. GAOR, 40th Sess., U.N. Doc. A/RES/40/32 (1985).

[3]   As Waldron points out, "one of the most important circumstances of politics in general is that people disagree about justice and rights." (Jeremy Waldron, "Moral Truth and Judicial Review" (1998) 43 *Am. J. Juris.* 75 at 77.

[4]   Aharon Barak, "A Judge on Judging: The Role of a Supreme Court in a Democracy" (2002) 116 *Harv. L. Rev.* 16 at 21.

[5]   See, for some major examples: Alec Stone Sweet, *Governing With Judges* (Oxford: Oxford University Press, 2000); Dan Keleman, "The Limits of Judicial Power" (2001) 34 *Comparative Political Science* 622; Carlo Guarnieri and Patrizia Pederzoli, *The Power of Judges* (Oxford: Oxford University Press, 2002); Neal Tate and Torbjorn Vallinder, *The Global Expansion of Judicial Power* (New York: New York University Press, 1995); William A. Bogart, *Courts and Country* (Oxford: Oxford University Press, 1995); Martin Shapiro, *Courts: A Comparative and Political Analysis* (Chicago: University of Chicago Press, 1986); Theodore Becker, *Comparative Judicial Politics: The Political Functionings of Courts* (Chicago: Rand McNally, 1970). For a critical perspec-

cial reform, we consider it only in terms of the key institutional values identified previously: independence, accountability and legitimacy.

The important of judicial independence has long been emphasized as key to maintaining the integrity of the judiciary in its role as a site of accountability for executive power. Alexander Hamilton believed that limitations on government "can be preserved in practice no other way than through the medium of courts of justice."[6] But as K.D. Ewing argues, independent monitoring is not the only foundational role of the judiciary. Courts not only restrain power – they also act as legislators, in their interpretation, application and, principally in common law jurisdictions, creation of legal rules. Such judicial lawmaking constitutes "a vast expanse of rule-making which remains completely untouched by the era of democracy, in the sense that the rules are made by a process from which the people are excluded, save only as litigants."[7] The legislative functions of the judiciary, like the lawmaking powers of the legislature and the executive, are only tenable when judicial power is in some way accountable. Only judicial accountability permits the appropriate and legitimate exercise of the legislative function of the judiciary in balance with its role of independence.[8]

The relationship between independence and accountability is a complex one. In some obvious respects, the two ideals sit in direct tension. For instance, as one USAID colloquium noted, the use of "hierarchical systems of supervision, common for maintaining accountability in executive agencies," are clearly problematic from the perspective of independent decision-making.[9] However, accountability is a multi-faceted concept and in many other more subtle ways mechanisms for independence can be consistent with, or even supportive of,

---

tive on Tate and Vallinder's collection see Haltern's review in *7 Eu. J. Int'l L. 1*; and especially Reisinger's review in *6 Law and Politics Book Review 1*.

[6] Alexander Hamilton, *The Federalist* No. 78, at pp. 465–6 (Clinton Rossiter ed., 1961). K.D. Ewing has similarly referred to "the overriding need to sustain the independence of the judiciary." (K.D. Ewing, "A Theory of Democratic Adjudication: Towards a Representative, Accountable and Independent Judiciary" (2000) 38 *Alta. L. Rev.* 709.)

[7] *Ibid.* at 711.

[8] The meaning of a democratic judiciary is the subject of much recent and interesting work. Ewing (*ibid.*) laments the absence of a coherent theory of adjudication as one of liberal democracy's major and fundamental deficits. Cass Sunstein's *Designing Democracy* (Oxford: Oxford University Press, 2002) considers that courts are related to participatory democracy as venues of deliberation, while Jeremy Waldron, in a number of essays in *Law and Disagreement* (Oxford: Clarendon Press, 1999), argues that judicial review, when not properly restrained, may actually "detract from the democratic character of the political system of which it is a part." (at p. 289).

[9] USAID, Office of Democracy and Governance, *Guidance for Promoting Judicial Independence and Impartiality* (Technical Publication Series (2002) at 19) [hereinafter *Guidance*].

judicial accountability.[10] Many traditional mechanisms used to ensure accountability threaten little, if any, interference with judicial independence: regularizing
appointments, following standards and procedures for the use of public resources, and ensuring public access to court decisions.[11] Moreover, some reforms
may improve both independence and accountability. Transparent selection and
promotion systems, for instance, generally considered mechanisms of independence, "can be thought of as a front-end mechanism of accountability,"[12] by
reducing the need for strong disciplinary mechanisms subsequently. Linn Hammergren argues for a different reason that "accountability in some sense also
strengthens independence. The need to account for its actions may reduce the
judiciary's vulnerability to external pressures, since in most cases the explanation
that 'the president made me do it' will not be an acceptable justification."[13]

Mechanisms for independence and accountability must also strike a delicate
balance in individual factual circumstances. Wartime or transitional government,
for instance, might prompt wide disagreements about the proper relationship
between the political and judicial branches.[14] Following Christopher Larkins,
we therefore acknowledge the importance of "regime relativity" in assessing

---

[10]   Martin L. Friedland, *A Place Apart: Judicial Independence and Accountability
in Canada* (Ottawa: Canadian Judicial Council, 1995) at 261.

[11]   But see Rogelio Pérez-Perdomo, "Judicial Independence and Accountability,"
Paper prepared for the *Meeting Comprehensive Legal and Judicial Development: Toward
an Agenda for a Just and Equitable Society in the 21st Century* Washington: World Bank
(June 5–7, 2000). Available online at: http://www4.worldbank.org/legal/legop_judicial/
ljr_conf_papers/Perez-Perdomo.pdf: "In practice, however, any accountability system
can be misused to punish independence, particularly if there is a double standard at work,
or different yardsticks for judges depending on their connections to the wielders of political power."

[12]   Ian Green, "Judicial Accountability in Canada," in P.C. Stenning (ed.), *Accountability for Criminal Justice: Selected Essays* (Toronto: University of Toronto Press, 1995)
ch. 15.

[13]   USAID, *Guidance*, *supra* note 9 at 152.

[14]   For instance, while Owen Fiss argues, with reference to the case of Argentina
after the dirty war under *Peronismo*, that new democracies should always dismiss,
wholesale, the old courts, Larkins disagrees stating that dismissing old courts "... can
actually injure the long-term functional independence of the judiciary as an institution.
It is certainly difficult for the courts to evolve when they are continually being altered,
especially without precise cause ... [C]ourts need to institutionalize before they will be
able to more forcefully act upon their independent (*sic*) ... When the judicial body is
dismissed and reconstituted, it needs to begin its process of development all over again,
thereby delaying by many more years the establishment of a judiciary which can be a
forceful mechanism in the protection of the rule of law." See Owen Fiss, "The Limits of
Judicial Independence" (1993) 25 *University of Miami Inter-American Law Review* 57
at 69 and Christopher Larkins, "Judicial Independence and Democratization: A Theoretical and Conceptual Analysis" (1996) 44 *Am. J. Comp. L.* 605 at 623.

judicial independence, and we adopt, as a starting point, his general definition of judicial independence as: "the existence of judges who are not manipulated for political gain, who are impartial toward the parties of a dispute, and who form a judicial branch which has the power as an institution to regulate the legality of government behaviour, enact 'neutral' justice, and determine significant constitutional and legal values."[15] In our view, this definition is largely reflected in international pronouncements on the subject.

B. Independence

The United Nations Basic Principles on the Independence of the Judiciary (Basic Principles) adopted by the General Assembly in 1985, is the leading international instrument establishing guidelines for judicial independence.[16] The Basic Principles reiterate the importance of the UN Declaration of Human rights, particularly the principle of equality before the law, explicitly state that freedom of expression extends to judges like all other citizens, and provide guidance for conditions of service, tenure, remuneration, and disciplining of judges.

There are several key mechanisms for ensuring judicial independence. First is a transparent, merit-based appointment process. The Basic Principles require that candidates be "shall be individuals of integrity and ability with appropriate training or qualifications in law," and prohibit discrimination on grounds such as race, colour or sex. The Beijing Principles similarly require, in Articles 11–13, selection on the basis of "proven competence, integrity and independence."[17] However, neither provides further guidance, and indeed the Beijing Principles recognize in Article 14 that "different procedures and safeguards may be adopted to ensure the proper appointment of judges" in different societies. Following the English tradition, "professional politics plays a clear role in the choice of judges" in many common law countries where experienced, distinguished lawyers are recruited to be judges and "professional and political circles may have a say in the selection."[18] In the United States, the power of the President to appoint federal judges introduces an element of political con-

---

[15] Larkins, *supra* note 14 at 611.

[16] *Supra* note 2. See also *Procedures for the Effective Implementation of the Basic Principles on the Independence of the Judiciary* (UN Economic and Social Council Resolution 1989/60, 15th plenary meeting, May 24, 1989); Statement of Principles of the Independence of the Judiciary (adopted by the 6th Conference of the Chief Justice of Asia and the Pacific, Beijing, August 1995, comprising the Chief Justices of 20 states in the region; the "Beijing Principles").

[17] Beijing Principles, *supra* note 16.

[18] Rogelio Pérez-Perdomo, "Judicial Independence and Accountability," Paper prepared for the *Meeting Comprehensive Legal and Judicial Development: Toward an Agenda for a Just and Equitable Society in the 21st Century*, World Bank, Washington

trol of the judiciary. The President's power of appointment, however, is constrained: the constitutional requirement of Senate confirmation limits the power of the President over appointments, the life tenure of federal judges, who after changes of administration have no relationship with the President distance the judiciary from executive influence, and the protection against judicial salary reduction further guards against political vulnerability in the judiciary. In civil law countries, the appointment process is designed to keep politics out, selecting judges soon after finishing a specialized program of judicial studies based largely on their academic merit. Many Latin American countries have instituted judicial councils to increase the transparency of judicial appointments, particularly at the level of the highest court.

Difficulties arise in both common and civil law systems when it comes to ensuring independence in the promotion process. The Basic Principles require objective factors of ability, integrity and experience to determine promotions, but it is almost impossible to find a consensus on how to assess or evaluate such factors. Martin Friedland quotes an English judge who observed that, "A judge who often found against the government, or in some other way displeased the executive, might find that promotion did not come his way."[19]

Security of tenure is a foundational mechanism for ensuring judicial independence. As a USAID report notes, "It is universally accepted that when judges can be easily or arbitrarily removed, they are much more vulnerable to internal or external pressures in their consideration of cases."[20] Article 12 of the Basic Principles requires that judges "shall have guaranteed tenure until a mandatory retirement age or the expiry of their term of office, where such exists." As Article 12 intimates, the specific length of the judicial term may vary, as indeed it does across the world,[21] so long as it is "adequately secured by law."[22] The Beijing Principles elaborate further that "Judges should be subject to removal from office only for proved incapacity, conviction of a crime, or conduct which makes

---

(June 5–7, 2000). Available online at: http://www4.worldbank.org/legal/legop_judicial/ ljr_conf_papers/Perez-Perdomo.pdf.

[19]   Martin L. Friedland, *A Place Apart: Judicial Independence and Accountability in Canada* (Ottawa: Canadian Judicial Council, 1995) at 255.

[20]   USAID, Office of Democracy and Governance, *Guidance for Promoting Judicial Independence and Impartiality*, Technical Publication Series (2002) at 19 [*Guidance*].

[21]   While some countries, including the UK, Canada, and the US appoint judges for life, many other countries use fixed term appointments. Fixed terms may threaten judicial independence in that judges who are approaching the end of their term may be susceptible to outside influence as they seek their next position. USAID argues that where fixed terms are used, the time of appointment should not coincide with presidential elections to prevent incoming presidents from stacking the courts in their favour. (*Guidance*, *supra* note 20 at 23.)

[22]   Basic Principles, *supra* note 2, Article 11.

the judge unfit to be a judge." Such fitness requires a fair, public hearing[23] subject to independent review.[24]

Ensuring adequate financing of the judiciary is also key to achieving judicial independence. The Basic Principles are vague on this point, requiring only, in Article 11, that "adequate remuneration, conditions of service, [and] pensions ... shall be adequately secured by law." The Beijing Principles more bluntly hold that "It is essential that judges be provided with the resources necessary to enable them to perform their functions." Where economic constraints limit available funds, the judiciary should be accorded a "high level of priority in the allocation of resources."[25] Financing is important in order to attract and retain the most qualified applicants, protect against judicial corruption, and ensure access to basic legal materials, competent support staff, and physical and technological infrastructure.[26]

C. Accountability

Judicial accountability can be divided into three discrete domains: operational, decisional, and behavioural accountability. *Operational accountability* is concerned primarily with such matters as the number of cases handled and time spent per case. Achieving operational accountability requires transparency of court operations, including the subjugation of internal procedures such as budgets, use of resources, promotions, and salaries to pre-existing rules. Increased financial independence of the judiciary will not always ensure operational accountability: while the respective judiciaries of many developing countries have gained control over their resources this has not always led to complementary procedures to ensure responsible resource management.[27]

Moreover, as Judith Resnick points out, there is danger in giving judges too much discretion over case management, particularly when this discretion is not also independently monitored. "Managerial judges," as Resnick terms judges vested with case-flow management responsibilities and expectations, "negotiate with parties about the course, timing, and scope of both pre-trial and post-trial litigation. These managerial responsibilities give judges greater power. Yet the restraints that formerly circumscribed judicial authority are conspicuously ab-

---

[23] Beijing Principles, *supra* note 16, Articles 23–8. The Principles allow for *in camera* hearings, but in such a case require that the proceedings be publicized.

[24] Basic Principles, *supra* note 2, Article 20. Articles 17 through 19 elaborate standards for removal only in the case of unfitness in accordance with established codes of conduct pursuant to a fair hearing.

[25] Beijing Principles, *supra* note 16, Articles 40–41.

[26] *Guidance*, *supra* note 20 at 26.

[27] USAID, *Guidance*, *supra* note 20 at 153.

sent. Managerial judges frequently work beyond the public view, off the record, with no obligation to provide written, reasoned opinions, and out of reach of appellate review."[28]

Decisional accountability concerns the quality of actual decisions rendered, as well as the quality of the reasoning used to reach them. Decisional accountability is the most difficult of the three types of accountability to reconcile with the idea of judicial independence, as it implies hierarchical "inputs" from other government agencies – something the most widely accepted definitions of judicial independence consider anathema.[29] Even our own favoured minimalist definition of judicial independence stipulates values (neutrality and impartiality) which seem at odds with the idea of a judiciary whose verdicts fall under the direct or indirect surveillance of the executive and legislative branches. Nevertheless, prejudiced or incompetently rendered decisions are a serious concern, as they imperil the courts' reputation and diminish their authority to render decisions with "sticking power." Moreover, decisional accountability also mandates publications of proceedings, decisions and sentences, something which is critical to public access and understanding of the courts, yet is not automatically required by all court systems and judgments are sometimes only released to the parties and often comprise no more than a few sentences.[30] We therefore conclude, albeit not without qualification, that accountability must comprise some form of decision-making review, whether through surveillance by a constitutional court or a multi-level appellate court system. We do not go so far as to prescribe any such arrangement, or to identify which arrangement is indicated in which cases; rather, we consider such questions essential to ask and answer in analysis of judiciaries in developing countries.

Behavioural accountability concerns dereliction of duty, misuse of office and other more flagrant forms of judicial misconduct. The judicial hierarchy itself has been traditionally responsible for ensuring behavioural accountability, but some countries have transferred these responsibilities to external institutions such as judicial ombudsmen or judicial councils.[31] The standard of *behavioural*

---

[28]   Judith Resnick, "Managerial Judges" (1982) 96 *Harv. L. Rev.* 376 at 378.

[29]   Rosenn and Verner respectively define independence as: "the degree to which judges actually decide cases in accordance with their own determinations of the evidence, the law and justice, free from the coercion, blandishments, interference, or threats from governmental authorities or private citizens," and "[the ability] to decide cases on the basis of established law and the 'merits of the case', without substantial interference from other political or governmental agents." See Keith Rosenn, "The Protection of Judicial Independence in Latin America" (1987) 19 *U. Miami Inter – Am. L. Rev.* 1 and Joel G. Verner, "The Independence of Supreme Courts in Latin America: A Review of the Literature" (1984) 16 *J. Lat. Am. Stud.* 463.

[30]   USAID, *Guidance, supra* note 20 at 136.

[31]   *Ibid.* at 136.

accountability, for its part, reflects an intuition, in Lumet's words, that "it is probably safe to say that a broad consensus of the public expects judges to be answerable, one way or another, for broad categories of misconduct that include misuse of office, undignified behaviour, bias or prejudgment, harmful or offensive conduct, dereliction of duty, or disrespect for the law (including, of course, lawbreaking)."[32] Instances of constraints on such behaviour, Lumet considers, constitute little threat to independence. "[T]here can be no serious argument," he explains, illustrating with examples from recent American case-law, "that independence is compromised when a judge faces reprimand or suspension for using his office to coerce the payment of a debt to his daughter ... or attempting to recruit litigants as ... sales representatives to the judge's own financial benefit."[33]

Instruments of accountability must respect not only the ephemeral boundary between accountability and independence, but between the three domains of accountability as well. A tribunal of judicial misconduct, for instance, should not serve as an alternative venue for interrogating or appealing judicial decisions, except in the most flagrant cases of abuse of judicial office, and the design of such tribunals and their procedures should reflect this restriction. Similarly, operational accountability should not, in its fair exercise, impinge on judges' primary discretion. Nor should modes of behavioural and decisional accountability undermine judges' ability to fulfil their operational mandate, including the timely disposition of cases.

D. Legitimacy

Successful judicial reform also requires public acceptance of the judicial institution. Courts must be perceived as legitimate because they occupy a powerful position vis-à-vis the public. As an institution which can deprive citizens of their liberty or their property, it is critical that courts act as "dispensers of legitimacy" in order for rule of law institutions to be effective.[34] Without a public perception of legitimacy in the court system, individuals may be more likely to choose to "exit" and employ alternative or traditional means of dispute resolution.[35] In

---

[32] Stephen Lumet, "Judicial Discipline and Judicial Independence" (1998) 3 *Law and Contemporary Problems* 61 at 61–2.

[33] *Ibid.* at 62.

[34] Jose Juan Toharia, "Evaluating Systems of Justice Through Public Opinion: Why, What, Who, How, and What For?," in Erik G. Jensen and Thomas C. Heller (eds) *Beyond Common Knowledge: Empirical Approaches to the Rule of Law* (Stanford, CA: Stanford University Press, 2003) at 26.

[35] Rosa Ehrenreich Brooks, "The New Imperialism: Violence, Norms, and the 'Rule of Law'" (2003) 101 *Mich. L. Rev.* 2275 at 2300.

addition, lack of respect for the court system may result in decreased compliance with judicial decisions, compounding enforcement problems, and further decreasing public respect for the courts.

The legitimacy of governmental authority generally derives from some notion of popular consent via democratic elections. However, while some US states utilize elections as a mechanism of judicial selection, it is not clear that such a process is desirable:

> Most US judges and court reform organizations regard elections as a poor method for selecting judges. They believe judges can be influenced by the fear of electoral retaliation against decisions that conform to the law but not popular preferences. They also fear that judges may compromise their independence by incurring obligations to those who provide financial support to their election campaigns.[36]

It may be that judicial legitimacy can be achieved by ensuring a transparent and merit-based appointment process via a democratically elected government. However, democratically elected governments are not ubiquitous to developing countries, and successful judicial reform may need to acquire legitimacy by other means. Many of the mechanisms of reform discussed above in the context of judicial independence and accountability play an important role in ensuring judicial legitimacy. A dependent and unaccountable judiciary is unlikely to garner or maintain much public legitimacy.

II.   EXPERIENCE WITH JUDICIAL REFORMS

A.   Latin America

According to Joseph Thome:

> Even a superficial over-view of Latin America's legal history reveals a judiciary with little social relevance, subservient to the executive on most important political issues as long as its corporative prerogatives were preserved, and mostly engaged in routine activity. Indeed, the image of the judge largely remains that of a faceless bureaucrat adverse to innovation. Despite some important exceptions such as Costa Rica and some clearly dedicated and innovative judges, Latin American judiciaries have yet to show a genuine commitment to the full panoply of democratic institutions and rights.
>
> In most of Latin America, judicial systems traditionally were politicized, usually intertwined with or dependent on the executive, even as they retain substantial corporative autonomy. The role of the judiciary became relatively minimal, as important conflicts were aired and resolved in other arenas – administrative agencies, semi-autonomous state enterprises, or the offices of the Minister or the President himself.

---

[36]   USAID, *Guidance, supra* note 20 at 140.

The courts were relegated to such functions as deciding debt collection cases, or to processing common criminals (white collar crime was largely ignored).

In most countries of Latin America, the judiciary is a public civil service career, but nevertheless has been traditionally organized as a closed system. While externally subject to varying degrees of political control by the Executive, Supreme Courts generally exercise iron-hand control over internal court administration, including entry-level selection and promotion of lower court judges.[37]

Judicial reform in Latin American countries is a story of mixed success, often beset by conflict internally within the judiciary, with other branches of government and sometimes even the public. Public opinion has suffered: as a 2004 report from the Justice Studies Center of the Americas (JSCA) found, public confidence in the judicial branch stood at only 34%. Even this response was an improvement over previous years, in which survey results fluctuated between 20% and 27%.[38]

According to Bryant Garth, in Argentina the violence of political struggle has left little room for investment in the autonomy of the law. Judges are first and foremost members of political parties chosen for their ability to reward their political friends and punish their political enemies. Each new regime transforms the judiciary – and indeed the entire state apparatus, including the public law school leadership – in accordance with this political warfare.[39]

At least two significant judicial reforms were included in the 1994 revision of the Argentinean Constitution. The first initiative was the creation of a judicial council consisting of judges, legislators, academics and a representative of the executive, with the mandate to oversee the nomination process for judicial appointments, enact regulations for judges, and hear disciplinary cases against judges.[40] The council has had a significant workload, working slowly and unable to fill judicial vacancies, leading it to be described by Mark Ungar, as well as by USAID, as "unwieldy".[41] Second, the Constitution included modified pro-

---

[37] Joseph Thome, "Heading South But Looking North: Globalization and Law Reform in Latin America," (2000) *Wisconsin L. Rev.* 69. See also Susan Rose-Ackerman, "Public Administration and Institutions in Latin America" (October 29, 2007), *Law and Economics Workshop Series*, Faculty of Law, University of Toronto.

[38] Justice Studies Center of the Americas, "Public Confidence in Justice Increases in Latin America" (September 6, 2004), online at: http://www.cejamericas.org/cejacommunity/?id=360&item2=840.

[39] Bryant Garth, "Building Strong and Independent Judiciaries for the New Law and Development: Behind the Paradox of Consensus Programs and Perpetually Disappointing Results" (2003) 52 *DePaul L. Rev.* 383.

[40] Disputes over composition delayed deployment, but by 1998 the council was operational.

[41] Mark Ungar, *Elusive Reform: Democracy and the Rule of Law in Latin America* (Boulder, CO: Lynne Rienner Publishers, 2002) at 181; USAID Office of Democracy

cedures for appointment of Supreme Court justices, requiring a two-thirds majority of the Senate to approve the President's judicial nominees. Other initiatives have focused on training and competence. USAID has sponsored the creation of "judicial conferences, at which individual judges are able to participate in discussions on issues of professional concern."[42] The organization argues that promoting active involvement in discussion encourages a culture of individuality, thus enhancing judicial independence. Argentina also established 12 judicial training schools in the late 1990s. These latter initiatives were part of the more general workings of the Center of Judicial Studies (CEJURA), created to provide "technical support to the provincial courts through publications, research, training, and consulting services on judicial administration",[43] although Hammergren is sceptical of the efficacy of many judicial training programs.[44]

Argentina has been an example *par excellence* of the kind of conflicts surrounding judicial independence noted above. The first instance of conflict developed in 1994 when the newly established judicial council sparred with the Supreme Court over their respective boundaries of authority. The Supreme Court resisted these changes, and asserted exclusive jurisdiction over disciplinary procedures and salary determination. The council responded by signing a resolution affirming its disciplinary authority,[45] but the Supreme Court rejected it and continued to hear disciplinary cases.[46]

A second, far more dramatic instance of conflict developed in 2001 and 2002 against a backdrop of severe economic crisis. In December 2001, with the country facing a massive debt and financial emergency, the government instituted restrictions on bank account withdrawals in an effort to avoid a mass exodus of funds from the financial system.[47] The restrictions quickly became a contentious public issue, and in early 2002 the question of their constitutionality came before

---

and Governance, *Achievements in Building and Maintaining the Rule of Law: MSI's Studies in LAC, E&E, AFR, and ANE* (Occasional Paper Series, November 2002, PN-ACR-220) at 34 [*Achievements*].

[42]   *Achievements*, *supra* note 41 at 34.

[43]   *Achievements*, *supra* note 41 at 34.

[44]   Linn Hammergren, "Judicial Training and Justice Reform" (Washington, DC: USAID Centre for Democracy and Governance, August, 1998); see also Linn Hammergren, "International Assistance to Latin American Justice Programs: Toward an Agenda for Reforming the Reformers," in Jensen and Heller (eds), *supra* note 34.

[45]   An interesting note is that 18 of the 19 judicial council members signed the resolution. The one missing signature was that of the council president, the one member appointed unilaterally by President Carlos Menem. The constitution of the Supreme Court at this time heavily favoured the Menem government.

[46]   Ungar, *supra* note 41 at 178–9.

[47]   In mid-2002, BBC reported that "[p]olls consistently show that the majority of Argentines now have so little faith in their financial institutions that in future they will stuff their savings under the mattress as soon as they can get access to them." Peter

the Supreme Court. When the Court supported the restrictions, long-held public apprehensions about the Court's independence[48] came to the fore and protests erupted.[49] On February 1, in a dramatic about-face, the Supreme Court in *Takko, Adolfo Ismael v. Freddo S.A. s/ despido* struck down the decree.[50] Accusations followed that the decision was formulated as a political tool to regain public support and stem calls among the public for a purging of the Court.[51] President Duhalde described the decision as "politically motivated" and the Court as "'totally discredited,'"[52] claiming that members of the Court had approached the legislature offering a government-friendly decision in exchange for an end to impeachment proceedings.[53] Duhalde then announced the launch of a congressional investigation into the activities of the Court with the goal of impeaching all nine members for malpractice.[54] Two days later, the government announced that all bank deposits held in US dollars were to be "pesified," that is converted to pesos, at a rate 29% lower than the market rate.[55] Through the rest of 2002,

---

Greste, "Argentina Bank Freeze Party Lifted," *BBC News* (June 1, 2002), online: http://news.bbc.co.uk/1/hi/business/2021075.stm.

[48] This apprehension is often traced to the Presidency of Carlos Menem, who in 1989 initiated a series of changes to the judiciary that were widely perceived to be derogations of its independence. Most relevantly, he increased the size of the Supreme Court from five to nine judges and therefore, along with one retirement and one protest resignation, was able to appoint six judges on a nine-judge court. The public perception of the judiciary in 1989 had already been quite poor, and a series of government-friendly judgments during the Menem years sorely aggravated this perception. Ungar, *supra* note 41, at 147–8.

[49] Alfred Hopkins, "Argentina: Running out of Patience," *World Press Review* (February 27, 2002), online: http://www.worldpress.org/Americas/380.cfm.

[50] Becky L. Jacobs, "Pesification and Economic Crisis in Argentina: The Moral Hazard Posed by a Politicized Supreme Court" (2003) 34 *U. Miami Inter-Am. L. Rev.* 391 at 402.

[51] Professor Jacobs notes the argument that the decision was a "politically calculated stab at the executive," also reviewing alternative explanations for the Court's about-face (*ibid.* at 412–13). See Geronimo Perez, "Argentina's Supreme Court Enters the Political Fray in a Move Aimed at Surviving the Public Calls for Impeachment" (2001) 8 *Sw. J. of L. & Trade Am.* 357 at 368–72, for a comparison between *Takko* and the two previous decisions in arguing that the *Takko* decision could not have been anything but a politically motivated decision.

[52] "Argentina Faces Court Challenge," *BBC News* (February 2, 2002), online: http://news.bbc.co.uk/2/hi/americas/1797868.stm.

[53] Marcela Valente, "Argentina in Limbo with Reviled Court and Frozen Accounts," *IPS News* (January 31, 2002), online: http://www.ipsnews.net/terraviva/03_argen_eng.shtml.

[54] "Argentine Judges Face Corruption Probe," *BBC News* (February 7, 2002), online: http://news.bbc.co.uk/2/hi/americas/1807705.stm.

[55] The Argentinean peso had been pegged to the US dollar in 1989 by then President Carlos Menem.

as constitutional challenges to pesification swirled through the lower courts, the justice system was stuck in something of a stalemate; the Duhalde government held the threat of impeachment and the judiciary the threat of a ruling of unconstitutionality which, according to the government, held potentially disastrous effects for the country's economy. The value of the peso collapsed to 30% of its pre-February value by October, and restrictions on withdrawals forced citizens to face the rapid disappearance of their savings. The government was ultimately pressured by the IMF to cease all impeachment proceedings and in December 2002 the restrictions on account withdrawals were abolished. In March 2003, pesification was struck down by the Supreme Court as unconstitutional, prompting further claims that the Court was acting out of political motivation.[56] The conflict abated only in May 2003, when Duhalde was voted out of office.[57]

Judicial reform in El Salvador has taken place against the background of a 12-year civil war, ending with peace talks in 1992. A truth commission found that the "judiciary ... fell victim to intimidation ... ; since it had never enjoyed genuine institutional independence from the legislative and executive branches, its ineffectiveness steadily increased until it became ... a factor which contributed to the tragedy suffered by the country."[58] In the 1980s, partially motivated by the unresolved killings of US citizens in El Salvador, USAID spent 5 million dollars to promote judicial reform by improving judicial efficiency and reforming criminal law in the country. As Popkin explains, these early efforts at reform were largely unsuccessful because of a lack of domestic political will for reform, failure of Salvadoran agencies to cooperate with USAID, and the emphasis of USAID on technical rather than political solutions.[59] By the time peace negotiations proved successful in 1991, the country's warring factions had found

---

[56] Hernan Etchaleco, "Argentine High Courts Overturn Government's Economic Program," *Pravda* (March 6, 2003), online: http://english.pravda.ru/world/2003/03/06/44068.html.

[57] As one of his first items of business, President Kirchner overturned a decree issued by Menem and supported at the time by the Supreme Court granting amnesty to a group of "military officers accused of abuses during the 1976–1983 dictatorship." During the Menem years, this had been one of the administration's most politically charged decisions and the Court's acquiescence a major hindrance to judicial independence. "President Overturns Decree Granting Former Military Officers Immunity," *Salt Lake Tribune* (July 26, 2003), http://www.sltrib.com/2003/Jul/07262003/nation_w/78699.asp.

[58] Margaret Popkin, "Efforts to Enhance Judicial Independence in Latin America: A Comparative Perspective" (2001), online at: http://www.dplf.org/Judicial_Independence/LAComparative_eng.htm. Popkin is the Executive Director of the Due Process of Law Foundation, an NGO working to promote judicial reform in the West. This paper is the later version of an article that appeared in USAID Technical Publication, Guidance for Promoting Judicial Independence and Impartiality (2001).

[59] Margaret Popkin, *Peace Without Justice: Obstacles to Building the Rule of Law in El Salvador* (University Park, PA: Pennsylvania State University Press, 2000) at 71.

themselves in a "strategic stalemate"[60] and with UN support, incentives on the salient parties to compromise were strong. Provisions in the new Constitution allocated a fixed 6% of national revenue for the judiciary, removed the executive and legislature from the Supreme Court nomination process and set a fixed term of nine years for Supreme Court judges. Supreme Court nominations were vested in a joint effort of the national judicial council and the practising bar, each of which is to submit one list of nominations, with final selection to be voted on by a two-thirds majority of the legislative assembly for staggered nine-year terms.[61] The council was also involved in the selection of lower court judges through the preparation of a three-candidate list for any given vacancy, from which the Supreme Court makes a selection. The composition of the council was initially problematic, as early versions were dominated by the Supreme Court. A 1999 legislative amendment dissociated the council from the Court, as well as the other two branches of government, and the six-member council is now composed of academics and members of the profession.

In 2001, some friction between the council and the Supreme Court was reported, however, as the Court "frequently transferred, promoted, or named to permanent positions judges who had temporary appointments"[62] without consulting the council. As of 2001, disciplinary procedures had not yet been fully placed within the jurisdiction of the council. Though the council performs judicial evaluations, it has the power only to recommend discipline, as final decisions remain with the Supreme Court. There has, therefore, been a debate, if not a struggle, between the Supreme Court and the judicial council over selection, discipline and council composition.

In Bolivia, reform assistance began with USAID projects in 1986 aimed at basic training, study of potential reform initiatives, and the establishment of law libraries and provision of technical assistance. A judicial council came into effect in 1998 but has faced fierce opposition from both the Supreme Court and political actors. Composed of five members led by the President of the Supreme Court, the council has the authority to "propose candidates for most courts, formulate the judicial budget and administer resources, and investigate and discipline all judicial personnel."[63] Final appointments for Supreme Court justices are made

---

[60]   Chuck Call, "Police Reform, Human Rights and Democratization in Post-Conflict Settings: Lessons from El Salvador" (Paper presented at the USAID Conference After the War is Over, What Comes Next? Promoting Democracy, Human Rights and Reintegration in Post-Conflict Societies, October 30–31, 1997) at 3. Call offers a brief description of the "nature of the conflict" and its termination on 3–4.

[61]   "Would You Trust this Court?" (*IDBAmerica*, Magazine of the Inter-American Development Bank, November–December 1999).

[62]   Popkin, *supra* note 58.

[63]   Ungar, *supra* note 41 at 182.

by a two-thirds majority vote of Congress, while lower court judges are appointed by colleagues in higher courts.[64] From 1998 to 2002, the council reviewed more than 10,000 nominations for judicial positions, and in its first 15 months sanctioned close to 100 judicial personnel for accepting bribes and other inappropriate behaviour. Such sanctions, however, previously unknown in Bolivian history, have been received with great political hostility. The Supreme Court has accused the council of abuse of power, while Congress, following a decision of the Constitutional Court finding that the dismissal of a court officer for collaboration with drug traffickers violated his right to due process, removed the council's power of dismissal. Agencies previously in charge of functions such as budgeting, now controlled by the council, have reacted adversely to claims of financial mismanagement. The Senate and the Supreme Court have accused the council of corruption and overpayment for various resources, mimicking many of the accusations made by the council of its predecessors. In February 2000, the council retaliated, accusing the judiciary of undermining its work "and even threatening its members' lives."[65] When members of the council accused various legislators of corruption, they were subpoenaed to appear before the Senate; the meeting quickly collapsed, as council member Luis Paravicini issued writs of habeas corpus against members of the Senate, and the Justice Minister demanded the resignation of all council members. These problems have been exacerbated by an apparent conflict of interest, as the President of the Supreme Court leads the judicial council. Ungar views the Bolivian experience as a partial success, noting that the council has refused to submit to the judiciary or Congress but that "the ensuing resistance to its efforts makes it a case study of how underlying processes limit a new institution's effectiveness."[66]

In Peru, judicial reform efforts began in 1990 with the election of President Alberto Fujimori. For decades, the system had been "increasingly characterized as corrupt, incompetent, inefficient, or simply irrelevant."[67] The judiciary was especially vulnerable throughout the civil war of 1979 to 1992, as "extreme political violence initiated by both the Shining Path group (Sendero Luminoso) and the Tupac Amaru Revolutionary Movement (MRTA)"[68] exposed judges to

---

[64]   Centro de Estudios de Justicia de las Américas website, http://www.cejamericas. org/newsite/forochat/material03_ing.html.

[65]   Ungar, *supra* note 41 at 183.

[66]   Ungar, *supra* note 41 at 184.

[67]   Linn A. Hammergren, *The Politics of Justice and Justice Reform in Latin America: The Peruvian Case in Comparative Perspective* (Boulder, CO: Westview Press, 1998) at 135 in Jeffrey A. Clark, *Building on Quicksand: The Collapse of the World Bank's Judicial Reform Project in Peru* (Lawyer's Committee for Human Rights) at n. 15.

[68]   Daniel C. Préfontaine and Joanne Lee, "The Rule of Law and the Independence of the Judiciary" (Paper presented to the World Conference on the Universal Declaration

intimidation by the warring factions. Elected on a reform platform, President Fujimori attempted to secure a series of emergency executive powers purportedly aimed at the endemic problems of terrorism facing the judiciary, but was rebuffed by Congress. Unable to secure the cooperation of the legislature, the President launched the so-called *autogolpe*, or self-coup, dissolving Congress, suspending the Constitution, and instituting rule by decree. He

> then embarked on a sweeping purge of the judiciary, firing 13 Supreme Court Justices, all members of the Constitutional Tribunal, all members of the National and District Councils of the Judiciary, and the Attorney General. Likewise, "130 judicial personnel in the Lima and Callao district were fired, including superior court judges, chief prosecutors, judges in court districts, provincial prosecutors and juvenile court judges." ... Now dominated by members appointed by the Fujimori government, the Supreme Court began evaluating all remaining Peruvian judges; the majority were thereafter dismissed. Another evaluation process led to the dismissal of some 166 prosecutors and 646 administrative personnel. Fired judges and prosecutors were replaced by provisional appointees, subject to dismissal and transfer at any time, without cause.[69]

These early years of President Fujimori's term of office were fraught with uncertainty. On the one hand, the initiatives represented significant change from the heavily troubled judicial system of the past, providing new resources to the courts, seeking to rationalize court administration, replacing judges and vesting in a new National Council of the Judiciary (NCJ) sole authority to select, dismiss and ratify or confirm the country's judges and prosecutors.[70] The Council was composed of seven members, appointed one each by the Supreme Court, the Board of Supreme Public Prosecutors, the public universities, the private universities, and three by various organizations of legal professionals. On the other hand, while the creation of the NCJ depoliticized the appointment process, opportunities for judicial review of executive action were highly circumscribed in a variety of ways. The Ministry of the Attorney General (the "Public Ministry"), the body empowered to initiate Constitutional challenges, was placed under the leadership of an ally to the President. Other legislation exempted from constitutional scrutiny a controversial 1995 amnesty law excusing armed forces personnel for human rights abuses, and in 1996 required that rulings from the newly reconstituted Constitutional Tribunal – initially closed after the *autogolpe* – be made with a super-majority of six of its seven members. In May 1997, three members of the Tribunal were dismissed by the government following public

---

of Human Rights, Montreal, Quebec, December 1998) at 20, online: http://www.icclr. law.ubc.ca/Publications/Reports/RuleofLaw.pdf.

69 Clark, *supra* 67 at n. 27.
70 Clark, *supra* 67 at n. 58.

comments to the effect that the law did not permit President Fujimori to run for a third time.[71] As Hammergren argues, the Fujimori reforms were aimed principally at enhancing the technical qualifications of appointees, not at strengthening the judicial institution as a mechanism of executive oversight: "it is not worth discussing the judiciary as a check to governmental abuses and illegalities. It clearly is not and is not intended to be one."[72] A 1993 report of a commission of international jurists found that on the whole "the effect of these measures [was] 'to grievously erode, if not eliminate, the institutional independence of the civilian judiciary.'"[73]

Throughout this period of uncertainty, discussion at the World Bank focused on whether a monetary grant aimed at judicial reform should be approved for the Peruvian government. Despite legislation in 1996 usurping the authority of the NCJ and transferring certain of its powers to the executive, the Bank approved the program in 1997 with the goal of improving judicial training and selection as well as court efficiency[74] and supporting "key activities of the National Council of the Judiciary (NCJ)."[75] The support of the World Bank mirrored to an extent that of the populace, as "twin victories over left-wing insurgents and hyperinflation" earned President Fujimori popular support, including an "overwhelming victory" in the 1995 elections. As time progressed, however, "a growing number began to voice concern that [Fujimori's authoritarian] methods were being employed against his democratic opponents." In March 1998, "Law 26933 transferred disciplinary power over judges and prosecutors from the NCJ to Executive Commissions of the Judicial Branch and Public Ministry, respectively."[76] The law became a "lightning rod for resistance to the project,"[77] and almost immediately the Bank postponed planned loan disbursements. In the face of demands that powers of the NCJ be restored, the Peruvian government eventually withdrew from the loan, ending the experiment.

Costa Rica embarked on an ambitious agenda of judicial reform starting in 1989. Prior to 1989 the Costa Rican Supreme Court demonstrated an unusually high level of judicial independence for the region, including effective life tenure of Supreme Court judges, financial independence, with a constitutional guaran-

---

[71]   Clark, *supra* 67 at section IVB, "Judicial Review."

[72]   L. Hammergren, *The Politics of Justice and Justice Reform in Latin America: The Peruvian Case in Comparative Perspective* (Boulder, CO: Westview Press, 1998) at 194–8.

[73]   Clark, *supra* 67 at n. 35.

[74]   Judicial Reform Project, World Bank Projects Database, online: http://web. worldbank.org/external/projects/main?pagePK=104231&piPK=73230&theSitePK=40 941&menuPK=228424&Projectid=P040107.

[75]   Clark, *supra* note 67 at n. 53.

[76]   Clark, *supra* note 67 at n. 106.

[77]   Clark, *supra* note 67 at n. 55.

tee of 6% of the government's annual budget, and control over the appointments of lower court judges. Nonetheless, before 1989 the Costa Rican Supreme Court was a timid and insignificant actor in Costa Rican governance, and "was effectively moribund."[78] The 1989 reforms brought a new activist style to the Supreme Court by creating a fourth chamber, Sala IV, with significantly expanded powers to assess the constitutionality of national laws. The mandate of Sala IV is to "guarantee the supremacy of the norms and constitutional principles, international law, and community law in force in the republic, their uniform interpretation and application of fundamental rights and freedoms consecrated in the constitution." Since the creation of Sala IV there has been a marked increase in constitutional cases filed with the Supreme Court, with 750 cases filed in the first 27 months of the Sala IV's operation, compared with 347 cases filed in the 51 years preceding the creation of the new chamber.[79] Sala IV has been a highly activist court, and "[t]his vertiginous increase in the number of cases reveals an increased willingness on the part of the court to act aggressively in opening access to the court system."[80] As the Costa Rican Supreme Court already enjoyed significant judicial independence, the increasingly activist stance of this court since 1989 can be attributed to the mandate of Sala IV, including broad habeas corpus and investigative powers, and its ability to render unappealable constitutional rulings that are binding on all other chambers of the Supreme Court. Bruce Wilson *et al.* also emphasize the role of the 1989 reforms in increasing citizen's confidence in and accessibility to the Supreme Court.[81]

As part of their rule of law reforms, many Latin American countries[82] have created independent judicial councils primarily to oversee the selection and promotion of judges, and in some cases also to administer the courts. In a 2002 paper assessing the efficacy of judicial councils in strengthening the judiciary in Latin America, Linn Hammergren finds that the promise of judicial councils in creating an independent judiciary may have been overstated.[83] Hammergren finds that judicial councils have been successful in removing outside influence on the appointment process and increasing transparency of appointments. Re-

---

[78]   Bruce M. Wilson, Juan Carlos Rogríguez Cordero and Roger Handberg, "The Best Laid Schemes ... Gang Aft A-gley: Judicial Reform in Latin America – Evidence from Costa Rica" (2004) 36 *J. Lat. Amer. Stud.* 521.

[79]   *Ibid.* at 518.

[80]   *Ibid.*

[81]   *Ibid.* at 522.

[82]   As of 2002, only Chile, Guatemala, Honduras and Nicaragua had not implemented judicial councils and Venezuala and Uruguay implemented a judicial council but subsequently abolished it.

[83]   Linn Hammergren, Carnegie Endowment, "Do Judicial Councils Further Judicial Reform? Lessons from Latin America," Working Paper 28 (2002); see also Hammergren, *supra* note 44.

quiring councils simply to announce vacancies, hold a competition, and make the results of the competition public has greatly increased the transparency of appointments. However, Hammergren also finds that real institutional independence has been more difficult to attain, and many judicial councils have been paralyzed by internal divisions and external conflicts with the courts as the councils have struggled to delineate their powers and responsibilities. Hammergren argues that the emphasis on the judicial council as a mechanism for increasing judicial independence has led to incomplete reform of Latin American judiciaries. She finds that the creation of judicial councils has simply changed the protagonists without addressing the underlying failures of judicial governance and the need for greater internal and external independence and accountability, including better oversight of judicial performance, stronger administrative management, and improved judicial policy in the sense of strategic planning and being able to respond to changes in the external environment.

Another major objective of judicial reform has been the improvement of court operations and the introduction of public, oral and adversarial trials and hearings. The Dominican Republic has undergone a dramatic reform of its judiciary since 1997 when 85% of the sitting judges were replaced and a National Judicial Council was implemented to appoint Supreme Court judges, who would then appoint lower court judges. USAID has provided support for the modernization of court administration, including: a new method for tracking and managing cases, heightened security for court records, which previously had often been "lost", and an improved filing and retrieval system for records, and random assignment of judges to a case via a computer-generated system.[84] In Argentina in 1992 reforms to the penal process code instituted oral procedures, often thought to be more efficient than written procedures. Over 200 oral courts were established, and while oral procedures did in fact prove faster, the reforms faced obstacles in the form of a judicial culture accustomed to the written format.[85] Argentinean Supreme Court justices encouraged a USAID project aimed at the development of "modern information and case reception and tracking systems,"[86] observing that such experiments were beyond the limits of their budgetary resources. The World Bank continued these efforts in 1998 with the launch of its Model Court Development Project. With the objective of improving court efficiency and reducing case backlog, twelve federal courts were chosen as pilot projects to revamp administrative procedures, separate administrative from judicial functions, purge inactive cases, and train judges and court staff in case management, information technology, human resources, and other critical

---

[84]   *Achievements*, *supra* note 41 at 56–7.
[85]   Ungar, *supra* note 41 at 148.
[86]   *Achievements*, *supra* note 41 at 34.

areas. In 2002 Honduras implemented a new criminal procedure code, and US-AID is providing support in the transition to oral trials.

In Chile, before the advent of USAID support, criminal procedure was based on an inquisitorial system limited exclusively to written submissions; under this system, the judge "investigates, accuses, determines guilt, and sentences the convicted"[87] and "the entire criminal case can be completed on paper without the input or even appearance of a defense attorney."[88] A new criminal procedures code was passed in 2000 and early reports suggest that "the system is working relatively well."[89] Reform in Chile also included administrative changes like those in Argentina. The Judicial Branch Administrative Corporation was established as a body of administrative professionals handling various administrative functions previously performed by judges, and computers and email accounts were set up for all judges and some staff. The Justice Studies Center of the Americas (JSCA) observes that some resistance to both the administrative and procedural changes has been encountered from judges accustomed to the written, formalized procedures and unaccustomed to following processes laid out by administrators and not by judges themselves. For instance, some judges insist on no longer required formal procedures that delay trials.[90]

USAID has sponsored similar reforms of criminal procedure throughout Latin America, including Guatemala, Bolivia, Honduras, El Salvador, Peru, Ecuador, Colombia, Nicaragua, Venezuela, Costa Rica, and Mexico. A recent review of these reforms finds significant impacts in most cases on a variety of indicators including rates of preventive detention; speed of trials; structural changes such as number of public prosecutors and public defenders; and availability and use of alternative sentencing.[91]

B.   Central and Eastern Europe

In the former Soviet Union, the judiciary was notoriously subservient to the Communist Party. Eugene Huskey argues that Soviet courts were "little more than an extension of executive power. In theory, judges were independent and

---

[87]   *Achievements*, *supra* note 41 at 42.

[88]   *Ibid*.

[89]   *Achievements*, *supra* note 41 at 44.

[90]   Cristián Riego, *Comparative Report: "Judicial Reform Processes In Latin America" Follow-up Project* (Judicial Studies Center of the Americas: 2003) at 9–11, online:http://www.cejamericas.org/.

[91]   Lisa Bhansali and Christina Biebesheimer, "Measuring the Impact of Criminal Justice Reform in Latin America," in Thomas Carothers (ed.), *Promoting the Rule of Law Abroad: In Search of Knowledge*, (Washington, DC: Carnegie Endowment for International Peace, 2006).

subject only to law; in practice, they conformed to the expectations, and occasionally the explicit commands, of the Communist Party, the Procuracy, the Ministry of Justice, and even local Soviets."[92] The Soviet legal system is often described as an embodiment of "telephone justice", as judicial decisions were sometimes made with the input of a discreet telephone call from a party authority. Judicial training in the Soviet system was sparse[93] and, as frequently noted, the position was held in low regard within the legal community.[94]

In Russia, early reforms addressed the kinds of fears inherited from the Soviet regime. Judicial appointments at all levels were made, subject to a three-year probationary period, for life, and a Judicial Qualification Committee (JQC) was established, entrusted with selection of and disciplinary procedures against judges. All judges were made immune to so-called administrative liability, such as traffic violations, as well as to criminal prosecution, subject to waiver at the discretion of the JQC.[95] Court budgets were protected in the abstract under the Constitution, and neither the total budget of the judiciary nor the salaries of individual judges could be reduced by unilateral executive or legislative action. Judges were also guaranteed housing within six months of their appointment to the bench.[96]

To what extent these formal improvements have enhanced actual judicial independence is a matter of debate. While Solomon notes that through the 1990s nearly 80% of cases against public officials were won by the private claimants,[97] he concedes that during the same period "the independence of judges in Russia was compromised by inadequate financing by the federal government, which led to the 'sponsorship' of courts by regional and local governments and private firms."[98] Foglesong blames dire financial constraints within the Russian government for the fact that "in 1996 and 1997 the money allocated to the courts barely

---

[92] Eugene Huskey, "Russian Judicial Reform After Communism," in Peter H. Solomon Jr. (ed.), *Reforming Justice in Russia 1864–1996: Power, Culture, and the Limits of Legal Order* (Armonk, NY: M.E. Sharpe, 1997) at 326.

[93] Lisa Halustick, "Judicial Reform in Ukraine" (1994) 1 *Parker Sch. J. E. Eur. L.* 663 at 665.

[94] See, for instance, Peter H. Solomon Jr. and Todd S. Foglesong, *Courts in Transition: The Challenge of Judicial Reform* (Boulder, CO: Westview Press, 2000) at 93.

[95] Peter H. Solomon Jr., "Putin's Judicial Reform: Making Judges Accountable as well as Independent" (2002) 11:1/2 *E. Eur. Const. Rev.* 117 at 118 [Solomon, "Accountable"].

[96] Todd Foglesong, *The Dynamics of Judicial (In)dependence in Russia* in *Judicial Independence in the Age of Democracy: Critical Perspectives from Around the World* (Charlottesville, VA: University Press of Virginia, 2001) 62–88 at 67, Foglesong, *Dynamics*. A desperate need for adequate housing is often cited as a tool of coercion held over judges by Party members in Soviet times.

[97] Solomon, "Accountable," *supra* note 95 at 119.

[98] *Ibid.* at 118–19.

covered judges' wages; virtually nothing was left to pay for operating costs (paper, stamps, telephone service, heating, and electricity), not to speak of repairs and improvements."[99] Financially desperate courts thus became "substantially dependent on local government authorities for subvention, credits, and in-kind assistance."[100] Financial support has similarly come from private sources, and in a 1997 survey of judges 22% admitted "that the support had some influence on their handling of cases."[101] Similarly, the JQC was forced to "rely on favours from 'sponsors', private donations, and government subventions, all obtained through negotiations."[102] The national/regional dynamics at play seem to be a critical factor; in Foglesong's words, "interagency conflict…between national and subnational governing bodies repeatedly have subverted efforts to make Russian courts financially autonomous."[103]

Facing allegations of endemic corruption in the judiciary, President Vladimir Putin in 2000 assembled a group of economists to examine the problem. One major reform "was the commitment of the Putin administration to a dramatic increase in spending on the courts … totalling 43,962,200,000 rubles over five years."[104] Among other things, the increased funding was earmarked to raise judges' salaries, repair buildings and add needed staff. Second, the Putin reforms sought to control corruption by striking a more acceptable balance between the autonomy and accountability of judges than had been achieved in the reforms of the early 1990s. The team proposed the substitution of 15-year non-renewable terms for lifetime appointments, the partial removal of immunity from administrative liability, and the loosening of restrictions on the criminal prosecution of judges. The Judicial Qualification Commission and top judges complained to the press; they invoked images of the powerful Soviet procuracy, claiming that to reinstitute administrative liability would be to subject judges to extortion by police. The judicial community argued further that the system of self-discipline worked effectively, pointing out that in the previous five years, approximately 100 judges per year had been removed for misconduct by the JQC. The recent conviction and sentencing of Mikhail Khordorkovsky and his partner Platon Lebedev has raised concerns about the influence of the state on the judiciary and has been compared to the show trials of Stalin's Russia.[105]

---

99 Foglesong, *Dynamics, supra* note 96 at 69.
100 *Ibid.* at 70.
101 *Ibid.* at 71.
102 *Ibid.* at 73.
103 *Ibid.* at 73.
104 Solomon, "Accountable," *supra* note 95 at 121.
105 Marsha Lipman, "The Soviet Spirit Lives On," *Washington Post* (June 1, 2005) http://www.carnegieendowment.org/publications/index.cfm?fa=view&id=17013 &prog=zru.

In Ukraine in 1994, a system of judicial qualification committees (JQC) was established to oversee judicial selection. Local committees were created with a chairman and 12 members, of whom six were elected by current judges and only two by the local executive. A Higher Judicial Qualification Commission, established to hear appeals from local commissions, comprised a chairman and 18 members, appointed by a combination of the Parliament, fellow judges, and only three by the executive. Judicial tenure was set at ten years, an improvement over Soviet times, but inadequate according to some demanding life tenure. Judges could be removed within these terms for misconduct either by the Ukrainian Parliament or by a judicial qualification commission and were granted immunity from criminal liability, which could be waived only with the consent of Parliament.[106] Salaries were not set at a minimum level or specifically allocated a certain fixed percentage of the national budget, but were prohibited from reduction.[107] In 1996, Ukraine enacted a new Constitution guaranteeing "the independence ... of judges."[108] Despite these progressive legislative initiatives, Kim Ratushny finds overall that "progress has been slow in reforming the Ukrainian judiciary to conform with Western notions of an independent judiciary."[109] Noting the subordinate position of judges under the Soviet regime, she observes that "Ukrainians remain cynical of the judicial system as a means to resolve their disputes, to assert their interests, or to address their grievances against either private citizens or the state."[110]

---

[106]   Halustick, *supra* note 93, seems reluctant to defer to the wisdom not just of the executive but also of Parliament. Particularly when discussing the composition of the JQCs, she seems to cast the role played by Parliament in a negative rather than a positive light. Given the important role for Parliament in the JQC process, advantages gained by judicial councils may be compromised to the extent that new Parliaments are comprised of former Soviets. More fundamentally, the issue raises concerns as to the inherent value of judicial councils and warns against the belief in such councils as a panacea for judicial corruption and politicization. Ultimately, judicial appointments must be made by one body or another, and the pervasiveness of corruptive elements in a political system is likely to be a threat irrespective of institutional control. The question becomes particularly pointed when comparing Russia with a country such as Canada, where judicial independence is less of an apparent problem yet judicial appointments were made (until recently), in essence, by executive fiat.

[107]   *Ibid.* at 666–73.

[108]   Ukrainian Constitution, in Kim Ratushny, "Towards the 'Independence ... of Judges' *in Ukraine*" 62 *Sask. L. Rev.* 567 at 568.

[109]   *Ibid.* at 568.

[110]   Ratushny, *supra* note 108 at 568–9. Ratushny describes the passage of the 1992 Law of Ukraine on the Status of Judges, which sets standards for judicial qualifications, selection, immunity, and so forth; constitutional commitments to civil and political rights; entrenchment of principles of fairness in judicial proceedings, such as open hearings and a right to appeal; and others.

In Poland, the 1997 Constitution formally recognized "the separation of, and balance between, the legislative, executive and judicial powers."[111] Included in the Constitution was the National Council of the Judiciary, its membership consisting of 25 people, including 15 judges from throughout the court system elected by general assemblies of the judiciary, four Members of Parliament, two Members of the Senate, and four others. All members hold equal power, and the judiciary holds a majority of the seats. The mandate of the council includes the nomination of judges for appointment, binding review of motions to transfer judges to other posts, and the authority to "express its opinion" on a variety of issues.[112] Each regional and appellate court has a President appointed by the Minister of Justice but only with the consent of the assembly of the judiciary. Judges are selected through a four-step process involving at least 4.5 years of training and a judicial examination, but governed primarily by the appellate court president and the ministry. Judicial tenure is guaranteed for life, and removal requires a court order. Judges are generally not to be transferred to different posts without their consent, although the Minister may transfer a judge for temporary three-month stints with no restriction on successive uses of this power.[113] Criminal and administrative proceedings against judges can be instituted only with leave of the court, and disciplinary actions are initiated by the "disciplinary spokesman, a judge elected by the college of an appellate court from among the judges of the same college."[114]

The Open Society Institute (OSI)[115] argues that the National Council of the Judiciary has been relatively successful in supporting the judicial independence of individual judges, but that independence in Poland is threatened on a more

---

[111]   Constitution of the Republic of Poland, Article 10 in Open Society Institute, "Judicial Independence in Poland" (Monitoring the EU Accession Process: Judicial Independence, 2001), online at: http://www.eumap.org/reports/content/20/616/judicial_poland.pdf [Judicial Independence in Poland].

[112]   The Council may "(4) make pronouncements on issues involving the professional ethics of judges; (5) express its opinion on proposals to change the organisational structure of courts as well as other matters pertaining to the way courts function; (6) acquaint itself with draft normative acts pertaining to the judiciary; (7) express its opinion on training programs for legal apprentices and the manner in which examinations for prospective judges are conducted; and (8) express its opinion on matters relating to judges and courts submitted for the Council's deliberation by the State President and other state organs, as well as by general assemblies of judges." Judicial Independence in Poland, *supra* note 111 at n. 24.

[113]   Judicial Independence in Poland, *supra* note 111 at 111.

[114]   *Ibid.* at 344.

[115]   OSI is a US NGO funded by philanthropist George Soros that, through its EU Accession Monitoring Program (EUMAP), prepares comprehensive annual reports on behalf of the EU in order to track the progress towards democracy of various Central and Eastern European nations.

institutional level given executive control over so-called administrative functions of courts. More specifically, it refers to the ministry's supervision over the enforcement of case rulings, "efficient case handling," inspection visits, and "review of complaints about judges' behaviour or rulings."[116] While many administrative matters, including periodic evaluations of judges and taking "necessary measures in the event" of flaws or infringements, are in the hands of court presidents, OSI seems to take exception to the relationship between these court presidents and the executive. However, OSI does not offer a clear solution. This is perhaps in recognition of the tensions outlined in the Russian context between autonomy and accountability, and an explicit acknowledgement that "administrative powers must vest in some body."[117] Significant problems are identified further with respect to judicial budgeting. While the Supreme, Constitutional, and Administrative Courts are budgeted separately, the budget of the ordinary courts is derived from that of the Ministry of Justice without the input of the judiciary. There is also a concern that poor working conditions, as courthouses become more dilapidated and court space becomes more cramped, could act as a threat to judicial independence to the extent that such conditions encourage "reliance on the branches that control funding decisions or on outside parties."[118]

In 1994, Belarus adopted a new Constitution "that enshrined democratic values and contained important human rights protections."[119] According to Human Rights Watch (HRW), "[i]n the early 1990s, the human rights situation in Belarus improved significantly," and the "judiciary began to function more independently."[120] In July 1994, Aleksandr Lukashenko was elected President in free elections. HRW argues that over the next two years, Lukashenko "sought to maximize executive power and minimize that of the legislature and the judiciary … systematically ignored rulings by the Constitutional Court declaring presidential decrees unconstitutional, and ordered the Cabinet of Ministers and other government institutions to ignore such rulings."[121] In November 1996, President Lukashenko held a referendum proposing a number of constitutional amendments. Just before the referendum was to begin, the Constitutional Court ruled that the referendum was not binding on Parliament. Lukashenko superseded the Court's findings, passing two presidential decrees establishing the

---

116   Judicial Independence in Poland, *supra* note 111 at 327.
117   *Ibid.*
118   *Ibid.* at 332.
119   Human Rights Watch, "Republic of Belarus: Crushing Civil Society" (1997), online at: http://www.hrw.org/reports/1997/belarus/Belarus-03.htm at n. 3 [Belarus HRW 97].
120   *Ibid.* at n. 3.
121   *Ibid.* at n. 6.

binding nature of the referendum, but Parliament, the US State Department, the Organization for Security and Co-operation in Europe (OSCE) and the EU all refused to recognize its validity. Nevertheless, the referendum passed, and was widely faulted for falsified votes and other illegalities. The Council of Europe issued a statement declaring the 1994 Constitution the "only legitimate supreme document of the Republic of Belarus."[122] On November 19, 1996, Parliament retaliated by initiating impeachment proceedings against President Lukashenko before the Constitutional Court. One week later, the case was withdrawn when a sufficient number of members of the Supreme Soviet withdrew their names from the petition under significant pressure. Pastukhov notes that the President has "given himself the right to appoint and remove from office all the judges of the Belarus Republic, and also to determine the financial and material support to be given to courthouses."[123] On a related note, the establishment of separately operated Constitutional Courts has been a frequent aspect of judicial reform in the region, with the goal that such a court will be successful in monitoring and preventing executive abuses of power. While recognizing the contribution of the Court in the foregoing example,[124] the events in Belarus demonstrate the importance of adequate enforcement mechanisms. Notably, five judges of the Constitutional Court resigned in protest in November 1996, a sixth being dismissed by presidential decree for expiration of term despite being three years into an 11-year appointment. The Court was subsequently reconstituted with a majority of presidential appointees.[125]

Another major object of judicial reform is the operation of the court system, often expressed in terms of its efficiency. In Hungary, Maria Dakolias finds that "[t]he number of cases filed from 1990 to 1996 increased by 521%, with a 259% jump in 1993 alone. The number of cases disposed of increased 263% ... probably in reaction to the rise in cases filed. The court, however, also experienced a steep rise in pending cases, with a 336% jump to 5,203 in 1993 and reaching 9,891 in 1996. This increase occurred because the rise of the filing rate outpaced the rise of the disposal rate."[126]

---

[122] Mikhail Pastukhov, "Presidential Abuse of Powers in Belarus" 4 *Parker Sch. J. E. Eur. L.* 479 at 481.

[123] *Ibid.* at 496.

[124] The Court, for instance, helped alert the Council of Europe to concerns with the legality of the 1996 referendum, and was generally a voice of opposition. Notably, while its rulings and authority were often superseded, it does not appear to have voluntarily ceded to presidential pressure.

[125] Belarus HRW 97, *supra* note 119 at n. 12.

[126] Maria Dakolias, "Court Performance around the World" (1999) 2 *Yale H.R. & Dev. L. J.* 87 at 39. The Stability Pact argues that "[t]he recent and dramatic increase of the number of cases, especially of civil and economic disputes, has created a huge backlog and has almost paralysed the judiciary in several countries." Stability Pact, *Framework*

One approach to this problem has been to attempt to improve judicial capacity. In 1997, the Hungarian Constitution was amended to allow for an extra appellate level between the county and Supreme Courts,[127] but by November the government claimed that the changes would be too costly and would actually slow down the judicial process.[128] The government argued further that "the introduction of appellate courts will weaken local courts, since the more experienced local judges will replace the county court judges promoted to the Courts of Appeals",[129] thus leaving a void at the lower level. The National Judicial Council challenged the decision as unconstitutional, but in 1999 the government amended the 1997 revisions, repealing the new appellate level.[130] In 2001 the Constitutional Court held that the government's decision not to create the new appellate level violated the Hungarian Constitution[131] and in June 2002, the government capitulated to the Supreme Court, pledging to begin establishing appellate level courts by 2003.[132]

Other recent reforms in Hungary to enhance judicial efficiency have also included the enlargement of administrative staff and the enhancement of case management information systems. Though the number of judges was roughly constant over the time period, the number of court secretaries increased by 25% in 2001 alone, the number of clerks showed a slight 4% increase, and the government established a new "legal secretary" position. Through 2002 implementation progressed on the Court Information System, which "provides

---

Document for Judicial Reform in South Eastern Europe (January 23, 2002) at 2, online at: http://www.southeasteurope.org/documents/Judicial%20Reform%20In%20SEE. doc.

[127] The court system had been a three-tiered system, local courts as a court of first instance, county courts as an appellate level court from local courts and a court of first instance in more serious matters, and all non-constitutional appeals (there was, and is, also a Constitutional Court) going straight to a heavily overburdened Supreme Court. European Commission, *2002 Regular Report on Hungary's Progress Towards Accession* (COM 2002 700), online: http://europa.eu.int/comm/enlargement/report2002/hu_en. pdf.

[128] It is not perfectly clear what the basis of this argument was. Perhaps it was premised on the notion that cases would be required to pass through an extra level to reach the Supreme Court.

[129] EECR, "Constitution Watch: Hungary" (1997) 6:2 *E. Eur. Const. Rev.* 16 at 17, online at: http://www.law.nyu.edu/eecr/vol6num2/constitutionwatch/hungary.html.

[130] EECR, "Constitution Watch: Hungary" (1998) 7:4 *E. Eur. Const. Rev* 15 at 17, online at: http://www.law.nyu.edu/eecr/vol7num4/27.html – it is not clear what the basis of this argument is or what degree of validity it held. Perhaps it was premised on the notion that cases would be required to pass through an extra level to reach the Supreme Court.

[131] Open Society Institute, *Judicial Capacity in Hungary* (EU Accession Monitoring, 2002) at 110.

[132] *Ibid.* at 24.

access to Internet and on-line access to CELEX ... and is now operational at 18 county courts, the Budapest Municipal Court, the Supreme Court, and the National Council of Justice."[133] The European Commission also finds, however, that difficulties in locating appropriate staff to fulfil the legal secretary positions as well as continuing budgetary restrictions have hindered reforms. Budget problems are in part due, according to OSI, to the fact that "although the judiciary now has the right to draft its own budget proposal, the executive routinely submits a parallel proposal, which in practice Parliament accepts."[134] Consequently, as of 2002 Hungarian judges were required to "ensure material conditions for court operations, hire and manage court personnel, oversee financial operations, and implement regulations of the National Judicial Council;"[135] in particular OSI finds that 58% of judges' time is "devoted to administrative tasks such as management, statistics and dictation of trial records."[136]

In Poland, judicial capacity problems were prevalent throughout the 1990s. In 1995, USAID found "insufficient capacity of the judicial system to handle increased organized and violent crime."[137] In 1997, "[d]elays of up to 4 years in reaching first instance judgements in civil matters [were] not uncommon,"[138] and in that time period the European Court of Human Rights (ECHR) found Poland in violation of the right to be tried within a reasonable time. In 2000, the government created a new jurisdictional layer to deal with so-called petty offences and reduce caseload pressures, establishing 200 new chambers throughout the country with jurisdiction over minor criminal and civil matters.[139] In 2002, the court system became even more specialized, establishing 40 labour and social security courts[140] and in 2000, procedural amendments were introduced to simplify and expedite civil cases.[141] Significant improvements were also made with respect to staffing. In 2001–02 the positions of judge's assistant and "'court director' [were] introduced. Court directors will assume the function

---

[133] *Ibid.*
[134] Judicial Capacity in Hungary, *supra* note 131 at 115.
[135] *Ibid.* at 118.
[136] *Ibid.* at 119.
[137] USAID website, *USAID Mission to Poland: SEED Assistance Summary 1995*, http://www.usaid.gov/pl/1995.htm.
[138] European Commission, *2002 Regular Report on Poland's Progress Towards Accession* (COM 2002 700) at 10, online at: http://europa.eu.int/comm/enlargement/report2002/pl_en.pdf.
[139] European Commission, *2000 Regular Report on Poland's Progress Towards Accession* (COM 2000 700) at 17–18, online at: http://europa.eu.int/comm/enlargement/report_11_00/pdf/en/pl_en.pdf.
[140] Poland 2002 Regular Report, *supra* note 138 at 25.
[141] *Ibid.* at 17–18.

of managing the court's financial matters and property."[142] In 2000, 295 "referendarz" were hired as clerks to work in court record offices, and an additional 300 were hired by 2002. The number of judges increased by 5% in 2001.

The overall effect of these reforms on judicial efficiency was mixed. In the words of the European Commission,

> [a]t this early stage in their implementation such measures have helped to stem the tide but have not yet managed to reverse its flow ... During 2000, the courts settled almost 10% more cases than in 1999 ... However, as a result of the increase in cases referred to the Court there was a very small increase in the backlog ... It should be noted, however, that in some categories of cases, the average duration of the legal procedure has been reduced. This is particularly true for real-estate registration cases, which lasted an average of 3.3 months in 2000 compared to 3.7 in 1999, and for civil cases in district courts (4.3 months in 2000, 4.7 months in 1999) and in regional courts (5.6 months in 2000, 5.9 months in 1999).

While these numbers are somewhat equivocal, on the whole they appear to demonstrate a shift towards more efficient processes.[143]

In Russia, there have been two closely related and heavily discussed reforms directed at court procedure, specifically the reinstitution of jury trials[144] and the enactment of a new Code of Criminal Procedure.[145] The traditional Soviet system of criminal court proceedings had demonstrated a fierce accusatorial bias,[146] arguably related to its civilian-style inquisitorial system under which the role of both the prosecution and defence are subordinated to that of the judge. In the context of the Soviet Union, where judges were notoriously weak and subservient to the procuratorial function, the supremacy of the judges effectively allowed for the supremacy of the prosecution.[147] Reformers have, therefore, sought to shift the system of criminal justice from inquisitorial towards adversarial. This

---

[142] *Ibid.* at 25.

[143] One exception appears to be Warsaw, which has consistently demonstrated delays several times higher than in the rest of the country.

[144] Jury trials had been part of the pre-Communist legal system, but were abandoned after the revolution. The jury trial has been described as a "hallmark of the adversarial system." Scott P. Boylan, "The Status of Judicial Reform in Russia" (1998) 13 *Am. U. Int'l L. Rev.* 1327 at 1337–9.

[145] In place of the jury system, Soviet courts had generally operated by way of a judge aided by two lay assessors.

[146] See the chapter on Prosecution for more detail.

[147] The context of the Soviet Union is emphasized; indeed the system in and of itself "is a fine system of criminal justice that has served well in democracies throughout the world, including nations such as France, Germany, and Switzerland." James W. Diehm, "The Introduction of Jury Trials and Adversarial Elements into the Former Soviet Union and other Inquisitorial Countries" (2001) 11 *Journal Transnational Law & Policy* 1 at 4.

goal has included the reinvention of the Russian jury trial. Early proposals for the reinstitution of jury trials were met with great hostility.[148] The enabling legislation was opposed by various factions, most notably the procuracy and, to an extent, the judiciary, both being in a position to lose substantial power from any shift towards an adversarial system.[149] When the law finally did pass, jury trials were only initiated in eight of 89 regions, and only for the most serious of charges. Though the intention had been to phase in jury trials in the rest of the country after this initial trial stage, it was a full decade before the project continued.[150] Under Vladimir Putin, the move towards an adversarial system has gained considerable momentum.[151] In 2001, a new Code of Criminal Procedure was enacted, guaranteeing the extension of jury trials throughout the country, and in January 2003 this process began.[152]

Despite the successes of several judicial reform projects in increasing judicial efficiency in many Central and Eastern European countries, a recent paper by Wade Channell criticizes these reforms for overemphasizing judicial reform at the expense of improving judicial enforcement.[153] As Channell writes, "[w]here court reform programs have been effective, they have resulted in faster, better,

---

[148]   A much-heralded document is the "Conception of Judicial Reform," a manifesto of sorts written in 1991 by a group of Russian academics and jurists setting out their vision of the Russian legal system to come. It included a distinct adversarial focus and the re-establishment of jury trials.

[149]   Justin Burke, "In Russia, Jury Still Out on Trial by Jury," *Christian Science Monitor* (June 14, 1993).

[150]   Richard T. Andrias, "CEELI Contribution" 11:2 *Criminal Justice* 20 at 21.

[151]   Solomon Accountable, *supra* note 95.

[152]   The Code of Criminal Procedures contained a series of critical reforms with respect to bail, individual rights, defendant's rights, and so forth. The Code has been described by Professor Leonard Orland as a "revolution". To the extent that the code affects judicial independence and accountability it is dealt with above; to the extent that it affects other aspects of the judicial system it is beyond the scope of this chapter. For a detailed summary and analysis of the new Code and its provisions, see Leonard Orland, "A Russian Legal Revolution: The 2002 Criminal Procedure Code," (2002) 18 *Conn. J. Int'l L. 133;* for further background, see Hon. John C. Coughenour, "Canary in the Coal Mine: The Importance of the Trial Jury: Reflections on Russia's Revival of Trial by Jury: History Demands that we Ask Difficult Questions Regarding Terror Trials, Procedures to Combat Terrorism, and Our Federal Sentencing Regime" (2003) 26 *Seattle Univ. Law Review* 399 at 407; for articles on jury trials occurring in Russia in 2003, see Fred Weir, "Russia Embraces Trial By Peers" (*Christian Science Monitor*, March 5, 2003) online: http://www.csmonitor.com/2003/0305/p06s01-woeu.html; Mark McDonald, "Russia Begins New Twist on Trials: Juries" (Knight Ridder Newspapers, February 17, 2003) online at: http://www.cdi.org/russia/johnson/7065-2.cfm.

[153]   Wade Channell, Carnegie Endowment, "Lessons Not Learned: Problems with Western Aid for Law Reform in Postcommunist Countries," Carnegie Paper No. 57 (2005).

more predictable decisions that *still cannot be enforced*."[154] For example, in Bosnia, rule of law reforms redrafted civil procedures and court processes, but overlooked practical problems of enforcement, and as a result it can take several years to enforce a final judgment. This problem has begun to receive attention from legal reformers. Channell argues that this attention, while commendable, is unnecessarily late, a result, he suggests, of segmentation in rule of law reforms that entails focused interventions but ignores systemic problems.

C. Africa

The quality of judicial independence varies considerably across African nations and across indicators. For example, the judiciary in Botswana is seen by legal practitioners as being relatively free from political influence as far as the ap-pointment process is concerned, in spite of the relatively short tenure of judges there.[155] In Cameroon, by contrast, the short tenure of high court judges there constitutes a far greater threat to judicial independence, in view of "the failure to ensure that those who are appointed are apolitical and fully equipped with the legal skills needed to deal with often complex issues of constitutional inter-pretation."[156] Both Botswana and Kenya have compulsory retirement regimes for judges – as do most countries – yet Botswana is regarded as having a more independent judiciary.

As such evidence suggests, the modalities of judicial independence in Africa are complex, and frustrate its implementation. As recently as the 1990s, judicial independence was perceived as something of a novelty in Africa:

> During the colonial era, the judiciary was an integral branch of the executive rather than an institution for the administration of justice. The colonial administration was mainly interested in the maintenance of law and order. It had no respect for the independence of the judiciary or for the fundamental rights of the ruled. The judiciary was that part of the structure which enforced law and order. It was therefore identifiable as an up-holder of colonial rule. To an average citizen, the judiciary, as an instrument of control of the executive power, lacked credibility and therefore enjoyed little respect.[157]

In recent years, however, the ascendance of constitutionalism and rights dis-course in the developing world has seen the role of courts in many African states

---

[154]   *Ibid.*

[155]   Charles M. Fombad, "Protecting Constitutional Values in Africa: A comparison of Botswana and Cameroon" (2003) 36 *Constitutional and International Law Journal of South Africa* 99.

[156]   *Ibid.*

[157]   Yash Vyas, "The Independence of the Judiciary: A Third World Perspective" (1992) *Third World Legal Studies* 131.

shift from one of maintenance (in concert with the executive, the constabulary and the military) of law and order to one of rights invigilation.[158]

A thorough account of the entrenchment of judicial independence in an African state is offered in Jennifer Widner's biography of Francis Nyalali, the first post-colonial chief justice of Tanzania's highest court.[159] Widner considers that a number of contingencies (economic and political crises), coupled with pressure for reform from foreign aid agencies, created "openings;"[160] that is, opportunities for judges "to renegotiate the relationship between branches and engage in institution-building,"[161] and secure the independence they considered important. However, as Widner also argues, the longevity and public acceptance of these changes depended to a large extent on the goodwill and dedication of a few judicial professionals and, ultimately, the dedication of Nyalali himself.

Ironically, in order to secure judicial independence, Nyalali arguably infringed upon it, by waging a political campaign against the executive excesses of President Julius Nyerere. As Mary Dudziak notes, "Nyalali acted politically to create a constituency for judicial review."[162] In creating this constituency, Nyalali made populist appeals to Tanzanian nationalism, and connected judicial independence not only with Tanzania's nascent nationhood, but also to the broader African liberation struggle and to pan-Africanism itself. While eschewing narrow conceptions of history, Nyalali made shrewd use of the *zeitgeist* of pan-Africanism by rhetorically connecting Tanzanian constitutionalism and judicial review with "a history of the internalization of the principles and values of a world-wide liberation movement."[163]

Moreover, Nyalali astutely recognized the enormous importance of family law as the best substantive area of law with which to establish constitutional precedent, and attract attention and an air of relevance to the court's activities. At a time when, as Widner points out, mortality from AIDS and civil conflict was "scrambl[ing] the conventional division of labour, as well as norms governing succession and inheritance, ... women's participation in the family, community and economy was often restricted in ways that impeded adaptation

---

[158] For a serviceable, though somewhat outdated, bibliography of literature on the independence of the judiciary in relation to liberalization in the developing world, see *ibid*. 132.

[159] Jennifer Widner, *Building the Rule of Law* (New York: W.W. Norton & Co., 2001) [*Rule of Law*].

[160] *Ibid*. at 151.

[161] *Ibid*.

[162] Mary L. Dudziak, "Who Cares about Courts? Creating a Constituency for Judicial Independence in Africa" (Princeton University Program in Law and Public Affairs Working Paper No. 03-002, 2003, Social Science Research Network electronic library (SSRN) reference # 380281, p. 5).

[163] Widner, *Rule of Law*, *supra* note 159 at 183.

to changed new circumstances."[164] Litigation on family law thus brought customary and constitutional law into direct conflict. The open disposition of these conflicts by Nyalali and his fellow justices helped to establish the court as the proper venue for reconciling Tanzania's past with its future, and for mediating the competing claims of authority, tradition and rights, and did much to enhance its popular legitimacy.

Resource constraints are also of significant concern in African courts. Insufficient resources manifest themselves in a variety of ways, such as a lack of legal materials, including case law, and low levels of judicial remuneration. Both of these encourage judicial corruption, the former by rendering monitoring more problematic[165] and the latter by encouraging rent-seeking.[166] A lack of proper resources can also have a more direct impact on court operations: "[t]o the extent that a court has to adjourn when it rains" because it has no roof, "this impacts on its performance."[167]

Some reform efforts have sought to address the problem of resource scarcity. For instance, as of November 2002, USAID's judicial reform activities in Liberia, now emerging from a long period of civil war and repressive government, focused on access to legal materials for judges. The agency has provided financial and technical assistance for the publication and distribution of legal documents, such as the rules of criminal and civil procedure, the compiling of Supreme Court case-law and the distribution of codes of ethics to all lawyers and judges. According to USAID, prior to these projects, few legal professionals in Liberia had access to these materials.[168]

Court operations have similarly improved. The Supreme Court is now fully operational, eight of 15 counties have established functioning circuit courts, and one civil court and three criminal courts are fully operational in Montserrado County. However, many significant problems remain, most of which derive from

---

[164]   *Ibid.* at 336.

[165]   USAID, *Guidance, supra* note 20 at 45.

[166]   *Ibid.* at 52.

[167]   Ziyad Motala, "Judicial Accountability and Court Performance Standards" (2001) 34 *Comparative and International Law Journal of Southern Africa* at 177. Jennifer Widner offers a similar anecdote from the International Criminal Tribunal in Rwanda; "[n]o paper was available, so prosecutors had to buy it out of pocket. There was also no transportation or clerical support, and judicial personnel often had difficulty finding places to live." (Jennifer Widner, "Courts and Democracy in Post Conflict Transitions: A Social Scientist's Perspective on the African Case" (January 2001) 95 *American Journal of International Law* 68. ["Courts and Democracy"]) However, Motala also cautions that "the appropriate standards for the evaluation of trial court performance can be a matter of great debate [and] each jurisdiction [has] to determine its own standards against the goals it seeks to accomplish." (at p. 177).

[168]   USAID, *Achievements, supra* note 41 at 132.

a lack of resources. For example, the recently established circuit courts require 21 judges to be fully functional, and only 11 positions have thus far been filled. The lack of human resources extends to the availability of lawyers – there are five qualified prosecutors and ten public defenders. Furthermore, only 40% of the 146 magistrates' courts are operating. Even though many international donors have expressed an interest in funding legal reform initiatives, as of April 2005 no such funds had yet been received.[169]

Malawi is one of the poorest countries in the region and, according to USAID, the judiciary faces significant resource limitations that have led to a shortage of personnel and poor administration.[170] In 2000, USAID provided technical and financial assistance to the High Court and 2,000 more cases were processed than in the previous year. The agency also sponsored a study entitled the *Rose Report* that examined court management. The *Rose Report* led to the creation of a reform program, and the position of chief courts administrator was established to oversee the reform process in the coming years. An example of a minor reform that has already been implemented as a result of the report is a modification to the court register based on guidelines given in the *Rose Report*. The resultant standardization of record-keeping contributes to good management as well as to increased transparency and accountability, by allowing the creation and tracking of performance indices.

Ethiopia has an inexperienced and untrained judiciary as a result of decades of civil war and poverty. In response, USAID began a training program for judges in 1997 that focused on "short-term, emergency training." In 2001, 880 judges underwent training and 1,500 were scheduled for training in 2002. As of 2002, USAID was unable to gauge the success of the then-nascent program, but emphasized that it was the first time that judges in Ethiopia had received any training. Another project involved the publication of government codes and procedures, law journals, case law and similar materials to improve access for the judiciary. At the time, USAID found anecdotal evidence indicating that the publications were being used.[171] Continued optimism was expressed through 2003, when the Federal Supreme Court trained 1,244 judges in criminal law, labour law, tax law, family and succession law, contracts and torts, criminal procedure and execution of decrees, and USAID printed and distributed a further 7,912 copies of legal reference materials.[172] However, more recent documenta-

---

[169] *National Transitional Government of Liberia: Results Focused Transitional Framework* (United Nations/World Bank, April 2005), at 41–3, online at: http://www. reliefweb.int/library/documents/2005/ntgl-lib-30apr.pdf.

[170] *Achievements, supra* note 41 at 134.

[171] *Achievements, supra* note 41 at 130.

[172] USAID, "'Democracy and Governance' Program in Ethiopia," 2004–05 Datasheet, online at: http://www.usaid.gov/policy/budget/cbj2005/afr/pdf/663-010.pdf.

tion appears to suggest that the program was discontinued as of 2004.[173] While no direct explanation is provided, the 2007 USAID profile of Ethiopia suggests a possible readjustment of priorities, stating the agency's main objective as "overcom[ing] the threat of deadly recurring famine."[174]

USAID has also sponsored more narrowly focussed judicial training in the context of trials in the 1970s "Red Terror" genocide, which have been ongoing for years.[175] In 2000, USAID organized and sponsored a conference on international humanitarian law in Ethiopia that was intended to teach the judiciary about fair trial process. According to USAID, this conference enabled 80 judges in the Red Terror trials to "establish a common legal framework for rendering decisions." The training provided at the conference enhanced the judiciary's ability to process genocide cases. In addition, short-term funding was provided by USAID to the judiciary and law schools to process cases during the summer holidays in order to clear case backlogs.[176]

Efficiency-oriented reform efforts in Mozambique have focused on the training of judges and other court personnel. A training project that started in 1997 began with an assessment of the justice sector on the basis of which USAID staff organized seminars for members of the Supreme Court and the head of the Maputo City Court. Further assistance to the Maputo City Court included measures such as the creation of model forms for debt and eviction that allow for faster case processing, the development of a computerized case-tracking system and periodic courses on the interpretation and application of the civil code. These measures are being adopted by other courts in the country.[177]

In Mali, the Economic Reform and Development Program (PRED), financed by USAID, sought to assist in judicial reforms designed to improve the investment climate beginning in 1991.[178] Towards this end, PRED and the government of Mali implemented measures intended to improve efficiency in commercial courts. For example, the eligibility guidelines for members of commercial courts were expanded to include individuals from previously ineligible categories such as bankers, industrialists and insurers; this was done in order to create more

---

[173] USAID Ethiopia Profile, online at: http://www.usaid.gov/policy/budget/cbj2007/afr/pdf/et_complete.pdf. The first page of the profile shows that funding under "Democracy and Governance" ceased after FY 2004. Prior documentation suggests that judicial reform efforts took place under the auspices of the Democracy and Governance project. See note 172, *supra.*

[174] USAID Ethiopia profile, *supra* note 173.

[175] *Achievements, supra* note 41 at 129.

[176] *Achievements, supra* note 41 at 129.

[177] *Achievements, supra* note 41 at 137.

[178] Shantayanan Devarajan, David Dollar and Torgny Holmgren (eds), *Aid and Reform in Africa: Lessons from Ten Case Studies* (Washington, DC: The World Bank, 2001) at 257.

specialized commercial courts.[179] These members were made subject to the same disciplinary proceedings as presiding judges in order to discourage corruption and decrease case processing time.[180] Logistical support was provided in the form of equipment such as computers, legal database software and photocopiers.[181] Five years after the reforms were implemented, it was found that the judiciaries in commercial courts were still not functioning properly. Renewed reform efforts are looking to expand training for judges and impose strict sanctions for violations of a code of ethics for judges created in 1999.[182]

Another issue in a somewhat different vein is the relationship between formal courts, usually the target of judicial reform efforts, and more traditional "neighbourhood forums" of adjudication. In many African states, these more informal forums are efficient, highly legitimate sites of dispute resolution. In Botswana, for instance, the best African performer on indices of judicial efficiency and independence for the past 40 years, most "land disputes, differences of opinion about the identity of rightful heirs, stock-theft cases, and petty criminal matters [are] effectively and quickly resolved in neighbourhood forums, which are more accessible and less expensive than state courts and whose personnel are better acquainted with local conditions."[183]

Mediating the relationship between state courts and local forums has implications for efficiency, legitimacy and independence. In Uganda, collaborative enterprises between state and local council courts have been at best only partially successful in enhancing efficiency. Inadequate record-keeping and inconsistent norms among neighbourhood forums have often required the state courts to hear a vast number of appeals.[184] Where failed trials ended up before the state courts *de novo* anyway, some Ugandan local council courts did nothing to improve efficiency. Moreover, some Ugandan council courts "ignored the law and showed bias, charged fees even though they were supposed to be free, and were not responsive to women's interests."[185] In Somalia, conversely, Australian peacekeepers had success in balancing the need for a centralized court system with popular approval by inviting elder councils to nominate personnel, and making appointments only with community approval. As a result, uniformity and adherence to standards of best practice were ensured, resources expended

---

[179]   *Ibid.*

[180]   The decrease in case processing time was an intended result of including a reference to due diligence in the codified ethical obligations of members of the court.

[181]   John-Jean Barya and J. Oloka-Onyango, *Popular Justice and Resistance Committee courts in Uganda* (Kampala: Makerere University, 1994).

[182]   *Ibid.*

[183]   Widner, "Courts and Democracy," *supra* note 167 at 65.

[184]   Barya and Oloka-Onyango, *supra* note 181.

[185]   *Ibid.*

on recruitment were somewhat reduced, and popular legitimacy of candidates was enhanced.[186]

D.   Asia

Judiciaries across Asia are at very different stages of development. While some countries have achieved near independent status in their judiciaries and elimi- nated almost all corruption, in other countries court systems are nascent and rife with corruption.

In China, judicial reform starting in the late 1980s focused primarily on the development of a modern adversarial trial system, mostly ignoring the need to establish an independent judiciary.[187] Law was viewed primarily as a tool to achieve government objectives such as economic reform, and was therefore closely linked to Chinese Communist Party (CCP) policy. The 1982 People's Republic of China (PRC) Constitution explicitly mandated that judges exercise their discre- tion to achieve a "correct ideological result" consistent with Party policy.[188]

In the mid-1990s, discussions about the need for legal reform began to gain momentum among Chinese legal scholars, who recognized the importance of rule of law reform for the country's modernization drive.[189] Subsequent years witnessed several signals of reform from government actors. In 1995, China enacted a Judge Law stipulating that judges have the right to exercise their powers without interference by any administrative organ, public organization, or individual.[190] In 1997, the 15th Congress of the CCP amended the Party's charter to include "governing the country according to law" and "establishing Socialist rule of law" as major objectives by the year 2010.[191] At the 16th Con- gress of the CCP in November 2002, General Secretary Jiang Zemin's report to Congress contained two key conceptual breakthroughs. First, the report rec-

---

[186]   Martin R Ganzglass, "The Restoration of the Somali Justice System," in W. Clarke and J. Herbst (eds) *Learning From Somalia: The Lessons of Armed Humanitarian Intervention* (Boulder, CO: Westview Press, 1997) 20–41 at 27.

[187]   Chris X. Lin, "A Quiet Revolution: An Overview of China's Judicial Reform" (2003) 4 *Asian-Pacific L. & Pol'y J.* 180 at 182 ["A Quiet Revolution"]; see also Donald Clarke, "Empirical Research into the Chinese Judicial System," and Hualing Fu, "Putting China's Judiciary into Perspective: Is It Independent, Competent and Fair?," in Jensen and Heller (eds), *supra* note 34.

[188]   James Hugo Friend, "The Rocky Road Toward Rule of Law in China" (2000) 20 *NW. J. Int'l L. & Bus.* 369 at 373.

[189]   "A Quiet Revolution," *supra* note 187 at 185–6.

[190]   Li Zhenghui and Wand Zhenmin, "The Developing Human Rights and Rule of Law in Legal Philosophy and in Political Practice in China, 1978–2000," available at http://dex1.tsd.unifi.it/jg/en/index.htm?surveys/rol/wang.htm [hereinafter Li and Wand].

[191]   "A Quiet Revolution," *supra* note 187 at 185–6.

ognized the Constitution as the supreme law of the land, thus subordinating the Party, at least in principle, to law. Second, the report emphasized procedural justice and judicial reform, recognizing the importance, in American terms, of "due process," as a complement to substantive law.[192]

However, these formal developments did little to improve judicial independence, as governments continued to exercise undue control in the funding of the courts and the appointment of judges. Chinese courts are dependent on local congresses and governments for personnel, financial, and material support,[193] and governments maintain control over appointment and removal of judges.[194] This close relationship has led to a great deal of local protectionism, as courts have been under pressure to rule in favour of local interests and have been reluctant to enforce unfavourable judgments against local interests.[195] The Political-Legal Committee of the Chinese Communist Party also interferes directly in certain cases – particularly those cases which are politically sensitive or of great economic importance – by making recommendations about the outcome to the court.[196]

The judicial appointment process also highlights the lack of independence of the Chinese judiciary. The Judges Law specifies that the president of a court is appointed by the People's Congress of the same level as the court, while the other members of the court are appointed by its president. In practice, however, the Party Organization Department maintains substantial control and veto power over all judicial appointments, while the appointment process specified in the Judges Law is merely a formality.[197]

Judicial corruption is another related problem. In one much-publicized 1999 case, *Cangman County v. Long Gang Rubber*, a county court was accused of entering judgment in favour of the county department of treasury only because the department funded the court.[198] The case provoked outrage among prominent

---

[192]   "A Quiet Revolution," *supra* note 187 at 187. Lin characterizes this change as a fundamental one, reflecting a shift from "rule by law" to "rule of law" – the former meaning merely that substantive rules govern behaviour, the latter being a statement on how rules are applied and, relatedly, on the relationship of government to law. While the link is not expressly made here to judicial reform, it seems to presume the need for a legal decision-making organ separate and independent from government.

[193]   Li and Wand, *supra* note 190.

[194]   Selection and retention of chief judges at each level in the hierarchy is decided by the People's Congress of the corresponding level. Charles Baum, "Trade Sanction and the Rule of Law: Lessons From China" (2001) 1 *Stan. J. E. Asian Aff.* 46 [hereinafter Baum].

[195]   Stanley Lubman, "Looking for Law in China" (2006) 20 *Columbia Journal of Asian Law* at 31.

[196]   Randall Peerenboom, *China's Long March Toward Rule of Law* (Cambridge: Cambridge University Press, 2002) 306–7 [hereinafter Peerenboom].

[197]   *Ibid.* at 305–6.

[198]   "A Quiet Revolution," *supra* note 192 at 220.

Chinese legal scholars, even prompting calls to curb judicial independence, on the theory that increasing the autonomy of incompetent and corrupt judges is likely to result in even more wrongly decided cases.[199] Although the central government has been running anti-corruption campaigns and punishing corrupt judges, a culture of corruption remains, as judges frequently accept bribes and various gifts from the parties to a case.[200]

A number of reforms have sought to counteract these effects by making modifications to various aspects of judicial decision-making. As part of a five-year plan to address local political interference in the judicial system,[201] the Supreme People's Court (SPC) has introduced an open trial system and has begun to publish decisions of selected cases on the court's website.[202] In a similar effort to enhance transparency, a Shanghai court in *Henan Securities v. Shanghair KeJiao* published a dissenting opinion for the first time.[203] There have also been more substantive changes to judicial decision-making. In July 2002, the District Court of Zhongyuan introduced a system of *stare decisis*,[204] and the following month, Tianjin City was the first Chinese court to adopt the precedent system at the provincial level. It is difficult to predict, however, whether this trend will expand to other jurisdictions across China. The current constitutional framework places the judiciary under the control of the legislature, which has the exclusive power to interpret laws, including the creation of binding precedent. This constitutional structure is therefore an impediment to open adoption of a system of judicial precedent.

In addition to corruption and political interference, the Chinese judiciary also faces problems of competence, which stem in part from its rapid development after 1978. In 1979, there were some 58,000 people working in the courts in China. Of these 58,000, the number of legally trained professional judges is unknown, but it is estimated to have been minimal. By 2002, there were approximately 310,000 people working in the various courts, of which over 210,000 were judges. The government sustained this rapid expansion by recruit-

---

[199]   Randy Peerenboom, "Judicial Independence and Judicial Accountability: Preliminary Thoughts on Our Empirical Study of Individual Case Supervision" (Fall 2004) The Workshop on Chinese Legal Reform: Yale Law School.

[200]   Ting Gong, "Dependent Judiciary and Unaccountable Judges: Judicial Corruption in Contemporary China" (Fall 2004) *China Review* 4: 2.

[201]   Mei-Ying Hung, "China's WTO Commitment on Independent Review: An Opportunity for Political Reform" (Carnegie Endowment for International Peace, Working Paper No. 5, 2002), cited in Stephanie Wang, "Funding the Rule of Law and Civil Society" (Human Rights in China, Issue Paper No. 3, 2003), available at http://iso.hrichina. org/download_repository/ 2/HRIC_issues_paper3.2003.pdf.

[202]   *Ibid.*

[203]   "A Quiet Revolution," *supra* note 187 at 225.

[204]   *Ibid.*

ing retired officers of the People's Liberation Army (PLA) to the bench, despite their lack of formal legal or academic training. It has since amended the Judges Law to require that new judges pass a qualifying exam before being appointed to a judicial position.[205]

The educational requirements for becoming a judge were also rather limited, though they have been improving in recent years. The 1995 Judges Law required that all judges have a college education, but there was no requirement that the individual have a law degree. Many judges filled this requirement through the completion of a two-year technical degree.[206] The Judges Law was later amended to require that new judges have a bachelor's degree as well as legal experience prior to becoming a judge, and existing judges were supposed to upgrade their educational skills to the same standards.[207]

In June 1998, the United States and China issued a joint statement announcing their intention to cooperate in six specific areas of law reform, including judicial and lawyer training.[208] Since this announcement, little has been done. Other organizations, however, including the Ford Foundation, the Canadian International Development Agency (CIDA), and the United Nations Development Program (UNDP) have all sponsored training programs for judges. The Ford Foundation initiative offered young judges the opportunity to study in other countries. Participants were selected by the Supreme Court's Senior Judges Training Centre with the hope that trainees would return to China and join the Centre's teaching staff upon completion of the program. While some did, a significant number took up opportunities in the private sector, their original courts, or abroad. Newer judicial training programs, such as the program at South Central University of Political Science and Law in Wuhan and the Shanghai Judges Training Centre, emphasize fostering professional values and legal skills, rather than substantive law.[209]

Anecdotal evidence shows that training programs may have had a positive effect on the competency and independence of China's judges. At South Central University, staff and law students conduct "before and after" interviews with

[205] He Weifang, "Tongguo sifa shixian shehui zhengyi: dui zhongguo faguan xianzhuang de yige toushi" ("The Realization of Social Justice through Judicature: A Look at the Current Situation of Chinese Judges") cited in Baum, *supra* note 194.

[206] Peerenboom, *supra* note 196 at 291.

[207] *Ibid.*

[208] Matthew Stephenson, "A Trojan Horse Behind Chinese Walls? Problems and Prospects of U.S.-Sponsored 'Rule of Law' Reform Projects in the People's Republic of China" (2000) 18 *UCLA Pac. Basin L. J.* 64 at 71.

[209] Aubrey McCutcheon, "Contributing to Legal Reform in China," in Stephen Golub and Mary McClymont (eds), *Many Roads to Justice: The Law Related Work of Ford Foundation Grantees Around the World* (2000) at 17. Available at http://www.fordfound.org/publications/recent_articles/ docs/manyroads.pdf.

trainees in order to assess the impact of their program. Prior to participating, one judge described his duty as "to protect the rights and views of the government." Upon completion of the course, he described his responsibility as a judge to be a neutral "arbiter between views of parties, even if the government is a party." Staff at the Shanghai Judges Training Centre relate a story about how one of their training sessions emboldened a judge to resist repeated requests from a local official to delay enforcement of a judgment against one of the official's associates.[210]

Judicial reform efforts have also sought to enhance court efficiency through modifications to trial processes. The majority of trials in China are presided over by a panel of judges. Cases heard by a collegiate panel in a certain court will then be reviewed and decided by its trial committee. The purpose of this system is to prevent abuse of judicial discretion, as the collegiate panel serves as a check against abuses of power by individual judges.[211] However, in light of China's overburdened court system and limited judicial resources, in 1999 the Intermediate Court of Qingdao in the Shandong Province initiated a new system in which only the most important cases are decided by a panel, with the rest being decided by a single judge.[212] Such reforms need to be followed by reforms which increase the enforcement rates of court decisions; significant inefficiencies in the enforcement of court decisions have presented a continuing impediment to the development of a judiciary to which citizens can turn for effective dispute resolution.[213]

In the Philippines, each judge constitutes a "branch" of the trial court, with branches grouped together in "stations" of varying sizes. In an effort to prevent corruption, cases are filed at a single point in the station and then assigned to judges by lottery.[214] Trial judges are monitored by the Supreme Court through administrative circulars and regular statistical reports. In 2001, in an effort to encourage foreign investment, the Philippines Chief Justice set out a five-year Action Program for Judicial Reform with judicial autonomy, improved access to justice, and judicial transparency as its primary goals.[215]

The Filipino judiciary faces a significant problem of delay and congestion in the court system. The annual inflow of new cases has increased dramatically in recent years. Between 1989 and 1999, there was an increase of 14.4% in the

---

[210]   *Ibid.*

[211]   *Ibid.* at 236.

[212]   *Ibid.* at 237.

[213]   See generally Donald Clarke, "Power and Politics in the Chinese Court System: The Enforcement of Civil Judgments" (1996) 10 *Columbia Journal of Asian Law* 1.

[214]   Rosemary Hunter, "Reconsidering 'Globalization': Judicial Reform in the Philippines" (2002) 6 *LTC* 41 at 49.

[215]   *Ibid.* at 45.

Regional Trial Courts (RTC) and an increase of 106.3% in the Municipal Trial Courts (MTC).[216] Moreover, there is a shortage of judges, as more than one quarter of trial court branches are vacant.[217] This shortage is at least partially related to the low salaries, high workloads, and low prestige of the profession, rendering recruitment difficult.

The 1987 Constitution sought to address some of these concerns with provisions relating to funding, judicial appointments and trial processes. Article 8, section 3 states that the judiciary shall enjoy "fiscal autonomy," prohibits reductions in funding below previous years' levels, and states that the amount allocated shall be "automatically and regularly released." Section 8 establishes a Judicial and Bar Council mandated to make recommendations for judicial appointments, and composed of a representative of the bar, a professor of law, a retired member of the Supreme Court and a representative of the private sector.[218] The Constitution also requires that trial processes be expedited, and a 1989 reform established "continuous trials," which required that cases be completed within 90 days of their first day in court.[219]

These reforms have been only partially effective, however, in part because the Department of Budget and Management (DBM) has continued to control the disbursement of funds from the national budget to the judiciary. Along with other government agencies, the judiciary receives an annual allotment from Congress. However, despite the constitutional requirement that funding be "automatically and regularly released," the DBM requires the judiciary to justify individual expenditures, leading to both delay and opportunities for rent-seeking.[220] Most detrimentally, perhaps, the process has compelled lower courts to accept subsidies from local governments. Under the Local Government Code,

---

[216]   *Ibid.* at 51.

[217]   *Ibid.* at 52.

[218]   Rosemary Hunter, "Philippines: Formulation of Case Decongestion and Delay Reduction Strategy Project Phase 1," Draft Final Report (2003), available at http://www. apjr-sc-phil.org/pub-reports.

[219]   Previously, a "piecemeal" trial system, in which judges habitually granted innumerable delays and continuances, contributed greatly to endless cases and huge backlogs on court dockets. Only trial lawyers, who collected fees on a per-appearance basis, seemed to benefit.

[220]   Email from Elsie Louise Pfleider Araneta, Senior Counsel, Asian Development Bank (May 5, 2004) (on file with author) [hereinafter Araneta]. Recent studies on the caseload of the Filipino judicial system indicate that delays occur throughout the court system, as shown by the high caseload of judges, low clearance rates and the incidence of archiving and transfer of cases, particularly in the lower courts. The duration of court proceedings remains very long, with an average two years between filing of information to judgment (Cristina E. Torres *et al.*, "A Survey of Private Legal Practitioners to Monitor Access to Justice by the Disadvantaged" (2003). Available at http://www.apjr-sc-phil. org/pub-reports [hereinafter UNDP Survey 2003]).

local governments units (LGUs) have the discretion to determine whether, how much and what kind of support will be granted to courts within their jurisdiction. As a result, courts turn to LGUs for the flexibility their own budgets lack, leaving them vulnerable to influence.[221] Moreover, the Judicial and Bar Council's rules and procedures are not transparent.[222]

Other projects, funded by donors such as The Asia Foundation (TAF) and the Ford Foundation, have been directed to training personnel. Early efforts in the 1990s sponsored international exchanges and consultancies for lawyers and judges. These programs were mostly unsuccessful because they failed to account for incentives on lower-level employees, who continued to benefit from the legal or illegal fees derived from delay and mismanagement.[223] The programs also failed to address judicial vacancies: even where sitting judges benefited from the training, one-third of posts in the lower courts remained vacant.[224]

TAF and the Ford Foundation therefore redirected their support to alternative law groups (ALGs), discussed in greater detail in Chapter 7 (Access to justice). The Ford Foundation reports that the greatest legal problems facing Filipinos "were of a social justice nature and were not necessarily handled by the courts, which in any event were backlogged, expensive, and hard to access."[225] For TAF, Ford, USAID and other donors that subsequently targeted legal issues in the Philippines, funding ALGs came to represent a more effective, if indirect, route to reform of the country's legal institutions. In a similar vein, donors also began supporting alternative dispute resolution (ADR) mechanisms. ADR has the dual benefit of alleviating congestion in the courts and providing a forum that is tailored to the needs of a certain kind of litigant. ADR mechanisms include mediation boards, neighbourhood counselling centers and binding arbitration schemes. Some are public, such as the *Barangay* Justice System, which the government introduced in 1978 to resolve disputes at the municipal level. Others take place in the private sector. For example, the Asia Foundation has worked with The Makati Business Club to develop commercial ADR mechanisms.[226]

---

[221]   *Ibid.*

[222]   Araneta, *supra* note 220.

[223]   Harry Blair and Gary Hansen, "Weighing in on the Scales of Justice: Strategic Approaches for Donor-Supported Rule of Law Programs," USAID Program and Operations Assessment Report No. 7 (1994), available at http://www.usaid.gov/our_work/democracy_and_governance/publications/pdfs/pnaax280.pdf.

[224]   This remained true as of 2003. UNDP Survey 2003, *supra* note 220 at 4.

[225]   Mary McClymont and Stephen Golub, "Many Roads to Justice: The Law Related Work of Ford Foundation Grantees Around the World" (2000) Ford Foundation, available at http://www.fordfoundation.org.

[226]   *Ibid.*

The government of the Philippines has also been operating its own judicial reform project, the Judicial Reform Agenda, which the Supreme Court has implemented through its organization, the Action Program for Judicial Reform (APJR). The APJR has had a hand in a wide range of reform efforts addressed at independence, accountability and efficiency. One project completed in December 2004 and entitled Strengthening the Independence and Defining the Accountability of the Judiciary included a comprehensive examination of seemingly every element of the Filipino judiciary, from budgeting to human resources, independence, appointments, physical assets and more.[227] In 2004 and 2005, APJR in conjunction with AusAID completed a "training needs assessment," which led to a set of recommendations for future training programs.[228] Other initiatives, though not all a matter of judicial reform, abound.[229] However, these programs suffer from a lack of awareness: fewer than half of the lawyers surveyed in 2003 knew of the existence of the Judicial Reform Agenda. Of those who did know about it, 38% were of the opinion that the reforms were inadequate.[230] This may change, however, with additional foreign funding, of which US$21.9 million was allocated by the World Bank in 2003.[231]

Law in Korea was traditionally seen as an instrument of political control,[232] and the current independent judiciary in Korea has only been in existence since the country's liberation from Japan in 1945. The 1987 Constitution requires that judges exercise their authority "according to conscience, free from any pressure or coercion from outside judicial administrative agencies,"[233] and establishes a system of checks and balances among the three branches of government. However, the judiciary does not exercise the autonomy guaranteed by the Constitution. While no judge is dismissed or forced to retire during good behaviour, the system of assignments and promotion allows the chief justice to move judges to undesirable positions. Furthermore, tenure for lower court judges is only ten years. According to a 1980 survey by the Seoul Lawyers' Association, 67% of judges believed that independence was not fairly achieved.[234] There is also a shortage of judges in Korean courts, as low salaries and high educa-

---

[227] See the downloadable list of report components at http://www.apjr-sc-phil.org/article/articleview/115/1/2/.

[228] Access the final report on the APJR website at http://www.apjr-sc-phil.org/article/articleview/134/1/2/.

[229] See the 2004 APJR annual report, online at: http://www.apjr-sc-phil.org/article/articleview/137/1/2/.

[230] UNDP Survey 2003, *supra* note 220 at 5, 49.

[231] http://www.idlo.int/texts///IDLO//mis6783.pdf.

[232] Chang Soo Yang, "The Judiciary in Contemporary Society: Korea" (1993) 25 *Case Western Res. J. Int'l L.* 303 at 311.

[233] *Ibid.*

[234] *Ibid.* at 312.

tional requirements harm recruitment and retention. There is only one judge for every 42,000 citizens, compared to the international average of one judge for every 1,000 citizens.[235] As a result, courts are overburdened and there is a large backlog of cases.

Legal reforms in Cambodia take place against the particularly bleak legacy of the Khmer Rouge, which devastated the legal system in the 1970s, killing or forcing into exile judges, lawyers, and other legal professionals.[236] It was not until the 1980 ousting of the Khmer Rouge that the government began to rebuild a formal court system. As of 1993, judicial monitoring of executive authority was virtually non-existent, as courts did not have the authority to review the legality of government decrees. Judicial competence was equally problematic, as most judges had only a high school education and had completed a three to five-month law course offered by the Institute of Public Administration and Law.[237] In these circumstances, the UNDP has focused on preliminary efforts at laying the groundwork for reform, including the development of reform planning and expertise. For instance in 2005, the agency initiated a US$231,000 project with several related objectives, including capacity development for individuals and institutions, such as the salient ministries, who would be largely responsible for reform programs, and instigating research into potential ways in which to "interface between formal and informal justice systems."[238]

Vietnam's judiciary has historically been highly decentralized, leading judges and courts to focus on maintaining good relations with local Party cadres.[239] In an early set of reforms in 1992, the government attempted to remedy this situation by centralizing authority over the legal system, and control over appointments was removed from local officials and vested in the President.[240] However, already facing an overburdened workload, the President's office was unable to perform this function and in practice relied on local governments for selections, which were subsequently rubber-stamped by the President. With judicial appointments fixed at five-year terms with the potential for reappointment, this local control over selection provided significant opportunity for government influence. Even where judges acted independently, government

---

[235]   *Ibid.* at 310.

[236]   Dolores Donovan, "Cambodia: Building a Legal System from Scratch" (1993) at 445.

[237]   *Ibid.* at 456.

[238]   UNDP Project Factsheet, "Legal and Judicial Reform (Preparatory Assistance)" http://www.un.org.kh/undp/?url=/undp/project_fact_sheet/gov_legal.asp.

[239]   Brian Quinn, "Vietnam's Continuing Legal Reform: Gaining Control Over the Courts" (2003) 4 *Asian Pacific L. & Pol'y J.* 355 at 359.

[240]   *Ibid.* at 362.

influence was felt through the use of "citizen jurors," a method of criminal trial in which cases are decided by a three-person panel composed of one judge and two "citizen jurors." Citizen jurors serve five-year terms, but sit at the pleasure of the Communist Party, and are explicitly selected on criteria of "political loyalty and reliability."[241] Finally, the 1992 reforms did nothing to change budgeting systems, which remained within the control of local government units.

In 2002, the government instituted a new round of reforms.[242] Mirroring the 1992 efforts, the 2002 reforms included the centralization of management of court personnel and budgets under the Supreme People's Court in Hanoi. Provincial governments resisted, claiming judicial independence would be sacrificed in two ways: by rendering local courts dependent on the Supreme Court, and by linking courts too closely with the central government. As Quinn argues, however, this latter position ignored the relationship of courts to local governments under the prior arrangement. The 2002 reforms also made adjustments to selection and appointment processes. Judges were no longer to be appointed by the President, but by the provincial chief judge, who was in turn appointed by the provincial government. Furthermore, prospective judges require approval by a Nominating Committee. There are numerous such committees, and each has a different composition; but in Quinn's view the composition of the committees generally send an "ambiguous signal," with one such committee staffed by a judge, a representative of the bar, and several representatives of the executive.[243]

The Singaporean judiciary is one of the most successful in the region. Public confidence in the fair administration of justice is as high as 97% according to one survey,[244] and the "judicial system consistently obtains high ratings in international and national surveys."[245] The Singapore Constitution contains numerous safeguards for judicial independence, insulating judges from political pressure, fixing tenure at 65 years, guaranteeing against adverse salary changes, and requiring the approval of a tribunal of current and former Supreme Court justices before dismissal of upper court judges is permitted.[246] Nevertheless, concerns about the independence of its judiciary still exist. Despite the mandatory retirement age of 65, judges past this age tend to be re-hired on contract, extensions which are not automatic. Furthermore, the lower levels of the judici-

---

[241] *Ibid.* at 363–6.

[242] *Ibid.* at 373.

[243] *Ibid.* at 378.

[244] Dakolias, *supra* note 126 at 131.

[245] Karen Blocglinger, "Primus Inter Pares: Is the Singapore Judiciary First Among Equals" (2000) 9 *Pac. Rim. L. & Pol'y* 591 at 591 [hereinafter "Primus Inter Pares"].

[246] Li-ann Thio, "Lex Rex or Rex Lex? Competing Conceptions of the Rule of Law in Singapore" (2002) 20 *UCLA Pac. Basin L. J.* 1 at 17.

ary are not granted tenure and are actually a part of the executive branch of government, as an exception to the separation of powers. These judges are appointed by the Prime Minister on the nomination of the Chief Justice, and are "routinely shuffled between the executive and judicial branches."[247]

Reform efforts in Singaporean courts in the past 15 years have focused principally on improvements to judicial efficiency and reductions in litigation delay. Former Chief Justice Yong Pung How spearheaded a series of reforms throughout the 1990s, including case management, the introduction of mediation as a form of dispute resolution, and the application of information technology in the courts. These efforts appear to have been successful: the rate of case disposition has increased, backlogs have been eliminated, and restrictions on the automatic right to appeal have diminished the appellate level caseload.[248] Blocglinger argues for various reasons that these successes have come without costs in terms of access to justice.[249] However, she does note a number of side-effects that seem to be of concern, including the equity implications of both restrictions on the automatic right to appeal and the use of court fees as a way to discourage lengthy litigation, and the fact that seven out of ten lawyers surveyed felt they no longer had sufficient time to prepare for trial.[250]

III. CONCLUSION

Impediments to the realization of an independent, yet accountable and legitimate, judicial branch come in a variety forms. Levers of influence may exist on the institutional level, through non-transparent selection regimes or executive control over budgets, or individually through promotions, salaries and threats of discipline. The wielders of such influence vary from private actors, to central governments, to local government officials operating below the radar of judicial reforms. Accountability may be threatened in all three of its forms – operational, behavioural and decisional – by low competence, a lack of transparency, insufficient funding and poor budgeting or case management skills. Legitimacy is threatened by all of these hazards. In each case, the relevant confluence of factors will generally be relatable to historical context and the role of the judiciary in previous – or current – undemocratic regimes: structural factors determining court funding, the level of legal or judicial expertise, a culture of judicial independence or of executive impunity.

---

247 *Ibid.* at 21.
248 "Primus Inter Pares," *supra* note 245.
249 *Ibid.* at 612–14.
250 *Ibid.* at 613. See also Dakolias, *supra* note 126 at 131–4.

Resource constraints impede judicial reform in two clear ways. First, an absence of resources renders it more difficult to improve efficiency and reduce court backlogs. Needed resources include money, as in Hungary, human resources, as in Liberia, China and the Philippines, or technical expertise in budgeting, criminal procedure or case management, each of which has been the target of reform efforts. Even where both efficiency and capacity are improved, a judiciary may still face resource constraints and backlogs where success in enhancing popular legitimacy causes radical growth in the number of cases filed and, therefore, the workload facing the judiciary. Moreover, even where court backlogs are reduced, both effectiveness and legitimacy can be harmed where there is a failure to ensure a concomitant growth in capacity for enforcement, leading to a proliferation of unenforceable court orders. Second, insufficient resources threaten judicial independence by encouraging reliance for funding on relatively unaccountable branches of government, such as local or administrative entities, or on private parties.

Cultural, historical and social values can also impact upon reform in various ways. Close historical relationships between the judicial and executive branches, for instance, can hamper the development of popular legitimacy, as the public remains sceptical of the judiciary as a site for fair dispute resolution and may justify the creation of new or alternative dispute resolution fora to break with the existing judicial culture.[251] Indeed, it often seems that the key task of judicial reform – even where reform attempts develop as a power clash between competing institutional bodies – can be recast as a struggle to establish legitimate authority. Claims from political, judicial or purportedly neutral bodies, such as judicial councils, about appropriate forms of selection, dismissal, or more fundamentally, tribunal jurisdiction, will necessarily be evaluated against prior public experiences with each institutional form. It is in this way that "regime relativity," introduced at the outset of this chapter, will be effected in particular circumstances. Unsurprisingly, where reforms originate from within the country and attempt to encourage public support for the value of judicial independence – and where domestic values are properly captured in the design of the new system, for instance by maintaining local forms of dispute resolution – the legitimacy of the new institution can be greatly enhanced. In completely different ways, resistance to change can arise simply out of habit, as in Chile, where judges were reluctant to abandon inefficient formal procedures, even after they were removed from the relevant legislation. Similarly, experience in Guatemala demonstrates that a failure to achieve ju-

---

[251] See Thomas Heller, "An Immodest Portrait," in Jensen and Heller (eds), *supra* note 34.

dicial consensus can harm the implementation of otherwise well-designed procedural reforms.[252]

The political economy of judicial reform is a significant issue, as adjustments in judicial structures can have significant implications for the authority of a variety of judicial and political actors. Judicial councils have faced considerable opposition wherever they have purported to usurp the authority of either higher court judges or politicians, and have sometimes, as in Bolivia, become involved in direct struggles for authority with political bodies. Crude power struggles have also ensued between judicial and executive branches where, as in Peru or Belarus, governments have asserted unilateral control over key elements of independence such as appointments or funding, or in some cases merely refused to recognize the legal authority of the courts. The relationship between the judicial and the political branches has been particularly prone to blurring where crisis emerges in the broader political or economic context. Argentina is an interesting example, by some accounts at least, of the role of public opinion in encouraging judicial opposition to executive policy even where such popular opinion was incapable of affecting policy choices more directly. In these cases, it is worth noting, it becomes difficult not only to moderate the political power of the executive but also to identify the legitimate boundary of judicial or legal authority. In the efforts of Chief Justice Nyalali in Tanzania or of the judicial council in Bolivia, we witness attempts to establish legitimate legal authority that seemed to have brought those institutions into direct political contestation. Modifications to criminal procedure such as a move to adversarial proceedings or the institution of jury trials have also engendered opposition where such changes imply a reduced role for entrenched interest groups.

Resistance to reform is manifested by interest groups in other, subtler ways as well. In both former Soviet states and certain African countries, local–national dynamics have been an important element of reform efforts, albeit in different ways. In African states, national courts attempting to standardize procedures have been unable to attain the efficiency or legitimacy of local forums for dispute resolution, and have therefore struggled to integrate with, rather than usurp, their authority. In former Soviet states, the threat to independence occasioned by resource constraints has manifested itself through corruption by local government actors resistant to modes of accountability implemented by central government entities. As in the Philippines, resource dependence can also vest influence in administrative bodies charged with distributing resources, even where sufficient funds are formally allocated by the legislature.

---

[252] See Malcolm Feeley, *Court Reform on Trial: Why Simple Solutions Fail* (NY: Basic Books, 1983).

3. Police

I. NORMATIVE BENCHMARKS

A. Re-conceptualizing the Role of the Police in Developing Countries

The law and development movement of the 1960s and 1970s and the initial stages of the subsequent rule of law reform revival focused on judicial independence, procedural reforms and the transition from written to oral advocacy, and largely ignored the role of the police in promoting the rule of law. Such an oversight was detrimental to rule of law reform as reformers underestimated the critical role played by the police in reforming the justice system. As the most visible arm of the justice system, the police provide a key link between the public and the rule of law, and effective reform of the police provides a critically important opportunity for increasing the legitimacy of rule of law reform. Before examining institutional mechanisms to ensure independence and accountability of police in developing countries, it is important to understand the history of police in developing countries and the consequent need to re-conceptualize police forces as democratic, civilian-oriented services.

International organizations, particularly the United Nations, have articulated standards for police behaviour. The United Nations Code of Conduct for Law Enforcement,[1] adopted in 1979 by the General Assembly, recognizes the crucial role that police play in protecting human rights and ensuring equal treatment of citizens before the law. Subsequent UN documents, including Guidelines for the Effective Implementation of the Code,[2] and the Basic Principles on the Use of Force and Firearms by Law Enforcement Officials,[3] adopted in 1990, provide further guidance on the appropriate role of police. Despite the existence and wide formal endorsement of these international principles, police reform

---

[1] United Nations Code of Conduct for Law Enforcement Officials, adopted by the General Assembly in 1979, G.A. Res. 34/169, U.N. Doc. A/34/46.

[2] Guidelines for the Effective Implementation of the Code of Conduct for Law Enforcement Officials, adopted by the Economic and Social Council on May 24, 1989.

[3] Basic Principles on the Use of Force and Firearms by Law Enforcement Officials, adopted by the Eighth United Nations Congress on the Prevention of Crime and the Treatment of Offenders, Havana, Cuba, August 27 to September 7, 1990, online: http://www.ohchr.org/english/law/pdf/firearms.pdf.

as an area of rule of law reform was largely ignored until the past 15 years and remains a sensitive topic. Early Cold War involvement of the major powers with the police forces of developing countries had left a bitter legacy of providing assistance to foreign police forces. The United States actually prohibited US agencies from training foreign police under section 660 of the Foreign Assistance Act, and only began exempting certain countries from this ban in the late 1980s.[4]

The legacy of history for police institutions in developing countries should not be underestimated. The police in many societies evolved from states' efforts to assert their sovereignty. While the police in developed countries have moved away from protecting the interests of state, this separation has been stunted in many developing countries. In Latin America the predominant role of the military and the implementation of National Security Doctrines to combat civil unrest and guerrilla movements blurred the distinctions between the police and the military and between common criminals and threats to the state. As Rachel Nield writes,

> This lumping together of all "enemies" has had lasting repercussions. Intelligence activities and social control policies expanded exponentially … As police dedicated themselves first and foremost to protecting the regime, normal police work in law enforcement and crime prevention was neglected. Basic police work remains appallingly shoddy and police-community relations are still characterized by hostility and fear for majority sectors of the population.[5]

In post-socialist countries, newly independent states are struggling with a legacy of police as part of the oppressive force of the Communist state. Under Soviet rule, the police operated as a tool of the Communist Party often directed against political opposition.[6] While there is much diversity amongst the post-Soviet states, Louise Shelley identifies a common legacy of "demoralized and corrupt police forces with little or no respect for citizen's rights."[7] An equally troubling legacy exists in post-colonial countries, where the colonial governments instituted local police forces to defend the interests of the colonizers.

---

[4]   David Bayley, *Democratizing the Police Abroad: What to Do and How to Do It* (Washington: US Department of Justice, 2001) at 3 [Bayley, *Democratizing*].

[5]   Rachel Nield, "Confronting a Culture of Impunity: The Promise and Pitfalls of Civilian Review of Police in Latin America," in Andrew Goldsmith and Colleen Lewis (eds), *Civilian Oversight of Policing: Governance, Democracy and Human Rights* (Portland, OR: Hart Publishing, 2000) at 226.

[6]   Louise I. Shelley, "Post-Socialist Policing: Limitations on Institutional Change," in R.I. Mawby (ed.), *Policing Across the World: Issues for the Twenty-first Century* (New York: Garland Publishing, 1999) at 76–7.

[7]   *Ibid.* at 76.

Even after independence, citizens in many post-colonial states continue to perceive the police as oppressive, often with good reason.[8]

Despite the diversity of experiences in developing countries there is a common theme running through the experience of many developing countries with police institutions. The role of the police in many developing countries posits a politicized role for the police acting against citizens, whether as tools of the Communist Party, an authoritarian government, or a colonizing government. The police were alienated from citizens because of the exclusive focus of the police on securing social order and defending ruling interests.[9] Driven by the primary goal of public order policing, police in such conditions had little interest in protecting basic human rights or upholding the rule of law: police were responsible only to the ruling interests, who, in turn, were often unaccountable to the citizens and whose interests lay in regime maintenance.

As Paul Chevigny writes, the police legacy in many developing countries has produced a misconception of the role of the police that "blinds them to the simple perception that the police are citizens, as are those with whom they work, and that there is no enemy."[10] The dominant conception of police in developed countries is that of a service to citizens. The ideal-type of police in developed countries is multi-faceted and police are required to:

- Prevent and control conduct widely recognized as threatening to life and property;
- Aid individuals who are in danger of physical harm, such as the victims of violent attack;
- Facilitate the movement of people and vehicles;
- Assist those who cannot care for themselves, the intoxicated, the addicted, the mentally ill, the physically disabled, the old, and the young;
- Resolve conflict, whether it be between individuals, groups or individuals, or individuals and their government;
- Identify problems that have the potential for becoming more serious problems;
- Create and maintain a feeling of security in communities.[11]

---

[8]   Etannibi E.O. Alemika, "Police, Policing and Rule of Law in Transitional Countries," in Lone Lindholt, Paulo de Mesquita Neto, Danny Titus and Etannibi E.O. Alemika (eds), *Human Rights and the Police in Transitional Countries* (The Hague: Kluwer Law International, 2003) at 74.

[9]   *Ibid.* at 63.

[10]   Paul Chevigny, "Defining the Role of the Police in Latin America," in Juan E. Méndez, Guillermo O'Donnell and Paulo Sérgio Pinheiro (eds), *The (Un)Rule of Law and the Underprivileged in Latin America* (Notre Dame, IN: University of Notre Dame Press, 1999) at 49.

[11]   H. Goldstein, *Policing a Free Society* (Cambridge, MA: Ballinger, 1977).

These various functions of the police reveal a conception of police acting in the service of citizens. Such a service-oriented conception of the police is recognized in the UN Code of Conduct for Law Enforcement, which states that the role of police is fulfilled by "serving the community," including "rendition of services of assistance to those members of the community by reason of personal, economic, social or other emergencies are in need of immediate aid."[12] One mechanism for ensuring that serving citizens is the top priority for police is by instituting an emergency telephone system. As David Bayley writes, with a 911 system "any citizen with access to a telephone can summon a uniformed representative of the state imbued with the authority of the law and equipped with instruments of force to attend to his or her particular need."[13]

As it is the interests of citizens that police are protecting, service-oriented policing naturally lends itself more easily to the protection of human rights and maintenance of the rule of law or what has been termed democratic policing. Peter Manning writes that democratic policing "eschews torture, terrorism, and counterterrorism; is guided by law; and seeks minimal damage to civility."[14] Democratic policing thus has both a substantive and procedural component. Democratic police must be guided by law, but they must also protect basic human rights, including freedom from torture and cruel, inhuman or degrading punishment and treatment, and freedom from arbitrary arrest and detention. Lone Lindholt argues that accountability is also a critical aspect of democratic policing,[15] as will be explored below.

The substantive component of democratic policing potentially places officers in countries that lack constitutional guarantees of human rights in a situation where the twin demands of democratic policing conflict. In such a case, a law that is procedurally valid may violate human rights, and since police cannot modify laws, they will be forced to choose between upholding the law and protecting human rights. While such a situation no doubt places the police officer in a difficult position, it should not be interpreted to preclude the application of democratic policing to states that lack constitutionally protected human rights. Moreover, the term democratic policing is not reserved for democratic countries. While democratic policing is easier to achieve in a political democracy,[16] democratic policing is still a valuable model to follow in non-democratic countries, in that it can limit the most egregious human rights violations, if only by increasing transparency and accountability, provide a signpost for the reform process

---

[12] Article 1, Code of Conduct, *supra* note 1.
[13] Bayley, *Democratizing*, *supra* note 4 at 13.
[14] Peter K. Manning, "The Study of Policing" (2005) 8(1) *Police Quarterly* 23.
[15] Lindholt *et al.*, *supra* note 8 at 19.
[16] Bayley, *Democratizing*, *supra* note 4 at 13.

to aspire to and may be more effective in achieving the goals of the police institution.

This last rationale for encouraging democratic policing even without a democratic system of government is perhaps the most interesting and potentially far-reaching. David Bayley finds that police in general often feel pressure to overstep their authority, violating human rights and infringing the rule of law, in order to ensure public safety and achieve what they perceive to be natural justice.[17] In developing countries the inclination of police to overstep their authority may be even greater, given the high crime rates that are prevalent in much of the developing world and the public and political pressure for security. In Latin America, where crimes rates have soared, citizens are often supportive of unlawful police behaviour and perceive human rights protection as being soft on crime. But as Paul Chevigny points out, the police and citizens supporting such policies are misled. Violating the rule of law and human rights is an ineffective means of reducing crime because "society cannot obtain 'security' through police lawlessness, precisely because it is lawless."[18] As an example, Chevigny argues that torture is often used by police in Latin America for corrupt purposes, such as to retrieve a stolen object, which is then sold back to its owner. In such a situation, security is not being achieved as criminals are left outside of the justice system and police fail to develop skills in investigating crimes.[19]

Research by David Bayley supports the conclusion that upholding the rule of law is in the self-interest of the police. Bayley demonstrates that violating the rule of law contributes marginally to deterrence: "'getting tough on crime' by overstepping legal boundaries produces very small, if any, gains in reducing criminality."[20] Further, he shows that by violating the rule of law the police are actually making their job harder in that it alienates the public and lessens the willingness of citizens to aid the police. Additionally, Bayley argues that lawless behaviour by the police wastes community resources, puts police officers at risk, and weakens the authority and legitimacy of the law. Taken together, Bayley concludes that "in short, a stronger, evidence-based case can be made that defending human rights enhances police effectiveness more than doing so hampers it. Illegality in policing is a risky and generally unproductive strategy."[21]

An attractive feature of this instrumental argument for respect for the rule of law by police in developing countries is that it appeals to the pre-existing interest of officers in achieving security and can thereby avoid the legitimacy problem

---

[17]   David Bayley, "Law Enforcement and the Rule of Law: Is There a Tradeoff?" (2002) 2(1) *Criminology & Public Policy* 133 at 136 [Bayley, "Tradeoff"].

[18]   Chevigny, *supra* note 10 at 60.

[19]   Chevigny, *supra* note 10 at 61.

[20]   Bayley, "Tradeoff," *supra* note 17 at 138.

[21]   *Ibid.* at 146.

that can occur when reforms conflict with prevailing social norms. Studies of police reform, and rule of law reform more generally, often conclude that cultural, social, and political norms impede the reform process. For example, in her studies of police reform in Brazil and Argentina, Mercedes Hinton concludes that "efforts at police reform to date have been at odds with the patterns of patronage, clientelism, unholy alliances and impunity that continue to prevail at the highest levels of the executive, legislative and judicial branches of government."[22] While recognizing that the continued presence of a culture of corruption is a serious problem, effective police reform does not have to wait for large-scale institutional change. By following the instrumental, self-interested approach advocated by Chevigny and Bayley reformers can advocate the rule of law by appealing to the interests of police institutions. Moreover, maintenance of the rule of law by police in developing countries, even if for instrumental reasons, can encourage systemic normative change. The presence of a police force, who are providing service-oriented policing, upholding the rule of law and protecting human rights in the daily lives of citizens, can greatly enhance the legitimacy of the police and the justice system.

B. Independence

Given the history of many developing countries, ensuring the independence of the police is critical to overcoming public perceptions of the police as an oppressive instrument of the ruling interests and to ensuring that police serve the interests of citizens. One of the strongest mechanisms for ensuring the independence of the police is by promoting and solidifying support for the rule of law. Separating the police from the interests of the state is only half of the equation. In order to achieve independence of the police, the police must then be subordinated to the law. The tradition of constabulary independence in Anglo-American policing elucidates this point. Here a police officer is said to be independent in that he does not exercise delegated authority and is not responsible to government for his action; rather the officer exercises original authority by virtue of his office and is individually responsible for the consequences of his actions. The principle of constabulary independence was affirmed by Lord Denning in *R. v. Commissioner of Police of the Metropolis*; *Ex Parte Blackburn* who stated, "The commissioner was as every constable in the land, independent of the executive ... but in all things he is not the servant of anyone, save of the law itself."[23]

---

[22]   Mercedes S. Hinton, "A Distant Reality: Democratic Policing in Argentina and Brazil" (2005) 5(1) *Criminal Justice* 75 at 95.

[23]   *Commissioner of Police of the Metropolis; Ex Parte Blackburn* [1968] 2 QB 118 in John Avery, *Police: Force or Service?* (Scarborough, ON: Butterworths Ltd, 1981) at 69.

The independence of the police allows officers to exercise wide discretion in fulfilling the duties of their office. Individual officers work with limited supervision and apply the law selectively.[24] It is not clear that police can (or should) always enforce the law – the costs of law enforcement, resource limitations, including too few police officers, and the prevalence of so-called victimless crimes such as gambling, drug use, and prostitution – all contribute to the discretionary enforcement of the law. As John Avery writes, "It is obvious that some discretion is necessary because no legislature has succeeded in formulating a set of laws which clearly excludes all other conduct."[25]

While recognizing that this discretionary element is part of the nature of police work, this capacity for discretion provides the opportunity for police to be unduly influenced by the state or private interests. Safeguarding the police from undue influence by the state is of great concern to many developing countries overcoming a legacy of a police force entangled with the interests of the state. Developed countries have instituted different mechanisms for ensuring the independence of the police from the interests of the state. The source of the police budget often provides one of the most difficult areas in which to maintain the principle of police independence. Britain has found a workable balance, where half of the police budget comes from the national government and the other half comes from local taxes via local police authorities. While the national government is a significant financial contributor to the police budget, the national government can only direct police officers to ensure conformity with the national administration of justice. Appointment of Chief Police Constables is the responsibility of local police authorities composed of elected officials, magistrates and community leaders. The Chief Police Constable's term lasts from four to seven years and he or she can be removed only under exceptional circumstances.[26] The guaranteed minimum term, and the fact that the expiration of the term is not designed to coincide with political elections provides stability to the office and a platform for independence. But even with these institutional barriers, governments may still attempt to influence the police action. For example, in Britain, the Thatcher government was accused of attempting to direct police action during the miners' strike of 1984/85.[27]

Police officers must also be protected from undue influence from private interests. Low salaries are often cited as enabling conditions for bribery and

---

[24]   David Bayley, *Police for the Future* (New York: Oxford University Press, 1994) at 5–6 in Hinton, *supra* note 22 at 82.

[25]   Avery, *supra* note 23 at 66.

[26]   Hinton, *supra* note 22 at 87.

[27]   B. Loveday, "Government and Accountability of the Police," in R.I. Mawby (ed.), *Policing Across the World: Issues for the Twenty-first Century* (New York: Garland Publishing, 1999) at 135.

corruption, as they increase the susceptibility of officers to turn a blind eye or even actively participate in criminal offences. Increasing financial resources to police departments and ensuring that police officers are adequately compensated are necessary steps to reducing corruption, although improved financial resources on their own will not ensure insulation of the police from bribery or other forms of corruption. In its evaluation of the New York Police Department, the Mollen Commission cited lack of commitment and unwillingness to investigate as the key impediments to corruption control:

> In a Department with a budget of over one billion dollars, the basic equipment and resources needed to investigate corruption successfully were routinely denied to corruption investigators; internal investigations were prematurely closed and fragmented, and targeted petty misconduct more than serious corruption; intelligence-gathering was minimal; integrity training was antiquated and often non-existent.[28]

In a recent literature survey, Newburn identifies several mechanisms for reducing police corruption[29] in addition to ensuring adequate financial resources. One mechanism identified by Newburn for reducing corruption is improved human resource management via more stringent admissions standards, such as increasing the minimum age of candidates and seeking out those with an adequate education level and improved training and ethics. Newburn points out that effective ethical training requires full and realistic discussion of the problem of corruption accompanied by specific examples. Another mechanism for reducing corruption identified by Newburn is through ethical codes and ethical commissions that officers can confidentially appeal to if they face an ethical dilemma. Newburn also identifies reform of police procedures as a means to reduce corruption, arguing that the nature of some police procedures, for example, unrealistic productivity targets, as policies that may encourage corruption.[30] Strengthening of accountability mechanisms, such as civilian oversight, also serves as a mechanism for reducing corruption, and will be discussed in the following section.

Newburn emphasizes the critical role played by police managers in combating corruption by providing "positive symbolic leadership" where managers who are open about internal misbehaviour, fully cooperative with external agencies, and committed to running a "clean" organization serve as role models for in-

---

[28]   T. Newburn, *Understanding and Preventing Police Corruption: Lessons from the Literature* (London: Home Office Research Development and Statistics Directorate, Policing and Reducing Crime Unit, 1999). Available at: http://www.homeoffice.gov.uk/rds/prgpdfs/fprs110.pdf.

[29]   *Ibid.*

[30]   *Ibid.*

tegrity.[31] The critical role played by senior management in combating corruption is echoed by David Bayley and is extended to all other areas of police reform. Bayley writes that the most frequently repeated lesson of police reform is that "sustained and committed leadership by top management, especially the most senior executive, is required to produce any important organizational change."[32] But Bayley is also careful to point out that reforms will not be successful unless they are perceived as legitimate throughout the police ranks. He recommends the use of task forces composed of all ranks to aid in the reform process and sharing the proposed plans with all units and departments before implementing the new program.[33]

C. Accountability

Ensuring the accountability of the police is a critical issue for countries throughout the world. The discretionary nature of policing and the autonomy of individual police officers raise the crucial question of *'Quis custodies custodiet'* or who will guard the guardians?[34] The distribution of power within a state can provide checks and balances on police action: the legislature controls police via public policy, and the judiciary monitors police performance, for example, by excluding evidence that is improperly obtained. Many developing countries, however, do not enjoy a tradition of strong checks and balances or of strong government institutions committed to the rule of law and have consequently been unable to ensure police accountability through the distribution of state power. Speaking of the potential for parliamentary oversight over the police in Latin America, Rachel Nield writes:

> While the age of politically subordinate "rubber-stamp" parliaments has largely ended, many parliaments have been and continue to be poorly equipped, with few staff and almost non-existent research or investigative capabilities. Police frequently resist parliamentary oversight, denouncing parliamentary efforts to reform legislation or increase oversight of public security police as an unwarranted political interference.[35]

---

[31]   M. Punch, "Rotten Barrels: Systemic Origins of Corruption," in E.W. Kolthoff (ed.), *Stategieen voor corruptie-beheersing bij de police* (Arnhem: Gouda Quint, 1994) cited in Newburn, *supra* note 28.

[32]   Bayley, *Democratizing*, *supra* note 4 at 20.

[33]   *Ibid.* at 22.

[34]   Avery, *supra* note 23 at 63.

[35]   Nield, *supra* note 5 at 232. For example Argentina has approximately 559 police officers for every 100,000 inhabitants, whereas Canada has 186 police officers for the same number of inhabitants. While Argentina only has 4.74 judges per 100,000 inhabitants, Canada has 6.47. See Office on Drugs and Crime, *United Nations Surveys of Crime*

The judiciary too has a poor track record in disciplining police misbehaviour in many developing countries. Judges generally are deferential to police actions, only questioning police in cases of obvious and extreme illegality. Rachel Nield suggests that this deference of judges to police action may stem from the lower ratio of judges to police in developing countries: while some developing countries have more police officers per capita than developed countries, developing countries only have one judge for every 74 police officers (compared to one judge for 24 police officers in developed countries).[36] The inability or reluctance of judges to effectively hold the police to account indicates that police reform is intimately tied to reform of other rule of law institutions. For example, without reform of the judiciary, such accountability mechanisms as human rights ombudsmen, which often rely on the courts to hear complaints, may be ineffective.

Holding the police to account can also involve more direct accountability mechanisms, including: civilian oversight of police activity, disciplinary and employee management procedures, auditing and financial accountability, and transparency in police activities. Given the culture of impunity that pervades police forces in many developing countries, civilian oversight bodies offer an attractive mechanism for ensuring accountability in police activities. The "civilianization" of police accountability involves citizens external to the police force in the assessment of citizens' (and sometimes police) complaints regarding police conduct. This can take the form of an institution devoted solely to the processing of complaints against the police, or can be included in the mandate of a human rights ombudsman who processes complaints against any state official, including the police. Civilian oversight institutions provide an alternative to police-run complaints mechanisms, and are often instituted as a response to police scandals, corruption or use of excessive force.

As with most bureaucracies, police departments tend to be conservative and resistant to change and are particularly reluctant to support reforms that they perceive as entailing external interference with police activity. In a survey of civilianization reforms across the world, Andrew Smith and Colleen Lewis conclude that the concrete effects of civilian oversight bodies in terms of more effective accountability are difficult to substantiate.[37] As Colleen Lewis writes, "there is a wide gap between civilian oversight the principle, and civilian oversight the practice."[38] According to Lewis, implementation of the idea of civilian

---

Trends and Operations of Criminal Justice Systems, covering the period 1990–2002. Available online at: http://www.unodc.org/pdf/crime/eighthsurvey/5678sc.pdf.

[36]   Nield, *supra* note 5 at 227.

[37]   Andrew Goldsmith and Colleen Lewis (eds), *Civilian Oversight of Policing: Governance, Democracy and Human Rights* (Portland, OR: Hart Publishing, 2000).

[38]   Colleen Lewis, "The Politics of Civilian Oversight: Serious Commitment or Lip Service?," in Goldsmith and Lewis, *supra* note 37 at 20.

oversight runs into two major impediments: police influence and government inaction. The vested interests of the police combined with the influential role that police have over the civilian oversight body, where police often retain the investigative function for public complaints, impedes the ability of the civilian oversight body to provide effective accountability. Governments, while enthusiastic at the idea of civilian oversight, often retreat to timid supporters as civilianization is implemented and acquiesce to demands of police officers. For example, in the establishment of the Police Complaints Board in the United Kingdom, where despite early enthusiasm by the government for ending police control over the complaints process, the government made key concessions to the police before the board was implemented – the police retained control over the investigation of complaints, and maintained the criminal standard of proof in disciplinary hearings.[39]

How then does one minimize the gap between the idea of civilian oversight and its implementation and enable civilian oversight bodies to provide effective accountability? Adequate resources are critical to the success of the institution to ensure sufficient staffing and expertise and to ensure that the public are made aware of the organization.[40] Who is selected to sit on the oversight committee is also critical: inappropriate appointments such as a police union official would contradict the external nature of the oversight body.[41] Philip Stenning outlines several criteria for a sound legislative framework for civilian oversight of complaints against the police,[42] including a clear statement of principles and objectives, of which he provides an example:

> To ensure that anyone having a complaint against the police service or any of its members has an opportunity to have such complaint impartially investigated and fairly and justly resolved; to ensure that any police officer against whom a complaint

---

[39] *Ibid.* at 25. Note that the Police Complaints Board was replaced by the Police Complaints Authority and the standard of proof was eventually modified to a balance of probabilities.

[40] *Ibid.* at 32.

[41] *Ibid.*

[42] Philip C. Stenning, "Evaluating Police Complaints Legislation: A Suggested Framework," in Goldsmith and Lewis, *supra* note 37. Stenning identifies several factors that are key to a sound legislative framework for civilian oversight: a clear statement of principles and objectives, accessibility, fairness and respect for rights, openness and accountability, timeliness, thoroughness, impartiality, independence, balance between the public interest and the interests of parties involved in a complaint, balance between formal and informal procedures for dispute resolution, balance between remedial and punitive dispositions, balance between internal management and external oversight of complaints, generation and provision of information about systemic problems or weaknesses in police services, and integration and compatibility with internal disciplinary and grievance processes.

has been lodged has a full and fair opportunity to respond to such complaint before an impartial tribunal; to maintain or restore public confidence in the police services ...[43]

In practice, one of the most controversial criteria to implement is impartiality[44] as there is much debate over whether police can ever be sufficiently impartial to investigate public complaints against other officers. Canadian courts have rejected this concern[45] stating that bias cannot be automatically presumed simply because the investigating officer may be part of the same organization as the subject of the complaint, and some commentators argue that a requirement for external complaint investigation is unnecessarily expensive, and may be less effective in that police officers may be more resistant to outside investigators and senior police management would not be responsible for complaints.[46] On the other hand, as Stenning points out, there is sometimes a problem of impartiality in having fellow officers investigate complaints, and for this reason, internal investigation units are often separated from the regular command structure, external investigations are often used for the most serious investigations, and civilian oversight bodies typically possess some capacity to review complaints investigation conducted by police.[47]

While there is ongoing debate regarding the ideal model of civilian oversight, it is important to recognize that the very process of civilianization plays an important legitimating function in societies that lack public confidence in the police. By involving civilians in the review of police activity, citizens are made active participants in the reform process and this can lead to improvements in police–community relations. Civilianization also aids in the re-conceptualization of police as a service to citizens as civilians are placed in a position of oversight of the police. Civilian oversight bodies can contribute to organizational learning by collecting and providing important information to the police leadership, such as types and patterns of complaints, which, if employed by the police leadership, can improve police services and help to restore public confidence in the police.

---

[43]   *Ibid.* at 148.

[44]   It is important to note that impartiality and independence are closely related but distinct concepts, where it is possible for an individual to be impartial but not independent in that she is unbiased and is not partial to one side of a dispute (she is impartial) but is subject to influence or direction from others (she is not independent).

[45]   *Trumbley and Pugh v. Metropolitan Toronto Police* [1987] 2 SCR 577 45 DLR (4th) 318 cited in Stenning, *supra* note 42 at 155.

[46]   David Bayley, "Accountability and Control of Police: Lessons for Britain," in T. Bennett (ed.), *The Future of Policing* (Cambridge: Institute of Criminology, 1983) cited in Stenning, *supra* note 42 at 155.

[47]   Stenning, *supra* note 42 at 155–6.

II. EXPERIENCE WITH POLICE REFORMS IN DEVELOPING COUNTRIES

A. Latin America

In Argentina, the various police forces existing prior to the 1983 termination of military rule are described as having "steadily acquired power because of ongoing civil strife, repressive executives, a powerful military, the weakness of the legislature and the judiciary, the lack of established oversight bodies, and, finally, the police's acquisition of power itself."[48] Immediately following the democratic transition, top police officials were replaced and habeas corpus regulations were instituted. In the face of "low remuneration, poor training, weak discipline, and … institutional dependency on the executive,"[49] however, there was little improvement. In fact, Ungar argues that, at least initially, democracy increased police corruption by loosening "the military regimes' stricter mechanisms of internal functioning to prevent common corruption."[50] Though restrictions on police discretion did exist, not only did the police act with impunity with respect to those restrictions but the courts were very generous in validating police action.[51] In 1991 and 1992 amendments to penal procedures and restrictions on detention were enacted, but neither had a substantial effect on police practices. Exacerbating the problem was that in the face of continually increasing crime, the public generally favoured "iron fisted" policies advocating "policing 'outside the law'"[52] and the performance of criminal acts by police officers. As crime continued to increase, however, and hard-line policies failed to deliver promised results, public opinion began to shift against the hard-line position. In July 1996 the police were restructured with a civilian chief, decentralized units aimed at reducing central control, and citizen forums at the lowest level were designed to advise newly decentralized units about community policing programs. Counterbalancing these reforms was "violent resistance"[53] from officers, including death threats directed at supporting politicians, the election of key anti-reform political candidates, and still-low police salaries encouraging further corruption. Aggravating this atmosphere of conflict was the debate over police edicts, a set of vaguely worded offences which allowed police broad discretion to impose up to 30 days pre-trial detention for very trivial, vaguely

---

[48]   Mark Ungar, *Elusive Reform: Democracy and the Rule of Law in Latin America* (Boulder, CO: Lynne Rienner Publishers, 2002) at 74.

[49]   *Ibid.* at 82.

[50]   *Ibid.* at 83.

[51]   *Ibid.* at 84.

[52]   *Ibid.* at 87.

[53]   *Ibid.* at 88.

worded, non-criminal acts. Law and order concerns had previously exerted pressure to retain the edicts but they were ultimately limited in scope in 1998 by the Urban Coexistence Code. Though a step towards greater human rights protection, it was found that a lack of personnel and infrastructure required to implement the code, such as prosecutors and judges, left substantial effective power with the police.[54] Further, in 1999 the Code was partially undermined when by executive decree the police were given the power to arrest for many of the same "crimes" which had characterized their powers under the edicts.

Venezuelan police before the 1980s were highly intertwined with the military. Officers received little or no training, inadequate pay and worked long hours. Oversight mechanisms rarely produced systematic change and complainants rarely knew what sanctions, if any, were imposed. Also, vagueness in Venezuelan law surrounding the proper roles of the police and the judiciary effectively vested in the police discretion to initiate and maintain secrecy about certain judicial proceedings. Consequently, police officers were in a position to falsify evidence and confessions and bring false charges,[55] a situation that persisted despite a democratic political regime in Venezuela.[56]

Reform attempts throughout the 1980s concentrated on coordinating the myriad Venezuelan bodies responsible for law reform, but faced opposition from existing agencies unwilling to sacrifice power. A wave of reform efforts surfaced after elections in 1993, but again died, this time due to more pressing political concerns. Ungar argues that the most significant police reform in Venezuela came with regard to the LVM, a 1939 law whose main thrust was the legislative entrenchment of preventative detention for unspecific offences, effectively vesting in the police broad discretion over extra-judicial detention. But despite claims of unconstitutionality by the Inter-American Court of Human Rights and other international organizations, high crime rates and political hardliners conspired to reinforce support for the law. Venezuelan public opinion demonstrates the same paradox as that in Argentina, as overwhelming majorities are fearful of both police violations of individual rights and criminal victimization. Even before crime rates sharply escalated in the early 1990s, however, surveys demonstrated support for greater violence in combating crime.[57] It was only in 1997 that the Supreme Court, with a newly appointed president, struck down the law; but while a new constitution in 1999 entrenched civil rights, it also vested new powers of law enforcement in the police. According to Ungar, "all societal sectors have repeatedly prioritized order over rights and supported strong

---

[54]   *Ibid.* at 95.
[55]   *Ibid.* at 104–5.
[56]   *Ibid.* at 98–101.
[57]   *Ibid.* at 107.

policing."[58] Ungar argues further that changes in the judiciary brought about by President Chavez since 1999 reduce the ability of and likelihood that the courts will act as a check on these new police powers. Citing significant problems of patronage and corruption in the judiciary and public administration, President Chavez undertook a number of extreme measures; among others, he assumed the power to dismiss judges (previously vested in Congress and the judiciary) and abolished the Senate, prompting the resignation of the President of the Supreme Court. These changes shifted the balance of power between the executive and the judiciary, arguably limiting the potential for control of executive action.

In El Salvador, at the conclusion of civil war in 1992 the existing law enforcement agency was the military itself and reform efforts "essentially threw out what went before and started anew."[59] The composition of the new force, the Policía Nacional Civil (PNC), was set at 60% newly trained officers, and 20% each from the two warring factions, resolving a dilemma that pits the desire to eliminate corrupt elements from an existing force against the need for experienced officers to fight crime. The 1992 reforms also established a police academy for the training of new officers, providing six months of training for all PNC officers. Call argues that, in El Salvador, the economic elites who might traditionally oppose police reform had come to the realization in the late 1980s that the military was no longer effective in protecting their interests. Desire for police reforms therefore cut across socio-economic lines and resistance came primarily from the army.[60] In the face of public consensus, military opposition was unsuccessful, and the PNC was established, albeit a few months late.[61]

The human rights gains resulting from the purge of the military could be described as qualifiedly positive. The 1992 Peace Accords included both internal (Inspector General for the PNC; an Internal Control Unit within the PNC for investigating corruption; a Disciplinary Unit within the PNC to investigate and make recommendations of administrative sanctions for abuses by PNC personnel; and a Disciplinary Tribunal within the PNC for acting on those

---

[58] *Ibid.* at 111.

[59] Linn Hammergren, *Institutional Strengthening and Justice Reform* (USAID PN-ACD-020) at 216–7.

[60] Chuck Call, "Police Reform, Human Rights and Democratization in Post-Conflict Settings: Lessons from El Salvador" (Paper presented to the USAID Conference After the War is Over, What Comes Next? Promoting Democracy, Human Rights and Reintegration in Post-Conflict Societies, October 1997) at 7. Call offers a brief description of the "nature of the conflict" and its termination at 3–4.

[61] "The first class at the academy was to begin on May 1, 1992, under the terms of the peace agreement, but the first class of recruits was not installed until August 31, 1992." *Aid to El Salvador: Slow Progress in Developing a National Civilian Police* (GAO/NSIAD-92-338, September 22, 1992) at 5.

recommendations) and external oversight mechanisms (press, NGOs, legislative oversight, and the exercise of civilian courts' authority over cases of police abuses). Call explains that while internal mechanisms have experienced government interference,[62] external safeguards have eliminated corrupt elements and on one occasion thwarted the appointment of a government-friendly candidate to the Inspector-General position of the PNC.[63] On the whole, while Brody identifies "several occasions" on which the government has acted in contradiction to the Peace Accords,[64] both he and Call adopt the position that the "end of the war resulted in a dramatic improvement in the human rights situation of the country. In contrast to police practice during and before the war ... cases of torture, 'disappearances,' and politically motivated killings have become the exception rather than the rule."[65] Call notes further that in a 1995 survey, "49 percent of respondents thought the PNC's conduct was better than the old National Police ... and 18 percent thought it worse."[66] With respect to crime, some statistics suggest dramatic improvements over the last decade. "From 1992 to 1994 ... reported homicides rose from 3,229 annually to 9,135." In 1995, "deaths by homicide exceeded the average annual number of deaths during the 12-year war"[67] and 95% of Salvadorans ranked crime as a "very serious" problem. However, international experts point out that "five years is a minimum reasonable time frame for deploying a self-sustaining police force,"[68] and in 1998, Interpol reported 2,340 murders, below the 1992 level cited by Call. Murders fell to 2,270 in 1999 and 2,196 in 2001.[69]

USAID, in cooperation with the Department of Justice's International Criminal Investigative Training Assistance Program (ICITAP) and the Department of States, has assisted in the development of the PNC since the end of the civil war in El Salvador. ICITAP worked with the UN to establish a de-politicized training center for the PNC and has also assisted in the creation of a 911 emergency response system, modernization of the PNC's case management system, and the development of a comprehensive strategy to address the escalating problems of

---

[62]   Call, *supra* note 60 at 11.

[63]   *Ibid.* at 17. Reed Brody, "The United Nations and Human Rights in El Salvador's 'Negotiated Revolution'" (1995) 8 *Harvard Human Rights Journal* 153 at 173. The Inspector General is one of the newly created internal oversight mechanisms referred to just above.

[64]   *Ibid.* at 175.

[65]   Call, *supra* note 60 at 10.

[66]   *Ibid.* at 11.

[67]   *Ibid.* at 5.

[68]   *Ibid.* at 12.

[69]   The dramatic drop in crime in only two years does seem suspect. Call cites as his source the Director of Statistics, State Prosecutor's Office, online: http://www.interpol.int/Public/Statistics/ICS/downloadList.asp.

youth gang violence in El Salvador. Policing in El Salvador continues to meet major challenges, including high violent crime and homicide rates stemming from gangs, which are estimated to be responsible for 60% of all crime in El Salvador, problems retaining officers in the PNC due to a ten-year freeze on police salaries, and a $5 million reduction in the PNC's budget.[70]

In Panama, when 21 years of military rule ended in 1989, one of the first acts of reform was the "replacement of the PDF (Panama Defense Force) by a civilian national police force and the conversion of the investigative secret police into a judicial police."[71] A police academy was also formed to train new officers, over 90% of whom were from the PDF.[72] Officers underwent training including instruction on forensic and physical evidence, thus decreasing the focus on confessions, which have been a source of human rights violations in other countries. Coordination between police and the prosecution has been enhanced, by both the formal integration of certain branches of the police into the prosecution as well as the creation of jointly run complaint centers offering information on victim services and staffed by trained officers whose interrogation skills improve the extraction of useful investigative information. Violent crime in Panama has fallen sharply, from 16.14 murders and 13.48 sexual assaults per 100,000 citizens in 1995 to 1.95 murders and 10.65 sexual assaults per 100,000 citizens in 1998.[73] In 2001, a joint USAID-IADB project planned continued focus on institutional linkages between the police and the prosecution, and the "transformation from military to civilian police forces is generally considered a success."[74] Even so, the country still has a high number of pre-trial detention prisoners.

Despite reform efforts throughout the 1990s and the assistance of foreign donors, crime continues to be a major problem throughout Latin America and the police are often seen as part of the problem rather than the solution. A 2004 Latinobarmetro poll found that only one in three Latin Americans had confidence in their domestic police. A study by a Mexican think-tank, the Center for Research for Development, found that 96% of crimes went unpunished between 1996 and 2003, and many Mexicans do not even report crimes, with officials

---

[70]   "El Salvador," online: International Criminal Investigative Training Assistance Program at http://www.usdoj.gov/criminal/icitap/elSalvador.html April 4.

[71]   USAID Office of Democracy and Governance, *Achievements in Building and Maintaining the Rule of Law: MSI's Studies in LAC, E&E, AFR, and ANE* (Occasional Paper Series November 2002, PN-ACR-220) at 81 [Achievements].

[72]   US General Accounting Office, *Aid to Panama: Improving the Criminal Justice System* (GAO/NSIAD-92-147: Washington, May 1992) at 3.

[73]   Interpol crime statistics, online at: http://www.interpol.int/Public/Statistics/ICS/downloadList.asp.

[74]   Achievements, *supra* note 71 at 83.

estimating that 75% of crimes are not recorded.[75] Citizens have sometimes voiced their discontent with the police by taking to the streets: for example, in Brazil protests were held when it was discovered that police officers were bribed to overlook the kidnapping of a student.[76] Reform efforts have been criticized for ignoring the relationship between the police and the community. USAID has recently announced support for "community policing programs" that seek to improve the relationship between the police and the public in El Salvador, Jamaica, Guatemala and Colombia.[77] Such programs emphasize capacity building at the local level and engaging civil society and the private sector. But the promise of such programs in improving public confidence in the police and combating crime should not be overstated: without improved training, leadership and anti-corruption initiatives, it will be difficult to garner public support for the police. In addition, the efficacy of exported community policing programs to developing countries has been questioned. Mike Brogden argues that community policing programs are implemented "generically rather than specifically," and are often reducible to three basic Western policing strategies of watch schemes, police community forums, and problem-solving policing. As Borden states, "the tripartite structures ... are promoted irrespective of local exigencies and realities. The West determines the policing programs to be adopted."[78]

B.   Central and Eastern Europe

In Russia, the modern state of policing is closely linked with the past and the continuity of certain structures in reform-era Russia. In the Soviet Union, as a "one party regime that controlled all legal economic activity, natural market forces went underground" and bribery and corruption of state officials "became a standard and unofficially accepted means of survival."[79] The KGB and the *militsiya*[80] are widely seen as having been highly corrupt, and the KGB has been

---

[75]   "The Americas: The Battle for Safer Streets; Crime and Policing in Latin America" (October 2, 2004) *The Economist* 53.

[76]   *Ibid.*

[77]   "USAID's Franco Advocates Community Policing as a Growing Component of Development," online: USAID, Latin America and the Caribbean, http://www.usaid.gov/locations/latin_america_caribbean/franco_csis.html.

[78]   Mike Brogden, "'Horses for Courses' and 'Thin Blue Lines': Community Policing in Transitional Society" (2005) 8 *Police Quarterly* 71.

[79]   J. Michael Waller, "Police, Secret Police, and Civil Authority," in Jeffrey D. Sachs and Katharina Pistor (eds), *The Rule of Law and Economic Reform in Russia* (Boulder, CO: Westview Press, 1997) 95–121 at 98.

[80]   The Soviet security system was composed of two parts: the KGB, responsible for a broad range of functions from foreign espionage to military counter-intelligence,

characterized as an "'organized crime' operation"[81] in itself. When internal security organs of the new Russian Federation were established, President Yeltsin "reversed earlier insistences that the KGB be broken apart."[82] The *militsiya* remained in place as the national police force, while the KGB was divided into five key new organizations in charge of internal and external intelligence, communications, border patrol and government security. Waller identifies this process as the roots of the endemic problems of organized crime in modern Russia, and alludes to the entrenchment of former security forces in the new Russia as a critical impediment to reform.[83] He argues further that reforms throughout the early and mid-1990s were heavily stalled by the vested interests of top political figures, particularly President Yeltsin, who sought to use the reach and authority of the KGB for personal and political ends.[84] There have been some indications that President Putin is more serious about police reform,[85] but there does not as yet seem to be significant evidence of improvement.

Against the backdrop of corruption described above, improprieties of the police have had a direct effect on the population. "[U]nder great pressure to produce confessions,"[86] Russian police have repeatedly been accused of a wide range of torture, including prolonged beatings, asphyxiation, suspension by the arms or legs, and electroshock.[87] Police torture has been chronicled by multiple organizations including Human Rights Watch, Russian NGO Human Rights

---

prison administration, border security and more, and the MVD, or *militsiya*, responsible for more quotidian law enforcement duties.

[81]   Waller, *supra* note 79 at 101.

[82]   *Ibid.* at 103.

[83]   There have been a number of recent publications on the issue of organized crime in Russia. See generally, David Satter, *Darkness at Dawn: The Rise of the Russian Criminal State* (New Haven: Yale University Press, 2003); Vadim Volkov, *Violent Entrepreneurs: The Use of Force in the Making of Russian Capitalism* (Ithaca, NY: Cornell University Press, 2002); David Hoffman, *The Oligarchs: Wealth and Power in the New Russia* (Oxford; New York: Public Affairs, 2002).

[84]   See Waller, *supra* note 79 at 103–15 for a more detailed analysis of impediments to reform.

[85]   See, for instance, Jonas Bernstein, "Putin Speaks out against Police Corruption" (American Foreign Policy Council, *Russia Reform Monitor* No. 1011, February 7, 2003) online at: http://www.afpc.org/rrm/rrm1011.shtml; and Jonas Bernstein, "A Focus on Human Rights Abuses by Russian Police; Border Service Implicated in Assisting Criminal Flight" (American Foreign Policy Council, *Russian Reform Monitor* No. 1054, July 1, 2003) online at: http://www.afpc.org/rrm/rrm1054.shtml [Bernstein 1054].

[86]   Human Rights Watch, *Confessions at any Cost* (1999), online at: http://www.hrw.org/reports/1999/russia/.

[87]   Human Rights Watch's evidence of torture has come from interviews with victims, judges, and police officers themselves. One Russian judge estimated that at least 40% of those defendants before him have been tortured, while another estimates that 80% who persistently refuse to confess are tortured.

Center,[88] and Amnesty International.[89] Long-awaited reforms in the code of criminal procedure were finally enacted in 2001 and came into effect in July 2002; though reforms in the new code were not explicitly directed at police reform, they purport to improve aspects of the process closely linked to the above problems. Article 16 entrenches the right to counsel, while Article 51 provides that

> no one shall be obliged to give incriminating evidence [against himself]. ... Article 48(2) specifies that "any person detained, taken into custody, [or] accused of committing a crime shall have the right to receive assistance of a lawyer (counsel for the defense) from the moment of detention, confinement in custody or facing charges accordingly." ... Article 7(3) declares that "a violation of the rules of this Code by a court, procurator, investigator, inquiry agency, or inquiring officer in the course of criminal proceedings shall cause the evidence thus obtained to be inadmissible," while Article 75(1) reinforces the rule that evidence "obtained in violation of the requirements of this Code shall be inadmissible."[90]

Professor Orland, despite a highly positive view of the new code, warns that it "would be naive to assume that ... due process provisions of a criminal procedure code can transform a nation steeped in oppression into one which embraces the rule of law."[91] An early evaluation of the effects of the code finds that

> [m]any reports have emerged of illegal interrogations, especially outside Moscow and St. Petersburg. A detainee who is beaten or tortured during interrogation must

---

[88] Bernstein, *supra* note 85.

[89] Amnesty International USA, "Torture and Ill-treatment in Russia", online at: http://www.amnestyusa.org/countries/russia/campaign/torture.html.

[90] The Code of Criminal Procedure contained a series of critical reforms with respect to bail, individual rights, defendants' rights, and so forth. The Code has been described by Professor Leonard Orland as a "revolution." To the extent that the code affects judicial independence and accountability it is dealt with above; to the extent that it affects other aspects of the judicial system it is beyond the scope of this chapter. For a detailed summary and analysis of the new Code and its provisions, see Leonard Orland, "A Russian Legal Revolution: The 2002 Criminal Procedure Code" (2002–03) 18 *Conn. J. Int'l L.* 133; for further background, see Hon. John C. Coughenour, "Canary in the Coal Mine: The Importance of the Trial Jury: Reflections on Russia's Revival of Trial by Jury: History Demands that we Ask Difficult Questions Regarding Terror Trials, Procedures to Combat Terrorism, and our Federal Sentencing Regime," (2002–03) 26 *Seattle Univ. Law Review* 399 at 407; for articles on jury trials occurring in Russia in 2003, see Fred Weir, "Russia Embraces Trial By Peers" (*Christian Science Monitor*, March 5, 2003) online: http://www.csmonitor.com/2003/0305/p06s01-woeu.html; Mark McDonald, "Russia begins new twist on trials: juries" (Knight Ridder Newspapers, February 17, 2003) online at: http://www.cdi.org/russia/johnson/7065-2.cfm.

[91] *Ibid.* at 155.

undergo a forensic medical examination to prove the abuse, but the only way to obtain an examination is by seeking a referral from the police or the prosecutor ... Reports of police torture remain common, and in many cases, the courts have ignored the abuses and refused to throw out coerced testimony.[92]

Further, "[a]ccording to the Independent Council of Legal Experts, defense lawyers in almost every region of Russia have been frequent targets of intimidation and coercion. The police and security forces have resorted to beatings and arrests"[93] of defence attorneys. Despite calls for a law explicitly prohibiting police torture, Parliament has declined to act and a draft bill to that effect was defeated in 2002.

The human rights situation has, to some extent, been both catalyzed and sustained by the uncontrolled crime problems discussed above. Richard Monk, a senior advisor with the Organization for Security and Co-operation in Europe (OSCE) heavily involved in police reform, observed that in certain countries, "there may be a tendency for police officers to view effectiveness in combating criminal activity as more important than respecting the rights of its citizens."[94] In September 2003, Russian Minister of the Interior Boris Gryzlov demanded amendments to the new Russian Code of Criminal Procedure, complaining that detainees could not be held for more than 48 hours and requesting preliminary detention of up to 30 days for suspects held in connection with terrorism-related activity.[95] This demand came despite a ruling from the Constitutional Court in early 2002 in anticipation of the Code, finding detention for more than 48 hours without judicial approval to be unconstitutional. It also arises in the broader context of the high Russian crime rate; from 1995, when post-Soviet crime rates were causing grave concern, until 2002, crime has dropped only slightly overall while increasing on some measures.[96]

When the 1992–95 conflict in the former Yugoslavia ended, the UN established an International Police Task Force (IPTF) for an initial period of 12 months with a staff of 1,721 officers. The mandate of the force was to monitor,

---

[92]   Mark Kramer, "Rights and Restraints in Russia's Criminal Justice System: Preliminary Results of the New Criminal Procedure Code" (May 2003) *PONARS Policy Memo 289*, Harvard University at 3.

[93]   *Ibid.* at 5.

[94]   Richard Monk, "OSCE Police-Related Activities" (speech delivered before the United States Commission on Security and Cooperation in Europe (Helsinki Commission), October 27, 2003) online at: http://www.csce.gov/briefings.cfm?briefing_id= 270.

[95]   Ilya Zhegulev, "United Russia Leader Wants Curb on Human Rights" (*Gazeta. ru*, September 24, 2003) online at: http://www.gazeta.ru/2003/09/24/UnitedRussia. shtml.

[96]   Interpol Crime Statistics, online at: http://www.interpol.int/Public/Statistics/ICS/ downloadList.asp#R.

train and inspect law enforcement personnel, "assessing threats to public order," and "accompanying the Parties' law enforcement personnel as they carry out their responsibilities."[97] In mid-1997 Security Council Resolution 1107 established a human rights office within the IPTF, designating 120 officers to discharge, under an earlier resolution, "responsibilities relating to the investigation of allegations of human rights abuses by police officers or other law enforcement officials of the various authorities of Bosnia and Herzegovina."[98]

One of the first tasks of the IPTF was to purge from the existing police force elements implicated in war crimes and the military more generally. Existing officers were required to reapply to the force and undergo an evaluation process. Applicants were nominated by local authorities, filled out a questionnaire examining their past, and completed a series of tests administered by the IPTF. The names of all applicants were placed on a list subsequently published in local newspapers so that victims of human rights abuses could provide IPTF with additional information to complement its own background check on each officer. At this stage, successful applicants were hired for a one-year probationary period, and at all times IPTF recommendations as to admission to the force were binding. The human rights mandate, as distinct from the police-restructuring mandate, consisted of

> "interviews [of] arrested/detained persons" ... and required monitors to "[assist] citizens who express concerns about policing and criminal justice activities and may be afraid to directly contact local police." ... [T]he IPTF had the authority "at any time to visit prisoners and detainees to talk to them ... without anyone being present, ... to appear in any of the courts during trial ... [or] visit ... any of our institutions for the implementation of law (Courts, Institutions for Social Behavior) [without] previous permission of [the] Ministry of Justice; ... [and] whenever they ask ... to be given [a] copy of [court] records, adjudications, ... and the exact time and place of those proceedings, etc.[99]

After two years of implementation, 40 officers were dismissed and a further 280 were under investigation out of a force of about 11,000. But while the foregoing discussion reveals an activist role envisaged for the IPTF, several factors conspired to hinder its practical implementation. First, political resist-

---

97 NATO website, http://www.nato.int/ifor/gfa/gfa-home.htm; there is debate as to whether this re-examination actually vested the IPTF with human rights oversight powers or simply clarified the powers they already had, but in any event from at least this date the IPTF was vested with a human rights mandate in Bosnia.

98 UNMIBH website, http://www.un.org/Depts/DPKO/Missions/unmibh/unmibhM.htm.

99 Human Rights Watch, *Bosnia and Hercegovina: Beyond Restraint: Politics and the Policing Agenda of the United Nations International Police Task Force* (June 1998) at n. 35, online at: http://www.hrw.org/reports98/bosnia/.

ance manifested itself in candidate lists presented to the IPTF, which, according to Human Rights Watch, were deliberately restricted in size, forcing IPTF officials to select candidates with questionable links to local authorities. Second, the goal of the IPTF was not to take over the task of policing but rather to monitor and train local civilian police forces. In 1997, IPTF Commissioner Manfred Seitner declared that "if an individual was unwilling to report [an] incident to the police, there would be no investigation and consequently no case,"[100] a position that poses obvious difficulties where police officers are themselves the transgressors. A third, related problem was that "the distribution of responsibilities within IPTF stations appears to make it difficult for monitors to reconcile the conflict of interest which arises between the duty to conduct human rights investigations and the duty to improve relations with the local police."[101] Human Rights Watch is concerned generally with a "reluctance of many police officers to pursue evidence that might incriminate a fellow officer" and one IPTF official reported more overt resistance in that "[a]s soon as he attempted to collect information for purposes of monitoring, he was threatened and denied access to materials."[102]

Another issue facing police reformers in Bosnia has been a substantial lack of accountability. Serious allegations of overt involvement in gross violations of human rights have been levied against the IPTF, in particular in the thriving Bosnian human trafficking market.[103] Officers have been accused of recruiting women, facilitating their transfer to Bosnia, selling them to brothel owners, and stunting police raids. One reason why it has been difficult to impose sanctions on the perpetrators relates to jurisdictional complexities. Confusing domestic systems of jurisdiction often make it difficult to prosecute nationals for war crimes perpetrated overseas,[104] while UN officials are accorded a degree of immunity against prosecution in international arenas.[105] Another potential

---

[100]   HRW Bosnia, *supra* note 99 at n. 32.

[101]   HRW Bosnia, *supra* note 99.

[102]   *Ibid.* at n. 59

[103]   Jennifer Murray, "Who will Police the Peace-Builders? The Failure to Establish Accountability for the Participation of United Nations Civilian Police in the Trafficking of Women in Post-Conflict Bosnia and Herzegovina" (2003) 34 *Colum. Human Rights L. Rev.* 475 at 502.

[104]   See Douglas Cassel, "Empowering United States Courts to Hear Crimes Within the Jurisdiction of the International Criminal Court," 35 *New Eng. L. Rev.* 421 at 429–35.

[105]   While UN immunity for civilian staff is limited to so-called functional immunity – immunity for actions taken in the "course of the performance of their mission" – "involvement in serious crimes does not seem to constitute a *per se* 'unofficial' act". Remarkably, "[r]ecent ICJ jurisprudence indicates that there has not yet developed a customary international law 'exception' to jurisdictional immunity even in cases of gross

roadblock is a lack of political will in both domestic countries and the United Nations, manifested in reports of cover-ups including, in one case, the dismissal of a whistleblower employee of a private military firm hired by the United States to train IPTF officials.[106] Irrespective of the cause, however, the broader point is the issue of accountability.[107] It is significant to note that, in Bosnia, problems were partially attributed to the "the economic crisis and breakdown in government left in the wake of the war,"[108] a familiar circumstance in countries targeted for reform. If these conditions are more likely to lead to violations of fundamental human rights while simultaneously increasing the need for police reform, accountability becomes a significant concern.

C. Africa

In her comprehensive survey of policing reforms undertaken in Africa since the 1990s, Alice Hills argues that changes to policing have been largely superficial: The police, Hills generalizes bluntly, are still "notoriously corrupt."[109] Police forces formed from the remnants of post-conflict militaries subservient to their respective regimes during the African wave of democratization in the 1980s have not purged their military legacies. "Policing," she argues, "continues to be characteristically paramilitary [...] Discipline and protocol tend to be military in character, though there often appears to be an unwillingness among all ranks to accept personal responsibility for actions."[110]

Nor, it seems, has the function of policing changed from its conventional purpose of protecting the regime in power:

> African police generally focus on the protection of regimes from domestic security threats to a greater extent than police in many other regions; crime prevention and

---

human rights violations if an alternative forum for prosecution exists or may exist in the future." Frederick Rawski, "To Waive or Not To Waive: Immunity and Accountability in U.N. Peacekeeping Operations" (2002) 18 *Conn. J. Int'l L.* 103 at 111–13.

[106]   Murray, *supra* note 103 at 505–6.

[107]   Claudio Cordone, Senior Director of International Law and Organizations at Amnesty International and a former chief of the Human Rights Office of UNMIBH, argued in 2000 that problems of accountability still pervaded international police forces in Bosnia. Claudio Cordone, "Police Reform and Human Rights Investigations: The Experience of the UN Mission in Bosnia and Herzegovina," in Tor Tanke Holm and Espen Barth Eide (eds), *Peacebuilding and Police Reform* (London, Portland, OR: Frank Cass, 2000) at 207–9.

[108]   Murray, *supra* note 103 at 502.

[109]   Alice Hills, *Policing Africa* (Boulder, CO: Lynne Rienner Publishers, 2000) p. 15.

[110]   *Ibid.*

the protection of life, cultural or religious values, and property continue to be much less important.[111]

This focus makes policing inherently subservient to the wills of the executive and legislative branches. Ironically, in many cases, liberalization has only entrenched this dependence: "policy reforms related to structural adjustment, market liberalization and privatization"[112] that have accompanied democratization in African states have been "heavily policed,"[113] with many transitional regimes making deliberate use of the constabulary to quell opposition.

Additionally, as Hills notes, the application of force is complicated by "the unwillingness or incapacity of insecure regimes to organize the police into efficient units. Thus, force is often applied in arbitrary and unpredictable ways at the hands of underpaid and undisciplined agents."[114] The inability or unwillingness of African regimes, by and large, to reform the police, coupled with their tendency to vest the police with coercive power to the extent that it suits their own objectives, has led to a paradoxical relationship between regimes and their police forces. On the one hand, the police are more subservient to the regimes they serve. On the other hand, they have learned to make use of their monopoly on coercive force to hold power in their own right. The result, in many cases, is a constabulary which is both manipulable by state officials and yet only marginally accountable to them.[115] In no way are the police directly or even indirectly accountable to the ordinary citizens whom they ought to be protecting. The African police often behave more as paramilitaries than as constabularies. Ugandan President Yoweri Museveni's 1996 use of the army and security forces for the purpose of harassing opponents[116] is but one stark example of the dangerous enmeshing of police and military bodies which prevails in many African states.

This "African police system," as just described, is a consequence of the more general political systems of many African states. For cultural, historical and economic reasons too complex to do full justice to here, many of these systems cannot sustain competitive political pluralism, and are instead characterized by cycles of order and fragmentation, mediated by intervals of paramilitarism. These paramilitaries are typically reified as the constabulary once the temporary phase of order is achieved. They retain much of their power and prominence under the pretext of maintaining transitional peace; consequently, their para-

---

[111] *Ibid.* at 15–16.
[112] *Ibid.* at 18.
[113] *Ibid.*
[114] *Ibid.* at 19.
[115] *Ibid.* at 185–7.
[116] *Ibid.* at 91–3.

militaristic character and objectives do not change substantially. It thus seems that as long as highly precarious personal rule and "no-party democracy" prevail in African states, and as long as political competition is perceived as a threat to the fragile order established by individual regimes, it seems likely that such regimes will rely heavily on the police to bolster them, and, in the process, foster both their dependence on the police, and the police's dependence on them. As Hills concludes, as a consequence of these dynamics, it is simply "not in the interests of African regimes to build strong, efficient, or 'professional' forces."[117]

Another problematic feature of policing in Africa is that the powers conferred on or taken by police are often overbroad. States often lack the institutional capacity to constrain police actions.[118] For example, the punishment practices that are often used by police officers – such as torture and the beating of suspects – are violations of human rights that are not always authorized by law. For example, in Lagos, Nigeria, thieves are publicly executed in what is known as the "Palm Beach Shows." The overwhelming presence of crime on the continent has led to a sense of complacency towards, and even support for, such violations. The levels of violent crime are significantly higher in Sub-Saharan Africa than in cities in Asia and Latin America whose crime rates in turn rank among the highest in the world. Severe sanctions are both an attempt by the authorities to indicate some level of effectiveness in policing to the public, as well as a way for citizens to vent their frustration with the lack of security on scapegoats.

Uganda, as a state which has been the subject of numerous policing reform efforts, serves as an exemplary case study of the problems of police paramilitarism and unaccountability. Uganda gained independence from Britain in 1962, but the Ugandan Police Force continued to receive training from Britain and other democracies through the 1960s and 1970s. Though the force was large and well-organized, it engaged in abusive and repressive conduct which was considered to be an extension of executive power and therefore legitimate. During the military regime of Idi Amin (1971–79), when several thousand Ugandans were killed, the police were implicated in many of the abuses that occurred. A consequence of the regime was that the police forces were assimilated into the military.[119] Subsequent to the fall of Amin's regime, attempts were made at separating the police from paramilitary forces but they were generally unsuccessful. In addition, stagnating economic conditions led to rising crime rates that the police were unable to control. After several regime changes, the National Resistance Army took control in 1986 and made changes to the Ugandan Police

---

[117] *Ibid.* at 186.
[118] *Ibid.*
[119] *Ibid.* at 90.

Force.[120] The size of the police force was expanded. The forces were trained in various ways because training was provided by France, North Korea and Britain, and the police forces remained as paramilitary forces.[121] In the 1990s, attempted reforms included the consolidation of the police force and the involvement of the public in policing. When Yoweri Museveni, the head of the National Resistance Army, took power, he promised that the government would seek to protect human rights, including checking the abuses perpetrated by state agents.[122] The success of these reform attempts has been limited by resource constraints and lack of public support. However, though the violations of human rights perpetrated by police continue, they are no longer officially condoned by state officials as they were in the past.[123]

The Ethiopian People's Revolutionary Democratic Front (EPRDF) has held political power in Ethiopia since 1991 and the party is dominated by the Tigray People's Liberation Front (TPLF). Although the federal constitution allows for the decentralization of power to nine regional states defined along ethnic lines, the central government is able to maintain a strong hold on the national population. The police force, as well as the army, helps maintain this control. The EPRDF did not establish a formal police force until 1994; the policing function was largely carried out by the party's military wing. In 1994, policing power was gradually transferred to newly created local and regional police forces, with soldiers from the TPLF forming many of the new police recruits. The adoption of the federal constitution in 1995 and the decentralization of power resulted in more of the policing function being transferred from the military to police forces. The Ministry of Internal Affairs was abolished and the national police force was placed under the auspices of the Ministry of Justice in order to indicate the government's commitment to policing that is more respectful of human rights. However, the military continues to participate in internal security matters. The training conditions and standards for new recruits are uneven, reflecting the resource constraints faced by the government. Police officers do not have the right to join unions, and are often underpaid in relation to the work they do. Thus the significant problems facing the Ethiopian police forces are the budgetary constraints on police forces and the advantages granted by the government towards the Tigray in order to facilitate the EPRDF's control over the population. These problems, combined with the proliferation of guns and the inadequacy of penal measures for police officers that engage in corrupt or repressive conduct, has led to a fragile sense of internal security in Ethiopia. Though the police force has

---

[120] *Ibid.* at 91.
[121] *Ibid.* at 95.
[122] *Ibid.* at 97.
[123] *Ibid.* at 98.

become less politicized since 1994, it appears unlikely that the quality and effectiveness of the police force will improve in the near future if economic conditions and political influences in the country remain the same.[124]

The historical relationship between the executive authorities and the police forces described above, where the latter act primarily as agents of the former rather than of the citizenry, has resulted in many Africans turning to non-state mechanisms for personal security. Even where the police forces are not acting as agents of a repressive central authority, their inability to control emerging forms of criminality further contributes to dissatisfaction on the part of the citizenry. Overall, the trend appears to be towards the privatization of security so that it is becoming the task of the citizen to maintain peace and order rather than the responsibility of the state. One consequence of this is that the level of security a person has is becoming contingent on his or her level of personal wealth. Wealthier citizens are more likely to hire private security firms, install private security systems and receive greater protection.

The provision of security services is a growing business in African countries.[125] Many employees of private security firms are ex-soldiers who are now available for employment due to the demobilization of armies and cessation of fighting in parts of the region.[126] Private security guards are also often trained by state police – for example, the national police training school in Zambia offers training to the staff of private security firms as a revenue-generating scheme.[127] Institutional incapacity has even led police forces themselves to rely on private security firms. For example, in 1998, the Kenyan police turned to private security firms for help in containing riots that the police were unable to control.[128] It should also be noted that private security guards generally receive better compensation than the state-funded police forces.

For those without the finances to pay for private security guards and security measures such as alarm systems, self-policing is an alternative to full reliance on state security mechanisms.[129] For example, two-thirds of the people living in Lagos, Nigeria, have community watch schemes. Such a scheme has involved the hiring of night watchmen, setting up barriers to close off streets at night and community patrolling. Though such schemes may effectively supplement state mechanisms, they are often subject to collective action problems.[130] Perhaps

---

124   *Ibid.* at 98–110.
125   Hills, *supra* note 109 at 166.
126   Ejakait S.E. Opolot, *Police Administration in Africa* (Lanham, MA: University Press of America, Inc., 2001) at 132–3.
127   Hills, *supra* note 109 at 167.
128   *Ibid.*
129   *Ibid.* at 168–9.
130   *Ibid.* at 168.

more significantly, they can deteriorate into a form of vigilante justice where those suspected of committing crimes are subject to treatment whose violent nature is disproportionate to the severity of the crime and in violation of human rights. In addition, vigilante groups have been at times co-opted by ruling political forces in order to exercise social control.[131]

A recent reform project that responded to the problem of police ineffectiveness that results from police corruption in a different manner from the methods described above was the creation of an oversight body in Nigeria with constitutional and statutory powers in November 2001. The Nigerian Police Service Commission (PSC) is responsible for appointments, promotions and discipline of police officials. Given the extent of the PSC's powers, the commission could have a significant influence on the quality of policing in the country. The Monitoring of Police Conduct During Elections project, funded by the Open Society Justice Initiative, offered short-term financial and technical assistance to the PSC during the spring 2003 election period in Nigeria. A successful performance by the PSC would increase the body's credibility with the public as well as provide guidelines as to how to proceed in the future. On a preliminary assessment, the performance of the PSC as seen at the elections was successful in increasing police knowledge of codes of conduct, raising public awareness of the PSC, showing that the PSC could act efficiently and limiting the excesses of police power seen in past elections in Nigeria.[132]

D. Asia

Police forces in China suffer from corruption and abuses of civil rights. The revised Criminal Procedure Law, enacted in 1996, includes provisions that strengthen rights of the accused with regard to their treatment by police and law enforcement officials. Citizens now have the right to seek counsel at an earlier point after detention[133] and to report mistreatment to the relevant authorities.[134] Chinese authorities acknowledge that implementation of the new law has been

---

131   *Ibid.* at 170.
132   Open Society Justice Initiative, "Nigeria: Monitoring Police Conduct During Elections." Available online at http://www.justiceinitiative.org/activities/ncjr/police/nigeria_psc.
133   Aubrey McCutcheon, "Contributing to Legal Reform in China," in Mary McClymont and Stephen Golub (eds), *Many Roads to Justice: The Law Related Work of the Ford Foundation Grantees Around the World* (2000), 170, available at http://www.fordfound.org/publications/recent_articles/ docs/manyroads.pdf [hereinafter McCutcheon].
134   Li Zhenghui and Wang Zhenmin, "The Developing Human Rights and Rule of Law in Legal Philosophy and in Political Practice in China, 1978–2000," online: http://dex1.tsd.unifi.it/jg/en/index.htm?surveys/rol/wang.htm [hereinafter Li and Wang].

difficult.[135] Some admit that the text of the revised Criminal Procedure Law does not go far enough: Article 93 stipulates, "the criminal suspect shall answer the investigatory personnel's questions truthfully." The police sometimes use this provision as an excuse to use excessive force.[136]

In 2001, the United Nations Office of the High Commissioner for Human Rights (OHCHR) began holding workshops and roundtables in China on human rights and the police. These workshops included senior government officials, academics, judges, lawyers, prosecutors and the police.[137] However, these and similar programs suffer as a result of a lack of critical analysis of existing practices.[138] In her testimony before the Congressional Executive Commission on China, Susan Westin said, "Problematic areas, such as training police to implement improved criminal enforcement procedures, pose a particularly strong need for monitoring and benchmarks ... to ensure that these programs do not end up masking implementation problems or exacerbating human rights violations or abuses."[139]

International Bridges to Justice (IBJ), based in Geneva, is developing a legal aid practice manual on criminal investigation and defence. The organization also conducts on-site criminal defence skills training, and supports the use of technological tools, such as online networks and national websites, as well as the development of provincial legal aid centers established by the Chinese government.[140] IBJ is one of the few private organizations approved by the Chinese Ministry of Justice to engage in cooperation with the government and other state agencies and has a formal Memorandum of Understanding with the Ministry. IBJ calls its programs "extremely successful."[141] A May 2004 newsletter cites the following evidence of change on the ground: "Four years ago, police stations, prisons, and courts featured banners with large characters, saying, 'Confess – better treatment. Resist – harsher treatment.' Today, IBJ posters announce, 'If you are arrested, know your rights!' and go on to specify those basic legal rights."

---

[135]   McCutcheon, *supra* note 133.

[136]   Li and Wang, *supra* note 134.

[137]   "Observations on China's Rule of Law Reforms: Testimony Before the Cong. Executive Comm. on China," 107th Cong. (2002) (statement of Susan S. Westin, Managing Director, International Affairs and Trade, World Trade Organization), available at http://www.cecc.gov/pages/hearings/060602/westin.pdf.

[138]   McCutcheon, *supra* note 133.

[139]   Stephanie Wang, "Funding the Rule of Law and Civil Society" (Human Rights in China, Issue Paper No. 3, 2003), available at http://iso.hrichina.org/download_repository/ 2/HRIC_issues_paper3.2003.pdf.

[140]   Memorandum of Understanding between China's National Legal Aid Center, Ministry of Justice for China, and International Bridges to Justice, available at http:// www.ibj.org/memorandum_of_understanding.htm.

[141]   Email from Joan M. Darby, Deputy Director, International Bridges to Justice (May 4, 2004) (on file with author).

In an effort to control abuses in their law enforcement system, the Chinese central government has recently allowed and even encouraged press coverage of abuses and lawsuits. Furthermore, China's state-owned law journals and newspapers now publish incidents of police brutality.[142] As a result, China is slowly changing. Police harassments and summary executions are becoming a thing of the past. When four farmers were unjustly executed on the night of August 7, 1997, their families waged a year-long campaign for redress. In the past, police would have received praise for such acts and even perhaps a bonus for such "swift justice."[143] However, the families asserted their legal rights and the officers stood trial on murder charges.

In India, the police organization was established after the Indian mutiny in 1857 to curb dissent and serve the interests of foreign rulers.[144] The force was designed to be loyal and subservient to the rulers of the moment. The police force was structured in order to reflect the system of feudal values prevalent in society, thereby making the task of maintaining and defending the establishment easy. Those officers occupying lower posts were referred to as "inferior officers."[145] Although India has been independent for over 50 years, the police are still governed for the most part by the Police Act of 1861, despite recommendations by the National Police Commission and other expert bodies to replace the archaic law with new legislation. One of the main reasons that this police system has persisted is because what suited the colonial rulers also suited the new ruling classes who emerged after independence. As long as the executive maintains control over the police it is easy to misuse the police to further the interests of the ruling classes.[146] As a result the police system in India today is "politicized and politically polarized."[147]

More than 50% of complaints received by the National Human Rights Commission (NHRC) of India every year are against police personnel.[148] In 1999, over 74,322 complaints were received from the public against police personnel

---

[142]   Elisabeth Rosenthal, "Police Abuses Start to Get Attention in China," *New York Times* (March 18, 1999) available at http://fox.rollins.edu/~tlairson/intro/CHINA6. HTML.

[143]   *Ibid.*

[144]   Doel Mukerjee, "Police Reforms and You," in G.P. Joshi and Deepti Kapoor (eds), *Commonwealth Human Rights Initiative* (New Delhi: Print World, 2003) at 2 [hereinafter Mukerjee].

[145]   "Police Practices: Obstructions to Poor People's Access to Justice" (2003) available at http://www.humanrightsinitiative.org [hereinafter "Police Practices"].

[146]   *Ibid.*

[147]   *Ibid.*

[148]   "Police Reforms in India: A Distant Dream," Indiainfo.com Law, available at http://lawindiainfo.com/miscellaneous/police-reforms.html.

in the country.[149] Furthermore in 1999–2000, the NHRC received reports of 177 deaths in police custody, 1,157 illegal detentions and arrests, 1,647 false implications and 5,783 other police excesses.[150]

In a study on the "Image of the Police in India," over 50% of the respondents mentioned non-registration of complaints as common malpractice in police stations.[151] One of the main reasons police fail to register complaints is because police performance is evaluated on the basis of crime statistics. As the department and the government are both keen to report that crime is under control, they underreport crimes in order to bring down the figures. Other important reasons for this practice include corruption, a heavy crime load, and inadequate staffing. Police departments in many states have launched drives to ensure full registration of complaints. However, when such initiatives have been undertaken, crime registers a big jump causing an outcry in the press and government. Police then revert to concealing crime and artificially manipulating crime figures.

In 1973, the government introduced the New Code of Criminal Procedure to replace the old code formulated during the British rule in 1898.[152] The new code made it mandatory to provide a copy of the First Information Report to the complainant free of charge and provided that any person who met with a refusal on the part of the police to take down their complaint could send its substance in writing to the District Superintendent of Police, who would then take the necessary action to investigate the case.[153] However, as neither of the two initiatives entailed effective sanctions, they did not succeed in curbing non-registration problems.

The existence of corruption in the police force is another major obstacle to the implementation of the rule of law in India. A recent field study of corruption faced by the common person in India revealed that the police was by far the most corrupt of the ten sectors of the public domain, including education, health, railways, etc., included in the study.[154] Indian police collect weekly bribes, known as *hafta,* from traders and kiosk owners so that these petty vendors may carry on their activity. The police have been known to resort to violence when collecting these *hafta.* In 1996, a fruit vendor in Delhi was beaten to death by two policemen because he failed to pay the *hafta.*[155]

---

[149]   Mukerjee, *supra* note 144 at 12.
[150]   *Ibid.*
[151]   "Police Practices," *supra* note 145.
[152]   *Ibid.*
[153]   *Ibid.*
[154]   "Police Practices," *supra* note 145 from Transparency International India: Corruption in India – An Empirical Study, December 17, 2002.
[155]   "Police Practices," *supra* note 145.

Indian police resort to corruption and bribery in part because of their poor working conditions. There is only one police officer for every 746 people.[156] They receive low salaries and have poor social status.[157] The constabulary, which constitutes 88% of the police force, are treated as unskilled labour.[158] Finally, only 37% of the forces are provided with family accommodation. The majority of police officers have to live either in slum-like conditions or away from their families for most of their careers.[159]

The Central Vigilance Commission (CVC) recently launched a campaign against corruption in India. As a part of this initiative, the names of officers, including the Indian Police Service officers, who were found guilty of corruption charges were displayed on the CVC's website.[160] By doing this, the CVC hoped to promote transparency, build public confidence that action would be taken, encourage deterrence and motivate the government to take action. While the public at large welcomed this initiative, unsurprisingly it was not well received by the police force.

Police brutality is a major problem in India. The problem persists because there are no effective accountability mechanisms. It is the police themselves that inquire into public complaints against police personnel.[161] Furthermore, the law itself is sometimes used to protect delinquent police officers. The Code of Criminal Procedure has a provision under which "a public servant cannot be prosecuted without the sanction of the appropriate authorities for acts done while acting or purporting to act in the discharge of his official duties."[162]

Indian police are also notorious for their biased practices when dealing with minorities. Although the Indian Constitution has provisions to protect the equality of Indian citizens, most of the responsibility for enforcing it is vested in the police.[163] As there are very few mechanisms in place to monitor police behaviour, police frequently act in a blatantly partisan manner towards members of the minority community. Allegations of biased police practices were made in November 1984 when Sikhs were massacred, again in October 1989 with the Bhagalpur carnage when the Bihar Police allegedly joined the marauders in acts

---

[156]   Mukerjee, *supra* note 144 at 6.
[157]   *Ibid.*
[158]   *Ibid.*
[159]   *Ibid.*
[160]   "Police Practices," *supra* note 145.
[161]   *Ibid.*
[162]   *Ibid.* from The Code of Criminal Procedure, 1973, Section 197.
[163]   William Eisenman, "Eliminating Discriminatory Traditions Against Dalits: The Local Need for International Capacity Building of the Indian Criminal Justice System" (2003) 17 *Emory Int'l L. Rev.* 133 at 138 [hereinafter Eisenman].

of arson, and in 1992–93 in communal riots in Bombay.[164] Police systematically collude with high-caste Hindus to prevent the lower-class Dalits from asserting their fundamental rights.[165] The most recent incidents of police bias against members of a minority community were the 2002 communal riots in Gujarat. Throughout these riots a large number of Muslims were killed and their property looted and destroyed. The police were complicit, by being inactive when they received desperate calls for help, and also by actively promoting or directing attacks.[166]

The United Nations Development Program (UNDP), the NHRC, and other organizations have developed initiatives to improve police organization in India. The main goal of these efforts has been to change police attitudes. Over 200 police personnel from different parts of the country have been sent to the United Kingdom and Singapore to study how the police system functions in those countries.[167] An UNDP sponsored project to improve the organization and management of the law enforcement system was launched in the late 1990s to improve law enforcement as well as to create a stronger police–public interface.[168] Furthermore, the NHRC has succeeded in persuading some state governments to set up Human Rights Cells in Police Headquarters to be headed by a senior officer.

The Supreme Court has also been proactive in promoting police reforms. In *D.K. Basu v. State of West Bengal*,[169] the Court set out ten points that addressed the rights of citizens when they came into contact with the police. However, since the state governments did not establish any mechanisms to monitor the implementation of the judgment, nor incorporate the safeguards in relevant laws or police manuals, the judgment was not effective in ending the misuse of powers of arrest.[170]

In the Philippines, the National Bureau of Investigation (NBI) and the Philippines National Police (PNP) are charged with the detention, identification and apprehension of criminals in the Philippines. The agencies investigate crimes and other offences against the laws of the Philippines, act as national clearing houses for information used by the country's prosecut-

---

[164] "In Search of Lost Credibility: The Carnage in Gujarat Underlines the Need for Police Reform," *Ind. Exp*, April 5, 2002, available at www.humanrightsinitiative.org.

[165] Eisenman, *supra* note 163 at 161.

[166] "Police Practices," *supra* note 145.

[167] Doel Mukerjee, "Police Reforms Initiatives in India" (2003) Commonwealth Human Rights Initiative: Police, Prison and Human Rights (PPHR) available at http://www.humanrightsinitiative.org.

[168] "Police Practices," *supra* note 145.

[169] AIR 1997 SC 610.

[170] "Police Practices," *supra* note 145.

ing and corrections agencies and maintain crime laboratories to assist in criminal investigation.[171] Law enforcement in the Philippines suffers from low salaries and benefits, a lack of transportation and communication facilities and deficient crime information systems. The duplication of functions between the PNP and NBI, moreover, results in potential institutional and operational conflict, conflicting investigation findings to support prosecution, inefficiency and wastage of manpower, time and financial resources. In view of these overlaps, some Congressmen have proposed the abolition of the NBI.[172]

Torture and other serious human rights violations by the police have long been a problem in Philippines. In 1986, after Corazon Aquino came into power, measures, such as the adoption of a new constitution, were taken to stop human rights abuses. However, despite these measures, torture persisted. Throughout the presidencies of Ramos, Estrada, and now Arroyo, torture has continued to be widely reported in the context of criminal investigations.[173]

The Filipino Criminal Code includes laws to help prevent torture. The extraction of confessions by means of torture is illegal.[174] However, the defence has the burden of proving that the confession was extracted by means of force, duress, promise or reward. Furthermore, in the past, judges have not taken proactive steps to order investigations into alleged or apparent torture.

In an effort to curtail corruption and abuse in the police force, the National Police Commission in collaboration with the PNP has set up a nationwide community-based oversight mechanism known as the People's Law Enforcement Board (PLEB). It is required by law that there be at least one PLEB for every municipality and/or for each of the legislative districts in a city.[175] According to the Human Rights Initiative, in terms of implementation and performance, the PLEBs are reported to be slowly having an impact.

In Cambodia, during the People's Republic of Kampuchea (PRK) and the State of Cambodia (SOC) regimes, the police acted as spies and enforcers for the ruling party. "As society came out of the closed chambers of the PRK and SOC regimes, the image of the police force as a repressive and abusive force

---

[171] Supreme Court of the Philippines, Department of Justice and United Nations Development Programme, "The Other Pillars of Justice through Reforms in the Department of Justice: Diagnostic Report IX" (2003), available at http://www.apjr-sc-phil.org/pub-reports at I.

[172] *Ibid.* at II.

[173] "Reparation for Torture: the Philippines" (May 2003) available at http://www.redress.org/studies/philippines.pdf at 2.1.

[174] *Ibid.* at 3.2.

[175] "Police Practices," *supra* note 145.

started surfacing."[176] In 1989, when the country began a process of political and economic liberalization, corruption and abuse became even more serious. Marcillino, a trained Filipino program officer, explains this increase in police abuse by an inability of the police force to adapt to a changing environment. "During the PRK and the SOC regimes, repression was absolute and no one would come against the state. But as soon as the political climate started opening up, the police started repression, as they had never been trained to deal with political opposition or demonstrations against the state. This was altogether new to the police force, which could not fit itself into the fast changes and took to repressive measures to curb all voices."[177] Furthermore, the legal and administrative frameworks in Cambodia were poorly defined in the period following the Communist regime.

Low salaries and poor working conditions also contribute to corruption in the police force. The highest salaries are around $30 to $40 a month.[178] Many officers have part-time businesses and the majority of low-ranking officials drive motorcycle taxis in the afternoon. Police are forced to rely on corruption and bribery to supplement their low incomes. There is also no accountability in the police force. Even at the highest levels, the police chiefs in the provinces are practically independent of the Ministry of the Interior and are accountable rather to the provincial governors. Furthermore, most of the provincial governors are old party veterans, making it difficult to establish an effective form of accountability.

The United Nations Commission on Human Rights (UNCHR) attempted an initiative which provided human rights training to the gendarmerie. However, after the coup and associated violence of July 1997, the program was terminated because the gendarmerie was heavily implicated in those events.[179] The UNHRC continues to work with local NGOs to train civilian police, but there are serious doubts as to the effectiveness of these programs.

The Australian government has recently funded the Cambodian Criminal Justice Assistance Project (CCJAP), a three-year program to support the government of Cambodia. The goal of this project is to improve operational, managerial, institutional and human rights conditions within the justice system of Cambodia. The project implements international standards of police conduct, while stressing practical training. It is too soon to evaluate the results of this program.

---

[176]   Muzamil Jaleel, "Cambodia: Cambodian Police and the Need for Reform," Asian Human Rights Commission – Human Rights Solidarity, available at http://www.ahrchk. net/hrsolikd/mainfile.php/1998vol108no11/1841/.

[177]   *Ibid.*

[178]   *Ibid.*

[179]   *Ibid.*

III. CONCLUSION

The experiences reviewed in this chapter suggest that many developing countries have encountered difficulties in instituting a professional, competent and non-corrupt police force which is dedicated to service to the community and addressing problems of conventional crime in their midst. Rather, the experience of many developing countries is that historically the police have been viewed as a form of paramilitary organization primarily dedicated to regime maintenance in societies dominated by military or authoritarian governments. This has made the conventional objectives of policing in developed countries of secondary importance in many developing countries and has led to support for, or at least acquiescence by, incumbent political regimes in extensive human rights abuses by police forces.

In terms of the three classes of impediments to rule of law reform identified in Chapter 1 of this book – resource constraints, social/historical/cultural values and practices, and political economy factors – it is clear that in many developing countries resource constraints have been an important source of the problem in developing an effective police force: police are often underpaid, under-qualified and under-trained, and lack various supporting resources for effective investigation of criminal activity. However, adequate resources should be viewed as a necessary but not sufficient condition for effective policing. Merely paying incompetent or corrupt police officers higher wages is unlikely to induce a more effective level of performance of their duties. The evidence suggests that changing incentive structures, through appropriate mechanisms of independence and accountability, are critical to changing police behaviour. In other words, institutional design that takes seriously incentives for public interest performance of policing responsibilities is critical. The precise nature of these mechanisms, is, to some extent, context-specific, but to echo William Easterly,[180] in the end, more resources without different incentive structures are likely to have a minimal impact on police behaviour and performance.

With respect to social/cultural/historical practices and values, it is true that deeply entrenched historical practices of assigning to the police a major mandate in political regime maintenance has entwined policing functions with those of the military and has raised major challenges in the process of disentanglement. However, it is difficult to view these historical practices as reflecting widespread social and cultural values, given that wide cross-sections of the community have been victims of such practices. A more salient social and cultural factor in many developing countries is widespread public concern over high and often rising

---

[180]   William Easterly, *The Uncertain Quest for Growth* (Cambridge, MA: MIT Press, 2002) Part III.

violent crime rates, where there appears to be an inclination to view respect for human rights on the part of police personnel as equivalent to a soft-on-crime outlook. In turn, the police and the incumbent political regimes, in order to assure the community that they are taking crime rates seriously, have often sought to demonstrate this commitment through forms of vigilante police justice. Here it seems that community attitudes to vigilante police justice in addressing high and rising crime rates are amenable to change through demonstrating that a lawless police force is in fact likely to be ineffective in reducing crime rates, and indeed some evidence from Latin America tends to suggest a growing community acceptance of this fact.

With respect to political economy factors, the central role of the police in many developing countries in political regime maintenance clearly reflects political economy factors and is unlikely to engender widespread community support. Here domestic political constituencies who support the role of police in providing a service to citizens (the community service model of policing) need to be supported and encouraged through financial aid and technical support, often provided by external organizations (a theme we return to in the concluding chapter of this book). It is obviously the case that this role of the police is more effectively advanced in a fully operational democracy, but steps towards this end are nevertheless achievable in less democratic regimes (although probably not in highly repressive or kleptocratic regimes, where police reform is simply one element in a much broader set of institutional reforms that are necessary if the welfare of the citizens in these societies is to be significantly advanced).

4. Prosecution

I. NORMATIVE BENCHMARKS

A. The Role of the Public Prosecutor

Prosecutors exercise the accusation principle of criminal law: they can accuse an individual of a crime and bring him or her before a court of law. The fair and consistent exercise of the prosecutorial function is critical to the success of rule of law reforms. As a report by the International Commission of Jurists finds, "[r]espect for human rights and the rule of law presupposes a strong prosecutorial authority in charge of investigating and prosecuting criminal offences with independence and impartiality."[1] The significance of the prosecutorial function lies in the prosecutor's responsibility to represent the public interest in criminal proceedings. As "representatives of the public interest,"[2] effective prosecutors are vital to improving public perceptions of the criminal justice system. According to Nelson Mandela, "[t]he challenge for the modern prosecutor is to become a lawyer for the people ... [and] to build an effective relationship with the community and to ensure that the rights of victims are protected."[3]

As with judicial and police reform, prosecutorial reform is centrally preoccupied with the twin values of independence and accountability. However, experience with prosecutors varies widely, and there is no universal checklist of steps to achieve either goal. The values of independence and accountability can also conflict as improvements in one may come at the cost of the other. Moreover, lack of public confidence or perceived illegitimacy of prosecutors

---

[1] "International Principles on the Independence and Accountability of Judges, Lawyers and Prosecutors: A Practitioners Guide," Practitioners Guides Series No. 1, International Commission of Jurists Geneva Switzerland, 2004, online at: http://www.mafhoum.com/press7/230S24.pdf.

[2] *Guidelines on the Role of Prosecutors*, Adopted by the Eighth United Nations Congress on the Prevention of Crime and the Treatment of Offenders, Havana, Cuba, September 1990.

[3] Christopher Stone *et al.* "Prosecutors in the Front Line: Increasing the Effectiveness of Criminal Justice in South Africa," online at: National Prosecuting Authority of South Africa, http://www.ndpp.gov.za/NPA/documents/NPA%20Front%20line%2008%2003.pdf.

may limit the gains that improvements in accountability and independence are designed to achieve.

The function of the prosecution is to represent the public in prosecutions against individuals charged with public offences. Public prosecutors are government employees or representatives who "seek justice,"[4] by "engag[ing] in truth-seeking and whose actions are constrained by rules that ensure fairness to defendants."[5] Such a characterization of the prosecutor emphasizes his role as a public servant, reflected in the historical creation of public prosecutors to mitigate the extremes of a purely adversarial system of criminal justice[6] through his responsibility not to simply seek convictions but to uncover the truth without violating the rights of the defendant.

The prosecutor's role varies considerably depending upon the mode of criminal procedure. Common law countries have an adversarial procedure, whereas civil law countries, including many Latin American countries, have, or had prior to recent reforms, an inquisitorial mode of procedure. A key aspect of rule of law reform in many developing countries, particularly in Latin America, has been a move to an adversarial mode of procedure, requiring significant changes to the role of the prosecution. In the Latin American inquisitorial system, "[t]he public prosecutor's office had a bureaucratic role, and active investigation was by law the responsibility of examining judges and in practice the work of police."[7] Prosecutors, consequently, were often described as the "fifth wheel" of the criminal justice system.[8] Reforms to develop an accusatorial model of criminal procedure have greatly changed the role of the prosecutor, who has assumed responsibility for conducting preparatory investigations of crimes.[9]

Some level of prosecutorial discretion seems inherent in the role of the prosecutor. Conceptually, it is possible to imagine a system where the legislature prescribes the criminal offences and requires that every offence is to be prosecuted. In practice, however, it is impossible for prosecutors to ensure that every single infraction of the respective criminal law is prosecuted: "Only an ideal system, provided with unlimited human, technical and financial resources could

---

[4]   Bruce A. Green, "Why Should Prosecutors 'Seek Justice'?" (1999) 26 *Fordham Urb. L. J.* 607 at 636.

[5]   Carolyn B. Ramsey, "The Discretionary Power of 'Public' Prosecutors in Historical Perspective" (2002) 39 *American Criminal Law Review* 1309 at 1317.

[6]   *Ibid.* The tradition of private prosecutions that was initially transplanted from Europe was "criticized as elitist, inefficient and vindictive," and public systems of prosecution have become the norm.

[7]   Maricio Duce, "The Role of the Public Prosecutor's Office in Latin America's Criminal Procedure Reform: An Overview," online: Centro de Estudios de Justice de la Américas, http://www.cejamericas.org/doc/documentos/reforma-mp2-ing.pdf.

[8]   *Ibid.*

[9]   *Ibid.* at 3.

reasonably fulfill this principle's ideal."[10] While full enforcement of every criminal law is impossible, Elizabeth Iglesias notes that full enforcement statutes limited to certain offences may be effective, for example in requiring police to arrest the batterer in domestic abuse cases.[11]

The degree of prosecutorial discretion varies significantly across jurisdictions and between modes of criminal procedure. Inquisitorial systems tend to bind prosecutors by the principle of mandatory prosecution, where the prosecutor must prosecute if there is sufficient evidence – though mandatory prosecution is generally softened by exceptions, such as the expediency principle, which allows the prosecutor to close investigations of minor offences if certain conditions are met.[12] In adversarial systems, prosecutors exercise broad discretion in deciding whether to prosecute, and if a decision to prosecute is made, what charge to prosecute the alleged offender with[13] and whether to negotiate and accept a plea bargain.

Elizabeth Iglesias frames the key challenge in relation to prosecutorial reform as a tension between independence and accountability. She writes: if we accept that "prosecutorial discretion is an unavoidable reality, the ultimate question is this: what legal rules and institutional arrangements will ensure that this tremendous power is exercised in a manner consistent with the values of due process and equal protection of the law?"[14] The objective of the UN *Guidelines on the Role of Prosecutors*, signed at the Eighth UN Congress on the Prevention of Crime and the Treatment of Offenders in 1990, is to "assist Member States in their tasks of securing and promoting the effectiveness, impartiality and fairness of prosecutors in criminal proceedings."[15] A review of the various recommendations in the UN *Guidelines* makes the importance of both accountability and independence to an effective prosecution clear.

---

[10]   Andrés José D'Alessio, "The Function of the Prosecution in the Transition to Democracy in Latin America," in Irwin P. Stozky (ed.), *Transition to Democracy in Latin America: The Role of the Judiciary* (Boulder, CO: Westview Press, 1993) 187 at 191.

[11]   Elizabeth M. Iglesisas, "Designing Institutional and Legal Structure of Prosecutorial Power," in *supra* note 10, 269 at 281.

[12]   K. Ambos, "The Status, Role and Accountability of the Prosecutor of the International Criminal Court: A Comparative Overview of 33 National Reports" (2000) 8 *European Journal of Crime, Criminal Law and Criminal Justice* 89 at 100.

[13]   Susanne Walther, "The Position and Structure of the Prosecutor's Office in the United States" (2000) 8 *European Journal of Crime, Criminal Law and Criminal Justice* 285.

[14]   Iglesisas, *supra* note 11 at 271.

[15]   *Guidelines on the Role of Prosecutors, supra* note 2.

B. Independence

The importance of prosecutorial independence to an effective prosecution is confirmed by the UN *Guidelines*, which seeks to ensure that the parameters of prosecutorial employment, including disciplinary investigations, are enshrined in law. The guidelines identify how prosecutors should be selected, promoted, remunerated and disciplined:

- Prosecutors should have appropriate qualifications and training, be selected without discrimination, and be made aware of the ethical duties of their office;
- Promotion of prosecutors should be based on objective factors, such as professional qualifications and experience, and assessed in accordance with impartial procedures;
- Remuneration, tenure, and pensions and age of retirement for prosecutors are to be legally provided for or in published rules;
- Disciplinary procedures for prosecutors must be based on law that guarantees an objective evaluation.

The *Guidelines* also seek to ensure the independence of prosecutors by placing responsibility on the state to protect prosecutors from intimidation, harassment or improper interference.

The location of the prosecution within the executive arm of government complicates greatly efforts toward prosecutorial independence. In common law countries, the chief prosecutor or attorney-general is appointed by the executive. Prosecutorial independence has been maintained in common law systems by prohibiting the executive from directing the prosecution on how to proceed in any given case or class of cases. Given this close yet segregated relationship between the executive and the prosecution, it is useful to follow Philip B. Heyman's suggestion and understand prosecutorial independence as a continuum

> between substantial independence and very substantial dependence on the orders of political superiors ... Few prosecutors' offices have the independence of the United States "Independent Counsel" in setting their own budgets. Few prosecutors' offices are subject to direct orders to bring or drop a case. Most prosecutors fall somewhere between these extremes.[16]

Even in countries where the rule of law has been firmly established, prosecutorial independence is not fully realized and threats to the independence of

---

[16] Philip B. Heyman, "Should Prosecutors be Independent of the Executive in Prosecuting Government Abuses?," in Stozky, *supra* note 10, 187 at 191.

prosecutors are still present. Tradition has largely guaranteed prosecutorial independence in Canada, where a constitutional convention allows the Attorney-General, a member of the executive, to issue broad policy directives for prosecutors to follow, but forbids him or her from becoming involved in day-to-day decisions relating to specific cases. But the tradition of prosecutorial independence has proven fallible in Canada. The Canadian *Royal Commission on the Donald Marshall, Jr., Prosecution* identified inadequate prosecutorial independence as a contributing factor to the wrongful conviction of Donald Marshall Jr. Philip Stenning summarizes the findings of the Royal Commission:

> To a great extent, the Inquiry characterized the problems collectively as an indication of an insufficient independence in the prosecutorial process and in the institutions charged with responsibility for prosecutorial decision-making. The independence from unacceptable partisan or personal influence of almost all those involved in the process was considered to be in question, as was the independence of the police from improper pressures by prosecutorial authorities.[17]

On the whole, however, prosecutors in common law countries are generally found to rank highly on the continuum of prosecutorial independence. In a comparative overview of prosecutorial systems in 33 countries, Ambos finds that prosecutors in common law countries are "virtually absolutely independent … demonstrated by the almost unlimited discretion of prosecutors in the common law system. On the basis of evidence presented by the police the prosecutor decides if he initiates proceedings or refrains therefrom."[18] In prosecuting individual cases, common law prosecutors are responsible only to their superiors within the office of the prosecution, and cannot be directed by other institutions, such as members of the executive.[19] While the executive may issue broad policy guidelines for the prosecution, prosecutorial independence is protected by the fact that government is unable to direct the prosecution in any particular case.

---

[17] P. Stenning, "Independence and the Director of Public Prosecutions: The Marshall Inquiry and Beyond" (2000) 23 *Dalhousie Law Journal* 385 at 387, 390. To remedy this dependence, The Royal Commission recommended the creation of a Director of Public Prosecutors (DPP) who would have limited independence from the Attorney-General. England and Wales have a similar Director of Public Prosecutions who oversees the Crown Prosecution Service throughout the country and is appointed by and responsible to the Attorney-General. The report recommended that the Attorney-General only intervene in individual cases after consultation with the DPP, and if the DPP advised against such intervention, the nature and extent of intervention of the Attorney-General be made public. When Nova Scotia implemented the DPP it required consultation with the DPP before the Attorney-General intervenes, but did not include public notice requirements on the extent of the intervention.

[18] Ambos, *supra* note 12 at 95.

[19] *Ibid.* This is known as the principle of hierarchy.

Distinguishing between individual case direction and broad policy direction has been critical to ensuring prosecutorial independence in developed common law countries. Questions have emerged as to whether this distinction can be easily sustained in countries lacking strong rule of law institutions. For example, in Nigeria, it has been reported that "it is not always possible to resist pressure or interference particularly from the executive arm of Government in the discharge of the Attorney-General's responsibilities … invariably the question becomes how far the public interest approximates to the interests of the regime or Government in power."[20] In such a case, the pervasiveness of the interests of the regime makes it difficult if not impossible to maintain a distinction between individual cases and broad prosecutorial policy.

The requirement for prosecutorial independence is not limited to independence from government interference. Individual prosecutors must feel independent within their own offices to exercise their own discretion and express their dissent if their office makes a decision with which they do not agree.[21] Independence from the police is another important concern as it is generally thought that the prosecutor should be removed from the initial investigation in order to make an objective decision on whether and how to prosecute a case.

The degree of dependence between the police and prosecutors in any given state will depend largely on the allocation of investigative functions between the two institutions. In the US, and most common law jurisdictions, police conduct investigations, and present the case to the prosecutor once they decide the investigation is complete and there appears to be sufficient evidence to warrant prosecution.[22] The prosecutor is not authorized to mandate a police investigation, other than to order further investigations once the prosecutor is already involved. The police monopoly over investigation is justifiable in that "[i]t is undesirable that the prosecution service be made formally responsible for the investigation of crime, as this would tend to blur the distinction between the investigation of crime and the dispassionate decision whether the facts of a given case merit prosecution."[23]

In practice, however, the day-to-day relationship between the police and the prosecution implies that prosecutors are often involved in the investigative proc-

---

[20]   *Ibid.* at 96.

[21]   D'Alessio, *supra* note 10 at 194.

[22]   In England and Wales the police function included making decisions on whether to prosecute and what offence should be charged until 1985 when the creation of the Crown Prosecution Services (CPS) required the CPS or barristers to present the case in court. It is still up to the police to make the initial decision to prosecute. See Andrew Ashworth, "Developments in the Public Prosecutor's Office in England and Wales" (2000) 8 *European Journal of Criminal Law* 257.

[23]   Ambos, *supra* note 12 at 114.

ess. Susanne Walther, describing the relationship of police and prosecutors in the US, argues, "the ever increasing complexities of substantive and procedural law make the former – the police – routinely depend on the latter – the prosecutor – for legal advice, a fact which in many jurisdictions has evolved into forms of cooperation that provide the prosecutor with considerable influence in the investigation process itself."[24] Changes in the type of crime, including increases in organized crime, drug-trafficking, and money laundering, combined with the inexperience of police in these areas, particularly in developing countries, have led prosecutors to play a more active role in the investigative process.[25]

The desirability of increased influence of prosecutors over the investigation process is controversial. On the one hand, blurring of the investigation and prosecutorial functions has given rise to concerns over the ability of prosecutors to distance themselves from the case to evaluate objectively its merits and then decide whether to prosecute. There is also concern that prosecutorial control over investigations threatens the institutional independence of the police and prosecution services. With respect to Latin America, Maurice Duce writes that "[t]he police have argued that this enters into conflict with their institutional chain of command," which not only threatens the institutional independence of the police but also fails to take into account the experience of police investigators in directing preliminary investigations.[26] However, by increasing cooperation between the prosecutors and police, prosecution-led investigations can increase conviction rates by improving investigation strategies and ensuring that potential problems with evidence are identified early on.[27] The term "prosecution-led investigations" "is not meant to suggest that prosecutors become investigators. Instead, the idea is that prosecutors should guide the strategy and tactics of police investigation, focusing on the collection of evidence that can be admitted in court, rather than simply on discovering facts."[28]

C. Accountability

The importance of prosecutorial accountability is reflected in the UN *Guidelines* in their emphasis on the prosecutor's responsibility to discharge his ethical and legal duties, enforced ultimately through disciplinary proceedings. The *Guidelines* specify that prosecutorial duties include accountability for adherence to human rights standards. Prosecutors must inform the court of, and refuse to take account of, evidence "that they know or believe on reasonable grounds was ob-

---

[24] Walther, *supra* note 13 at 288.
[25] Ambos, *supra* note 9 at 114.
[26] Duce, *supra* note 7 at 15.
[27] Stone *et al.*, *supra* note 3 at 34.
[28] *Ibid.* at 33.

tained through recourse to unlawful methods, which constitute a grave violation of the suspect's human rights."

The increase in prosecutorial responsibility that has accompanied the transition in several developing countries to adversarial systems of criminal justice has, in addition to its prospective benefits, also given rise to problems of prosecutorial accountability. Mauricio Duce finds that Latin American prosecutors in reformed systems exhibit a "general reluctance to make themselves publicly accountable for their performance."[29] While recognizing that this tendency stems from a variety of complex factors, Duce identifies the failure of prosecutors to conceptualize themselves as agents of the public as a leading factor: "[P]rosecutors do not fully comprehend the concept that society is in fact a client to which the public prosecutor's office is accountable. Personnel in these institutions tend to see themselves as mere judicial operators, and not as agents who fulfill an important social function and must satisfy the community or 'client's' expectation."[30]

There are a variety of mechanisms through which prosecutorial accountability can be achieved. Detailed national or sub-national guidelines governing the exercise of prosecutorial discretion can help to achieve prosecutorial accountability.[31] But as Ramsey points out, discretion "can never be completely formulaic."[32] In countries where prosecutors are agents of the Attorney-General, the Attorney-General may legitimately call on prosecutors for information or explanation regarding prosecutorial duties.[33] Professional disciplinary proceedings within the prosecutor's officer are an important source of accountability, as are more public forms of accountability, such as where prosecutors may need to explain their decisions to police officers investigating crimes, victims, bar associations,[34] and in some high-profile cases, the public at large.[35] In much of the US prosecutorial accountability to the public is easily visible, as misconduct by prosecutors or the District-Attorney herself will become an issue during the elections of the District-Attorney.[36] However, it is not clear that this form of

---

[29]   Duce, *supra* note 7 at 11.

[30]   *Ibid.*

[31]   Rory K. Little, "Proportionality as an Ethical Precept for Prosecutors in the Investigative Role" (1999) 68 *Fordham L. Rev.* 723.

[32]   Ramsey, *supra* note 5 at 1318.

[33]   D.A. Bellemare, "Public Confidence and Accountability in the Exercise of Prosecutorial Discretion," online: http://www.isrcl.org/Papers/2004/Bellemare.pdf.

[34]   In *Krieger v. Law Society of Alberta* [2002] 3 SCR the SCC held that prosecutors are not completely immune from the disciplinary procedures of the relevant law society.

[35]   Bellemare, *supra* note 33.

[36]   Fred T. Zacharias, "The Professional Discipline of Prosecutors" (2001) 79 *N.C. L. Rev.* 721 at 765.

public prosecutorial accountability is desirable. As one author suggests, a prosecutor should not become "the slave of his electorate ... [for] in many matters his duty clearly lies in the defiance of community pressures."[37] The whims of the electorate may not coincide with the duties of the prosecutor, for instance, since the electorate may often not be fully sensitive to notions of fairness to the defendant.[38]

One of the strongest mechanisms of accountability for prosecutors is through judicial review, where decisions made by judges act as a check on prosecutorial discretion. Judges may make rulings adverse to the prosecutor, dismiss the case, or even impose costs in the most egregious cases.[39] Prosecutorial discretion in accepting plea bargains is restricted by judges, who must consider whether to accept a guilty plea, and in the US, grand jury proceedings limit prosecutorial charging power.[40] Developing countries transitioning from inquisitorial systems to adversarial systems may be reluctant to emphasize judicial oversight as a means to achieve prosecutorial accountability as it may seem to resurrect the dominant role of the examining judge and the lesser role of the prosecutor under the inquisitorial system. Elizabeth Iglesias, however, argues that limits on prosecutorial discretion through judicial review can coincide with and support an effective prosecution in an adversarial system. In fact, she argues that the US experience shows that judicial review of prosecutorial conduct "is the most effective mechanism for ensuring that the norms restricting prosecutorial power are routinely respected in individual cases."[41] She cites the doctrine of presumptive vindictiveness as an example of an effective judicial check on prosecutorial discretion: a prosecutor's case will be dismissed if the defendant can overcome the presumption of good faith and non-discriminatory prosecution.[42]

D. Tensions between Independence and Accountability

The tensions between independence and accountability discussed in relation to the judiciary are equally of relevance to the public prosecutor: prosecutors are

---

[37] H. Richard Uviller, "The Virtuous Prosecutor in Quest for an Ethical Standard: Guidance from the ABA" (1973) 71 *Mich. L. Rev.* at 1152–3.

[38] Ramsey, *supra* note 5 at 1320.

[39] Prosecutors can also be subject to civil actions for malicious prosecution. See Bellemare, *supra* note 33.

[40] James Vronberg, "Decent Restraint on Prosecutorial Power" (1981) 84 *Harv. L. Rev.* 1521 at 1537–8.

[41] Iglesisas, *supra* note 11 at 274.

[42] To do so, the defendant must prove the following three elements: (1) that other similarly situated individuals have not been prosecuted; (2) that the defendant was consciously and deliberately singled out; and (3) that the basis upon which the defendant was singled out was arbitrary and invidious. See Iglesias, *supra* note 11.

integral to criminal policy and are linked to government, yet must also be distanced from the governmental process, treating all citizens equally and ensuring that prosecutions are not conducted for partisan purposes.[43] The *Royal Commission on the Donald Marshall, Jr., Prosecution* recognized this tension between prosecutorial accountability and independence, writing that "we reject the concept of a totally independent Director of Public Prosecutors (or Attorney-General) who would be accountable to no one except his or her conscience and the law … the challenge has been to find the model that best reflects the right blend of independence and accountability."[44]

The Italian experience with prosecutorial reform illustrates the difficult relationship between prosecutorial independence and accountability. In the post-war period, Italy steadfastly pursued prosecutorial independence to avoid government interferences of the kind that had occurred in the past. This had the effect of curtailing prosecutorial accountability. Italian prosecutors can take extended periods of absence without affecting their career trajectory, and several prosecutors have used these absences to run for political office, which paradoxically threatens the independence of the prosecution that the reforms were designed to achieve. Prosecutors can largely determine the location of their post even if the functional needs of the system call for transfers; and promotions of prosecutors occur automatically, raising the question of "to what extent protection of independence should be pursued at the expense of real, substantial guarantees of professional qualification and quality?"[45]

In discussing Italy's shortcomings in prosecutorial accountability, Di Federico recognizes the tension between the two values and expresses scepticism that both goals can be "reconciled at the operational level."[46] Nevertheless, he also identifies mechanisms for striking a balance between these values and "observe[s] the tendency to redress the balance between the values of independence and accountability through measures intended to render public prosecution less dependent on the expectations of the governing majority."[47] Distancing the prosecutor from the government is the goal of independence, while mechanisms outside the governing majority can help to ensure that this independence does not go unchecked. One such mechanism for prosecutorial accountability is private prosecutions, which can serve as a check on prosecutorial inactivity. For

---

[43]   G. Di Federico, "Prosecutorial Independence and the Democratic Requirement of Accountability in Italy" (1998) 38 *The British Journal of Criminology* 371.

[44]   Nova Scotia, *Royal Commission on the Donald Marshall, Jr. Prosecution, Commissioners' Report, Vol. 1: Findings and Recommendations* (Halifax: Royal Commission, 1989) cited in Stenning, *supra* note 17 at 389.

[45]   Di Federico, *supra* note 43 at 371.

[46]   *Ibid.*

[47]   *Ibid.*

example, if a prosecutor declines to investigate an individual, perhaps for partisan reasons, a private individual can bring the prosecution herself. For example, England and Spain have adopted this mechanism. In Germany, a judge can issue an order to initiate criminal proceedings if the prosecutor fails to do so. When the government itself may be directly implicated, that is, when high-ranking officials are subject to prosecution, special mechanisms may be necessary to ensure both independence and accountability. The US system provides for independent counsel to investigate high-ranking US officials accused of crimes. If the US Attorney-General believes there are reasonable grounds to warrant further investigation, he or she must first apply to a three-judge panel of the US Court of Appeal for the District of Columbia Circuit (often known as the Special Division) to appoint the independent counsel.[48]

E. Legitimacy

Lack of public confidence in the prosecution is unfortunately common in many developing countries where prosecutors must overcome a history of unequal application of the law. In countries with histories of human rights abuses, prosecution of the perpetrators of such crimes is a critical step in demonstrating the equal application of the law and can also serve as an important public rallying point in support of rule of law reforms. An impartial and effective prosecution service can lend legitimacy to rule of law reforms, particularly in countries transitioning from inquisitorial to adversarial modes of procedure, where the prosecutor can be an important leader in the move to oral advocacy.[49] Prosecutors can also help to anchor criminal justice reforms within the existing community by embarking on diversion programs and community education. Susanne Walther points out that American prosecutors are "political leaders in education, prevention and treatment efforts. In particular, in the vast area of 'diversion', i.e., the handling of cases not considered proper for formal accusation in court, prosecutors have authority to refer suspects who do not wish to contest the charges to pre-trial diversion programs aimed at prevention, education and treatment."[50]

Improving the relationship between prosecutors and crime victims is an important means for improving the legitimacy of the prosecution and the criminal justice system more generally. A study by the South African Law Commission reveals that victims often feel they have been treated rudely and insensitively by the police and ignored by prosecutors, who fail to keep victims

---

[48] Ambos, *supra* note 12 at 93.
[49] Duce, *supra* note 7 at 3.
[50] Walther, *supra* note 13 at 289.

up to date with the case.[51] The South African Law Commission finds that the prosecutors have a duty to "recognize and promote the interests of the victim."[52] Prosecutors can discharge this duty by keeping in contact with victims, updating them on the status of their cases, and informing them about the nature of the criminal justice process. Doing so not only benefits the victim, but can also aid the prosecution because victims who feel ignored by the prosecution often make poor witnesses as they are unprepared for examinations and unfamiliar with court procedures. In addition, better treatment of victims can improve the quality of the justice system as a whole: "It is hoped that crime victims who are treated well will be more likely to participate constructively during the investigation and trial ... and report crime in the future, even in the face of intimidation."[53]

II.   EXPERIENCE WITH PROSECUTORIAL REFORMS

A.   Latin America

The move towards oral advocacy described in Chapter 2 on judicial reform has broad implications for prosecutorial systems that often previously had very narrowly defined duties. The new adversarial systems have restrained the power of judges, who had exercised an almost complete monopoly over cases in the inquisitorial system, and has strengthened the role of prosecutors, who can now direct case investigations.

In Guatemala in 1986, before procedural reforms and while the country was still embroiled in civil war, there were 30 poorly paid, poorly trained prosecutors. In 1992 oral advocacy was introduced, and in 1994 the Public Ministry (prosecution service) was established as an entity formally independent of all three branches of government; by 2002 there were 175 prosecutors in the country. Nevertheless, Guatemala has often failed to redress military human rights violations of the past, a problem that gains particular importance due to the historical context of civil war. In the highly publicized murder case of Bishop Juan Gerardi, the prosecutor assigned to the case reported being subject to anonymous threats and military surveillance and, according to a local citizens' organization (FAMDEGUA), was forced into exile after serving subpoenas on

---

[51]   South Africa Law Commission, *Sentencing Restorative Justice: Compensation for Victims of Crime and Victim Empowerment* (Pretoria: SALC Issue Paper 7) cited in Stone *et al.*, *supra* note 3 at 26.

[52]   *Ibid.*

[53]   Stone *et al.*, *supra* note 3 at 26.

military officials.[54] In spite of threats, convictions of high-ranking officers were secured in 2001, but threats to prosecutors remain a problem nonetheless.[55] Further, serious allegations of corruption have been levelled against the Public Ministry. These accusations allege highly politicized appointments despite formal administrative separation and the permeation of the Ministry by former military personnel who, "[i]nstead of taking steps to protect witnesses ... have relayed ... second-hand threats"[56] to witnesses from the military. Finally, the Ministry is accused of incompetence. Unregulated, outdated legal education produces a weak pool of potential prosecutors, while low salaries and low esteem surrounding the prosecutorial office have made it difficult to attract experienced lawyers into the pool.

The effects of a new code of criminal procedure were particularly significant in Chile, where criminal justice had traditionally been run almost entirely by judges relying on written submissions. Establishing a public prosecution office meant the creation of a new institution,[57] and therefore the prosecutor's office is staffed primarily by young, inexperienced professionals. Further, the reform of the justice system produced a prosecutorial system lacking existing procedures; decisions as to whether and how to follow up on cases are left almost fully to the judgment and discretion of individual prosecutors, and the absence of upper echelon supervision creates few incentives to make timely decisions. In order to appease demanding private parties, and in the absence of instructions to act otherwise, prosecutors agree to leave open cases that might otherwise have been quickly closed; as a result, resources are wasted and more importantly prosecutorial caseloads grow to unmanageable levels. In cases where the Public Prosecutor's office has issued regulations, they have often been vague, restrictive and unresponsive to continuing experience.[58] Prosecutors in Chile have also faced some resistance from police. In much of Latin America, under the inquisitorial system police ran investigations quite freely and submitted their evidence to a judge.[59] With the new focus on the importance of prosecutors, police were

---

[54] Nathan Heasley *et al.*, "Impunity in Guatemala: The State's Failure to Provide Justice in the Massacre Cases" (2001) 16 *Am. U. Int'l L. Rev.* 1115 at 1142–3.

[55] USAID Office of Democracy and Governance, "Achievements in Building and Maintaining the Rule of Law: MSI's Studies in LAC, E&E, AFR, and ANE" (Occasional Paper Series November 2002, PN-ACR-220) at 70 ["Achievements"].

[56] Heasley *et al.*, *supra* note 54 at 1151.

[57] Cristián Riego, *Comparative Report: "Judicial Reform Processes In Latin America" Follow-up Project* (Judicial Studies Center of the Americas: 2003) at 8, online: http://www.cejamericas.org/.

[58] *Ibid.* at 14.

[59] Linn Hammergren, "Institutional Strengthening and Justice Reform" (USAID PN-ACD-020) at 35.

required to cooperate with and in effect were subordinated to the prosecutorial function.

In El Salvador, early attempts at prosecutorial reform were unsuccessful. In 1983, USAID reacted to an absence of prosecutorial investigation by providing training in sophisticated investigation techniques and establishing a special investigative unit; in the result, they were disappointed by the "ineffectual use of the former and the highly politicized and often abusive operations of the latter."[60] As discussion of a new code of criminal procedure began in the 1990s, reform efforts again focused on the prosecutorial institution, or *Fiscalia*, and found the system deficient in many ways. Remuneration was very low, thus hindering the attraction of qualified personnel, while any hiring or promotion that was done was based on political associations: "Political and personal pressures or simple bribes tended to decide the outcome of most cases – although the judges were the usual targets, *fiscales*[61] also participated in the process."[62] Further, while prosecutors were supposed to work with the police in an investigative role, in practice they rarely did so. Through the mid-1990s, reform was heavily focused on decentralizing organizational structures and training of prosecutors, and not surprisingly into the late 1990s problems persisted. Salaries were still low, staff in prosecutorial offices were lacking in basic administrative skills, and corruption "was a factor in such basic decisions as the distribution of cases."[63] After the new criminal procedures code was finally enacted in 1998 resistance similar to that described in Chile was felt from police unwilling to sacrifice power.[64] In more recent years, budgets have expanded in the *Fiscalia*, and throughout the justice system, officials found to be corrupt, including prosecutors, have been released. Nevertheless, it "is believed that many corrupt officials continue in office; this is a matter of intense public debate and the subject of a recent investigation and report by a special prosecutor."[65]

B.   Central and Eastern Europe

During Soviet rule, the prosecutorial function was vested in the Procuracy, a Russian institution holding broad powers of supervision over courts and admin-

---

[60]   *Ibid.* at 38.

[61]   Members of the *Fiscalia*, i.e. prosecutors.

[62]   Hammergren, *supra* note 59 at 39.

[63]   *Ibid.* at 41.

[64]   IADB, "I'll See You in Court!: New Oral Procedures Give Prosecutors and Defenders the Leading Roles in Criminal Trials" online at: http://www.iadb.org/idbamerica/archive/stories/1999/eng/e1299s8.htm.

[65]   "Achievements," *supra* note 55.

istrative branches of government. "Invariably party members in excellent standing, they were at the pinnacle of the local power elite,"[66] and are often described as the "eye of the party."[67] In its prosecutorial function, the procurator supervised criminal investigations, had absolute discretion in the granting of search warrants, prosecuted cases in court, and most importantly supervised the functioning of the courts, a power that added a severe accusatorial bias to proceedings and significantly disadvantaged the defence. Acting as a prosecutor in the Western sense has not been a substantial part of the procurator's duties; due to the inquisitorial nature of criminal procedure, as late as 1996 procurators would not even appear at over 50% of trials, as the judge could perform those functions in his or her place.[68]

In 1991, a group of nine academics published a detailed criticism of the Soviet judicial system, demanding that the procuratorial office be reduced to its prosecutorial functions. Forces within the procuracy fought these changes vigorously. Procurator General Valentin Stepankov pushed through a 1992 Law on the Procuracy of the Russian Federation, maintaining the procuracy as an institution "charged with 'supervising the implementation of laws by local legislative and executive bodies, administrative control organs, legal entities, public organizations, and officials, as well as the lawfulness of their acts.'"[69] In 1993, when a draft law circulated "calling for the creation of an independent investigatory agency,"[70] procuracy officials filed a case with the Constitutional Court alleging that a reduction in their authority was illegal. While the law was passed, Parliament failed, at least initially, to provide staff for the agency. In 1993, the office of the procuracy also protested the proposed institution of jury trials; although the law passed, it was a full decade before widespread implementation began. In 1995, the two sides of the debate each submitted draft laws to the Duma for a new law on the procuracy. Not surprisingly, one draft supported the transformation of the procuracy into a purely prosecutorial office and the institution of an adversarial system, and the other the retention of supervisory powers and the then-current system of justice.[71] Under the final law passed by the Duma, "the

---

[66]   Leon Aron, "Russia Reinvents the Rule of Law" (American Enterprise Institute Online, 2002) online at: http://www.aei.org/publications/contentID.2003020615462159/default.asp.

[67]   Stephen C. Thaman, "Reform of the Procuracy and the Bar" (1996) 3 *Parker Sch. J.E. Eur. L.* 1, at 5.

[68]   *Ibid.* at 13.

[69]   Gordon B. Smith, "The Struggle Over the Procuracy," in Peter H. Solomon Jr. (ed.), *Reforming Justice in Russia, 1864–1996: Power, Culture, and the Limits of Legal Order* (Armonk, NY: M.E. Sharpe, Inc., 1997) 348 at 358 [Smith, "Procuracy"].

[70]   *Ibid.* at 360.

[71]   Thaman, *supra* note 67 at 13–18.

Procuracy retained most of its traditional powers and functions,"[72] although it no longer supervised courts.

Smith points out that the battle over the procuracy was far more nuanced than the crusade of valiant reformers attempting to uproot a power-mongering elite. Supporters of the procuracy had argued that, executing a strangely dual function, the procuracy had always been charged not just with the implementation of party policy but also acted as the representative of the citizen against executive action; by way of "procuratorial protests," procurators would, for instance, invalidate the imposition of illegal administrative fines if they found a basis for a citizen complaint. As of 1996, the procuracy received over 100,000 complaints per year resulting in 13,000 formal protests; Smith argues that it is not entirely clear that a court system already experiencing severe backlogs and with its own questions with regard to independence is better placed to address these complaints.[73] Reformers countered that the procuracy often pursued complaints only when it was in the interests of the state, and certainly not when complaints related to powerful party interests.[74] Smith also acknowledges that there is an issue of citizen trust, as the procuracy's history of bias has made many citizens sceptical of its value.[75] The protracted nature of this debate seems to have indirectly impeded the evolution of the prosecution. Reluctant to sacrifice its powers of oversight and assume a greater role in prosecutorial functions, the procuracy fought against changes, such as the jury trial, which would have moved the Russian criminal system closer to an adversarial style.[76] It was only in 2002 that a new Code of Criminal Procedure was enacted. In the meantime, the American Enterprise Institute for Public Policy Research identified in 2002 as problems with the Russian prosecution "meagre salaries, insufficient education and training, and not infrequently outright incompetence among judges and prosecutors alike."[77]

The politicized nature of the procuracy, and hence the prosecution, is also exemplified in the experiences of a series of Procurators General. In 1993, relying on rising crime rates in Russia as a way of emphasizing the importance of a strong procuracy, the institution adopted a strict anti-crime stance. This position placed the procuracy in line with that of the anti-Yeltsin Duma majority

---

[72] Gordon B. Smith, "The Disjuncture between Legal Reform and Law Enforcement: The Challenge Facing the Post-Yeltsin Leadership," in Gordon B. Smith (ed.), *State-Building in Russia: The Yeltsin Legacy and the Challenge of the Future* (Armonk, NY: M.E. Sharpe, 1999) 101–22 at 110.

[73] *Ibid.* at 360–61.

[74] *Ibid.* at 353.

[75] *Ibid.* at 117–18.

[76] Thaman, *supra* note 67 at 9.

[77] Aron, *supra* note 66 at 12.

and pulled it onto the side of the Parliament in an emerging conflict between it and President Yeltsin. In April, Procurator General Stepankov arrested two top Yeltsin aides for criminal behaviour, and announced that the procuracy would focus on corruption in the executive rather than legislative branch. In May, the Supreme Court held that Stepankov had committed legal violations in a 1991 investigation; Yeltsin pressured him to resign, and Aleksei Kazannik, a professor with ties to Yeltsin, was appointed Procurator General. In 1994, the Duma awarded amnesty to organizers of the October 1993 coup. Yeltsin opposed the move and ordered Kazannik not to release the prisoners; when Kazannik refused, Yeltsin forced his resignation, and appointed Aleksei Iliushenko. The Duma attempted to frustrate the move by refusing to accept Kazannik's resignation or confirm Iliushenko's appointment, but Yeltsin simply left Iliushenko in place as the "Acting" Procurator General.[78] In 1995, Iliushenko was also forced to resign, and in 1996 was arrested on charges of bribery and abuse of office.[79]

In Bulgaria, the formal subordination of the procuracy to other branches of government and the relaxation of its dependence on the executive occurred more quickly and with less controversy than in Russia. As Holmes points out, the Russian procuracy was "a proud instrument of centralization" on which the "unsteered devolution of power to the regions ... has inflicted great strains;"[80] presumably this centralizing effect was less pronounced away from the upper echelons of the institution in Moscow. In fact, Zdravka Kalaydjieva seems to argue that in Bulgaria problems with the prosecution have stemmed from reform efforts that happened too quickly, without due regard for how a newly independent, depoliticized prosecutorial office would function. In Kalaydjieva's words, "[t]he primary concern of reformers, during this euphoric early period of democratization, was to emancipate the judicial power from executive supervision and to draw sharp lines between the three branches of government, rather than to spell out clearly their appropriate internal functions."[81] Procurators were given life tenure following a three-year probationary period, and were supervised by an independent Supreme Judicial Council. However, according to Kalaydjieva, due to poorly defined duties the oversight of the council has been illusory; for instance, two procurators who were subject to disciplinary procedures by the council and demoted to a lower position were simply re-hired by the Procurator to work in his office, "and the council had no legal means to overrule or even

---

[78] Smith, "Procuracy," *supra* note 69 at 361–7.

[79] Thaman, *supra* note 67 at 16–17.

[80] Stephen Holmes, "The Procuracy and its Problems" (1999) 8:1/2 *E. Eur. Const. Rev.* 76 at 78.

[81] Zdravka Kalaydjieva, "The Procuracy and its Problems: Bulgaria" (1999) 8:1/2 *E. Eur. Const. Rev.* 79 at 80.

protest his decision."[82] Further, little attention was paid to legally limiting the discretion of procurators or instituting judicial review of procuratorial action. Accused persons do not appear to have the right to judicial review until trial begins, and until 1998 did not have the right to challenge periodically pre-trial detention orders in court. While for most crimes there is a one-year limit on detention during the process of a criminal investigation, once the procurator has completed his or her investigation there is no maximum time within which an indictment must be heard in court. Procuratorial discretion has also been abused in "dozens" of criminal investigations of journalists who have criticized the procuracy in newspapers. One journalist was even arrested for asking the procurator "provocative questions" during an interview.[83]

In 1991 in Romania a new Constitution entrenched a series of principles of prosecutorial independence in an attempt to break away from the "strong procuracy and ... weak judiciary"[84] that characterized the system under Ceausescu. The prosecution is now a function within the Public Ministry, which is in turn accountable to the Ministry of Justice. Selection, promotion and discipline of both judges and prosecutors are vested in a new institution, the Superior Council of the Magistracy, composed of ten judges and five public prosecutors selected for four-year terms by a joint session of the Chamber of Deputies and the Senate.[85] Potential prosecutors must either undergo a training program at the new National Institute of the Magistracy or pass an examination administered by the Minister of Justice. The Constitution mandates that all selected magistrates are obligated to undergo continuing education at the Institute, but limited funds have restricted the number of courses available. Judges and prosecutors are forbidden by the Constitution to be associated with a political party, engage in public activities with a political official or participate in "the exercise of trading activities, (or) ... the administration or management of trading or civil companies."[86] Potential candidates left off the nomination list by the Council of the Magistracy have a right of appeal to the Supreme Court of Justice, whose decision is then final. According to Viorica Costiniu, Judge of the Bucharest Tribunal, most new prosecutors are young, recent graduates from the University,[87] a circumstance

---

[82]   *Ibid.* at 81.

[83]   *Ibid.* at 83.

[84]   Monica Macovei, "The Procuracy and its Problems: Romania" (1999) 8:1/2 *E. Eur. Const. Rev.* 95 at 95.

[85]   Recently altered to allow for 17 members.

[86]   Viorica Costiniu, "The Judiciary System in Romania" (presentation at the "Global Forum on Fighting Corruption: Safeguarding Integrity Among Justice and Security Officials," Washington, DC, February 24–6, 1999) at 3, online at: http://www.nobribes.org/Documents/GlobalForum99/Romania_Judiciary_GF99.pdf.

[87]   *Ibid.* at 2.

that may be partially responsible for an EC observation that Romanian prosecutors are in need of greater training.[88] More recently, in 2002, Romania established the National Anti-Corruption Prosecutor's Office. Formerly a department within the general prosecutor's office, it now holds a "special status" and operates independently of the General Office.

One frequent criticism of the Romanian system is that prosecutors have the right to bring extraordinary appeals against judicial decisions, a mechanism under which final decisions of the High Court of Cassation and Justice (formerly the Supreme Court) are invalidated by the Prosecutor-General and returned to the Court for retrial.[89] Commentators have argued that this power has often been invoked in property disputes in order to "restore the balance in favour of current tenants, among whom are many of the former communist elite."[90] Over the years, the bases under which the Prosecutor can initiate such an appeal have expanded and it has been suggested that judges of the High Court, in retrying such a case, feel enormous pressure to reverse the decision. One prosecutor in particular, Joita Tanase, has attracted attention as a specific example of a politicized prosecutorial function, as he "used the recourse of the extraordinary appeal to invalidate the election of a mayor running against the government party in a village, to rescue the generals who had ordered firing at demonstrators in 1989, and to protect the bankers who had crippled state banks with bad loans in 1994–96."[91] Extended powers under the new anti-corruption system, such as longer preventive detention, create the potential for even broader abuses of power. The EC argues that selection of members of the Superior Council of the Magistracy, charged with nominating proposals for prosecutorial appointments, lacks sufficient transparency. The EC argues further that the placement of the Institute of Magistracy within the Ministry of Justice compromises its independence by requiring approval of budgets and programs by the Ministry.[92]

---

[88] European Commission, "Justice and Home Affairs in the EU Enlargement Process – Romania," online at: http://europa.eu.int/comm/justice_home/fsj/enlargement/romania/printer/fsj_enlarge_romania_en.htm.

[89] Though, under Government Emergency Ordinance 58/2003, this power has been repealed in civil cases, it is still in force with respect to criminal decisions.

[90] EECR, "Constitutional Watch: A Country-by-Country Update on Constitutional Politics in Eastern Europe and the ex-USSR: Romania" (2002) 11:3 *E. Eur. Const. Rev.* 39 at 41.

[91] *Ibid.* at 41.

[92] European Commission, *2002 Regular Report on Romania's Progress Towards Accession* (COM 2002 700) at 25, online at: http://europa.eu.int/comm/enlargement/report2002/ro_en.pdf.

C. Africa

The crime rate in South Africa is one of the highest in the world while the conviction rate is among the lowest.[93] This scenario has led USAID to focus its legal assistance to South Africa on the criminal justice system. The agency describes the major changes that occurred in the prosecutorial system in the immediate post-apartheid period. Formerly separate prosecutorial systems were amalgamated into one system called the National Prosecuting Authority. Attempts have been made to tailor hiring so that it would be more inclusive of the marginalized black population, although this often resulted in the appointment of inexperienced prosecutors. To address this problem, USAID has assisted the government in establishing the Justice College. Since its inception in 1997, the Justice College has offered a period of training for aspiring prosecutors by experienced prosecutors. According to USAID, the feedback regarding this first stage of the program was "extremely positive," which led to the expansion of the program to include training for working prosecutors in 1999. This second stage operates with funding from USAID and other donors, and it is expected that the South African government will be responsible for it in the future. Prosecutors have also received salary increases with the hope of reducing their movement to the private sector. With assistance from USAID, a Sexual Offences and Community Affairs Unit has been established within the National Prosecuting Authority; it is intended that the Unit work with NGOs to increase public awareness of domestic violence, sexual offences and child support obligations.[94]

In 1996, 29 specialized courts that deal only with rape cases were established in response to the high number of rape cases and low rate of convictions. Prosecutors in these courts are specially trained in issues surrounding sexual assault and work exclusively in that area. This focus appears to have been successful: in the specialized courts relative to traditional courts, the average time to trial is lower and the conviction rate is higher. Due to these successes, the government plans to add many more such courts. Eventually, the plan is to prosecute all sexual assault cases through these courts.[95]

In 2002 USAID entered into an alliance with the Department of Justice (DOJ) and Business Against Crime (BAC), a non-profit organization. The purpose of the alliance is to render the DOJ more efficient through the decentralization of court support services and an improved case management system. The alliance

---

[93]   The conviction rate in South Africa is around 8%, online at: http://www.usaid. gov/locations/sub-saharan_africa/countries/southafrica/.

[94]   "Achievements," *supra* note 55 at 145.

[95]   "S. Africa Finds 'Rape Courts' Work," *The Christian Science Monitor* (January 29, 2003), online at http://www.csmonitor.com/2003/0129/p01s04-woaf.html.

also targets white-collar crime, which has had a particularly negative effect on the South African economy, accounting for 30% of all business failures and consuming 5% of business revenue, and discouraging foreign investment. This objective is addressed through the establishment of courts that are permanently assigned to deal exclusively with commercial crimes, including fraud and corruption. By 2002 the conviction rate in these commercial courts was 94%, with 50% of all accused pleading guilty, and 33% of convictions resulting in jail time with no option to pay a fine. Organized crime is also highly problematic in South Africa, and is therefore the target of a USAID/US DOJ combined project. Finally, given rampant violent crime, much of which is directed against women and children, USAID supports NGO initiatives that provide victim support services, prepare child victims to testify in court, and monitor cases involving domestic and other forms of violence against women and children as they move through the legal system.[96]

D. Asia

Criminal procedure in China was provided for in the 1979 Criminal Procedure Law (CPL) until revisions were made in 1996. Under the terms of the CPL, the procuratorate had discretionary powers to initiate a public prosecution, dismiss a case, exempt a case from prosecution, and remand a case for further investigation.[97] This broad discretionary power often led to abuse of power through corrupt practices by letting a guilty person off the hook or declaring an innocent person guilty. Under the revised CPL, the practice of exemption from prosecution was abolished because of criticism concerning its lack of due process and arbitrary nature. Furthermore, under the revised CPL, supplementary investigations were limited. Previously, there were no limits on the number of investigations the procuratory could request from the police. In theory, a suspect could be held indefinitely as long as the procuratory continued to request further investigations. Between 1997 and 1999, there was an increase in the number of defendants who received a lighter sentence, fine, probation, or other sentences without imprisonment.[98] The courts now handle many of the suspects that would have been exempt from prosecution.

The 1996 revisions to the CPL also introduced the presumption of innocence and the trial procedure moved from an inquisitorial to a more adversarial sys-

---

[96] Online at: http://www.sn.apc.org/usaidsa/uss01.html.

[97] Mike P.H. Chu, "Criminal Procedure Reform in the People's Republic of China: The Dilemma of Crime Control and Regime Legitimacy" (2001) 18 *UCLA Pac. Basin L.J.* 157 at 178 ["Criminal Procedure Reform"].

[98] *Ibid.*

tem.[99] In March 1997, the National People's Congress adopted a revised Criminal Code, granting equal protection under the law and a proportional sentencing scheme. In 1995, China's Procurates Law was introduced in order to protect prosecutors from public interference.

After the revised CPL took effect in 1997, acquittal rates rose from 0.66% to 1.03% in 1998 and dropped slightly to 0.97% in 1999.[100] Although the increase in acquittals seems minor, it is unprecedented in Chinese court rulings. The statistic suggests that after the change, judges were not as quick to convict defendants, which is consistent with the presumption of innocence. However, courts are still not free from political interference. In 1999, there was a slight decrease in acquittal rates which was likely caused by higher conviction rates faced by Falun Gong members during the government's crackdown on the organization during that year.[101] Furthermore, extensive investigations by the National People's Congress Standing Committee in six selected provinces, autonomous regions, and cities revealed that the CPL had not been fully implemented.[102] The committee attributed failures in the implementation of revised law to misunderstandings of the law by law enforcement officials.

The Chinese procuracy also continues to maintain broad powers to supervise individual cases. Under these supervisory powers, procuratorates can petition to have cases reconsidered, even when the normal appeal process has been exhausted.[103] In 1999, procuratorates had 14,069 cases reconsidered under such powers, and judgments were revised in 3,185 of these cases.[104]

In Indonesia, one of the greatest problems that the prosecution faces is a lack of education and training, which is part of the larger issue of competence. The Indonesian legal system does not work to advance those who are most competent. In fact, a recent Final Report of the Audit of the Public Prosecution Service of the Republic of Indonesia stated that performance is measured by "loyalty, honesty, and cooperation rather than tangible results."[105] Little has been done

---

[99]   Li Zhenghui and Wang Zhenmin, "The Developing Human Rights and Rule of Law in Legal Philosophy and in Political Practice in China, 1978–2000", online at: http://dex1.tsd.unifi.it/jg/en/index.htm?surveys?rol/wang.htm.

[100]   "Criminal Procedure Reform," *supra* note 97 at 187.

[101]   *Ibid.*

[102]   Mei-Ying Hung, "China's WTO Commitment on Independent Review: An Opportunity for Political Reform" (2002) Carnegie Endowment for International Peace, Working Paper No. 5.

[103]   Randall Peerenboom, *China's Long March Toward the Rule of Law* (Cambridge: Cambridge University Press, 2002) 313.

[104]   *Ibid.*

[105]   David Cohen, "Intended to Fail: Trials before the Ad Hoc Human Rights Court in Jakarta" (August 2003) The Occasional Paper Series, International Centre for Transnational Justice at 48 ["Intended to Fail"].

to redress this problem. On the formation of the Ad Hoc Human Rights Court, it was suggested that training be provided to public prosecutors.[106] However, most agencies viewed this training as unproductive as the government shows no will in prosecuting cases of violence. In 2000, the Asia Foundation began funding a training program for judges and prosecutors in Jakarta.

The Public Prosecution Service (PPS) in Indonesia has traditionally had a strong military culture. This militarization serves to ensure a commitment to "the values and goals of the state's policies rather than the legal system and values of justice that it normally serves."[107] This militarization has also led to corruption and undue influence within the prosecution. A recent self-assessment report pinpointed strengthening investigative and prosecutorial capacities by fostering inter-agency cooperation and ensuring that investigation and prosecution are free from improper pressures and controls as a necessary goal for Indonesia.[108] In an effort to achieve this goal, an agreement has been reached between the Public Servants Wealth Audit Commission and the Attorney-General and the police to collaborate in the future in providing training on conducting investigations.

In the Philippines, the National Prosecution Service (NPS) suffers from inadequate salaries, lack of core training, no institutionalized system for continuing legal education, lack of physical space, equipment and resources, absence of clear performance indicators, low morale, weak information services and lack of regional autonomy.[109] However, the greatest weakness of the prosecutorial body in the Philippines is that criminal prosecution is mostly privatized. Complainants are forced to hire "private prosecutors" to carry out the work of indolent, incompetent or suborned public prosecutors.[110] The Anti-Corruption Initiative for Asia-Pacific has approached the problem of corruption in the Philippines on three fronts, building up institutional resources, strengthening

---

[106]   Hilmar Farid and Rikardo Simarmatra, "The Struggle for Truth and Justice: A Survey of Transitional Justice Initiatives Throughout Indonesia" (2004) The Occasional Paper Series, International Centre for Transitional Justice at 49.

[107]   "Intended to Fail," *supra* note 105 at 49.

[108]   Jak Jabes and Frederic Wehrlé, "Anti-Corruption Policies in Asia and the Pacific: Self Assessment Report Indonesia," ADB/OECD Anti-Corruption Initiatives for Asia and the Pacific (2004) at 6.

[109]   Supreme Court of the Philippines, Department of Justice and United Nations Development Programme, "The Other Pillars of Justice Through Reforms in the Department of Justice: Diagnostic Report IX" (2003), online at: http://www.apjr-sc-phil.org/pub-reports.

[110]   Harry Blair and Gary Hansen, "Weighing in on the Scales of Justice: Strategic Approaches for Donor-Supported Rule of Law Programs," USAID Program and Operations Assessment Report No. 7 (1994), online at: http://www.usaid.gov/our_work/democracy_and_governance/publications/pdfs/pnaax280.pdf.

individual and institutional confidence, and strategic and enhanced private and public sector involvement.[111]

The biggest problem that the Korean prosecution faces is abuse of power. Korean prosecutors do not view their role as subordinate to that of the judge. They view themselves as equals, a mentality that is inconsistent with the adversarial system.[112] Korean prosecutors control prosecutorial powers under the Criminal Procedure Act and through indictments.[113] In the past, public prosecutors have indicted many political dissenters on charges of violating the National Security Law (NSL).

Legislation has been enacted to cut the ties between the prosecution and the ruling party. Previously, it was common practice for top prosecutors faithful to the President or his party to be appointed to prestigious public offices or recruited to the President's party after retirement. In 1997, an amendment to the Prosecution Act provided that the Attorney-General should not be appointed to public office for two years following retirement and it restricted participation by prosecutors in any political party.[114] However, later that year, nine high-ranking prosecutors challenged the constitutionality of the amendment. Korea's Constitutional Court agreed with the applicants, thus demonstrating the need for other measures to ensure the independence of prosecution.

In 2000, Korea adopted some of the recommendations of the Organization of Economic Cooperation and Development (OECD) from its convention on bribery into the Korean Criminal Code. Korea enacted a special law, the Foreign Bribery Prevention Act (FBPA), with the purpose of fully incorporating the OECD into its national law.[115] Currently the set of legal instruments available to combat transnational bribery is more powerful than those used to combat national bribery.

---

[111]   Simeon Marcelo, "Combating Corruption in the Philippines," ADB/OECD Anti-Corruption Initiative for Asia-Pacific, 4th Regional Anti-Corruption Conference for Asia and the Pacific.

[112]   Jae Won Kim, "The Ideal and Reality of the Korean Legal Profession" (2001) 2 *Asian-Pacific Law and Policy Journal* 45 at 55.

[113]   *Ibid.*

[114]   *Ibid.* at 57.

[115]   Jong Bum Kim, "Korean Implementation of the OECD Bribery Convention: Implications for Global Efforts to Fight Corruption" (2000) 17 *UCLA Pacific Basin Law Journal* 245 at 264.

III. CONCLUSION

The evidence reviewed in this chapter suggests that in many developing countries, particularly in Latin America and other countries with historical traditions of inquisitorial rather than adversarial criminal proceedings, prosecutors have played a minor role in prosecuting crimes, relative to the police and the presiding members of the judiciary. In other developing and transition economies, such as the former Soviet Union, prosecutors have played a much larger role and often have been the local eye of the incumbent political regime in overseeing broad applications of laws in local communities as well as legal institutions, including courts. Like police, prosecutors in many developing countries have often been poorly paid, poorly qualified, and poorly trained, and have been vulnerable to corruption by both members of incumbent political regimes and private parties.

With respect to the three classes of impediments to rule of law reform identified in Chapter 1, resource constraints have clearly been a factor in many developing countries, but again as with police reform, without changes in institutional structures and related incentive structures, effectuated by new mechanisms of prosecutorial independence and accountability, simply paying incompetent or corrupt prosecutors higher wages is unlikely to yield significant benefits in terms of improved prosecutorial performance.

With respect to social/cultural/historical practices and beliefs, the change from an inquisitorial to an adversarial form of criminal proceeding obviously necessitates a reconceptualization and expansion of the role of prosecutors. Progress that has been made in many developing countries in this respect suggests that entrenched mindsets as to the role of prosecutors, relative to police and the judiciary, are amenable to change over time. Where prosecutors have been conceived of as agents for the protection of the incumbent political regime (as in the former Soviet Union or China), disentangling the prosecutorial function from the executive arm of government is a larger challenge to the established role of prosecutors, but again experience suggests that at least in some countries (such as China) modest progress has been made in this respect.

With respect to political economy constraints on reforming the role of the prosecutor, obviously these are most acute in military or authoritarian regimes (such as the former Soviet Union), where the prosecutor has been viewed as the local eye of the incumbent political regime. De-politicizing the role of the prosecutor in these countries is obviously a major and largely unmet challenge. Again, as with police reform, external agencies through the provision of financial and technical assistance can support domestic political constituencies committed to a reconceptualization of the prosecutorial function (as we elaborate more fully in the concluding chapter of this book).

5. Correctional institutions

I. NORMATIVE BENCHMARKS

Several international documents elucidate how the rights guaranteed to all persons by the Universal Declaration of Human Rights and the International Covenant on Civil and Political Rights[1] translate into specific standards for the treatment of prisoners.[2] The United Nations Standard Minimum Rules for the Treatment of Prisoners, adopted by the UN Economic and Social Council in 1957, is the most comprehensive of these guidelines.[3] The Standard Minimum Rules set detailed standards for the condition of food, clothing, housing, medical services, discipline and punishment practices, institutional arrangements and other aspects of prison conditions. Other sets of standards, codes

---

[1]   Article 10 of the ICCPR states:

1. All persons deprived of their liberty shall be treated with humanity and with respect for the inherent dignity of the human person.
2.
(a) Accused persons shall, save in exceptional circumstances, be segregated from convicted persons and shall be subject to separate treatment appropriate to their status as unconvicted persons;
(b) Accused juvenile persons shall be separated from adults and brought as speedily as possible for adjudication.
3. The penitentiary system shall comprise treatment of prisoners the essential aim of which shall be their reformation and social rehabilitation. Juvenile offenders shall be segregated from adults and be accorded treatment appropriate to their age and legal status.

International Covenant on Civil and Political Rights, G.A. res. 2200A (XXI), 21 UN GAOR Supp. (No. 16) at 52, UN Doc. A/6316 (1966), 999 UNTS 171, entered into force March 23, 1976.
[2]   These documents include the United Nations Standard Minimum Rules for the Treatment of Prisoners, Body of Principles for the Protection of All Persons under any Form of Detention or Imprisonment, Basic Principles for the Treatment of Prisoners, the United Nations Standard Minimum Rules for the Administration of Juvenile Justice.
[3]   *Standard Minimum Rules for the Treatment of Prisoners*. Adopted by the First United Nations Congress on the Prevention of Crime and the Treatment of Offenders, held at Geneva in 1955, and approved by the Economic and Social Council by its resolution 663 C (XXIV) of July 31, 1957 and 2076 (LXII) of May 13, 1977.

of conduct and operations manuals from a wide variety of national governments, regional and international bodies and non-governmental organizations (NGOs) abound.[4]

The opposable ideals of independence and accountability do not appear to be as prevalent in the correctional literature as they have been, for instance, in relation to the judiciary or the prosecution. In fact, "independence" generally seems not to be of significant concern. In its place, however, is a serious preoccupation with achieving professional, civilian systems of corrections geared towards retribution and rehabilitation, while also maintaining basic protections for prison inmates. For instance, the first strategy of the *New Agenda for Penal Reform*[5] is to develop a system of "Restorative Justice," the

---

[4] *Draft Inter-American Declaration Governing the Rights and the Care of Persons Deprived of Liberty*, developed by the government of Costa Rica in conjunction with Penal Reform International, online at: http://www.penalreform.org/download/Declarati on%20interamericaine_eng.pdf; *Kampala Declaration on Prison Conditions in Africa*, adopted by 47 countries at the First Pan-African Conference on Penal Reform and Prison Conditions in Africa, Kampala, Uganda, September 1996 (adopted by the United Nations, Resolution 1997/36 of the Economic and Social Council, *International Cooperation for the Improvement of Prison Conditions*); *The Ouagadougou Declaration on Accelerating Prison and Penal Reform in Africa* and *The Ouagadougou Plan of Action* (both adopted by the African Commission on Human and Peoples' Rights, 34th Ordinary Session, 2003, in Banjul, the Gambia); Penal Reform International, *Making Standards Work*, 2nd edn (2001). *Making Standards Work* is a highly detailed document that discusses and elaborates on standards developed by other international bodies, such as the Standard Minimum Rules. It was drafted in four stages, including an international conference held in the Netherlands in 1994. (*Ibid.* at 1); American Correctional Association, *Standards for Adult Correctional Institutions*, 3rd edn (College Park, MD: American Correctional Association, 1990); Nancy Neveloff Dubler (ed.), *Standards for Health Services in Correctional Institutions*, 2nd edn (Washington, DC: American Public Health Association, 1986); Washington, DC : American Public Health Association Washington, DC : American Public Health AssociationInternational Center for Prison Studies, Guidance Notes, online at: http://www.kcl.ac.uk/depsta/rel/icps/downloads.html; European Committee for the Prevention of Torture and Inhuman or Degrading Treatment or Punishment, *The CPT Standards* (CPT/Inf/E (2002) 1 – Rev. 2004). *International Prison Policy Development Instrument* (1st edn, July 1, 2001). (This document is designed as a policy guide for correctional institutions. It is an initiative of the International Centre for Criminal Justice Reform and Criminal Justice Policy, founded by the Canadian government, in conjunction with representatives from several countries, particularly in Africa, as well as representatives of UN organizations. The document is based on existing UN prison standards.)

[5] The "New Agenda" is a document adopted in 1999 by governmental and non-governmental representatives from 50 countries across five continents at the International Penal Reform Conference. *A New Agenda for Penal Reform* ("International Penal Reform Conference," April 13–17, 1999, Royal Holloway College, University of London, Egham, Surrey, UK).

basic principle of which is to "restore the balance between the victim, the offender and the community."[6] Moreover the agenda encourages conceiving of the prison system "as a public service ... transparent and open to public scrutiny."[7] The *Draft Inter-American Declaration Governing the Rights and the Care of Persons Deprived of Liberty*[8] asserts that the principal aim of imprisonment "shall be to rehabilitate offenders and to establish in them the will to lead law-abiding and self-supporting lives after their release."[9] "Accountability" remains a major preoccupation, and is manifested in calls for effective mechanisms of oversight in order to ensure that correctional facilities properly execute their public functions.

Standards documents touch on many facets of prison management required to help build a public, law-abiding corrections regime. While there are varying points of emphasis from one to the next, at least the following four elements are prevalent throughout. The first, overriding, concern is with overcrowding and the state of accommodations.[10] The Standard Minimum Rules permit accommodation in both individual cells and dormitory-style rooms, but in the latter case prisoners are to be "carefully selected as being suitable to associate with one another in those conditions."[11] Sanitary conditions must be consistent "with the needs of nature."[12] Similarly broad and vaguely worded standards apply to the condition of bathing installations, the provision of toilet articles, clothing, bedding, food and exercise, and the sufficiency of light and ventilation.[13]

The Draft Inter-American Declaration proposes a number of measures for alleviating overcrowding. Article 11 proposes fixing a maximum capacity for

---

⁶   *Ibid.* at 8.

⁷   *Ibid.* at 12. The agenda specifies further that prisons should be civilian run, and independent from the military. Prison staff should be civil servants, rather than military or police personnel. (*Ibid.*)

⁸   *Supra* note 4.

⁹   Draft Declaration, *supra* note 4, Article 51.

¹⁰   See the Introduction to the Draft Inter-American Declaration, *supra* note 4: "Overcrowding is one of the most pernicious problems facing a penitentiary system. It has devastating effects on inmates and represents a significant source of abuse of the human rights of persons deprived of liberty. It aggravates all the other conditions, often rendering them inhumane. It also seriously undermines the ability of prison authorities to control the situation in their prisons: spread of disease becomes inevitable, violence is aggravated, infrastructure collapses, and inmates suffer severe mental and physical stress from living in such close quarters."

¹¹   Standard Minimum Rules, *supra* note 3, Article 9. In a related requirement in Article 8, prisoners in different sets of "categories" are required to be kept separate from one another. For instance, men and women, convicted prisoners and untried prisoners, and juveniles and adults "shall be kept in separate institutions or parts of institutions."

¹²   *Ibid.*, Article 10.

¹³   *Ibid.* See generally Articles 11–21.

each penitentiary, along with "adequate mechanisms," such as the possibility of early parole for minor offences, women with dependent children and the elderly, to avoid exceeding that capacity. In Article 12, the Draft endorses alternative conflict resolution, including alternatives to sentencing.[14] Alternative penal and sentencing mechanisms figure prominently in the *New Agenda for Penal Reform*.[15] Of the nine broad points of reform, four focus on alternatives to the criminal justice system: voluntary alternative dispute resolution, for instance through neutral mediation; informal, community-based justice aimed at reconciliation and compensatory outcomes, and sensitive to local community values; limiting more traditional custodial options such as pre-trial detention and detention for minor offences; and elimination of imprisonment for juvenile offenders except as a strategy of last resort.[16] Participants at the November 1997 International Conference on Community Service Orders in Africa, held at Kadoma, Zimbabwe, adopted the *Kadoma Declaration on Community Service*, encouraging the use of community service orders as an alternative to custodial sentencing. The Plan of Action developed in tandem with the declaration was subsequently cited by the UN Economic and Social Council in a resolution promoting the value of alternative sentencing.[17] The Draft Declaration also makes reference to limitations on pre-trial detention in Article 14, and in Article 15 calls for mechanisms to improve the efficiency and operational capacity of criminal justice systems.

The second concern is with health and medical services. The Standard Minimum Rules require that at least one qualified medical officer be available at each institution, and that full hospital facilities are available to any patient in need, either on site or by way of transfer to an appropriate institution.[18] Article 24 requires the segregation of prisoners suspected of infectious or contagious disease, an important problem tied closely to overcrowding.[19] The Draft Declaration reiterates the right to health and medical care in much the same terms, although it goes further in one respect, by involving public health

---

[14] See also *Abuja Declaration on Alternatives to Imprisonment* ("Alternatives to Imprisonment" Conference, Abuja, Nigeria, February 8–10, 2000); Penal Reform International, *Resolutions and Recommendations* ("Alternatives to Imprisonment in the Republic of Kazakstan" Conference, Almaty, Kazakstan, October 27–30, 1999).

[15] New Agenda, *supra* note 5.

[16] *Ibid.* at 8–10.

[17] UN Economic and Social Council Resolution, *International Cooperation Aimed at the Reduction of Prison Overcrowding and the Promotion of Alternative Sentencing* (1998/23, July 28, 1998).

[18] Standard Minimum Rules, *supra* note 3 at Article 22.

[19] Other interesting provisions include the requirement in Article 26 that the medical officer inspect the prison and advise the prison director about health-related lifestyle issues, such as food, sanitation and physical exercise. *Ibid.* at Article 26.

authorities in the administration and delivery of health care in detention facilities.[20]

The third focus is on the treatment of prisoners by prison staff, particularly in terms of discipline and punishment. The Standard Minimum Rules prescribe procedural and minimum substantive standards, requiring, for instance, that all offences and punishments be determined by law and prohibiting the use of cruel, inhuman or degrading punishments.[21] The Draft Declaration reiterates the basic human rights of prisoners numerous times, emphasizing the right to be free from torture[22] and the applicability of the Geneva Conventions and other similar foundational instruments.[23]

Ensuring compliance by prison staff with human rights standards requires effective training and adequate levels of remuneration,[24] and the Standard Minimum Rules establish a number of regulations regarding institutional personnel. Selection is to proceed "carefully," with due regard for "integrity, humanity, professional capacity and personal suitability for the work." Personnel are viewed as full-time, "professional prison officers," attracted by security of tenure, salaries adequate for recruitment, employment benefits and favourable working conditions.[25] All personnel are required to undergo training and testing, and are expected to maintain their professional capacities by in-service training through the course of their careers.[26] The Draft Declaration recognizes in Article 7 similar requirements for well-qualified, trained and remunerated employees, with a further focus on infrastructure support and technical cooperation at a higher institutional level.[27]

The final key issue relates to monitoring mechanisms. Under Article 55 of the Standard Minimum Rules, "there shall be a regular inspection of penal institutions and services by qualified and experienced inspectors appointed by a

---

[20]   Draft Declaration, *supra* note 4 at Article 26. See the Draft Declaration, Articles 25 to 30, on medical care more generally.

[21]   Standard Minimum Rules, *supra* note 3, Articles 27–34.

[22]   Draft Declaration, *supra* note 4 at Article 24.

[23]   Draft Declaration, *supra* note 4 at Articles 19–23, 46–50. In addition to the ICCPR and ICESCR, the Declaration invokes the American Convention on Human Rights and the *United Nations Code of Conduct for Law Enforcement Officers*, UNGA Res. 34/169, 1979. The applicability of the fundamental rights and freedoms to prisoners, "except for those limitations that are demonstrably necessitated by the fact of incarceration," is reaffirmed by the Basic Principles for the Treatment of Prisoners, UNGA Res. 45/111, adopted December 14, 1990.

[24]   The possibility that there would be an improvement in prison conditions if compensation for staff were higher is suggested in a recent report by Human Rights Watch. The report is available at: http://www.hrw.org/wr2k1/special/prisons.html#monitoring.

[25]   Standard Minimum Rules, *supra* note 3, Article 46.

[26]   *Ibid.*, Article 47.

[27]   Draft Declaration, *supra* note 4, Articles 6 and 8.

competent authority." Article 9 of the Draft Declaration identifies several over-sight mechanisms, including judicial authorities and a Public Ombudsman and the International Committee of the Red Cross. The Body of Principles for the Protection of All Persons under Any Form of Detention or Imprisonment[28] re-quires that "places of detention shall be visited regularly by qualified and experienced persons appointed by, and responsible to, a competent authority distinct from the authority directly in charge of the administration of the place of detention or imprisonment."[29] The Body of Principles is also replete with references to various kinds of informal oversight, through access to judicial process and legal counsel. In furtherance of these general principles, in the past few years the United Nations has been attempting to create a treaty that would establish a subcommittee mandated to make periodic and *ad hoc* visits to prisons and detention centers in party states. Due to disputes over content, the treaty is still in the drafting process.[30]

II. EXPERIENCE WITH CORRECTIONS REFORM

A. Latin America

Overcrowding in Latin American prisons has reached unprecedented levels, with one prison in Brazil, for instance, housing 192,000 prisoners with a capac-ity of 70,000.[31] This overcrowding has been attributed partially to rising incarceration rates throughout the region beginning in the 1980s, and rising rapidly in the 1990s, where, for example, Peru's new anti-terrorism measures coincided with a 50% increase in prison populations. Mark Ungar reports further that in almost every Latin American country pre-trial detention limits are rou-tinely violated, and the majority of inmates have not been tried due to slow criminal justice processes.[32]

Several Latin American countries have addressed prison overcrowding by releasing prisoners who have yet to be tried or have been convicted of minor offences. In Peru following the collapse of the Fujimori government in 2000, the transitional government released many prisoners still awaiting trial and in Ecuador, the country's 1998 Constitution provides for the release of unconvicted

---

[28] UNGA Res. 43/173, adopted December 9, 1988.

[29] *Ibid.*, Principle 29.

[30] Human Rights Watch website, http://www.hrw.org/prisons/united_nations. html.

[31] Mark Ungar, "Prisons and Politics in Contemporary Latin America" (2003) 25:4 *Human Rights Quarterly 909* at 912.

[32] *Ibid.*

individuals who have spent over a year in jail.[33] Many Latin American countries have included provisions for alternative sentencing, but such reform measures have encountered resistance from judges who prefer imprisonment.[34] Governments are also exploring criminal procedure reform as a method of reducing overcrowding. In Panama, laws enacted in 1991 placed limits on pre-trial detention, although institutional weaknesses in access to justice effectively prevented detainees from properly exercising their legal rights. In the early 1990s, Panama also dedicated over $2.5 million to new prison construction.[35]

Other reforms have focused on enhancing training for prison staff. In 2000 and 2001, the International Centre for Prison Studies (ICPS), a British organization funded by the UK Foreign and Commonwealth Office, conducted human rights workshops for prison staff from across Brazil.[36] A similar workshop was held in Venezuela, and a handbook for prison officials was planned as a follow-up.[37] Chilean prison authorities went beyond initiatives in Brazil and Venezuela, planning visits to the United Kingdom during which they observed the operations of British penal systems and underwent training workshops. The United Nations Latin American Institute for the Prevention and the Treatment of Offenders (ILUNAD) has also been involved in training efforts over a broader range of Latin American countries. Since 1999, prison officials from at least 17 countries have visited ILANUD headquarters in Costa Rica to attend lectures given by officials from penal NGOs based throughout the world.[38] In addition to participating in training efforts by ILANUD, the International Centre for Criminal Law Reform and Criminal Justice Policy, headquartered at the University of British Columbia in Canada, publishes the International Prison Policy Development Instrument, a comprehensive handbook providing in-depth guidelines for prison officials in developing countries.

Several states have also attempted to enhance conditions by improving prison monitoring. Eleven Latin America countries have created independent national ombudsmen, known as the Defensoría del Pueblo, which serve as a monitoring mechanism of prison conditions and an avenue for investigation of prisoner abuses.[39]

---

33   Ungar, *supra* note 31 at 916.
34   Ungar, *supra* note 31 at 917.
35   US General Accounting Office, *Aid to Panama: Improving the Criminal Justice System* (GAO/NSIAD-92-147: Washington, May 1992).
36   ICPS website, http://www.kcl.ac.uk/depsta/rel/icps/latin_america.html.
37   *Ibid.*
38   The United Nations Latin American Institute for the Prevention of Crime and Treatment of Offenders, *ILANUD Activities in 2002 and 2003 Work Programme*, online at: http://www.ilanud.or.cr/InformeING2002.doc.
39   This includes Argentina, Bolivia, Brazil, Colombia, Ecuador, Mexico, Panama, Peru, and Venezuela.

These reform efforts seem to be viewed by reformers with optimism.[40] However, they must compete with other domestic political pressures; as Ungar concludes, despite their sound design, the effectiveness of many of these reforms may be impeded by broader weaknesses in the rule of law and "pressures emanating from public clamour for law and order amid increasing crime."[41]

B. Central and Eastern Europe

The Soviet penal system was heavily predicated on the extraction of labour from prisoners. Yuri Kalinin, head of the Russian Prison Administration (GUIN) in the immediate post-Communist era, argues that the system was "founded first and foremost on the concept of deriving profit from the labour of convicted prisoners"[42] and consequently that prisoner rights and the state of prisons were secondary to ensuring maximum output from prisoner labour. With the fall of the Soviet Union, the corrections system was inherited by the Yeltsin government along with two particularly serious problems: overcrowding and poor health.

In 1992, the first legislative reform with respect to prisons was adopted with a series of amendments to enhance rights of prisoners. In 1993 a Federal law laid out the aims and objectives of various correctional institutions and in 1995 a government document was published supporting the extension of rights and privileges of prisoners. Real improvements were slow, however, and Krajick counts this period (from 1991 to 1998) as a time of worsening conditions in Russian prisons.[43] The Moscow Center for Prison Reform (MCPR), a local NGO, observes that beginning in 1991 overcrowding in SIZOs (pre-detention centers) worsened,[44] and in 1998 a government official noted that some prisoners actually ask to be killed rather than put in prison. Kalinin observes that most of the above reforms were not implemented and identifies two main reasons. First, he argues that prison reforms took place ahead of other legal and judicial reforms without which prison reform was made very difficult.[45] Second, Kalinin

---

[40]   International Centre for Prison Studies, *Projects: Central and Latin America*, online at: http://www.kcl.ac.uk/depsta/rel/icps/latin_america.html.

[41]   Ungar, *supra* note 31 at 910.

[42]   Yuri Kalinin, "The Russian Penal System: Past, Present and Future," Lecture delivered November 2002 at King's College, London, 4, at http://www.kcl.ac.uk/depsta/rel/icps/russian_penal_system.pdf.

[43]   Kevin Krajick, "Russia's Prison Meltdown," Ford Foundation report, summer 2001; available at http://www.fordfound.org/publications/ff_report/view_ff_report_detail.cfm?report_index=291.

[44]   Moscow Center for Prison Reform website, http://www.prison.org/english/mcpr-work.htm.

[45]   Though Kalinin fails to elaborate, one might posit a connection to the prevalence of pre-trial detention. Pre-trial detention in 1998 was reported to average ten months,

points to the placement of the prison administration system within the Ministry of the Interior. Being responsible for crime fighting and maintaining public order, Kalinin argues that for the Ministry of the Interior prisoner rights were of second-order importance. Human rights activist Valery Abramkin concurs, noting an improvement in prison conditions following the transfer of responsibility for prisons from the Ministry of the Interior to the Ministry of Justice, a civilian rather than military arm of government, in 1998. Abramkin also attributes the failure of reform through the mid-1990s to an increased crime rate, leading to an aggressive police reaction that aggravated the overcrowding problem.[46]

In 2001, a new Federal law introduced reforms that relaxed penal sentences for minor crimes, extended the grounds for parole, and increased the possibility of obtaining bail.[47] The International Center for Prison Studies (ICPS) initiated a program in 2000 under which prison staff in Moscow undergo training and exchange programs with staff in UK prisons. MCPR, arguing that a core problem with Russian prisons is its poor treatment of vulnerable groups, has attempted to educate prison staff through, for instance, a 2001 instructional seminar for staff at female penal colonies.[48] Penal Reforms International (PRI) has focused substantial attention on developing alternatives to prison. It held a two-day conference in 2002 at which academics, lawyers, and representatives of the prosecution, the courts, Parliament, and other branches of government gathered to discuss ways to direct new convicts away from the prison system. To this end, PRI has also provided training seminars to improve the skills of inspectors who carry out probation and community service orders. In evaluating the success of these initiatives, Kalinin points to a reduction of 205,000 prisoners in recent years, but Krajick attributes the drop to a one-time amnesty of 176,000 prisoners in May 2000. He argues that such amnesties are a band-aid solution, and that the "whole system has to adopt a more reasonable attitude."[49] To further illustrate his point, he notes that parole releases by GUIN increased seven-fold from 1990 to 2001 to 90,000 per year, yet prison populations are still growing. Duma member Sergei Popov argues that fundamentally, "[w]e are used to detaining people for little reason."[50]

---

and with no time limit within which judges were required to hear cases, sometimes stretched as long as four years. With a consistent stream of pre-trial detainees exacerbating the overcrowding problem and reforms on pre-trial detention lagging behind prison reform, Kalinin's point is well taken; Khadine L. Ritter, "The Russian Death Penalty Dilemma: Square Pegs and Round Holes" (2000) 32 *Case W. Res. J.* 129 at 155–6.

[46]   Krajick, *supra* note 43.
[47]   For a list of such reforms, see Kalinin, *supra* note 45, at 14–16.
[48]   MCPR web, *supra* note 44.
[49]   Krajick, *supra* note 43.
[50]   *Ibid.*

Closely connected to overcrowding is a serious problem with prisoner health. The infection rate for tuberculosis (TB) is 100 times higher in prisons than in the general population, while strains of TB found in prisons are becoming more resistant to existing drugs. With increased efforts to release as many prisoners as possible, resistant strains of TB are being incubated in Russian prisons then released into the country, a problem described as a "medical Chernobyl."[51] HIV has also become a problem. Eighteen per cent of all HIV cases in Russia are found in prisoners and at some points in time were increasing as quickly as 15% every two months.[52] From 1999 to 2002, new space was made for the treatment of 15,500 TB patients, laboratories have been constructed for diagnosis of drug-resistant TB, and a program initiated in 1998 devoted $2 billion roubles over six years to the fight against TB.[53] In the fight against HIV, professionals from organizations such as PRI and Médecins Sans Frontières have in recent years visited prisons and in the Nizhnii Novgorod region of Russia conducted training seminars on HIV care and prevention.[54] Doctors on these visits identified overcrowding as the most significant source of problems with respect to health. Kalinin identifies a 13% reduction in TB infection rates, and though the problem is still severe it does seem to be receiving increasing recognition.

In Kazakhstan, PRI reports the third highest per capita rate of imprisonment in the world, and that, despite reform efforts and periodic amnesties, prison populations have continued to grow. The TB problem is even more pervasive in Kazakhstan than in Russia, with a 15% infection rate.[55] As in Russia, PRI finds that many prisoners held in pre-trial detention are "charged with offences not posing a great danger to society"[56] and to whom alternative measures could be applied. PRI also identifies a lack of funding as a significant impediment to reform. In 1998, a two-pronged reform project was initiated in the Pavlodar region of Kazakhstan aiming first to enhance prison management and human rights, and second to control the TB problem. More specifically, the project trained prison officials in international human rights norms and practices such that there

---

[51] *Ibid.*

[52] Penal Reform International, *Newsletter of the Penal Reform Project in Eastern Europe and Central Asia*, Issue 6 (1999); at http://www.penalreform.org/english/nlece-ca6_3.htm#Russia [PRI Newsletter 1999].

[53] Kalinin, *supra* note 45 at 24.

[54] PRI Newsletter 1999, *supra* note 52.

[55] Penal Reform International, *Alternatives to Imprisonment: Resolutions and Recommendations*, Conference, October 1999, at 4.

[56] Penal Reform International, *Resolutions and Recommendations* ("Alternatives to Imprisonment in the Republic of Kazakstan" Conference, Almaty, Kazakhstan, October 27–30, 1999).

is now a group of local officials who work as experts in other regions.[57] In this way, it has effectively constructed a set of operating standards against which these prison staff now hold themselves accountable. PRI has also accelerated the rate of training by adopting a "train the trainers" program. In September 2002 a group of 20 people from the country's prison service underwent training and beginning in November they, in turn, led seminars attended by over 200 people in nine cities. Further, PRI has encouraged media coverage of the prison situation by offering financial awards to journalists and authors of articles on the state of the country's prisons and the desirability of alternatives to imprisonment. Pyotr Posmakov, the Prison Director General of Kazakhstan observed that "in 2002, there was five times more press coverage about the prison service than in the last five years together."[58] Finally, drawing from recommendations developed during a 1999 conference, PRI has encouraged the use of alternatives to imprisonment. A working group composed of members from Parliament, the Supreme Court, and certain ministries worked through 2001 on researching existing programs in Western European countries offering alternatives to imprisonment. One by-product has been that the "Supreme Court issued several documents that encouraged judges to widen the use of alternatives to imprisonment."[59]

In Poland, Holda notes that "[o]vercrowding was a permanent feature of Poland's communist-era correctional system" and that "[i]n reality, the exploitation of [prisoners'] work was the main purpose of the prison administration."[60] Early reform efforts demonstrate the importance of the connection of correctional reforms to the rest of the criminal justice system. In 1981 a wave of protests gripped Polish prisons and over 50% of prisoners demonstrated their dissent. Two prison associations were formed to lobby for prisoner rights, and improvements were achieved in prisoner living conditions. But in December 1981, political conditions changed and "Martial Law was proclaimed as the communist regime attempted to defend the status quo and the power and privileges of the ruling elite."[61] Criminal penalties became more severe, a series of independent associations including the two prison activist groups identified

---

[57] International Center for Prison Reform, Kazakhstan Project website; http://www. kcl.ac.uk/depsta/rel/icps/kazakhstan.html.

[58] Regional Summary, Central and Eastern Europe, PRI website at http://www.penalreform.org/english/frset_region_en.htm.

[59] PRI, Kazakhstan initiatives website, at http://www.penalreform.org/english/region_central.htm#kazakstan.

[60] Zbigniew Holda, "The Law of Corrections in Poland," in Stanislaw Frankowski and Paul B. Stephan (eds), *Legal Reform in Post-Communist Europe* (Netherlands: Kluwer Academic Publishing, 1995), 351–67 at 353–4.

[61] *Ibid.* at 355.

above were outlawed, the number of political prisoners increased, and the total prison population grew almost 50% in five years. As in Russia, where, arguably, both increased crime rates and the prevalence of pre-trial detention led indirectly to poorer prison conditions, the state of Polish prisons seems to have been strongly influenced by factors extraneous to prison administration. In both cases, the place of prisons within the criminal justice system left prison conditions sensitive to both political and other situational factors even if no vested interest overtly resisted reform. This effect can also be seen in more recent news on Polish prisons. In the fall of 2000, the Minister of Justice called for restrictions on the use of bail, while the deputy head of Parliament called for substantial increases in sentences for a series of violent crimes.[62] Just a few months later, the total number of prisoners in already overcrowded jails was recorded at a level almost 25% higher than a year earlier, while remand prisons were overcrowded by 103%.[63] Though there is no obvious link between the overcrowding and the demand for harsher sentences – indeed we have no evidence that these demands were actually acted upon – the fact that political pressure to lengthen pre-trial detention coincided with such a serious overcrowding problem in remand prisons demonstrates how prison conditions can sometimes be a political afterthought within a criminal justice system with other priorities.

C. Africa

At the First Pan-African Conference on Penal Reform and Prison Conditions in Africa, held in Kampala, Uganda in 1996, delegates from 40 African countries formulated the *Kampala Declaration on Prison Conditions in Africa*, setting broad objectives for a wide range of penal reforms, including prison conditions, alternative sentencing and prison staff.[64] The Second Pan-African Conference on Penal Reform and Prison Conditions in Africa, in Ouagadougou, Burkina Faso, in 2002, produced *The Ouagadougou Declaration on Accelerating Prison and Penal Reform in Africa*, another high-level document establishing seven key principles of prison reform.[65] *The Ouagadougou Plan of Action*, also adopted at the Second Conference, elaborates on the Declaration by proposing

---

[62] PRI, *Newsletter of the Penal Reform Project in Eastern Europe and Central Asia*, Issue 10 (Autumn 2000), online at: http://www.penalreform.org/english/frset_lib_en.htm.

[63] PRI, *Newsletter of the Penal Reform Project in Eastern Europe and Central Asia*, Issue 11 (Winter 2000–01).

[64] *Supra* note 4.

[65] See *ibid*. These included: Reducing the Prison Population; Applying the Rule of Law to Prison Administration; and Promoting an African Charter on Prisoners' Rights.

strategies to help achieve the broader principles.[66] These continent-wide statements of reform are complemented by a continent-wide monitoring mechanism in the form of the Special Rapporteur on Prisons and Conditions of Detention in Africa, established by the African Commission on Human and People's Rights.[67] The Special Rapporteur investigates prison conditions and reforms in African states and releases periodic reports; it seems that approximately 15 reports have been issued since 1997.[68]

In Malawi, the 1994 Constitution guarantees a wide variety of rights and freedoms including, in Article 42, the rights of detained and arrested persons. Detained persons are, *inter alia*, to be held "under conditions consistent with human dignity, which shall include at least the provision of reading and writing materials, adequate nutrition and medical treatment at the expense of the State." Prison monitoring is undertaken by a variety of institutions including the Special Rapporteur, the Centre for Human Rights and Rehabilitation (CHRR),[69] the Malawi Human Rights Resource Centre (MHRRC)[70] and the Inspectorate of Prisons established under the Malawian Constitution.[71]

Nevertheless, reports consistently document overcrowding, poor conditions and instances of mistreatment. In a 2001 report, former Special Rapporteur Vera Chirwa found a broad range of both domestic and international violations. Dr Chirwa, a former Malawian prisoner, said the following:

> It should be mentioned that Malawi is the very country where the Special Rapporteur on Prisons and Conditions of Detention in Africa has spent 11 years in prison as a political prisoner during Dr. Banda's regime. After visiting Malawi prisons this year,

---

[66]   See *ibid.* Many of these mirror those considered *supra*, in the discussion of Normative Benchmarks.

[67]   See the Commission's website, at http://www.achpr.org/english/_info/index_prison_en.html.

[68]   See PRI website at http://www.penalreform.org/english/frset_theme_en.htm. See also *16th Activity Report of the African Commission on Human and People's Rights* at p. 9; and *18th Activity Report of the African Commission on Human and People's Rights* (EX.CL/199 (VII), Sirte, Libya, July 2005) at p. 4.

[69]   The CHRR is a self-described "leading human rights non-governmental organisations in Malawi," founded in 1995 by a group of "former student exiles" who returned to Malawi following the reintroduction of multiparty elections in 1994 (http://www.chrr.org.mw/).

[70]   The MHRRC is funded, among others, by the Danish Institute for Human Rights. The Centre "provides training, project grant funding, [and] supports research initiatives and study tours" with the broad objective of strengthening human rights through civil society capacity-building" (http://www.sdnp.org.mw/mhrrc/).

[71]   Under Article 170 of the Malawian Constitution, the Inspectorate is to be composed of: a judge appointed by the Judicial Service Commission; the Chief Commissioner for Prisons; another member of the Prison Services Commission; another magistrate appointed by the Judicial Services Commission; and the Ombudsman.

the Special Rapporteur can confirm that prison conditions have deteriorated since she was released in 1993. This confirms a view that the Inspectorate of Prisons expressed and documented in its report dated May 2000.[72]

The most serious problem identified by the Special Rapporteur was overcrowding. According to the report, prison populations had increased from 5,557 in 1997 to 7,800 at the time of her visit in June 2001. Zomba, the country's largest prison, held 1,912 prisoners with a capacity of 800.[73] Of the total prison population, 35% were remand prisoners, with some prisoners still awaiting trial after four to ten years' detention.[74] Despite this – or perhaps the reason for this – the report claims that only seven lawyers were to be found in the entire country of 10–11 million.[75] The report goes on to note several standard incidents of overcrowding, such as unhygienic conditions, contagious diseases[76] and poor ventilation.

One major reform initiative was the introduction in May 2000, with the assistance of PRI, of Paralegal Advisory Service (PAS), which aims to provide assistance to all remand as well as convicted prisoners. The paralegals are culled from a number of organizations, including CHRR, and facilitate prisoner release by educating prisoners about basic criminal procedures, and monitoring trials and other detentions in order to alert courts and prosecutors when prisoners are due to be released.[77] The paralegals work under a Code of Conduct and under the supervision of a national coordinator. In addition, an Advisory Council composed of personnel from the correctional system as well as other legal institutions – the judiciary and the prosecution – provides guidance to the PAS.[78] As of December 2002, the PAS was operating in 13 prisons across Malawi, comprising 84% of the total prison population, and had facilitated the release of more than 1,000 prisoners.[79] Paralegals have also been involved in developing "micro-projects … such as soap-making and carpentry, to improve conditions

---

[72]   Vera Mlangazuwa Chirwa, Special Rapporteur on Prisons and Conditions of Detention in Africa, "Prisons in Malawi: Report on a Visit June 17–28 2001," African Commission on Human and Peoples' Rights: Series IV, No. 9 at 4.

[73]   *Ibid.* at 9.

[74]   *Ibid.* at 7.

[75]   *Ibid.* at 8.

[76]   *Ibid.* at 35. See also George Ntonya, "NTP Trains Prison Officers for TB Screening (Malawi)," *National Online*, January 15, 2007. Center for Human Rights and Rehabilitation, *Malawi Human Rights Report: 2003–04* (Lilongwe, Malawi: CHRR, 2005) at 26.

[77]   "Penal and Prison Reform in Africa," Volumes 13–14 (*PRI Newsletter*, April 2001) at 5.

[78]   *Ibid.*

[79]   "Access to Justice: The Role of Paralegals in Providing 'First Aid'" (*PRI General Newsletter*, Issue 51, December 2002). See Chirwa, *supra* note 72 at 42.

at low cost and to allow prisoners to develop skills which will benefit them on their release."[80]

Another cluster of efforts surround increased use of community service orders (CSO) as an alternative to imprisonment, most obviously through the founding of the Malawian National Committee on Community Service. PRI finds that although statutes had permitted the imposition of "public work" orders, "the practice of the courts imposing such orders had long fallen into disuse."[81] Legislative reforms in 1999 approved more specifically of the use of community service orders, and a number of pilot projects followed. An early PRI progress report in October 1999 found that although somewhat successful, the projects had faced obstacles principally in relation to personnel: judicial scepticism, a lack of training, confidence or interest, and insufficient personnel for supervision.[82] Community service has also been an element of the Malawi Safety, Security and Access to Justice Programme (MaSSAJ), funded by DFID, and geared towards wide-ranging reforms in the Malawian crime and justice sector. A 2003 progress report identifies success in promoting CSOs and recommends increased prominence for the program,[83] as does the Special Rapporteur.[84] Another, somewhat less typical reform has been the development of prison farms. According to Dr Chirwa, prison farms, open prisons in which prisoners are employed in food production, generally hold prisoners in the later stages of their sentences and act as an incentive for good behaviour.[85] Dr Chirwa appears to view the farms as a positive development both for their value as "productive and cost effective"[86] imprisonment and because they tend to alleviate severe food shortages faced across Malawian prisons. However, she also finds troubling complaints about forced work and very poor living conditions.

Despite these efforts it is important to note that prison populations continue to rise at an alarming rate. The 2003–04 CHRR report identifies an increase in prison population to 9,000,[87] and the UK Home Office reports a further rise to 10,389 as

---

[80] PRI Summary of Activities in Sub-Saharan Africa, see Malawi, online at: http://www.penalreform.org/english/frset_region_en.htm (cached version on file with author).

[81] Community Service in Malawi, PRI website, http://www.penalreform.org/english/cs_malawi.htm.

[82] *Ibid.*

[83] DFID, *Malawi Safety, Security and Access to Justice Programme: Output-to-Purpose Review* (September/October 2003) at 26.

[84] Chirwa, *supra* note 72 at 43.

[85] *Ibid.* at 41.

[86] *Ibid.*

[87] CHRR 2003-04 Report, *supra* note 76 at 30.

of March 2006[88] – an increase of 80% over 1997 statistics, as reported by Dr Chirwa. The CHRR report notes that a variety of factors are responsible for this increase; however "the major factor is the failure of the criminal justice system to clear the backlog especially those on homicide remand."[89] These statistics lead to the most conspicuously absent reform: the construction of new prison facilities or upgrading of existing ones.[90] The March 2006 UK Home Office report refers to an April 2004 program in conjunction with international donors to renovate the country's four major prisons, and an ongoing project to construct a new prison, due to open in early 2006.[91] We are uncertain of the status of this latter project.

An interesting example of backlog and its relationship with high levels of remand – and consequent reform efforts through innovative criminal procedure and community service orders – can be found in Rwanda. The Rwandan correctional system faces special challenges due to the aftermath of years of civil war and genocide. Over 110,000 defendants are awaiting trial on charges of genocide and will be tried in Gacaca tribunals, an *ad hoc* institution created partly in response to the implications of adding this burden to a prison system already in "crisis."[92] Gacaca tribunals, based on a "semi-traditional" model of community justice, have been heavily supported by international donors such as the European Union, which views the tribunals as an appropriate compromise given the constraints of the Rwandan system of criminal justice and the importance of the need for prosecution.[93] However, early criticisms expressed concern that the tribunals have taken an overly expeditious approach and sacrificed the right to a fair trial in the zeal to prosecute.[94] The Rwandan perspective on this

---

[88]   Home Office Immigration and Nationality Directorate, Operational Guidance Note: Malawi (Malawi OGN v1.0 Issued March 21, 2006) at 6. An interesting discrepancy is that the UK Home Office report finds there to be 10,389 prisoners as against a total capacity of 7,000, an overcrowding of approximately 50%. However, other earlier reports, such as Dr Chirwa's, find overcrowding in some of Malawi's larger prisons to be in excess of 100% – despite citing lower prison populations, and without any indication that new prison facilities were built and counted in the calculations of the UK Home Office. This discrepancy may be explained at least in part by a reference in Dr Chirwa's report to an imbalance whereby some facilities operate under capacity – as low as 50% – despite overall overcrowding (at p. 11).

[89]   CHRR 2003-04 Report, *supra* note 76 at 30.

[90]   *Ibid.*

[91]   Home Office report, *supra* note 88 at 7.

[92]   "Rwanda: Gacaca Tribunals Must Conform with International Fair Trial Standards," Amnesty International Press Release, December 17, 2002, online at: http://web.amnesty.org/library/Index/ENGAFR470052002?open&of=ENG-332.

[93]   Interview with David McRae, EU representative in Kigali, April 13, 2005 (Unrepresented Nations and Peoples Organization (UNPO), online: http://www.unpo.org/news_detail.php?arg=10&par=2313).

[94]   Amnesty International, *Rwanda: Gacaca: A Question of Justice* (2002).

point is valuable because it presents the obverse of an oft-heard prison reform dilemma, that inefficiency in criminal justice systems, by increasing the population of remand prisoners, is a key cause of prison overcrowding.

PRI has assisted in the introduction of community service as one of the sentencing methods available to the Gacaca, for instance through recruitment and training of experts to advise government officials on sentencing.[95] Smaller projects undertaken by PRI in Rwanda in 2001 include the introduction of income-generating work and skills-training work for prisoners and the training of prison staff on human rights.[96]

In South Africa, there have been efforts to align national regulations on sentencing and detention with international standards, particularly in relation to the treatment of juveniles. For instance, a court has held that regard is to be had to international instruments on juvenile detention,[97] and the South African Law Commission has frequently advanced proposals for juvenile justice reform based on international benchmarks.[98] However, broader conditions in South African prisons continue to fall short of international guidelines.[99] At a 2005 conference on criminal justice, Inspector Judge of Prisons Hannes Fagan noted that while the overcrowding rates in South African prisons have decreased, they still remain double the world average. Fagan identifies two major sources of this overcrowding. The first, which is actually decreasing, is the number of prisoners on remand. Any decrease in this first factor, however, is offset by the second, which is an increase in the length of minimum sentences.[100]

Some modest, on-the-ground reforms appear to have been successful. The Centre for the Study of Violence and Reconciliation (CSVR), a South African NGO, sponsors the Criminal Justice Programme, focused on reforms to institutions within the criminal justice system. CSVR has conducted research involving

---

[95] "Penal and Prison Reform in Africa," volume 17 (*PRI Newsletter*, April 2003) at 1–2.

[96] April 2001 PRI Newsletter, *supra* note 77 at 1.

[97] Dirk van Zyl Smit, "The Impact of United Nations Crime Prevention and Criminal Justice Standards on Domestic Legislation and Criminal Justice Operations" (presented at "The Application of the United Nations Standards and Norms in Crime Prevention and Criminal Justice" Expert Group Meeting, Burgenland, Austria, February 10–12, 2003) at 136.

[98] Zyl Smit, *supra* note 97.

[99] In one remarkable anecdote, Professor van Zyl Smit relays a personal experience with international standards in the South African correctional system, whereby "prison authorities would crowd three prisoners into a single cell because Rule 9(2) of the SMR [Standard Minimum Rules] forbade them from housing two prisoners in a single cell." (*Ibid.* at 138.)

[100] Hannes Fagan, "Our Bursting Prisons" (presented at "Consolidating Transformation" Conference, Gordon's Bay, Western Cape, South Africa, February 7–8, 2005), online at: http://www.csvr.org.za/confpaps/fagan.htm.

prisoners and ex-prisoners aimed at understanding the types of environment that lead to violence in prisons, especially sexual violence. This research has led to a better understanding of the spread of HIV in prison populations and forms the basis of a future strategic response to prevent increasing rates of HIV infection. The Programme has also held workshops for prisoners in order to help them develop skills with respect to surviving in prison and in society upon release. Feedback regarding the workshops from prisoners and prison officials suggested that the workshops had resulted in positive behavioural changes in the prison population, and the CSVR continues to offer them. In conjunction with Penal Reform International and the Deputy Chairperson of the Human Rights Commission, CSVR also conducted a study on racism and discrimination, which found that issues of discrimination affecting both staff and inmates needed to be dealt with by prison administrations.[101]

South Africa has also established a multi-layered system of accountability that involves the intertwined mandates of a series of governmental institutions.[102] The Corrections Portfolio Committee is one of many such "portfolio committees" created by the National Assembly as part of its obligation under section 55(2) of the Constitution to maintain oversight over the exercise of executive authority. Like all portfolio committees, the Corrections Committee is staffed by elected members and has a broad supervisory mandate over the Department of Correctional Services (DCS) encompassing budgeting, structure, policy, staff and even legislative amendments. The Committee's powers are similarly broad but, it seems, non-binding: it may "monitor, investigate, enquire into and make recommendations."[103] In practice it has exercised its authority in a wide number of ways, including, for instance, consultations on new corrections legislation, adopted in 1998 but only partially implemented; prison visits and advocacy with other government portfolios, such as Justice, regarding overcrowding and the state of South African prisons; and dialogue with civil society organizations. The second element in the accountability matrix is the National Council on Correctional Services (NCCS), established in 1991 and modified by the 1998 Correctional Services Act. Whereas the Portfolio Committee is a political oversight body, the NCCS serves an expert consultative function. It is composed of judges, members of the prosecution and the DCS, and has the authority to appoint experts in relevant fields such as penology, social work and psychology. The Council makes recommendations, at the request of the Minister or of its own ac-

---

[101]   Centre for the Study of Violence and Reconciliation, "Annual Report 2001/2002 Criminal Justice Programme" (2002). Online at http://www.csvr.org.za/annrep/anncjp.

[102]   See Amanda Dissel, *A Review of Civilian Oversight over Correctional Services in the Last Decade* (Centre for the Study of Violence and Reconstruction, 2003) for a detailed account.

[103]   Dissel, *supra* note 102 at 16.

cord, on penal policy such as the treatment, detention or release of prisoners, and moreover can make recommendations regarding individual prisoners. Under the 1998 legislation, the Minister is required to refer draft legislation and proposed policy changes to the Council for review. The final mechanism is in fact a group of institutions known as "Chapter 9" institutions, for the place of their constitutive provisions in the Constitution. These institutions are not focused on penal policy *per se*, but rather a broader policy goal – human rights (South African Human Rights Commission), gender equality (Commission for Gender Equality) – and, as part of their duties, apply their specific expertise to the penal context.

The success of these institutions depends to some extent on the person rendering the opinion. In the context of the Portfolio Committee, one writer found that perceived success among Committee members is stronger where the member being interviewed belongs to the governing party.[104] Constraints on the success of Committee work include technical shortcomings and capacity problems. Committee members sit on other committees, and both their engagement with the material and the regularity of committee meetings may suffer. The Committee may also be marginalized where its substantive positions, for instance on overcrowding, conflict with other public priorities such as crime-fighting.[105] Members of the NCCS have reported similar problems of capacity. They also note that, in contrast with the Portfolio Committee, which performs independent monitoring, the Council, as essentially an expert policy advisory body, processes information as provided by the Ministry.[106]

In Mozambique, two visits from the Special Rapporteur – one in 1997 by then Rapporteur E.V.O. Dankwa and a second in 2001 by Dr Chirwa – help track the progress of reforms. In 1997, the total prison population stood at 11,000. Of these, approximately 5,000 were held under the Ministry of the Interior and 5,800 by the Ministry of Justice.[107] Ministry of the Interior prisoners are under investigation by the police and are therefore all on pre-trial detention; prisoners are transferred to the Ministry of Justice upon transmittal of the file to the prosecutor from the police. The problems noted by the Special Rapporteur as of December 1997 were typical, including: significant overcrowding,[108] dilapidated prisons,[109] mixing of prisoners required to be segregated (juveniles and adults, sick and

---

[104] Dissel, *supra* note 102 at 30.

[105] *Ibid.* at 27.

[106] *Ibid.* at 49-50.

[107] E.V.O. Dankwa, Special Rapporteur on Prisons and Conditions of Detention in Africa, "Prisons in Mozambique: Report on a Visit December 14–24, 1997," African Commission on Human and Peoples' Rights: Series IV, No. 3 at 10.

[108] Maputo Central Prison is observed to hold 1,600 prisoners with a capacity of 800. (*Ibid.*)

[109] None had been built since the 1960s. (*Ibid.*)

healthy, remanded and convicted), shortages of food and other necessities, slow judicial processes marked by a dearth of judges, courthouses and lawyers, insufficient training in human rights standards,[110] and only sporadic provision of food and soap. Remand was restricted by law to 90 days, with exceptions in "complex" cases, with adherence to these standards seemingly varying from facility to facility. Disciplinary practices also varied, with some prisoners complaining about abuses and others reporting good relations with guards.

A number of reform efforts have been undertaken in Mozambique prisons, which – though improvements should not be overstated – seem to have led many to agree that at least some progress has been made. In 1996, the Mozambique Human Rights League (LDH), a local NGO, prepared a human rights training program for prison guards. The Ministry of the Interior agreed initially to the program but subsequently postponed implementation.[111] In 2001, Dr Chirwa notes in her report a significant gap in training as between prison staff in the Ministry of Justice, where over 90% of personnel are prison guards, and the Ministry of the Interior, staffed almost exclusively by policemen. Whereas the former undergo eight months of training and a 90-day internship, the latter had, at the time, no prison training at all.[112] Prison guard training includes human rights "sensitization," provided since 1996 by a local human rights NGO.[113] Salaries for Ministry of Justice prison guards are also noteworthy, reported by Dr Chirwa at US$60 per month.[114] Dr Chirwa found in 2001 that "by and large, prisoners did not complain about treatment by the guards and officers,"[115] though abuses have been reported in subsequent evidence from LDH and Amnesty International. While purely anecdotal, it is worth observing that these latter reports seem to focus more (though not exclusively) on police abuse in "jails," for instance in extracting confessions, than on prison staff or guards.[116]

---

[110] *Ibid.* at 13.

[111] Human Rights Watch, 1997 World Report, Mozambique: http://www.hrw.org/reports/1997/WR97/AFRICA-06.htm#P296_136171.

[112] Vera Chirwa, Special Rapporteur on Prisons and Conditions of Detention in Africa, "Prisons in Mozambique: Report on a Visit April 4–14, 2001," African Commission on Human and Peoples' Rights: Series IV.

[113] *Ibid.* at 20. Dr Chirwa does not specify, but this may be the LDH, which appears to be heavily involved in Mozambique penal reform and monitoring. Indeed the report notes later on the involvement of LDH in human rights training for prison staff: *Ibid.* at 34.

[114] *Ibid.* at 20. According to the US State Department, the 2004 average GNI in Mozambique was US$250, or approximately US$21 per month: US Department of State, Bureau of Africa Affairs, Mozambique Country Profile: http://www.state.gov/r/pa/ei/bgn/7035.htm.

[115] *Ibid.*

[116] Interview with Alice Mabota, President of LDH, in "Mozambique: Penal and Courts System Reform Needed to Improve Human Rights Record" (Integrated Regional

Other reforms have sought to address the most pressing problem – overcrowding. One approach has been the use of "Commissions to Strengthen Legality," a group of individuals who travel between prisons, meeting prisoners and recommending the release of those who are under the age of 16 and those who have been on remand for an excessive period of time.[117] Details of the program are sparse, and it is not clear when or on whose initiative it was begun, or more importantly, who sits on the so-called "Commissions." However, they have been analogized to the Paralegal Advisory Service, described in Malawi above.[118] Less successful have been attempts at increasing capacity by upgrading existing facilities and building new ones. One new prison construction project in Beira had been under construction since 1994, but was still not completed as of 2001, due, in the words of Dr Chirwa, to "administrative problems."[119] Several other prisons under the Ministry of Justice have significantly higher "theoretical capacity" than "actual capacity" but are in a state of disrepair such that they are closed and awaiting refurbishment.[120] At least one new prison was constructed in 1999, exclusively for women.[121] Other initiatives have been taken in the broader context of the Mozambique criminal justice system, for instance increased use of alternatives to imprisonment and construction of courts, which has expedited the trial process.[122]

Counteracting these various reforms have been spikes in levels of new detainees, due for instance to a period of increased prosecutorial vigilance in 1998[123] and an anti-crime initiative in 2001,[124] combined with slow investigatory and judicial processes. Approximately 75% of all Mozambique prisoners are remand prisoners.[125] Some prisoners also reported to Dr Chirwa that they

---

Information Networks (IRIN), May 11, 2005). Ms Mabota reports a decrease in abuses against detainees overall. Amnesty International, *2003 World Report*, Mozambique.

[117]   Chirwa, *supra* note 112 at 33.

[118]   Address by Baroness Vivien Stern, "Second Pan-African Conference on Penal and Prison Reform in Africa" (Ougadougou, Burkina Faso, September 18–20, 2002).

[119]   Chirwa, *supra* note 112 at 9.

[120]   *Ibid.* at 8. In Dr Chirwa's view, places of detention kept by the Ministry of the Interior are not in better condition; they are merely used despite being in a condition which requires that they be closed.

[121]   *Ibid.* at 11.

[122]   *Ibid.* at 33.

[123]   Human Rights Watch, *2000 World Report*, Mozambique Country Report.

[124]   Chirwa, *supra* note 112 at 12.

[125]   More recently, Dr Chirwa named the conditions in Mozambique's prisons as on a par with Malawi and South Africa: Michael Wines, "The Forgotten of Africa, Wasting Away in Jails Without Trial" (*New York Times*, November 6, 2005). Chirwa, *supra* note 112 at 8. Human Rights Watch attributed overcrowding in 2000 to a "lack of resources and space but also due to an overburdened criminal justice system." (Human Rights Watch, *2001 World Report*, Mozambique Country Report.)

had been detained merely for being unwilling or unable to bribe police officers.[126]

On the whole, these initiatives have been successful in reducing prison populations, as the number of prisoners in 2001 is reported to have decreased by 2,000, or about 18%, from 1997 levels. Nevertheless, while prison populations have gone down, overcrowding remains an extremely important problem. In Ministry of Justice prisons overcapacity remained at an average of 400%;[127] precise numbers were not available for Ministry of the Interior detention centers, but the more qualitative observations of Dr Chirwa were not optimistic.[128]

In Nigeria, PRI implemented follow-up projects to a previous two-year Prison Reform program that was concluded in December 2000. The follow-up projects focused on juvenile justice and the training of prison staff. Juveniles facing problems with the law in Nigeria generally are handled through the adult correctional system; thus, the attempt of PRI in that respect has been to implement juvenile justice structures and procedures within the criminal justice system.[129] To this end, the National Conference on Juvenile Justice Administration in Nigeria was held in July 2002 with the goal of developing a new set of policies on juvenile justice, and a National Working Group was established in order to research and advocate for juvenile prisoners rights. The working group has, *inter alia*, visited dozens of prisons across Nigeria to assess conditions, and successfully advocated the adoption of a new Children's Rights Bill in the National Assembly.[130] In August 2003, the Working Group introduced a draft National Policy on Child Justice Reform.[131] However, in April 2005, the UN Committee on the Rights of the Child criticized the Nigerian justice system for non-compliance with international standards in a variety of ways, including low minimum ages of criminal responsibility, the use of the death penalty against juveniles under the age of 18, and detention of juveniles together with adults. The Committee noted particularly the

---

[126] Chirwa, *supra* note 112 at 28.

[127] *Ibid.* at 8.

[128] Wines, *supra* note 125.

[129] PRI Activities in Sub-Saharan Africa, *supra* note 80, see Nigeria.

[130] Statutory Report of the National Human Rights Commission for the Year 2003 (delivered at the 2003 annual conference of the Nigerian Bar Association, Enugu, Nigeria, August 25–29, 2003). See also Chinwe R. Nwanna and Naomi E.N. Akpan, *Research Findings of Juvenile Justice Administration in Nigeria* (Constitutional Rights Project and PR I, 2003).

[131] "Child Justice Reform in Nigeria" (The International Child and Youth Care Network Newsletter, Issue 59, December 2003), online at: http://www.cyc-net.org/cyc-online/cycol-1203-Nigeria.html.

incongruence between certain international standards and Shariah law in force in parts of the country.[132]

The International Centre for Criminal Law Reform and Criminal Justice Policy (ICCLR), an NGO based in Canada, has also assisted in the implementation of several reform projects in the African region. In Uganda, the ICCLR, in conjunction with the Bowden Institution, undertook a Prison Needs Assessment Service. The purpose of the report – created in March 2001 – is to identify areas of need and possible solutions. The draft assessment report was discussed with Ugandan prison officials at a conference of Eastern, Southern and Central African Correctional Administrators (CESCA) in September 2001. In Namibia, the ICCLR collaborated with Tecknikon SA to organize a technical assistance seminar in September 2001. The seminar featured sessions and workshop presentations on Technology and Information Systems in Corrections, Prison Policy Development, Correctional Officer Training, Community Corrections and Juvenile Justice.[133]

The 2002/03 annual report of CESCA demonstrates an increase in the number of countries participating in programs to reform their correctional systems. For instance, a proposal was drafted for seminars to be conducted on how to improve the correctional system of Botswana. Additionally, following the 2003 CESCA conference, the Commissioner of the Zambian Prison Service initiated a process leading to the design of a needs assessment framework for the Zambian prison system. A three-phase program for improving the South African correctional system was also proposed. Phase I of the program is essentially needs assessment, Phase II policy implementation and Phase III the delivery of technical assistance.[134]

D.   Asia

In China, individuals who advocate freedom of expression or political change are systematically arrested and detained. While imprisoned, these individuals are often subjected to abuse and torture. While the Chinese government publicly condemns this type of behavior, they have been unable (or unwilling) to control it. In the words of the UN Committee on Torture, "China's judicial system has been unable to assert its authority over the police, the security system and the prisons."[135]

---

[132]   United Nations Committee on the Rights of the Child, Concluding Observations: Nigeria (38th session, April 13, 2005, CRC/C/15/Add.257).

[133]   International Centre for Criminal Law Reform and Criminal Justice Policy, Africa Region. Online: http://www.icclr.law.ubc.ca.

[134]   http://www.icclr.law.ubc.ca/Publications/Reports/September%202003%20%20 Progress%20Report% 20to%20the%20CSC.pdf.

[135]   Daniel Turack, "The New Chinese Criminal Justice System" (1999) 7 *Cardozo Journal of Int'l and Comparative Law* 49 at 64 [hereinafter Turack].

One particularly troubling tool is "re-education through labour," an "administrative penalty" ostensibly used to incarcerate those whose offences are not serious enough to justify criminal punishment, or where the police do not have enough evidence to make an arrest.[136] The program is unique in that no trial is necessary before the police impose punishment. As of 2001, approximately 300,000 people were being "reprogrammed" in nearly 300 camps nationwide. A third of these inmates are drug addicts, prostitutes, or brothel visitors, while another third are perpetrators of minor crimes such as larceny, fraud, or assault. The remainder consist of other types of inmates, including more than a thousand followers of Falungong, a spiritual movement banned as a cult by the Chinese government since 1999.[137] Even though the system is supposed to be applied to cases that do not merit criminal punishment, detention in a labour camp is often a much harsher punishment than some criminal punishments such as fines, surveillance, and criminal detention of one to six months.[138] In addition, human rights groups allege that torture and other forms of maltreatment are commonplace in the camps.[139]

Formal legal developments and public pronouncements have suggested a willingness to improve the treatment of prisoners. In December 1994, China promulgated and put into effect the Prison Law, which provides that the "human dignity of criminals shall not be humiliated, and his personal safety, lawful properties, and rights to defence, petition, complaint and accusation … shall not be violated." The Law also sets forth the rights of criminals with regard to their conditions of confinement, including the right not to be subject to corporal punishment and maltreatment, the right to exchange correspondence, meet relatives, receive education, rest on holidays, and earn just compensation for work, which is mandatory for those who are able.[140] In May 1996, at a meeting of the UN Committee on Torture, the Chinese state media quoted Xiao Yang, the Chinese Minister of Justice, as saying "the police must … not permit physical abuse or extraction of confession by torture."[141]

---

[136] Turack, *supra* note 135 at 58.

[137] Mei-Ying Hung, "China's WTO Commitment on Independent Review: An Opportunity for Political Reform" (Carnegie Endowment for International Peace, Working Paper No. 5, 2002), citing "Beijing to Introduce Reeducation-through-Labour Law this Year," Zhongguo Tongxun She, February 19, 2001 [hereinafter Hung].

[138] *Ibid.*

[139] *Ibid.*, citing Amnesty International, "Torture in China under the Spotlight at the UN" (2000), available at http://web.amnesty.org.

[140] Li Zhenghui and Wang Zhenmin, "The Developing Human Rights and Rule of Law in Legal Philosophy and in Political Practice in China, 1978–2000," available at http://dex1.tsd.unifi.it/jg/en/index.htm?surveys/rol/wang.htm.

[141] Turack, *supra* note 135 at 64.

However, the Chinese government creates significant obstacles to realizing these standards. For instance, independent monitoring of Chinese prisons or re-education through labour camps is not permitted. In 1994, the International Committee of the Red Cross (ICRC) began initial negotiations with the PRC to have access to Chinese prisons; but ultimately no concrete steps toward this end were taken.[142] Moreover, Chinese officials use the rhetoric of crime prevention to justify measures such as the re-education camps. Wang Yunsheng, Director of the Ministry of Justice Bureau of Re-education through Labour, maintained in 2001, "[f]or such a populous nation as China, [re-education through labour], which aims at stopping those on the verge of committing serious crimes, is an effective [system] for reducing crime."[143] Furthermore, in 1997, Justice Ministry official Xiao Yang boasted, "during the last five years, only eight percent of those released through the program committed crimes again."[144] The government is, however, currently considering whether to enact a law to improve re-education through labour by integrating the system with the country's criminal law and mainstream courts.[145]

In India, two reform projects have, in very different ways, helped to enhance the monitoring and accountability of the penal system. The first reform, driven by the Public Interest Litigation Movement (PIL), has broadened the concept of *locus standi* and opened the courts to a wider class of claimants.[146] This popular access to the court system has brought to light rights violations previously hidden from the public, including the torture of prisoners and police detainees, and in the process created an innovative tool of reform.

Results could be seen, for instance, in *Maneka Gandhi v. Union of India*,[147] where the Indian Supreme Court expanded the right to life and liberty guaranteed by the Indian Constitution.[148] The Court declared that life, even behind

---

[142]   *Ibid.* at 67.

[143]   *Ibid.*, citing "China Reviews Reeducation Through Labour System," *Deutsche Press-Agentur*, February 5, 2001.

[144]   Turack, *supra* note 135 at 61.

[145]   *Ibid.*, citing "Speed Urged for Judicial System Laws," *China Daily*, December 24, 2001. Veron Mei-Ying Hung, an associate of the Carnegie Endowment for International Peace, urges activists to settle for no less than total abolition of re-education through labour: "Although [the government's proposed] reform measures would alleviate some of the problems of the current system … Chinese courts are not independent enough to serve as an effective alternative to public security organs in imposing punishments under reeducation through labour." (Hung, *supra* note 137.)

[146]   Vijayashri Sripati, "Towards Fifty Years of Constitutionalism and Fundamental Rights in India: Looking Back to See Ahead" (1998) 14 *American University International Law Review* 413 at 454 [hereinafter Sripati].

[147]   AIR 1978 SC 597 [hereinafter *Maneka Gandhi*].

[148]   Sripati, *supra* note 146 at 146.

prison bars, "did not mean mere animal existence."[149] Death row prisoners were entitled to the basic necessities of life such as food, clothing, and shelter on a par with ordinary prisoners. Practices such as "torture, cruelty, arbitrary imposition of solitary confinement, use of iron chains, routine handcuffing of prisoners, denial of permission of prison inmates to have interviews with their attorneys and family members" were similarly outlawed.

In a second innovative reform effort, the Commonwealth Human Rights Initiative (CHRI) has worked to enhance accountability in Indian prisons by improving upon an informal watchdog program initially implemented by the British. Finding Indian prisons relatively inaccessible in its early reform efforts, CHRI discovered a prison visiting system enacted in the 1894 Prisons Act – still the key legislation governing prison administration – empowering state governments to appoint citizens as "prison visitors." Where state regulations implemented the visitor program, in most cases they have failed to set appropriate guidelines for the qualifications of visitor appointees.[150] CHRI has therefore spearheaded a program giving proper training to these visitors as a means of enhancing transparency and accountability in the prison system.[151]

The prison system in the Laos People's Democratic Republic is very closely controlled by government. While Lao authorities deny that inhumane practices occur in their prisons, no independent human rights monitors are permitted to visit and it is therefore difficult to collect independent evidence.[152] Amnesty International has raised concerns for years about conditions of detention, and, more recently, has managed to gather data by interviewing former detainees and their family members. Findings indicate that Lao citizens are regularly arbitrarily detained and that prisoners are subject to cruelty at the hands of prison officials. Moreover, prisoners and their families have reported the inadequacy of medical treatment. Detainees have become increasingly vulnerable to health problems because of malnutrition and, once they become ill, they are left untreated. This maltreatment and malnourishment is especially prevalent amongst the poor who are unable to bribe prison officials for proper care.[153] Amnesty concludes: "Whatever limited protection exists in Lao law to uphold the rights

---

[149]   *Ibid.*

[150]   "Prison Visiting System in India" (CHRI, 2005) at 1–3. See generally for a detailed discussion of the program, online at: http://www.humanrightsinitiative.org/publications/prisons/prisons_visiting_system_in%20India.pdf.

[151]   Doel Mukerjee, "Police Reform Initiatives in India" (CHRI Police, Prison and Human Rights (PPRH), July 2, 2003) at 7. Online at http://www.humanrightsinitiative.org/publications/police/police_reform_initiative_india.pdf.

[152]   Lao People's Democratic Republic: "The Laws are Promulgated but Have no Impact on the People: Torture, Ill Treatment and Hidden Suffering in Detention," available at http://web.amnesty.org/library/print/ENGASA260042002.

[153]   *Ibid.*

of the accused is not applied in practice, and individuals are at the mercy of a system which lacks transparency, clarity or reason."[154]

This situation is difficult to remedy, as there is "a complete lack of independent monitoring of the situation in places of detention or guidance from the international human rights bodies to the government of Laos."[155] Independent international monitors are not allowed into the country and therefore it is difficult to properly assess the situation. UN Special Rapporteurs have not received invitations to visit and conduct investigations.

Thai prisons are plagued by the practice of torture, overcrowding and a lack of adequate food, sanitation, and medical care. One of the main factors contributing to poor conditions is the lack of funding provided by the Thai government. Low prison staff salaries contribute to chronic understaffing, bribery of prison guards by prisoners and the abuse of power by unmotivated staff.[156] A weak chain of command in the prison system, such that the chief of the prison block is not accountable to the prison governor, exacerbates these problems. Underfunding is similarly a concern with regard to medical services. Despite a high incidence of infection of both AIDS and TB, the hospital medical director reports that hospitals only receive 200 Thai baht per year per patient, the equivalent of less than $US5.[157]

Government officials have been discussing the problem of prison overcrowding for several years, but to date very little has been done. Recent statistics show that 173,902 inmates were being held in 15 prisons with a capacity for only 90,000 people.[158] Prisoners awaiting trial are often held in the same facilities as those already convicted, in contravention of UN guidelines. While Amnesty International and the UN have made recommendations for improvement, very little action has been taken to date.

III. CONCLUSION

It becomes evident from a cursory review of the penal reform literature that reform efforts focus predominantly on reductions in prison populations. Given the far-reaching impact of prison overcrowding – infectious disease, insufficient food, poor ventilation, subhuman sanitary and living conditions – such a focus seems inevitable. However foreign-funded penal reforms in this respect are

---

[154]   *Ibid.*

[155]   *Ibid.*

[156]   Thailand: "Widespread Abuses in the Administration of Justice," available at http://web.amnesty.org/library/print/ENGASA390032002.

[157]   *Ibid.*

[158]   *Ibid.*

politically problematic because they are bound up, inevitably, with an independent, fixed, and quintessentially domestic constraint that fits uneasily into any of the three categories of obstacles to rule of law reform that have thus far been the focus of this book – namely, crime. Indeed, the reform effort most often noted in this chapter, substantive amendments to criminal sentencing, seems to extend beyond the procedural conception of rule of law reform elaborated in Chapter 1.

Given the institutional approach of this project, any discussion about obstacles to penal reform necessarily takes place against this background. To some extent, popular calls for harsh sentencing can be characterized as a cultural attitude in need of reform. This approach can be justified by the standards discussed at the beginning of this chapter, every one of which bespeaks a clear endorsement of alternatives to imprisonment. Nevertheless, at least on the approach adopted in this book, these reforms should be mindful of legitimate concerns about socially debilitating crime.[159]

The central role in penal reform of overcrowding, crime and the drive to reduce prison populations may also have some influence on the fact that, despite the egregious and widely known violations of the most basic standards of human rights occurring in prisons across the world, major lending organizations have not been heavily supportive of penal reform.[160] According to Thomas Carothers, the United States has avoided penal reform for domestic political reasons, as "the potential for criticism at home from Congress or human rights groups has scared away most US officials."[161] To understand the politically charged nature

---

[159] This tension is evident in Dr Chirwa's 2001 report on Mozambique, where the Special Rapporteur struggles to find the appropriate scope of her authority to comment on the country's sentencing practices. She says: "As mentioned by Dr. Edmundo Carlos Alberto, Deputy Attorney General, it would be unfair and unethical to say that a sentence is not the right one. However, the Special Rapporteur would like to draw the attention of the Attorney General's Office to the fate of the 51 young people detained in Mabalane who alleged that they were arrested and sentenced to three years' imprisonment for not being able to produce identity cards. These 51 persons are part of a wider group of people who have been and are being arrested in the course of the operations to fight criminality in Maputo, in particular ... The Special Rapporteur would like to draw the attention of relevant authorities to this situation and invite them to enquire into it and take all necessary actions to make sure that petty offenders are not sent to court but are rather dealt with inside the community through mediation for instance." (*supra* note 112 at 30–31).

[160] Including USAID, the European Commission (with the exception of Sub-Saharan Africa), the United Nations Development Program, the Inter-American Development Bank, the German Agency for Technical Co-operation and the World Bank. World Bank donor table, online at: http://www1.worldbank.org/publicsector/legal/donortable.htm.

[161] Thomas Carothers, *Aiding Democracy Abroad: The Learning Curve* (Washington, DC: Carnegie Endowment for International Peace, 1999) at 167.

of this issue for the United States, one need look no farther than domestic prisons, which house nearly half the world's prison population – and, at 713 prisoners per 100,000 residents, have far and away the highest incarceration rate in the world.[162] There is an obvious policy incongruence between the approach of the United States on this issue, and that of lead penal reform institutions such as PRI.

With these caveats in hand, obstacles to penal reform can indeed be identified in terms of all three factors enumerated in Chapter 1: resource constraints, cultural factors and political economy. Resource constraints manifest themselves most clearly in failures to build new prison facilities and upgrade existing ones. Prison construction projects have floundered in Malawi and Mozambique due to an absence of funding. Low salaries, another by-product of limited resources, can lead to understaffed prisons, untrained staff and an increased likelihood of bribery and corruption, such as in Thai prisons. More subtly, funding deficiencies across the legal system – a lack of qualified judges, lawyers, and courthouses – in part explain slow judicial processes that contribute to the number of remand prisoners, the principal source of prison overcrowding across a wide range of countries. The absence of these kinds of legal resources can also hinder penal reform in a different sense, by making enforcement of substantive legal rights more difficult for individual prisoners.

Cultural values also play a role in hindering penal reform. Subject to the comments above, public pressure for more stringent law enforcement in the face of already shocking prison conditions could reveal a general insensitivity to the human rights of convicts and pre-trial detainees. Similarly, where imprisonment has been historically dissociated from criminal procedure, efforts at penal reform may face attitudes among politicians and the public that trivialize the seriousness of imprisonment as a tool of criminal justice. Moreover, even where programs are properly enacted, staffed and funded, judicial attitudes may hinder practical implementation of novel forms of non-custodial, community-based sentencing.

Obstacles within the sphere of political economy can be observed on two levels: the relationship between prisons and the state, and incentives on individual actors such as police and prison guards. The first variant is most easily identifiable in former Soviet bloc countries and other states still lacking effective democratic institutions. The role of prisons in these contexts was not historically tied to crime, punishment or rehabilitation, but to suppressing political opposi-

---

[162]   Roy Walmsley, *World Prison Population List*, 6th edn (King's College, London, International Centre for Prison Studies, 2005). Aside from a cluster of former Soviet Republics (including Russia), only Bermuda and tiny Palau, with a combined population of 85,000, exceed 500, and none rises above 532.

tion and/or extracting labour from vast populations of captive workers. Reform efforts in this respect have focused on developing correctional institutions as professional, public institutions. Where basic democratic institutions have been established, as in Russia, these effects are not as overt as they once were, but evidence indicates a lingering impact where correctional facilities remain under the control of government departments linked to military or security rather than civilian justice. In other states, such as China and Laos, an almost complete absence of independent monitoring is the result of a strong political tradition of government secrecy. The various standards discussed above emphasize the broadly accepted importance of independent monitoring, and as the Special Rapporteur in Africa, the Defensoría del Pueblo across Latin America and the assortment of institutions in South Africa demonstrate, such mechanisms can be of substantial practical value.

The second variant relates to more quotidian forms of individual corruption. Police officers may abuse their powers of detention in order to extort bribes from civilians, and prison guards may use their positions of influence to destroy evidence or take commissions for funnelling funds to prisoners from their families. Guards may also accept bribes as payment for withholding discipline or poor treatment.

The most important lesson to be drawn from penal reform efforts may be their relationship to the broader criminal justice system. Correction, dealing as it does with a very small and marginzalized subset of the population, is, perhaps more than any other institution, inextricable from the broader successes and failures of rule of law reform. It depends, at least, on the efficiency of court processes, the effectiveness of law enforcement (not to speak of the broad complex of social factors determining crime rates more generally), a vigorous legal bar willing to defend prisoner rights and a culture of human rights robust enough to conceptualize prisoners within its ambit.

6. Tax administration

I. NORMATIVE BENCHMARKS

We focus on tax administration in this chapter as a proxy for the administrative apparatus more broadly, which, as a whole, we believe represents an important element in the institutional matrix. We do so for two reasons. First and foremost, tax administration is an example of a specialized law enforcement or regulatory function which all developing countries must perform (unlike less ubiquitous specialized law enforcement and regulatory agencies in, e.g., telecommunications and public utilities sectors, environmental protection, occupational health and safety, and competition policy). Second, for reasons we elaborate below, we believe that there is a particularly strong correlation between good tax administration and development.

Although it is difficult to identify the specific institutional and legal characteristics of "good" tax administration, an evaluation of the development and tax literature suggests a tentative list of normative criteria. Effectiveness and efficiency can be promoted by focusing on: simplicity; costs; voluntary tax compliance; self-assessment; effective enforcement; independent or semi-autonomous tax authorities; automation; and large taxpayer units. These normative criteria, and their individual links to development through the fiscal and rule of law channels, are explored in this chapter.

There is no universal definition of "tax administration" although several common understandings have been advanced. Tax administration includes activities relating to the ascertainment of tax liability, the collection of the tax, and the settlement of tax disputes and imposition of penalties for violation of tax laws.[1] This encompasses a wide range of action on the part of tax authorities. Ascertainment of tax liabilities, either calculated officially or voluntarily through taxpayer self-assessment, includes "determination of the tax base, submission of tax returns and the issuing of assessments."[2] Collection can be managed through a variety of channels, including through withholding at the income source, in conjunction with the filing of a tax return, or after the issuing

---

[1] Veerinderjeet Singh, *Malaysian Taxation: Administrative and Technical Aspects*, 2nd edn (Petaling Jaya, Malaysia: Longon Malaysia, 1994) at 82.

[2] *Ibid.*

of an assessment to the taxpayer.[3] Tax disputes can stem from a wide range of factors (incompetence, neglect, honest mistake, deliberate evasion) and administrative and judicial penalties will vary in form, from minor financial penalties such as interest on unpaid dues to imprisonment.[4] The variations on these general themes are as numerous as the tax authorities that implement them.

Stanley Surrey argued decades ago that "the concentration on tax policy – on the choice of taxes – may lead to insufficient consideration of the aspect of tax administration. In short, there may well be too much preoccupation with 'what to do' and too little attention to 'how to do it'."[5] Richard Bird has noted not only that in most developing countries "the administrative aspect of taxation is overwhelmingly important,"[6] but also, with Casanegra, that "in developing countries, tax administration *is* tax policy."[7] Bird's greatest concern with divorcing tax policy from tax administration lies in the consequent impracticality of policy prescriptions, evidenced by the fact that "the development tax literature has had relatively little operational impact."[8] An optimal tax policy bequeathed to a capability-constrained administration results in sub-optimal implementation. Yet, as Klun notes, "only a few authors have discussed the significance of tax administration."[9]

There are two primary ways in which a linkage can be drawn between the effectiveness and efficiency of a tax administration and broader economic development. First, better tax administration will aid the implementation of legislated tax policies, leading to an increase in fiscal resources. Second, because of its unique role as an intermediary between populations and their governments, better tax administration will improve institutional legitimacy and help inculcate a culture of compliance rather than a culture of corruption or non-compliance – in other words, broadly promote the rule of law. Neither of these effects is necessarily self-evident, nor are these phenomena well-explored in the empirical literature. "Deficiencies of statistical coverage are well-known and frequently

---

[3]   *Ibid.*

[4]   *Ibid.*

[5]   Stanley Surrey, "Tax Administration in Underdeveloped Countries" (1958) 12 *University of Miami Law Review* 158–88 at 158–9.

[6]   Richard Bird, *Tax Policy and Economic Development* (Baltimore, MD: Johns Hopkins University Press, 1992) at 14.

[7]   Richard Bird and Milka Casanegra, *Improving Tax Administration in Developing Countries* (Washington, DC: International Monetary Fund); cited in Parthasarathi Shome, "Taxation in Latin America: Structural Trends and the Impact of Administration," *IMF Working Paper 99/19* (Washington, DC: IMF, 1999) at 17.

[8]   *Supra* note 6 at 19.

[9]   Maja Klun, "Performance Measurement for Tax Administrations: The Case of Slovenia" (2004) 70 *International Review of Administrative Sciences* 567–74 at 568.

lamented"[10] in the context of economic development, something doubly true in the area of tax administration, which has received little academic attention. Even if the academic community had been deeply committed to the endeavour, the rule of law link would, in any event, be difficult to tease out in any statistically meaningful way.

A.   Administration, Tax Policy and Fiscal Improvements

It is something of a truism that more effective and efficient administration (defined in Section III) will facilitate the implementation of tax policy. For most governments the primary role of tax policy is the provision of revenues. Virtually all tax reform processes involve "the desire to improve the revenue-generating capacity of the tax system."[11] Judging these reform efforts in terms of their impact on revenues, they "appear to have been marked with some success."[12] The fiscal improvement, of course, is only an intermediate goal intended to facilitate government expenditures. It is tempting to suggest that the improvement of a government's fiscal position is itself a positive result in terms of development – this would make the connection between administrative reforms and development rather direct. Unfortunately, this convenient link is also unlikely to withstand robust examination. The manner in which government spends the revenues it collects will be the ultimate determinant of whether the fiscal benefit of administrative reform has a positive effect on overall development. A government that collects greater revenues in order to finance welfare-destroying activities, such as violent repression of the local population or military conflict, may certainly benefit from administrative reform, but such benefit has no salutary aspect for the population at large. This suggests that a more nuanced link is required on the fiscal front. A reasonable qualification therefore would be to note that where additional fiscal resources are directed towards development, more or less capably and in good faith, then the fiscal benefit of administrative reforms aids development. Such a contention is highly plausible. Extensive development programs and the ubiquitous scarcity of funds to implement them are commonplace. As the United Nations Economic Commission for Africa (UNECA) has emphasized, in developing countries, "governments continue to be challenged by the tension between the need to increase spending on poverty-reducing areas ... and to preserve macroeconomic stability within the context

---

[10]   Richard Bird and Oliver Oldman (eds), *Taxation in Developing Countries*, 4th edn (London: Johns Hopkins University Press, 1990) at 5.

[11]   Malcolm Gillis, "Tax Reform: Lessons from Postwar Experience in Developing Nations," in Malcolm Gillis (ed.), *Tax Reform in Developing Countries* (London: Duke University Press, 1989) at 493.

[12]   *Ibid.* at 494.

of their limited domestic resources."[13] The room for direct fiscal improvements is not insignificant. In the African context, the UN states that a 40% tax gap – the difference between tax payable and tax collected – is "caused by inefficient administration within the taxation system. Improving tax administration could reduce the gap and enhance fiscal revenue."[14] Provision of greater funds for other development programs is therefore a fundamentally important connection between tax administration and development.

Apart from a direct positive – though not easily quantifiable – effect on governments' fiscal balance sheets through better collection of revenues and lower costs, administrative reforms can advance the more substantive goals of tax policy generally. These can be varied, sometimes contradictory, and almost certainly ambiguous in terms of their ultimate benefit, and yet are important complements to the fiscal objective identified above. Regardless of the policy perspective, as Veerinderjeet Singh has emphasized, "a well-designed tax which is poorly administered can become an instrument of injustice; on the other hand, proper and effective administration can partially offset the demerits of a poorly designed tax."[15]

B. Administration, Rule of Law, and Development – A Complex Nexus

The connection between the rule of law and tax administration is twofold. First, the key values in a procedural conception of the rule of law – process values, institutional values, legitimacy values – help define what "good" administrative practice might look like.[16] *Process* values (transparency, predictability, stability, enforceability) and *institutional* values (independence/accountability) in particular are important elements of a well-designed tax administration, and help inform the discussion below of the constituent characteristics of effective and efficient tax administration.

Second, tax administrations that are properly informed by rule of law considerations will in turn influence the development program more generally, most likely by enhancing *legitimacy* values: "the level of *auctoritas* enjoyed by ... institutions; that is, their capacity to engender the belief that they deserve obedience and respect."[17] Thus there is a mutually reinforcing quality about tax administration reforms. While this is likely a characteristic of all administrative

---

[13]   UNECA, "Economic Report on Africa 2004" (available online at http://www.uneca.org, accessed February 10, 2006) at 44.

[14]   *Ibid.* at 203.

[15]   *Supra* note 1.

[16]   *Ibid.*

[17]   Jose Juan Toharia, "Evaluating Systems of Justice through Public Opinion: Why, What, Who, How, and What For?," in Erik G. Jensen and Thomas C. Heller (eds), *Beyond*

agencies, and indeed all rule of law institutions, it is, as noted above, particularly salient in relation to tax authorities, because of their distinctively visible interactions with members of the public.

This section presents a series of normative criteria against which the effectiveness and efficiency of tax administration may be judged, and outlines some mechanisms that can be used to gauge the benefits of different administrative practices. This discussion can be thought of as laying out a menu of administrative issues that a successful reform agenda should tackle. Throughout this section under each normative benchmark is a discussion of the link between the relevant feature and the development objectives (fiscal and rule of law) outlined above. In other words, from a development perspective, what makes for a "good" tax administration?

The OECD suggests in a Practice Note on the "Principles of Good Tax Administration"[18] that the mandate of "revenue authorities is to ensure compliance with tax laws"[19] – what Bagchi, Bird and Das-Gupta call the tax administration's "raison d'être."[20] It is relatively uncontroversial that tax authorities – indeed, any administrative body – should be *effective* and *efficient* in carrying out their mandate. There are many "partial approaches to the definition of an effective or efficient tax administration."[21] Tanzi and Pellechio propose that tax administration is effective when voluntary compliance with tax laws is high, and efficient when administrative costs relative to revenue collected are low.[22] This definition is the most common, although others have been suggested.[23] Frampton broadly follows Tanzi and Pellechio's demarcation, adding a "responsiveness" category for analyzing tax administration performance,[24] while Gnazzo defines

---

Common Knowledge: Empirical Approaches to the Rule of Law (Stanford, CA: Stanford University Press, 2003) at 24.

[18]   OECD (Centre for Tax Policy and Administration), "Principles of Good Tax Administration – Practice Note" (May 2, 2001) available online through http://www.oecd.org (October 21, 2005).

[19]   *Ibid.* at 3.

[20]   Amaresh Bagchi, Richard Bird and Aridnam Das-Gupta, "An Economic Approach to Tax Administration Reform," *Discussion Paper No. 3* (Toronto: International Centre for Tax Studies, Faculty of Management, University of Toronto, 1995) at 8–9; see also Jamie Vazquez-Caro, Gary Reid and Richard Bird, "Tax Administration Assessment in Latin America," Latin America and the Caribbean Technical Department, Regional Studies Program, Report No. 13 (Washington, DC: The World Bank, 1992).

[21]   Maja Klun, "Performance Measurement for Tax Administrations: The Case of Slovenia" (2004) 70 *International Review of Administrative Sciences* 567–74 at 567.

[22]   Vito Tanzi and Anthony Pellechio, "The Reform of Tax Administration," *IMF Working Paper 95/22* (Washington, DC: IMF, 1995).

[23]   *Supra* note 21 at 569.

[24]   Dennis Frampton, *Practical Tax Administration* (Bath: Fiscal Publications, 1993).

efficiency as the fulfilment of objectives at the lowest possible cost (echoing a typical economic definition).[25] An economic understanding of an efficient tax administration would require that the marginal benefit from tax collection (in terms of revenue) be equal to the marginal cost of collection.[26] The administrative definition suggested in the literature is looser than this, although the more technical definition is still applicable, since the ratio of administrative costs relative to revenue collected will be most favourable when the economic condition is satisfied.

Although a wide range of possible factors can be argued to influence the effectiveness and efficiency of tax administration, there is limited empirical clarity on the relative importance of specific factors, and, perhaps consequently, no single theory that can effectively map appropriate administrative practice and provide a blueprint for administrative reform in the context of broader economic development. The lack of a concrete prescription or recipe for success is not necessarily a detriment: no set of recommendations is likely to apply fully to all countries, let alone the subset of developing countries that often face unique institutional, political and economic challenges. Richard Bird has emphasized the futility of a "search for an optimal tax system suitable for all developing countries,"[27] and suggests that the relatively small operational impact of development tax literature is explained at least in part by overly ambitious attempts to create institutional and policy recommendations that are insufficiently responsive to individual country circumstances.[28] The approach here is to canvass the leading normative criteria for evaluating tax administrations, and contextualize these within the development framework suggested above, while recognizing that a successful tax administration may function without any specific enumerated factor, and that an administration that possesses all the enumerated characteristics of good administration might still fail due to particular economic, political or institutional circumstances.

---

[25] E. Gnazzo, "Tax Avoidance, Tax Evasion and the Underground Economy – The CIAT Experience," in A. Yoingco and M. Guevara (eds), *Tax Evasion, Tax Avoidance and the Underground Economy* (Manila: Council of Executive Secretaries of Tax Organizations, 1993) at 16–23.

[26] Robert McEwin (National University of Singapore) helpfully pointed out that the economic definition of efficiency is not explicitly applied in the tax administration literature, but that economic efficiency should nevertheless be applied in administrative settings.

[27] *Supra* note 6 at 19.

[28] *Ibid.*

A.   Simplicity

It can be argued that the simplicity of the tax system is more properly viewed as a matter of tax policy than administration. Despite our disinclination to undertake a detailed analysis of tax policy, the issues of complexity are so central to effective administration that their operational impacts must be considered. An exhaustive list of structural features that promote simplicity is not possible, although some stylized facts are appropriate. Silvani and Baer write in an IMF working paper that "a tax system with few taxes, a limited number of rates for each tax, limited exemptions, and a broad base has proven, in the context of many developing countries, to be much easier to administer and to result in higher compliance levels than a complex tax system."[29] The appeal of simplified tax rules for administrative authorities is disarmingly straightforward: simple, clear and concise rules facilitate administrative action. A simple rule requires less sophistication of tax officials and generally less complex administrative instruments – thus, the simplicity of the rule is transmitted through a simpler administrative apparatus. It is not only more likely that implementation will be more effective under a streamlined rule, but efficiency is also expected to improve as administrative costs are reduced. Bagchi *et al.* write that "simplification of the tax structure is a prerequisite for removing one of the major irritants for taxpayers – the complexity of tax returns and requirements regarding filing of supporting documents."[30] There is therefore a direct benefit in simplification that is captured by the time saved in filling out tax returns and providing relevant documents.

Simplicity comports well with the process and institutional values expounded earlier. Although the benefits of simplicity apply equally well to both developed and developing economies, the latter are particularly vulnerable to complex legislation. Lack of well-trained personnel in sufficient numbers makes implementing complex tax rules more difficult, suggesting that in the development context the case for simplicity is relatively stronger.[31] Complexity may also affect society's attitude towards tax authorities, which impacts compliance rates, and influences the legitimacy of legal mechanisms and institutions. Reviewing a series of government and consultancy studies relating to tax reform in Uganda, Odd-Helge Fjeldstad writes that lack of taxpayer culture derives from a perception of lack of fairness, which is driven in part by "a complex

---

[29]   C. Silvani and K. Baer, "Designing a Tax Administration Reform Strategy: Experiences and Guidelines," *IMF Working Paper WP/97/30* (Washington, DC: IMF, 1997) 10.

[30]   *Supra* note 20 at 34.

[31]   See David Newbery and Nicholas Stern, *The Theory of Taxation for Developing Countries* (Washington, DC: Oxford University Press, 1987) at 200.

and partly incoherent set of rules."[32] A lack of objective standards of evaluation can also encourage corruption by facilitating bribery and rendering the monitoring of tax authorities more difficult.[33] This suggests that simplicity, or "plainness," can foster greater fulfilment of tax obligations because taxpayers are better able to understand the specific rules that form the foundation of their tax burden. Finally, clarity has the added benefit of serving notice on taxpayers as to likely outcomes from filing claims – for those entitled to a tax refund (credit), this creates an incentive to file tax returns, while those expecting debits can either budget their financial resources accordingly, or alter the structure of their income activities to minimize the tax burden (in addition to the unfortunate possibility that clear notice of subsequent tax liabilities may induce non-compliance).

B. Costs

Keeping administrative costs in check can be a key factor in determining whether a tax system with a highly circumscribed budget can fulfil its objectives. Of course, costs will be highly influenced by the array of other factors canvassed here. Their independent enumeration should serve to highlight the importance of cost control in all other relevant areas, and the fact that cost ratios are a key measure of administrative efficiency. Although this is sometimes overlooked when focusing on the government bodies that administer taxes, significant costs are also borne by taxpayers, and a theory of costs should include an analysis of costs to both parties. Maja Klun has suggested that there are in fact three types of costs that require scrutiny: administrative costs, which deal specifically with how much the tax collection agencies must expend in order to collect revenues; compliance costs, which deal with the costs borne by taxpayers; and operative costs, which describe transition costs to administration and taxpayers due to changes in legislation.[34]

---

[32]   Odd-Helge Fjeldstad, "Corruption in Tax Administration: Lessons from Institutional Reforms in Uganda," *Chr. Michelsen Institute Working Paper* (2005), available at http://www.cmi.no (accessed April 10, 2006) at 3.

[33]   *Ibid.*

[34]   *Supra* note 21 at 571–2. Oddly, the actual definition of operative costs is not made explicit by Klun, and the one provided here has to be inferred from studying a table (at 571) listing this as a type of cost, and a cost discussion (at 571), where although it is not mentioned by name, the context suggests this is the appropriate definition. In any event, it works for the purposes of the current discussion, without being critical to it.

C. Voluntary Tax Compliance

The IMF has argued that "a broadly accepted principle in tax administration is that the ultimate goal … is to promote voluntary compliance,"[35] defined as "the timely filing and reporting of required tax information, the correct self-assessment of taxes owed, and the timely payment of those taxes without enforcement action." The key measure of voluntary compliance is the "tax gap," discussed earlier, which determines the difference between taxes that ought to have been collected, and those that actually were – although in the voluntary compliance situation this is done gross of any enforcement or corrective actions on the part of the tax authority. As with other factors, voluntary compliance is as much a result of proper administration as it is a contributing factor to such administration. Consequently, issues of effective enforcement mechanisms will determine the degree to which taxpayers feel the risk of non-compliance, automated administrative procedures will increase the chances of catching delinquent taxpayers, simplicity will make actual compliance less daunting, greater legitimacy of taxing institutions will ameliorate a distrust of government (a clear link with the rule of law), and so forth. At the same time, a number of initiatives can improve compliance that are not easily caught under some of the other headings in this section. For instance, the presence of taxpayer education programs, and easy access to authoritative and correct advice relating to filing a tax return are essential. This is part of the impetus behind the numerous digitization initiatives which aim to make tax information accessible online (of course, the irony of these policies is that in developing countries where they may be needed most, they are least likely to gain significant traction due to lack of complementary physical and human capital). Many of the process-oriented rule of law issues are particularly salient in increasing voluntary compliance. Transparency, predictability and relative stability can all promote a salutary behavioural response. Laws that individuals can understand are substantially more likely to be obeyed, all things being equal. When those laws additionally remain relatively stable, it gives administrations a chance to imprint a pattern of behaviour on populations, thereby giving the process of change a chance in areas least hospitable to the rule of law (for cultural, political-economy, or other reasons). Voluntary compliance is in many ways also self-perpetuating – the more people in society conform to a behavioural norm of compliance, the less likely deviation is by others.[36]

---

[35]   *Supra* note 29 at 11.

[36]   For a discussion of the economics of social conformity, see Matthew Sudak, "Conformity and Networks in a Simulated Society" (thesis), University of Calgary, 2003.

D. Self-assessment

"Voluntary compliance goes hand in hand with a system of self-assessment."[37] Although the benefits of voluntary compliance can be significant even in a non-self-assessment system, they are powerfully manifested when coupled with self-assessment. Under a standard deductive system of taxation, where the authorities calculate tax liabilities based on information provided by third parties, as is the case in Sweden, or as was the case in the United Kingdom prior to 1997,[38] voluntary compliance relates largely to the payment and processing of tax liabilities after assessments have been carried out. Although important, the greater benefit of voluntary compliance accrues when individuals are themselves responsible for reporting their tax liabilities to revenue agencies, in a timely and accurate fashion (and, of course, subsequently paying their liabilities). The benefit of this approach is not only that it allows a reallocation of limited administrative resources to other crucial areas, such as enforcement, but also that it shifts the assessment burden to the party that has the best and likely most cost-effective access to relevant tax information. It is useful to note, however, that self-assessment is generally not applied to taxes such as property tax, but rather is limited to major taxes such as personal and corporate income tax.

E. Effective Enforcement

Effective enforcement is vital to effective tax collection. Enforcement clearly has a punitive aspect aimed at catching and punishing non-conforming taxpayers, but its real power comes from the ability to induce voluntary compliance if the probability of being caught is high enough, and the severity of punishment significant enough. There are many ways that enforcement can be improved by tax authorities. It is clear that "the probable money value of a penalty is the product of the probability of its application and its amount."[39] Whereas administrative efforts speak to the probability portion, without a reasoned policy regarding level and forms of sanction any actual administrative action will be pointless. There are numerous other factors that need to be in place for enforcement to work. For one, specialized enforcement divisions that are well resourced are essential – something made substantially easier when self-assessment predominates, saving resources, although this may not be an available compromise in developing countries that lack both a culture of self-assessment and effective

---

[37] *Supra* note 29 at 12.
[38] *Ibid.*
[39] Richard Goode, "Some Economic Aspects of Tax Administration," in Richard Bird and Oliver Oldman, (eds), *Taxation in Developing Countries*, 4th edn (London: Johns Hopkins University Press, 1990) at 490.

enforcement. As Richard Gordon has observed, "while almost every developing country has enacted penalties for both negligent and intentional failure to comply with revenue laws, few civil, and virtually no criminal, penalties are ever assessed and collected."[40] Gordon goes on to outline some of the possible reasons for lack of effective enforcement: "penalties have no clear rationale" and are often too severe; enforcement is impossible unless there are mechanisms in place to discover underreporting; penalties "can be bargained away in the process of securing the tax deficiency."[41] In addition, tax administrations are susceptible to corruption, which further reduces the efficacy of enforcement. None of these issues is readily solved by an enforcement-only reform process, as they are closely interrelated to other aspects of tax administration and policy.

Concern about enforcement is doubly important when one considers the effects it can have on institutional legitimacy and the rule of law more generally. The failure to collect taxes and to enforce assessments can serve as yet another example of unfair process. A general perception that others are getting away with meeting their tax obligations can lead to a crisis of confidence in tax authorities, which is often a part of more broadly-based institutional legitimacy issues. By the same token, effective administrative efforts in this regard can go far to ensuring that fairness is not only implemented but also observed to be implemented.

F.   Independent or Semi-autonomous Tax Authority and Accountability

The questions of independence and accountability play an important role in tax administration design. As the OECD has noted, "the extent of an agency's autonomy is likely to have important implications for operational efficiency and effectiveness."[42] The key issues are: from whom is independence required, and to what end?[43] The primary actor against whom independence-enhancing administrative reforms are generally proposed is the government itself, as evidenced by "the worldwide trend towards the creation of semi-autonomous revenue authorities."[44] One reason why semi-autonomous revenue authorities

---

[40]   *Ibid.* at 459.

[41]   *Ibid.*

[42]   OECD, *Tax Administration in OECD Countries: Comparative Information Series* (2004) at 9.

[43]   See Chapter 1, *supra.*

[44]   Rosario G. Manasan, "Tax Administration Reform: (Semi-) Autonomous Revenue Authority Anyone?," *Philippine Institute for Development Studies Discussion Paper No. 2003-05* (June 2003) (available online at http://www.pids.gov.ph, accessed April 17, 2006).

are created is to facilitate a break with the "political favoritism, employment-generation and myriad other factors that account for masses of low-paid, poorly trained, poorly motivated public servants found in most developing countries."[45] In other words, the independence is not so much from the government itself, as it is from the culture that can permeate a line government agency. As Bird has pointed out, the creation of an elite or autonomous entity above the standard rank-and-file of government is unlikely to be effective or long lasting on its own.[46] The OECD identifies five areas in which powers and responsibilities can be delegated to tax authorities: tax law interpretation, organization and management, information technology, performance standards, and personnel.[47] There is a wide range of practice, both among OECD countries (about half of which have unified tax authorities with some effective degree of autonomy), and developing ones, where independence is more diversely interpreted.[48]

Another aspect of independence is independence from taxpayers themselves, and from their political friends – "delegating enforcement decisions to tax administrators and simultaneously providing them with a positive incentive to collect revenue helps provide a credible deterrent to tax evasion."[49] An organization that is insulated from the political repercussions of unpopular actions can commit much more credibly to tracking down tax evaders. A number of steps can be taken in this regard. Simplification of tax laws makes it more difficult for potentially corrupt practices to withstand a subsequent audit, since it generally will have the effect of limiting administrative discretion.[50] A strict functional division of labour within the administration, ensuring that different officers fulfil different roles (such as assessment, enforcement, auditing, etc.), and that officers making determinations are not the same as those officials who have contact with taxpayers (i.e., separate information gathering from enforcement application), can also enhance autonomy.[51]

As our empirical evidence will show, however, the gains achieved from autonomous revenue agencies can, for a variety of reasons, be eroded over time.

---

[45]   *Supra* note 6 at 195.
[46]   *Ibid.*
[47]   *Supra* note 42 at 9.
[48]   *Ibid.*
[49]   Arindam Das-Gupta and Dilip Mookherjee, *Incentives and Institutional Reform in Tax Enforcement: An Analysis of Developing Country Experience* (New Delhi: Oxford University Press, 1998) at 257; see also N. Melumad and D. Mookherjee, "Delegation as Commitment: The Case of Income Tax Audits" (1989) 20(2) *Rand Journal of Economics* 139–63.
[50]   *Ibid.* at 198.
[51]   *Ibid.*

G. Information Technology

The automation or computerization of tax administrations refers to the use of information technology to manage the copious amounts of data associated with collecting, storing and analyzing tax revenue and assessment information. The administration of a tax system is inherently an exercise in information collection and management. In many developing countries, where unskilled and ill-equipped revenue authorities are endemic, "most work is done manually, causing delays and mistakes ... many tax offices do not have computers, and those that have computers do not use them properly."[52] The lack of computerization causes a myriad of problems. Enforcement is made difficult, since auditing of tax returns is neither systematic nor widespread. Collection of statistical information on taxation is nearly impossible. Preventing "political intervention, collusion and corruption"[53] within the administration is extremely difficult to control without sophisticated information management systems, as is the implementation of various anti-graft initiatives (such as having different officers involved in different aspects of a case, which without computerized information management is a logistical nightmare). The rational use of computer technology can greatly aid in a number of functions, including, as Das-Gupta and Mookherjee emphasize, creating a tamper-proof information base, cross-matching different sources of information which can aid verification, improving accuracy, and facilitating administrative planning and resource allocation.[54]

The obvious concern that computerization is too costly to be affordable for developing nations is mitigated by the relatively quick return on investment associated with computerization programs, by the relatively small magnitude of investments required as a percentage of tax revenues to observe real improvements, and by the continually falling costs of information technology.[55] Although initial costs of equipment and training, which may include substantial imports and contracting for specialized technical services, might make significant investments too costly for the poorest nations, there is the potential of greatly increased administrative effectiveness and efficiency. Unfortunately, this potential has not always been realized. Among the more vocal skeptics of computerization as a "simple" solution to administrative problems have been Bird and Oldman. They write that although computerization can help, implementation is often negated by the lack of appropriate technology skills in the administration, and that "as experience has shown in all too many countries,

---

[52]   *Ibid.* at 143.
[53]   *Ibid.* at 149.
[54]   *Ibid.* at 270.
[55]   *Ibid.* at 274–5.

computerization of tax administration is a complex task that has, as yet, been successfully accomplished by few ... It is not hard to find instances in which the inappropriate introduction and use of computer systems has in some ways made matters worse."[56] They contend that computerization is likely to be of greatest benefit "where the tax administration is already well-organized."[57]

H. Small Fish Big Fish – Large Taxpayer Units

In most developing countries a small number of taxpayers account for a disproportionately large amount of tax liability. "There is strong evidence supporting the proposition that in developing economies revenue is concentrated in a limited number of the largest firms,"[58] and similar parallels exist for other forms of tax. As a recent report by Christophe Grandcolas, an IMF Tax Administration and Policy Adviser, notes, in some developing countries the portion of taxes collected from a very small portion of taxpayers can account for well over 90% of tax revenues.[59] In Brazil, 30,000 large taxpayers, representing 0.3% of all taxpayers, accounted for 92% of revenues, when withholding at the source is included.[60] Similarly, in Sri Lanka 2,024 large taxpayers, representing 2% of total taxpayers, accounted for the same portion of revenues (92%).[61] An efficient administrative response would be to devote a commensurately larger portion of resources to focus on these larger taxpayers.

One response to large taxpayers is to develop large taxpayer units (LTUs) within the tax administration that specifically target revenue collection from these units. This not only permits the development of specialized skills, but also can direct additional resources to this branch in a more organized fashion. The possibility for substantial benefits from such an organizational move explains

---

[56] *Supra* note 10 at 467.

[57] *Ibid.*

[58] Richard T. Ainsworth, "Digital VAT and Development: D-Vat and D-Velopment," *Tax Notes International* (August 15, 2005) at 627.

[59] Christophe Grandcolas, "VAT in the Pacific Islands," *Asia-Pacific Tax Bulletin* (January/February 2004) at 19.

[60] *Ibid.*

[61] *Ibid.* See also Katherine Baer *et al.*, *Improving Large Taxpayers' Compliance: A Review of Country Experience* (Washington, DC: IMF, 2002) at 6; McCarten notes that in Argentina, 0.1% of the population accounts for 49.1% of tax revenue (William McCarten, "Focusing on the Few: The Role of Large Taxpayer Units in the Revenue Strategies of Developing Countries" (presented at *The Andrew Youngs School's Fourth Annual Conference on Public Finance Issues in an International Perspective: The Challenges of Tax Reform in a Global Economy*, Georgia State University, May 24–25, 2004) at 9, online at http://isp-aysps.gsu.edu/academics/conferences/conf2004/McCarten. pdf.

why "LTUs are so popular among advisors on tax administration policy that, without an LTU, a tax administration is unlikely to be called modern."[62] In addition to the general development of LTUs to deal with large taxpayers, most countries also have special rules for how LTUs are treated, especially through the imposition of withholding tax obligations on businesses that qualify as LTUs. Withholding taxes, whereby the employer deducts income tax from employee wages and benefits, is much less likely to face significant compliance issues, and shifts some of the informational burden onto taxpayers rather than administrations. Larger taxpayers have a strong incentive to comply with tax laws, both because they are likely to be the focus of greater investigative scrutiny, with the prospect of significant penalties, and also because their financial dealings leave a more readily identifiable informational trail for the tax authorities to investigate.

I. Training and Skills Development

The size and abilities of human resources at tax authorities have been discussed in the context of numerous tax administration reforms. Available data suggest that there are significant economies of scale in tax administration,[63] and that increasing the professionalism of administrators is an important element in successful tax reforms.[64] For instance, among the many recommendations contained in an OECD Practice Note on "Principles of Good Tax Administration" are several that point to the critical importance of "competence" for tax authorities, including recruiting and promoting employees on the basis of merit, protecting them from arbitrary dismissal, providing sufficient remuneration, informing staff about changes in tax laws and emerging avoidance practices, and participating in international tax forums to develop and set international standards.[65] Consequently, it is essential that developing countries invest in creating a professional core of tax experts. This will not solve any administrative problems, but is the starting point to finding solutions, and is necessary in order for many of the other proposed reforms to be effective.

---

[62] Parthasarathi Shome, "Tax Administration and the Small Taxpayer," *IMP Policy Discussion Paper* (May 2004) at 2.

[63] *Supra* note 49 at 263.

[64] *Ibid.* at 264–5.

[65] OECD Centre for Tax Policy and Administration, "Principles of Good Tax Administration – Practice Note" (May 2, 2001) available online through http://www.oecd.org (October 21, 2005) at 8.

II. EXPERIENCE WITH TAX ADMINISTRATION REFORMS

A. Latin America

In Mexico, the tax collection system prior to 1988 involved over 60 often scarce, complex forms, and person-to-person communication between taxpayers and a large pool of collectors. The system was slow, taxpayers were confused about which forms applied to them, and low pay and low accountability encouraged corruption among tax officials. Reforms have been undertaken in order to improve communication and reduce corruption and lower-level collection officers were removed and partially replaced with increased reliance on computerized notices. Incentive schemes for audit officials were devised which tie bonuses to the amount of penalties collected, corrupt officials have been released, and audits which do not call for additional dues are re-evaluated by a third party in a different department. Resistance to change was anticipated from two fronts and avoided. First, many top and middle level managers were released at the time of reform, eliminating an element "that might have resisted changes in the department being imposed from above."[66] Second, fearing bureaucratic resistance to high salaries required for capable computer personnel, new information system capacities were outsourced to an external firm.

In Bolivia, three significant administrative reforms were instituted. First, the government introduced a new taxpayer registration system, the result of which was to double the number of taxpayers on file. Second, facing a financial crisis, the government increased enforcement efforts on the very largest taxpayers through computer monitoring, increased penalties for violation, and for the first time began closing businesses failing to give receipts for the value-added tax (VAT) sales tax. Finally, tax collection was turned over to commercial banks. Bank systems have better control over information and revenue and most importantly eliminate direct communication between taxpayers and tax officials, thus reducing the possibility of corruption.[67] Some have described the reforms of the late 1980s as characterized by a "near-obsession with simplicity."[68]

---

[66] Arindam Das-Gupta and Dilip Mookherjee, *Incentives and Institutional Reform in Tax Enforcement: An Analysis of Developing Country Experience* (Delhi, India: Oxford University Press, 1998) at 319.

[67] Richard Bird, "Tax Administration and Tax Reform: Reflections and Experiences," in Javad Khalilzadeh-Shirazi and Anwar Shaw (eds), *Tax Policy in Developing Countries* (Washington, DC: The World Bank, 1991) 38–56 at 45.

[68] *Supra* note 7 at 20.

As in Mexico and Bolivia, reforms in Colombia aimed to simplify procedures. In 1986, most itemized deductions, all personal exemptions, taxation of dividends, and the net wealth tax were all abolished. The reforms recognized "the constraints imposed on policy by administrative feasibility" and the "inevitable roughness (approximate nature) that can be attained in an open economy with severely limited administrative capability."[69] Unlike Bolivia, however, where dire financial crises drove reform efforts, radical improvements in tax administration were not instituted in the late 1980s. Though some reforms, like collection at banks, were initiated, reforms that focused on strict enforcement among the wealthiest taxpayers were not duplicated in Colombia.[70]

Several Latin America countries have addressed tax administration problems by creating independent or semi-independent revenue agencies (SARA). Peru was the first Latin American country to adopt this strategy in 1991, and Venezuela, Mexico, Bolivia, Guatemala, Argentina, and Columbia followed.[71] In 1988 Peru's tax revenue amounted to only 9% of GDP (compared to 14% in 1978), and the Peruvian government embarked on a sweeping reform of its tax administration, including the creation of a semi-autonomous revenue authority. The success of the Peruvian reforms, where tax revenue rose to 13% of GDP by 1997, has been attributed to the SARA, in particular the guaranteed fiscal autonomy of the organization (the organization was entitled to a certain percentage of taxes collected), strong political and managerial support, large changes in personnel, competitive salaries, and infrastructure and IT development.[72] McCarten reports, however, that more recent interference by the Ministry of Finance in the new tax organization contributed to a loss of public confidence in the SARA and tax revenue decreased to 12% of GDP in 2001.[73]

Large taxpayer units (LTUs) have also been popular among Latin American states. Argentina first implemented an LTU in 1970s, and has been copied by several other Latin American nations. However, the experience of Ecuador illustrates the susceptibility of the LTU approach to corruption. Ecuador established an LTU in 1995 and initially instituted procedural changes which facilitated tax payment. In 1999, a massive corruption scandal was uncovered, virtually every one of the 1200 national tax employees was replaced, and it was found that positions within "the LTU could apparently be 'bought' by corrupt officials for their personal gain."[74] Though the corruption problem was not

---

69   Bird, *supra* note 67 at 47.
70   *Ibid.*
71   McCarten, *supra* note 61 at 14.
72   *Ibid.* at 15.
73   *Ibid.*
74   Baer *et al.*, *supra* note 61 at 35.

limited to the LTU, it still serves to demonstrate the corruption risk associated with LTU's; "[t]he concentration of important and often sensitive cases ... in one unit may increase the risk that political pressure will be brought to bear on the LTU."[75]

B.   Central and Eastern Europe

The historical circumstance of Central and Eastern European countries as centrally planned economies (CPE) poses a peculiar dilemma for tax reformers. Since "[t]he private sector was outlawed and property taxes did not exist,"[76] taxes were levied primarily against state-owned enterprises. The government, acting in "a dual role as the owner of state enterprises and as the tax collector," faced "little opposition to otherwise controversial tax measures" and "could reportedly conduct a 100 percent audit each year to ensure compliance."[77] In essence, the system "did not tax individuals (or households) as such, but instead financed state expenditure by, in effect, diverting some enterprise profits to the government budget as they flowed through the banking system."[78] As a result, the difficulties inherent in the enforcement of taxation against a vast base of individual taxpayers were virtually unknown, and the institutions required to confront such difficulties were similarly absent.

One recent trend in tax administration reform in Central and Eastern Europe has been the consolidation of tax and customs departments into semi-autonomous revenue generation agencies. In Latvia, the State Revenue Service (SRS) was formed in 1994 by the merger of the State Finance Inspection Board and the Customs Department. Its long-term mission is to "implement the State fiscal and customs policies [and] to ensure the protection of the state economic border and collection of the planned revenue to the State budget." The organization emphasizes the goal of "[a]chieving voluntary timely assessment and collection of taxes, duties and other compulsory payments."[79] The Director General of SRS, who heads the agency and is responsible, among other duties, for the dismissal of employees in violation of the Anti-Corruption Act, approval of budget expenses, and the hearing of certain appeals, is essentially

---

[75]   *Ibid.* at 22.

[76]   Jorge Martinez-Vazquez and Robert McNab, "The Tax Reform Experiment in Transitional Countries" (International Studies Program, Andrew Young School of Policy Studies, Georgia State University, International Studies Program WPS, January 1, 2000) at 3, online at: http://isp-aysps.gsu.edu/papers/ispwp0001.pdf.

[77]   *Ibid.* at 3.

[78]   Anahit V. Mkrtchyan, *Tax Reform in Armenia* (Budapest: NISPAcee Occasional Papers in Public Administration and Public Policy, summer 2001) at 6.

[79]   SRS website, http://www.vid.gov.lv/eng/user/show.asp?ID=202&CId=2.

an executive appointment made by the Cabinet on the recommendation of the Minister of Finance. Agency staff are hired generally in accordance with the Latvian Labour Code and, although no special qualifications are required, 50% of staff have a post-secondary education and a further 33% have received "secondary-professional" training.[80] Decisions of tax officials may be appealed to three levels of review: from officials of regional offices to the Director General of the particular office, from the Directors General of regional offices to the Director General of the SRS, and from the Director General of the SRS to the courts. In each case the applicant must file his appeal within 30 days of the issuance of the decision. The agency is also empowered to form a seven-member *ad hoc* commission for the resolution of a "definite contestable matter;" the commission is to be headed by the Director General and must include two representatives of SRS regional offices.[81] The SRS has also undertaken to improve the transparency of the tax system through the publication of laws, policies, annual reports and organizational structures on its website, although it concedes that "Internet services are for the time being unavailable to the majority of taxpayers." Largely as a result of these reforms, the amount of tax collected increased by approximately 130% from 1994 to 2000. As might be expected, given the CPE context, the most significant increases occurred in personal income tax, collected against a wide base of individual people and households.[82]

Despite the substantial increase in income tax collected, Latvia still faced significant challenges in tax administration at the end of the 1990s. In particular, the Latvian government needed to keep up with the expansion of the private sector by expanding its tax base to lower compliance costs, decrease corruption and evasion, and improve and modernize the administration and organizational structure of the SRS. Although the customs and tax administrations had been combined in 1993, there was no unifying organizational structure between the two areas. In 1998 the Latvian government embarked on a comprehensive modernization project of its customs and tax administration, requesting and receiving the assistance of the World Bank and the European Union. The modernization project included an overall reformulation of the basic business process and organizational structure of the SRS, strengthening management

---

[80]   State Revenue Service: Annual Report 2001 at 4.

[81]   Article 22, Law On the State Revenue Service.

[82]   See graph on the SRS website (http://www.vid.gov.lv/eng/user/show.asp?ID= 202&CId=2). Personal income tax collected in 1994 was approximately 100 MLs. (as read from the graph), compared with 284 MLs. in 2001 as reported in the State Revenue Service 2001 Annual Report, *supra* note 80 at 20. Also consistent with the observations about taxation in former CPEs is that enterprise income tax, despite some fluctuation over the years, stood at approximately the same level in 2001 as it had in 1994.

capacity, automation of tax and customs administration, and reformulating the human resource strategy with an improved incentive structure, which along with a reduction in face-to-face interaction and the creation of an internal vigilance unit, reduced the potential for corruption. A 2004 report of the World Bank rates the program as a success, with a high likelihood of sustainability: since the implementation of the project Latvia has increased its tax and customs revenues from 28.8% of GDP in 2001 to 31.5% of GDP in 2003; tax arrears have been reduced from 4.7 to 2.4% of consolidated budget revenues; and a new organizational structure for the Financial Police Department has led to a decline in tax evasion and a 1.6 times increase in the number of criminal cases brought by the Financial Police.[83] Still, the Latvian State Revenue Service faces future challenges in its tax administration: despite attempts to improve the integration between the customs and tax branches, the two branches are under different management lines at the capital office in Riga;[84] and the 2003 EU report notes that Latvia needs to continue to improve its administrative capacity, implement IT systems, and meet further commitments to harmonize with the EU's VAT.[85]

The Polish tax system performed well throughout the 1990s, accumulating strong and continuous tax revenue to finance government spending. Poland introduced corporate taxation in 1989 and personal tax in 1992, but Poland, like Hungary and the Czech Republic, continues to rely more on social security contributions than the OECD average. Unlike other Central and Eastern European countries, Poland's tax revenue as a percentage of GDP has remained constant, at around 40%, from 1991–98, comparable to levels in European Union countries, but higher than the US and Japan. According to a 2000 OECD report, Poland was in need of tax reform, not simply to increase its revenue-generating capacity, but to ensure that its tax burden does not interfere negatively with its economic growth.[86] Poland spends a large portion of its revenue on social programs, particularly pensions that take up 14% of government spending – more than public spending on education, research and development and public investment. Poland is facing large costs in public infrastructure, NATO and EU

---

[83] World Bank, Poverty Reduction and Economic Management Unit Europe and Central Asia Region, *Implementation Completion Report in the Amount of $5.05 Million Equivalent to the Republic of Latvia for a State Revenue Service Modernization Project*, Report No. 30736-LV (2004).

[84] World Bank, *Implementation Completion Report*.

[85] European Union Online, "Latvia – Adoption of the Community Acquis," http://europa.eu.int/scadplus/leg/en/lvb/e10104.htm, January 14, 2004.

[86] Organization for Economic Cooperation and Development, Economics Department, Patrick Lenain and Leszeck Bartoszuk, "The Polish Tax Reform," Working Paper No. 234 (2000).

accession, but because of the high tax burden already imposed on those who comply, the continued presence of a large underground economy, and high taxes needed to sustain high social spending, Poland needed further tax reform. As the 2000 OECD report stated "[b]ecause the tax burden can no longer be increased, solutions need to be found to make room for these growth-enhancing outlays."[87]

In 2000, the Polish government embarked on a program of restructuring and reducing public expenditure, outlined in the "Strategy of Public Finance and Economic Development," for 2000–10. The program sought to reduce the tax burden by broadening the tax base and provide greater incentives for economic growth. Poland implemented several tax reforms, including a reduction in corporate income tax from 34% in 1999 to 22% in 2004, and harmonization of VAT and excise taxes with the EU. Poland appears committed to its reduction in corporate income tax, and has not readjusted the cuts even in the face of a growing budget deficit. In 2001 Premier Miller imposed a moratorium on readjusting brackets as a measure to cope with the growing deficit and imposed a new tax on personal savings accounts.[88] The reduction of corporate income tax appears to have been successful: despite the reduction of corporate tax, the revenue from corporate income tax in relation to GDP has remained stable due to increased compliance and a broader tax base.[89]

Other reforms in Poland have focused on the computerization and simplification of processes. In 2000 tax returns and other taxpayer information were made available online.[90] In 2001, the computerized system POLTAX went into effect in tax offices across the country, allowing tax officials to "automatically calculate and control the amount of tax due."[91] A 2002 improvement to the system

---

[87] Lenain and Bartoszuk, *supra* note 86 at 5.

[88] Poland Business Review Newswire, November 5, 2001 in "International Imperatives and Tax Reform: Lessons from Post Communist Europe."

[89] Jaroslaw Neneman, Under-Secretary of State and the Ministry of Finance, Poland, "Global Tax Reform: Who's Leading, Who's Lagging, and Is the U.S. in the Race?," Conference at the Tax Foundation, November 18, 2004.

[90] European Commission, *2002 Regular Report on Poland's Progress Towards Accession* (COM 2002 700) at 10, online at: http://europa.eu.int/comm/enlargement/report2002/pl_en.pdf at 52. The effectiveness of online information will be tempered by the extent to which Polish individuals have access to the Internet. Though data is scarce, one 2000 Ispos-Reid poll in Russia found that 83% had no access whatsoever to the Internet. "Internet Still Luxury in Russia," *Pravda: RU* (June 19, 2001), online at: http://english.pravda.ru/society/2001/06/19/8079.html. Another poll in 2003 finds 88% of Russian youths (generally the target demographic for Internet use) have never used the Internet. Online at: http://www.afpc.org/rrm/rrm1054.shtml.

[91] European Commission, *2001 Regular Report on Poland's Progress Towards Accession* (COM 2001 700) at 63, online at: http://europa.eu.int/comm/enlargement/report2001/pl_en.pdf.

perfected a tax enforcement module, which facilitates links between taxpayer information, their bank accounts and other taxpayers. A training program for tax officials was initiated, and a group of officials were charged with the training of 760 other personnel in the VAT and other tax policy issues. Finally, an amendment to the Law on Bailiffs and Enforcement enhanced court and administrative enforcement powers. A comment in the 2001 EC Regular Report on Poland noted that unnecessarily complex tax processes and forms had hindered compliance; it is not clear what, if any, progress has been made in this respect.

Another method of administrative improvement has been the creation of large taxpayer units (LTU) in several Central and Eastern European countries. In Hungary, the "experience with a large taxpayer unit has been one of the most successful among transition countries."[92] The LTU was established in 1996, and as of 2002 handled the files of 470 taxpayers, all in the greater Budapest area, accounting for 42% of domestic tax collection. Unlike in some other countries, in which the LTU focuses on a subset of tax enforcement functions, the Hungarian LTU is a "'full-service' office ... including returns and payments processing, audit, collection enforcement, and taxpayer services."[93] The results have been impressive. "Between 1996 and 1999, tax revenue collection for the LTU increased by about 40 percent, and grew from about 32 percent of total tax collection in 1996 to about 42 percent of total tax collection in 1999."[94] The number of delinquent taxpayers stood at 3% in 1999. Hungarian authorities attribute the success to a number of factors, including enhancement of voluntary compliance through more efficient processes, and the development of information systems supporting various administrative tasks.

In Bulgaria, the LTU was established in 1997. Katherine Baer finds that initial results were not as positive as those in Hungary, attributing this weakness to a "bottom-up approach (giving priority to restructuring field offices) instead of a top-down approach (giving priority to restructuring headquarters and strengthening the [LTUS]). As a result, headquarters' capacity to direct and support the operations of the [LTUs] and field offices was weak."[95] From 1998, results began to improve. In 1999, 3.9% of the total tax administration (i.e., the LTU) dealt with 842 taxpayers paying 51% of total taxes. This represented an increase from 44% in 1998 and corresponded to a reduction in tax arrears from 17% in 1998 to 11% in 1999 of domestic tax collections. One major reason for success identified by Bulgarian authorities is the enhanced quality of services offered to large taxpayers due to focusing these services on a small group of taxpayers.[96] In

---

92   *Ibid.* at 25.
93   *Ibid.*
94   *Ibid.*
95   *Ibid.* at 24.
96   *Ibid.* at 24–5.

several other countries, including Azerbaijan, Georgia, Latvia, Moldova, Tajikstan and Ukraine, LTUs have been established more recently. Baer does not attribute to the LTUs in these countries the same early success attributed to Bulgaria and Hungary. Along with poorly defined processes, she finds a major source of problems to be a focus by the LTU on a particular part of the process, for instance audit and enforcement, rather than a comprehensive system of administration for large taxpayers. She notes that in Latvia, the most successful of these six countries, the LTU is "full-fledged."

C. Africa

A significant constraint on tax administration reform in Africa is the severe scarcity of resources. One way of dealing with this situation has been the introduction of semi-autonomous revenue authorities which are not subject to the same resource constraints as other public service bodies. Such revenue authorities were established in Ghana in 1985 and Uganda in 1991, followed by Zambia, Kenya, Tanzania, and Rwanda. In recent years, other African nations have begun the process of establishing them.[97] For revenue administration bodies, autonomy can be measured with respect to several aspects of the organization including "legal character, financing, governance, personnel policy, procurement policy, and accountability relationships."[98] The legal character of the revenue body depends on its enabling statute and determines what assets it can own. For example, the South Africa Revenue Service and the Kenya Revenue Authority were both formed through Acts of Parliament and are, respectively, a public service organization separate from the public sector and a corporate body. Both revenue authorities were given the ability to own assets, which implies a greater degree of autonomy.[99]

The results of semi-autonomous revenue authorities are mixed. Studies indicate that, in Sub-Saharan Africa, they initially led to an increase in revenue and a decrease in the perception of corruption. However, whether these positive consequences are sustainable over the long term is called into question by evidence from Tanzania and Uganda where tax revenue as a percentage of GDP is on the decline, and there is an increase in the perception of corruption. This evidence is consistent with more general studies, which have found that although "the more successful and sustainable revenue authorities appear to be those that

---

[97] Richard Bird, "Administrative Dimensions of Tax Reform" (April 2003) Draft Module prepared for a course on Practical Issues of Tax Policy in Developing Countries, World Bank at 23.

[98] World Bank information on semi-autonomous tax authorities, online: http://www1.worldbank.org/publicsector/tax/autonomy.

[99] *Ibid.*

have a higher degree of autonomy ... there is some evidence that the gains in revenue performance tend to be eroded after some time."[100] An extensive survey conducted by Arthur Mann for USAID found that the benefits of autonomous revenue agencies have risen and receded, and have not proven to be quick-fixes in otherwise problematic administrative situations – "they do provide a platform from which tax administration efficiencies can be generated, but their mere establishment offers no guarantee of success."[101] A complete assessment of the success of the reforms in Tanzania and Uganda would be premature at this early stage, but reviewing trends provides insight into possible future outcomes.

In both countries, the introduction of semi-autonomous revenue authorities was motivated in large part by the presence of pervasive corruption in the public sector. In Uganda, the reforms not only included significant increases in the salaries of tax officials relative to other public sector employees, but also the replacement of senior management in tax administration. The former reform was intended to reduce incentives for taking bribes in exchange for favourable treatment, and the latter reform was intended to break down the "corruption networks" that characterized the administration.[102] In both countries, the reforms were followed by a six-year to eight-year period of success – measured in terms of increased tax revenue and a decline in the perception of corruption – which now appears to be on the increase. Declining tax revenues may be explained by many factors that need not have anything to do directly with the tax administration body, but indications that fiscal corruption is on the rise suggest that corruption may indeed be one cause of the decline in tax revenues.[103] Indeed, a recent World Bank examination of Uganda's tax regime identifies three factors that directly hinder revenue generation through internal taxation, none of which is directly the result of incapable administrations: (1) the large size of the informal sector, (2) a lack of reliable income data and (3) unequal income distribution. The Ugandan Tax Authority has been delegated responsibility for devising the policy solutions to these problems.[104]

---

[100] *Supra* note 44 at 1.

[101] Arthur Mann, "Are Semi-Autonomous Revenue Authorities the Answer to Tax Administration Problems in Developing Countries?," *USAID, Fiscal Reform in Support of Trade Liberalization Project* (available online through http://www.fiscalreform.net, accessed April 16, 2006).

[102] Odd-Helge Fjeldstad, Ivar Kolstad and Siri Lange, "Autonomy, Incentives and Patronage: A Study of Corruption in the Tanzania and Uganda Revenue Authorities" (2003) Chr. Michelsen Institute (CMI Report R 2003:9). Available for download at http://www.cmi.no/publications/publication.cfm?pubid=1688.

[103] *Ibid.*

[104] http://www.finance.go.ug/peap_revision/downloads/PEAP2004/PEAP%202005. pdf.

In examining the possible causes of the increase in corruption in Uganda, Fjeldstad *et al.* suggest three factors, involving the reduction of autonomy, the diminution of incentives and the "cultural logics of corruption." A brief discussion of these factors, which operating cumulatively might explain the resurgence of old problems, offers lessons about the reform of tax administration. Providing tax authorities with a significant degree of autonomy may not reduce political interference but rather provide incentives for interference due to the attractive compensation packages received by personnel in these bodies. With respect to incentives, the revenue authorities in Uganda and Tanzania failed to sustain the incentives that might have led to the initial period of success. For example, in both countries, initial wage levels were high but were reduced after a period of time due to an economic downturn. In addition, decisions regarding promotions – which are incentives for good performance – were made on the basis of "connections" and favouritism rather than merit. Finally, the "cultural logics of corruption" refers to the general acceptance of rent-seeking and self-serving behaviour in Uganda and Tanzania. The cultures of both countries are communalist in that a great deal of value is placed on one's kinship ties. In a sense, the granting of favours to those with whom one is connected is seen as an extension of these ties, which in other contexts may create socially desirable outcomes.[105] The factors outlined by Fjeldstad *et al.* present possible reasons for the decline in the success of reforms directed at increasing the independence of tax authorities.

The World Bank's involvement in Tanzania's economic development has resulted in the beginning of a significant restructuring of that nation's tax system. This includes the reduction or elimination of many agriculture and basic education-related taxes. Furthermore, in 2002 the government began examining reforms of much of its broader tax policy – with the purpose of reducing the tax burden on individuals and weaker sectors of the economy and increasing the tax revenue generated from high performance sectors of the economy.[106]

Reforms in Cameroon have been geared towards simplicity. Taxpayers have often had little familiarity with the taxes they were required to pay, and the complexity of business tax laws in particular has required frequent interaction with tax officials, thereby increasing costs for both businesses and the tax authorities. The government of Cameroon attempted to address these problems by utilizing information and communication technologies.[107] In November 2001, a website was launched which provided tax-related data, primarily aimed at

---

[105]   *Supra* note 102.
[106]   http://siteresources.worldbank.org/TANZANIAEXTN/Resources/2002_PRSP_ProgressReport.pdf.
[107]   World Bank Projects, online: http://www1.worldbank.org/publicsector/egov/cameroontax.htm.

business people including foreign investors. Besides information on the corporate tax structure of Cameroon, the website contains information about payment and refund schedules, as well as locations and other details about tax tribunals. The latter information was included in the hope of reducing opportunities for public officials to extract payments in return for providing the information as they had previously done.

Cameroon's web-based initiative has been called "a partial success."[108] The main impediment to it having a significant impact is the fact that the overwhelming majority of Cameroonians do not have access to the Internet. In addition, the website does not allow for transactions; allowing citizens to fill out their tax forms online would increase the value of the technology. However, making tax information public is a useful first step in that it provides an objective measure by which taxpayers can judge the information provided to them by tax officials, and it has facilitated communication between tax officials and interested members of the public.

D. Asia

Tax administration in Asia has experienced a wide range of reform initiatives, and a variety of problems that differ dramatically between countries, many of which have significantly different taxpayer cultures, levels of government corruption, and institutional structures. What is clear from the Asian experience is that "tax policy in a developing country constitutes an essential part of a development policy,"[109] since most countries have recognized that reforms in other areas of the economy and political system need to be complemented by progress in the area of tax administration.

In China, the biggest problem plaguing the tax system is tax evasion. According to an assessment done by the Wall Street Journal in 2001, the Chinese media revealed that none of the "ten richest Chinese" paid any income tax,[110] while citizens living on meagre incomes pay the majority of income taxes received by the Chinese government. The Vice President of the Chinese Taxation Society is of the opinion that a regulatory function must be introduced and strengthened

---

[108]   The author of the World Bank Report on the web-based tax initiative in Cameroon, Kenhago Tazo Olivier, argues in the report that the initiative was a "partial success."

[109]   Miranda Stewart, "Global Trajectories of Tax Reform: The Discourse of Tax Reform in Developing and Transition Countries" (2003) 44 *Harvard International Law Journal* 139 at 173.

[110]   *People's Daily Online*, "Income Tax Reform, Dreadful Not in Slowness But in Standstill: Analysis," available at http://english.people.com.cn/200207/10print20020710_99474.html.

while at the same time improving the progressiveness of the current tax system. However, he concedes that supervision and control on all sorts of incomes is a difficult task. Currently, there is no effective punishment imposed on tax evaders. China has a cash society, which makes the task of supervision even greater. Some experts have suggested that bankcards be used to monitor and regulate economic activity and thus reduce tax evasion.[111] The situation highlights the failings of the Chinese tax collection system in several of the areas we have examined, such as voluntary tax compliance, enforcement and focusing on large taxpayers. They also underscore, however, the impact that social norms, such as using cash, can have on reform efforts.

Prior to 1994, local governments in China collected virtually all of the taxes and remitted the funds to the central government according to a prescribed formula. However, as the PRC's economy has evolved from central government control to local government control, local governments had less incentive to collect taxes effectively if these taxes were to be remitted to the central government. In 1994, yielding to both internal pressures and external pressures from foreign investors and international institutions, the PRC announced a series of fiscal reforms.[112] Included among these was a major reorganization of the PRC's tax administration that included a two-level system of tax collection. Post-1994, the State Administration of Taxation's (SAT) national tax offices collect taxes throughout the PRC while local governments maintain a separate system of tax collection offices. From the perspective of administrative independence and accountability, this reform can be seen as a distinctive one. Whereas reforms generally try to enhance the independence of tax administrations, the intent in this case was to align the incentives of the tax collection administration with those of the government for which they were collecting, a result seen as desirable in the circumstances. While the reforms have had a major impact on improving tax enforcement and administration, many taxes still go uncollected in the PRC.[113]

The Indian tax system has been a prime target for institutional reform.[114] The majority of India's taxpayers are salaried employees working for the government or private firms whose salaries are taxed at source.[115] In total, only about 2% of

---

[111]   *Ibid.*

[112]   Richard Cullen and Hua Ling Fu, "July 1, 1997: Hong Kong and the Unprecedented Transfer of Sovereignty: Fiscal Reform in China: Implications for Hong Kong" (1997) 19 *Loyola of Los Angeles International & Comparative Law Journal* 389 at 402.

[113]   *Ibid.*

[114]   Soutik Biswas, "Reforming India's Maddening Tax System" BBC News South Asia, July 5, 2004, available at http://news.bbc.co.uk/2/low/south_asia/3868073.stm.

[115]   *Ibid.*

India's population pays taxes.[116] This is facilitated, much as in China, by a large underground economy that operates on a cash basis, which makes it difficult to detect concealed income, gather statistics, or even estimate the tax gap. Although cash transactions are present in all economies, industrialized economies, such as members of the OECD, are dependent on a much smaller portion of them. These systemic issues are compounded by a notoriously corrupt tax administration and a complex tax system, each of which provides significant disincentives for citizens to report income. The system is so complicated that a tax consultant is often required to file even the least complicated returns, further raising the costs of compliance. An assessment of India's tax situation conducted by the World Bank in 2004 suggests a three-faceted reform to its tax regime: (1) the introduction of a state-level VAT, (2) tapping into India's growing professional population as a significant revenue-generating base and (3) inter-state revenue coordination as a means of streamlining the tax process and reducing the potential for corruption.[117]

In 2002, the Sri Lankan Minister of Finance, Nairman Choksy, announced, "Sri Lanka's tax regime is bedevilled by complexity. Simplification and deregulation are a critical necessity."[118] Choksy proposed a series of reforms to improve tax administration, including strengthening the Large Taxpayer Unit (LTU), creating a revenue authority to oversee Inland Revenue and the Customs and Excise departments, and restructuring the board of investments (BOI) and rationalizing tax incentive programs.

The LTU in Sri Lanka, which handles all taxes owed by the 1,200 or so largest taxpayers, was first created in 1995 and was reformed in 2002. As a part of the reform effort, assessors and tax officers are reorganizing their work to allow specialization in certain types of businesses. One substantial benefit is that it facilitates the development of specialized skills within different groups. Previously, one firm might have a different assessor for each type of tax obligation, which would result in a duplication of effort (the same firm would be assessed numerous times by different people) and provide an opportunity to manipulate the numbers (since no one team of tax assessors were looking at all of a firm's tax liabilities). Under the current regime, LTU tax teams are responsible for all taxes payable by a firm, improving the ability to

---

[116] *Ibid.*

[117] Stephen Howes *et al.*, *State Fiscal Reforms in India: Progress and Prospects* (World Bank Report No. 28849-IN, November 10, 2004).

[118] Jo Beth Mertens, "South Asia FDI Roundtable: Tax Administration" (Discussion Draft, Foreign Investment Advisory Service, Maldives, April 9–10, 2003). Online at: http://www.fias.net/ifcext/fias.nsf/AttachmentsByTitle/Conferences_SouthAsia_Maldives_Apr2003_030403+Mertens.pdf/$FILE/Conferences_SouthAsia_Maldives_Apr2003_030403+Mertens.pdf.

effectively monitor and enforce tax liabilities.[119] However, without complementary auditing and review procedures, the system also creates opportunities for abuse, since teams could with greater ease come to a private understanding with the taxed entity.

Another aspect of the Sri Lankan reform initiative, which at least partially addresses this point, is the creation of a National Revenue Authority, which oversees the work done by Inland Revenue, Customs Department and Excise Department. The goal of the Revenue Authority is to reduce duplication of work and increase communications between the three departments, improve efficiency and transparency, evaluate procedures, and recommend reforms. While the Ministry of Finance places great confidence in the ability of the Revenue Authority to make changes in the three departments, Martens finds that many of those working within the departments know very little about the role of this authority and how it will affect their positions. In these circumstances, she emphasizes the importance of securing buy-in from department heads.[120]

After an economic crisis, which started in late 1997, South Korea was forced to initiate a series of comprehensive economic reforms to overhaul the economy. As a part of these reforms, the government made a number of changes to the tax laws and tax administration.[121] One problem related specifically to the high number of returns done on the basis of estimated income. For instance, in 2000, 53% of tax returns were based on estimated income, while only 42% were based on bookkeeping.[122] However, in terms of total revenue, bookkeeping taxpayers contributed 67.4% of taxes received, while taxpayers with estimated income paid only 20.8%. In 2002, the Korean government recognized that in order to improve the tax system, the taxing authority must increase the number of bookkeeping taxpayers. The government has since implemented a number of incentives to encourage bookkeeping. Taxpayers who keep their books receive a 10% deduction and an exemption from tax audits for two years. Conversely, taxpayers who do not keep their books receive a 10% penalty. The ultimate goal was not only to encourage voluntary tax compliance, but to simultaneously facilitate enforcement.[123]

In 1996, with the introduction of global financial income taxation, Korean tax administration made a "full-scale change in the tax-return based administra-

[119]   *Ibid.*

[120]   Mertens, *supra* note 118 at 11.

[121]   Ilho Yoo, "Experience with Tax Reform in the Republic of Korea" (2000) 7:2 *Asia-Pacific Development Journal* 75 at 81.

[122]   Dae Hee Song, "Korean Tax Reform for the Global Era" (2002) Korea Institute of Public Finance, available at kipfweb.kipf.re.kr/lis/livedb/etc/tax_r/%EC%86%A1% EB%8C%80%ED%9D%AC_3%EC%A3%BC%EC%A0%9C.pdf.

[123]   Dae Hee Song, *supra* note 122 at 32–3.

tion system."[124] In September of 1999, National Tax Service (NTS) abolished region-based tax administration and required the submission of tax-related data from other government agencies and financial institutions. Korean businesses operate mainly on a cash basis, which, unlike credit, provides little transparency to the government. In order to increase incentives for credit card users, NTS introduced some measures, like income tax credit for credit card users, and began a credit card lottery.[125] All of these measures have helped to improve transparency and predictability and have made many hidden tax bases public.

While Korea has experienced success in its administrative reforms up to now, many areas of the administration remain in need of improvement. The current penalty tax rate for filing a false tax return in Korea is relatively low as compared to the US – 20% of the tax amount due and a five-year statute of limitation, whereas in the US, the penalty rate for the same violation is 75% and the statute of limitation is lifelong.[126] This speaks to the need for further fine-tuning in order to create appropriate incentives for voluntary tax compliance. Another problem has to do with the general public view of the tax system as unfair, in part because tax auditing has in the past been abused for political reasons. A significant part of this apprehension is due to the fact that the tax audit does not have a strong base in law and there is a lack of transparency in the selection process of tax audit subjects.[127]

Many Asian countries have begun modernizing their tax administration through the introduction of electronic processing and payment systems, with Singapore serving as an exemplar. The Inland Revenue Authority of Singapore (IRAS) introduced an imaging system to electronically process the paper-based returns filed by citizens in 1992, which was later improved to allow filing by phone, and then by Internet.[128] The new electronic processing system improved the efficiency of the administrative process, facilitated "back end" auditing, and eliminated unnecessary paper shuffling. Filing by phone was introduced in 1995, although few individuals initially made use of the option. In 1998, Singapore introduced direct electronic filing of income taxes via the internet. While taxpayers did not embrace the new system immediately, by the year 2000, 30% of all

---

124   *Ibid.* at 35.
125   *Ibid.*
126   *Ibid.*
127   *Ibid.*
128   Subhash Bhatnagar, "Modernizing Tax Administration in Singapore" (The World Bank Group, December 19, 2000) online at http://web.worldbank.org/WBSITE/ EXTERNAL/TOPICS/EXTINFORMATIONANDCOMMUNICATIONAND TECHNOLOGIES/EXTEGOVERNMENT/0,,contentMDK:20486053~menuPK: 1767268~pagePK:210058~piPK:210062~theSitePK:702586,00.html, or http://unpan1. un.org/intradoc/groups/public/documents/APCITY/UNPAN003581.pdf.

taxpayers filed electronically, and a further 10% filed over the telephone.[129] Moreover, about 60% of individual taxpayers made payments electronically, up to 80% of simple assessments were made automatically and the time needed to issue these assessments fell from 12 to 18 months to three to five months.[130] Staff turnover has decreased, tax arrears have fallen, property valuations have been kept current, and the audit function has been strengthened. The success of the new system can be attributed to Singapore's high per capita income and technologically sophisticated population and infrastructure, as well as strong support from political leaders, dedicated and skilled managers, the development and implementation of a strong business plan, and the creation of a semi-independent Revenue Authority. However, it is important to remember that Singapore's success was not immediate. The IRAS system took eight years to build, and is still undergoing improvements. It is also important to recognize that the factors that led to success in Singapore are by no means ubiquitous in developing countries.

While Singapore was very successful in implementing a computer system, other countries have been less fortunate. In February 1992, the World Bank signed a loan agreement to carry out a large and complex Information Technology (IT) project in the Revenue Department of Thailand.[131] The project differed from the computerization project in Singapore in that it focused on back-end computerization without any element of online delivery – something likely to be appropriate for a large portion of the population without relative easy and secure Internet access or literacy. The project was to be completed by the end of 1996, but in 1993 the software contractor defaulted and forfeited the contract.

Prior to the failed attempt at computerization, the tax systems used to collect and process tax revenues were slow and inefficient. Only about 38% of the 6.5 million tax returns received by the Revenue Department were computer-processed.[132] There was virtually no tax data retrieval capability to assist auditors in data processing or applying audit criteria to tax returns. In January 1992, the government introduced a major tax-restructuring program meant to increase the efficiency of the tax system. The national computer system was expected to

---

[129] *Ibid.*

[130] *Ibid.*

[131] Robert Schware and Subhash Bhatnagar, "Thailand's Troubled Tax Computerization Project" (The World Bank Group, February 22, 2001) available at http://web.worldbank.org/WBSITE/EXTERNAL/TOPICS/EXTINFORMATIONAND COMMUNICATIONANDTECHNOLOGIES/EXTEGOVERNMENT/0,,contentMDK: 20486040~menuPK:1767268~pagePK:210058~piPK:210062~theSitePK:702586,00. html.

[132] *Ibid.*

decentralize tax administration, introduce a single Tax Identification Number (TIN) to integrate all taxes and returns for each tax entity, and provide computerized billing and collection of all taxes.

The project was to be completed within three years, with a provision of two additional years for facilities management and system management. However, the project faced delays from the start. Initially, there were delays in the specification and design of suitable software applications. By the time the Revenue Department Consortium (RDC) finally delivered the software, the hardware that had been purchased had become outdated and had to be repurchased. In 1993, the software contractor defaulted on the contract, forfeiting its bond and leaving other RDC partners responsible for the delivery of the application software. In 1994, a major restructuring of the project was proposed. However, the problems by this point were overwhelming.[133]

As there was no centralized milestone reporting, there was no single point from which management could obtain a clear picture of project progress. While the RDC had assigned several senior managers to the project as well as a substantial support staff, the management responsibilities were not clearly defined. The implementation team lacked skills in system integration engineering, facilities management, applications development and software engineering. Furthermore, the team was under-resourced and pressured to achieve over-optimistic timelines. In 1995, after an independent audit report the World Bank placed the project under "intensive supervision."[134] In 1996 the Thai government proposed an extension of the project, but in view of the poor progress the World Bank decided not to grant the extension.

The Indonesian tax reforms of the 1980s were some of the most comprehensive undertaken by developing countries, and the new Indonesian system represented "a sharp departure from tax policies followed since independence in 1945."[135] Although 2000 and 2005 saw further reform efforts, these changes are minor compared to the sea change instituted in the 1980s.[136] They took place in an environment of overall government chaos, and in particular, opposition from the tax administration itself. Importantly, they are largely judged to have been a qualified success, even though there is significant room for additional reform. The World Bank judges that on the whole "the Indonesian tax

---

[133] *Ibid.*

[134] *Ibid.*

[135] Malcolm Gillis, "Comprehensive Tax Reform: The Indonesian Experience, 1981–1988," in Malcolm Gillis, (ed.), *Tax Reform in Developing Countries* (London: Duke University Press, 1989) at 79.

[136] For an overview see "Indonesia," Presentation at the Asian Development Bank 15th Tax Conference (2005) (available online at http://www.adb.org, accessed April 17, 2006).

reform program represents a substantial improvement over the pre-reform situation."[137]

As Malcolm Gillis writes, "the impetus for tax reform in Indonesia did not originate within the tax administration itself. On the contrary: in early 1981 there was initially no significant support for reform among any of the senior officials responsible for assessment and collection of taxes."[138] In part because oil revenues were at the time providing significant financing to the government, and in part because the administration had been accustomed to operating in a lax environment in which little was expected, there was limited impetus for reform. In addition to this, Gillis has suggested three other factors that worked against reform: low-income groups were largely ignorant of the costs of complicated indirect taxes, and in any event, the political system was unresponsive to popular pressure from them; high-income taxpayers paid very limited taxes; and "given the complexity of tax design and procedures, tax administrators had wide scope for securing irregular income."[139] Ultimate pressure for reform came from the Ministry of Finance and the government planning agency, with key considerations for reform including a belief that high oil prices would not be sustained, fear of inflation caused by the surge in oil revenues used to finance government expenditure on non-traded goods, and the belief that tax reform could be popular if accompanied by a reduction in nominal tax rates.[140]

Given the "extremely serious shortcomings in the machinery for assessing and collecting taxes,"[141] there was significant room for improvement. The ultimate reform experience encompassed initiatives in most of the benchmark areas we have discussed. Simplicity was a fundamental goal of the reforms, largely because of the salutary effects of such a change on tax administration. The simplification took place at the level of simplifying laws, but also streamlining administrative procedures in applying them. In fact, a completely new law was written consolidating all procedures for the assessment and collection of taxes.[142] This law contained two kernels: one was making procedures simple, and the second was depersonalization of the tax administration.[143] The latter of these points was essential in beginning to foster a culture of compliance, and allowing

---

[137]   Mukul Asher, "Reforming the Tax System in Indonesia," in Wayne Thirsk (ed.), *Tax Reform in Developing Countries* (Washington, DC: The World Bank, 1997) at 163.

[138]   *Supra* note 135 at 92.

[139]   *Supra* note 137 at 136. See also *supra* note 135.

[140]   *Ibid.*

[141]   *Supra* note 135 at 92.

[142]   *Ibid.* at 94.

[143]   *Ibid.*

for more effective enforcement. Depersonalization included limiting sharply direct contacts between taxpayers and tax authorities, and managing this conduct more closely, but also a marked reduction in administrative discretion (which was facilitated by the simplification). In addition, the reform also displaced the traditional government assessment of tax liabilities with a nascent system of self-assessment.[144] The move proved important in reducing the "routine workload on tax officials"[145] and "allowing for more and better audits of cases promising high revenue payoffs"[146] – in other words, large taxpayers become a focus of the tax authorities. The reforms also focused extensively on development of information technologies, including the introduction of a new computer management system.[147] This system got off to a very rocky start, although towards the end of the reform process the potential for efficiency gains was finally beginning to be realized, as field offices began to utilize the computer systems (technology directives were initially just ignored), and individuals developed a familiarity with the software.[148] About 75 tax officials were also sent for training internationally between 1981–88.[149] The government developed a strike force of auditors, largely composed of these foreign trained officials, who reported directly to senior levels of the administration and were charged with monitoring the behavior of large taxpayers reporting zero or negative tax liabilities.[150] The program was highly successful. During a one-year period starting in June 1986, at a cost of US$200,000, the auditors assessed a total of US$68 million in taxes, fines and penalties (not including amounts that were disputed), which amounts to 340 times the initial investment.[151] As Gillis points out, "this experiment yielded enough additional revenue to cover the costs of two other major investments in tax administration ... the overseas training of ... tax officials ... and the entire cost of all hardware and software used to date in the new computerized tax-information system."[152]

It is no surprise that the main administrative reform features overlap closely with the normative criteria outlined in this chapter: the inspiration for those criteria is largely based on international reform experiences. The changes instituted in Indonesia are not complete, and "there is still the opportunity to increase national revenue without increasing rates and by increasing the capacity of the

---

[144] *Ibid.*
[145] *Ibid.*
[146] *Ibid.*
[147] *Ibid.* at 92 and 111.
[148] *Ibid.* at 107–8.
[149] *Ibid.* at 111.
[150] *Ibid.* at 108.
[151] *Ibid.* at 108–9.
[152] *Ibid.* at 111.

tax administration …"[153] Nevertheless, the earlier reforms were largely deemed successful in improving administrative capacities.

III. CONCLUSION

Implementing an effective tax administration regime has been a challenge for many, if not most, developing countries. The importance of an effective tax administration to developing countries is critical, given that a constrained ability to raise revenues effectively also constrains governments in terms of expenditures on pressing developmental priorities. The gap between taxes nominally due and taxes actually collected is extremely large in many developing countries, suggesting the potential margins for improved tax administration performance. While the appropriate design of substantive tax policies is an important factor in enhancing a country's revenue-raising capacity, designing an effective tax administration regime is arguably even more important and has been relatively neglected in the development literature.

In terms of the three broad classes of impediments to effective rule of law reform in developing countries that we identified in Chapter 1 – resource constraints, social/political/historical values and practices, and political economy considerations – all three have played some role in explaining poor tax administration performance. First, with respect to resource constraints, low compensation rates for tax administration officials have affected the ability of governments to attract and retain suitably qualified personnel and have rendered existing personnel susceptible to corruption. Inadequate investments in information technology have further constrained the effectiveness of tax administrations in many developing countries. However, simply paying existing personnel more, without attending to appropriate prior education and training programs and on-the-job training opportunities, is unlikely to be effective. Moreover, in order to implement, manage and operate sophisticated information technology systems, broader investments in the requisite specialized human capital are necessary for these systems to be effectively utilized. Further, attending to the incentive structure of tax administration personnel is clearly important. More resources without changes in incentive structures are likely to have a limited impact. Appropriate forms of institutional independence are necessary to limit inappropriate forms of political interference in tax administration decisions. Incentive structures for personnel that reflect superior levels of performance, and compensation-based systems that reflect increased revenue collections legally due are also necessary.

---

[153] Mohamad Ikhsan, Ledi Trialdi and Syarif Syahrial, "Indonesia's New Tax Reform: Potential and Direction" (2005) 16 *Journal of Asian Economics* 1029 at 1.

In order to ensure accountability for due performance of tax officials' duties, simplification of substantive taxes and tax filing, auditing and collection procedures, and greater transparency in the administration of tax laws are important, as are effective avenues for challenging the front-line decisions of tax officials, both internally within the tax administration agency and externally in courts or other specialized appellate tribunals.

With respect to social/cultural/historical beliefs and practices, there is some evidence that more communalistic or patrimonial societies are more vulnerable to corruption in tax administration (and other aspects of public administration), through extrapolation of personalized kinship ties at the local community level to dealings with government officials. However, reforms in various developing countries that have minimized personal contact between taxpayers and tax officials have depersonalized much decision-making, including computerized processing of returns and simplification of rules and procedures that reduce the scope of administrative discretion and increase transparency for taxpayers, suggesting that over time these practices and values are amenable to change. However, simply setting up independent tax administration units, separate from line departments of government which are left unreformed, makes heroic assumptions about the ability of independent tax administration agencies to maintain themselves over time as islands of virtue in an otherwise corrupt or incompetent general public administration.

With respect to political economy considerations, clearly these have been a significant factor in many countries, in part because members of incumbent political regimes derive various perquisites from their ability to interfere in the administration of tax policies, and in part because large taxpayers, who have often been able to evade their tax obligations through incompetent or corrupt tax administration, are likely to resist effective administrative reforms. However, recognizing that ineffective revenue collection translates into constrained expenditure capacities for governments in developing countries, it seems reasonable to assume that a broad, if largely nascent, political constituency exists, or can be stimulated or nurtured, for effective tax administration reform. As we will explore in more detail in the final chapter to this book, the international community has an important role to play in supporting and nurturing such a constituency.

Finally, we note that many of the characteristics of good tax administration are likely to be replicated, in large part, with other specialized law enforcement or regulatory agencies – and are likely to face similar impediments.

7. Access to justice

I. NORMATIVE FRAMEWORK

A. Why "Access to Justice"?

The United Nations Development Program (UNDP) suggests that the importance of securing access to justice in developing countries lies in its links with establishing democratic governance and reducing poverty. It finds that democratic governance is undermined where access to justice for all citizens is absent. Access to justice is also closely linked to poverty reduction since being poor and marginalized means being deprived of choices, opportunities, access to basic resources and a voice in decision-making. Lack of access to justice limits the effectiveness of poverty reduction and democratic governance programs by limiting participation, transparency and accountability.[1]

In *Rethinking the Welfare State*, we propose that the normative justifications for state provision of legal services can be broken down into three broad notions: "the importance of equal access to the justice system from the point of view of liberal values and social solidarity; the necessity of access for the survival of the rule of law itself; and the role that the justice system plays in establishing and maintaining patterns of resource distribution."[2] Although the emphasis here is on the rule of law, it is important to consider the other justifications, as programs providing access to justice draw on all of these rationales.

The first rationale for access to justice is that it relates directly *to liberal ideals of equal freedom and dignity of individuals*. The common law adversarial system, in allowing parties to represent their own cause, is perhaps more often associated with the liberal ideal of individual autonomy. Despite this "*prima facie* preference for party autonomy, however, a state that is committed to liberal values will seek to ensure that each party has access to adequate and roughly equal legal representation."[3] In a liberal state that did not ensure access to justice

---

[1] United Nations Development Program, *Practice Note – Access to Justice* (Geneva: UNDP, 2004) at 3.
[2] Ronald J. Daniels and Michael J. Trebilcock, *Rethinking the Welfare State: The Prospects for Government by Voucher* (New York: Routledge, 2005).
[3] *Ibid.* at 80.

and the ability for individuals to adequately represent their cases, the goal of equal freedom and dignity of individuals would be threatened. This conception of access to justice will be most compelling in certain contexts, such as when the coercive power of the state is marshalled against individuals.

Related to the liberal ideal of equality of freedom and dignity is the liberal value that equal application of the law and respect for a diversity of viewpoints may be the only common value shared by a society. Liberal legalism posits that laws made through a pluralistic process should be applied equally to all citizens, and should also respect the vital interests of all groups in that society.[4] Without adequate access to justice, individuals may not be able to ensure that their vital interests are respected. Access to justice is therefore a vital aspect of the primary shared value of plurality and, relatedly, equal application of the law.

The second rationale is based on *the close relationship of access to justice to the rule of law*. If the rule of law is considered to be based on laws that are knowable and consistently enforced such that individuals are able to avail themselves of the law, then individuals must have the tools to access the systems that administer those laws. Hobbes argued that the rule of law must satisfy an obligation which Dyzenhaus has called the "publicity condition."[5] This means that individuals, in committing their obedience to the sovereign will, are promised the protection and benefits of law.

Dyzenhaus argues that the publicity condition is "not so much an external limit on the sovereign's legal power, but ... what the sovereign has to do in order to exercise power through the law."[6] Dyzenhaus argues further that part of the obligation that attaches to the rule of law, especially as that law becomes more complex, is for the government to provide the resources so that people can not only know the law, but also gain access to it.[7] However, the publicity condition does not imply that the state is under an obligation to ensure that every individual has a grasp of the entire set of laws.[8] Actual knowledge of the law is not considered a right under even the most progressive liberal theory, so long as every person has an opportunity to know the law.[9] This means that where individuals are unable to understand the law and its impact, the state has an

---

[4]   David M. Trubek and Marc Galanter, "Scholars in Self-Estrangement: Some Reflections on the Crisis in Law and Development Studies in the United States" (1974) *Wisconsin Law Review* 1062 at 1071–2.

[5]   David Dyzenhaus, "Normative Justifications for the Provision of Legal Aid," in John D. McCamus (Chair) (ed.), *Report of the Ontario Legal Aid Review: A Blueprint for Publicly Funded Legal Services* (Toronto: Queen's Printer, 1997) at 477.

[6]   *Ibid.* at 477.

[7]   *Ibid.*

[8]   *Ibid.* at 479.

[9]   Daniels and Trebilcock, *supra* note 2 at 81.

obligation to ensure that person has the resources to do so, but is not necessarily under an obligation to provide such resources where individuals have access to their own resources.[10]

The argument for access to justice following from the rule of law is based on access to the law, not access to justice. Access to the law requires that individuals can avail themselves of the laws of a state, with no requirement that those laws fit within a broader conception of justice. The other normative justifications of access to justice considered here include normative considerations of what justice is, either through liberal values such as freedom from deprivation of liberty, or through equality considerations in the redistribution of resources. Despite the indirect approach to justice, the rule of law approach has benefits because it "requires fewer controversial assumptions about the nature of political rights and duties, and the content of equality than does the liberal values approach."[11] In addition, the rule of law can include mechanisms that establish access to justice through mechanisms for challenging laws and policies, often based on constitutional rights. As an example, India has very liberal rules for public interest litigation, in a recognition that access to justice is limited for those who have the fewest resources and may be the victims of state-induced injustice.[12]

The third normative justification for access to justice relates to *principles of equitable distribution*. Where there are redistributive programs governed by law, access to justice may require that people seeking access to those programs be granted legal assistance to do so. Social welfare programs are generally derived from values of justice, and if there is no ability to access the law administering those programs then justice may not be served. Access to justice in this context requires that those who cannot understand or navigate the law pertaining to social welfare should have legal services provided by the state; otherwise the substantive equality goals of the social welfare programs cannot be attained. Other areas of law that safeguard equitable goals such as employment law and family law also create claims on the government to provide legal services. Employment law may ensure, especially to the lowest wage earners, access to gainful employment. Family law may ensure the well-being of women and dependent children. Anti-discrimination laws prohibit invidious forms of discrimination.[13]

The normative justifications for access to justice contribute to an understanding of what areas of the law should be given priority in the state provision of legal services. Government support for access to justice in any form must compete for scarce public resources. Thus, some ranking of priorities will be unavoidable.

---

[10]   Daniels and Trebilcock, *supra* note 2 at 81.

[11]   *Ibid.*

[12]   *PUDR [People's Union for Democratic Rights] v. Union of India* (1982) 2 SC 253 (Supreme Court of India).

[13]   *Ibid.* at 82.

Criminal law has been the area of law in which the provision of government services guaranteeing access to justice has been least controversial.[14] The consequences of a criminal conviction lead most directly to the deprivation of liberty by the state, thus implicating, in liberal terms, the defendant's negative liberty. From a broader philosophical standpoint, Dyzenhaus argues that one of the most important reasons that criminal law is often given priority in the provision of legal services is that it is the area of law with the most overlap of support from the different normative perspectives.[15] A further justification for emphasizing criminal law is that the individual is pitted against the full resources of the state.[16]

Yet there are several difficulties arising from the focus on criminal law. One is a strong gender bias, in that men are the primary users of legal services for criminal matters.[17] There are also concerns that in predominantly focusing on criminal law, and in particular the threat of incarceration, priorities may be misplaced. Legal outcomes in the realm of employment, immigration, family law or anti-discrimination law may be of equal or greater importance to many individuals.

Access to justice can play an important role where, as discussed above, the state provides social and welfare services. Where the idea of justice in a society is supported by legislation that redistributes resources, limitations on access to the law defining those benefits will constitute a limit on effective access to justice.

Status legislation is an important aspect of access to justice, as determinations of status in immigration and refugee cases can affect one's very membership in society and participation in its system of law. A determination of status can also be seen to infringe on negative liberty where a person is under threat of deportation.

Family law matters embrace a wide range of issues, but often touch on the breakdown of marriage and custody of children, as well as support and division of assets. Although negative liberty is not generally at stake, these outcomes can be critically important for those who have few resources and are dependent on a partner for support. Moreover, family law matters are especially important for women and dependent children, thus implicating the interests of gender equality.[18]

[14] Dyzenhaus, *supra* note 5 at 483.

[15] *Ibid.*

[16] F.H. Zemans and P.J. Monahan, *From Crisis to Reform: A New Legal Aid Plan for Ontario* (North York, Ontario: Osgoode Hall Law School, York University Centre for Public Law and Public Policy, 1997) at 120.

[17] National Association of Women and the Law, "Research Proposal – Women, Legal Aid, and Access to Justice," Submission to the status of women of Canada, the funding agency (1996).

[18] Mary Jane Mossman, "Gender Equality, Family Law and Access to Justice" (1994) 8 *International Journal of Law and the Family* 357 at 358.

Civil law disputes are often the lowest priority in the consideration of access to justice. Where there are private disputes between parties, however, those with fewer legal resources are often at a great disadvantage. Private disputes relating to contract, property, consumer protection, or landlord/tenant law may have important repercussions, yet be relatively inaccessible for low income people.

B.   International Human Rights Law

A number of international human rights instruments implicitly recognize a right to access to justice through requirements that individuals have access to remedies where their rights are violated. For example, the International Covenant on Civil and Political Rights (ICCPR) requires states to ensure that an individual whose rights or freedoms as recognized by the Covenant are violated has "an effective remedy". Further, states are required to ensure that a person claiming such a remedy has their case "determined by competent judicial, administrative or legislative authorities, or by any other competent authority provided for by the legal system of the State, and to develop the possibility of judicial remedy."[19] A number of other international human rights instruments also implicitly recognize the importance of access to justice in this manner, including the European Convention on Human Rights,[20] the African Charter of Human and People's Rights,[21] and the American Convention on Human Rights.[22]

With respect to criminal matters at least, access to legal representation is an important aspect of the right to access to justice as incorporated in international human rights instruments. The ICCPR requires in Article 14 that everyone have the right to legal assistance in criminal proceedings, including without payment where they do not have sufficient means to pay for it. Similarly, the *United*

---

[19]   International Covenant on Civil and Political Rights, Adopted and opened for signature, ratification and accession by General Assembly resolution 2200A (XXI) of December 16, 1966, entry into force March 23, 1976, Article 2(b). Available online: http://www.ohchr.org/english/law/ccpr.htm.

[20]   Articles 6 (right to a fair trial) and 13 (right to an effective remedy). Convention for the Protection of Human Rights and Fundamental Freedoms as amended by Protocol No. 11, Rome, 4.XI.1950. Available online at the European Council: http://conventions.coe.int/Treaty/en/Treaties/Html/005.htm (date accessed: October 12, 2006). See also *Access to Justice in Central and Eastern Europe: A Source Book* (Public Interest Law Initiative, 2003) at 159–174.

[21]   Article 7 (an individual's right to have their cause heard). African Charter of Human and People's Rights, available online at African Commission on Human and People's Rights: http://www.achpr.org/english/_info/charter_en.html (date accessed: October 12, 2006).

[22]   Article 8 (right to a fair trial). American Convention on Human Rights, available online at the Organization of American States: http://www.oas.org/juridico/english/treaties/b-32.htm (date accessed: October 12, 2006).

Nations Basic Principles on the Role of Lawyers state that in criminal matters, all persons should have access to lawyers and legal services, and that governments should ensure that legal services for poor and disadvantaged persons receive sufficient funding.[23] The Charter of the Organization of American States specifically requires that all persons receive "due legal aid" in order to secure their rights but does not specifically limit the right to criminal matters.[24] In addition, the European Court of Human Rights, the Council of Europe, and the European Union all reiterate this right in various ways.

The right to counsel in criminal matters has been constitutionalized in a number of countries, including South Africa. Some states have also recognized a right to counsel in civil cases. For example, in *Airey v. Ireland*, the European Court of Human Rights recognized a right to counsel in civil matters.[25] In India, Article 39A of the Constitution includes a broad notion of "equal justice and legal aid" which has been interpreted by the Indian Supreme Court as extending to some civil matters.[26] In South Africa, a constitutional right to legal representation in land tenure security matters has also been recognized.[27]

C. Obstacles to Accessing Justice

Cappelletti and Garth's *Florence Access to Justice Project*, published in 1978, refers to the so-called "access to justice movement" and note that a key challenge for this movement is to find new ways and means of making the rights citizens already possess both effective and enforceable.[28] The *Florence Access to Justice Project* was structured around the metaphor of three "waves" in the

---

[23]   *The Basic Principles on the Role of Lawyers*, adopted by the Eighth United Nations Congress on the Prevention of Crime and the Treatment of Offenders, Havana, Cuba, September 1990 online: http://www.ohchr.org/english/law/lawyers.htm.

[24]   Article 45, Charter of the Organization of American States, online: http://www.oas.org/juridico/English/charter.html.

[25]   32 Eur. Ct. H.R. (ser. A) 592 (1979), available at www.worldlii.org/eu/cases/ECHR/1979/3.html (date accessed: October 25, 2006).

[26]   Jeremy Perelman, "The Way Ahead? Access-to-Justice, Public Interest Lawyering, and the Right to Legal Aid in South Africa: The Nkuzi Case" (2005) 41 *Stanford International Law Journal* 357 at 394–5. Perelman notes that in the US, the Supreme Court has refused to recognize a constitutional right to counsel for civil litigants.

[27]   *Nzuki v. Government of South Africa*, No. LCC 10/01 (LCC 2001). See discussion in Jeremy Perelman, "The Way Ahead? Access-to-Justice, Public Interest Lawyering, and the Right to Legal Aid in South Africa: The Nkuzi Case" (2005) 41 *Stanford International Law Journal* 357.

[28]   Kim Economides, "2002: A Justice Odyssey" (2002) 34 *Victoria University of Wellington Law Review* 1 at 11. Discussing Mauro Cappelletti and Bryant Garth, *The Florence Access to Justice Project, 4 Volumes* (Alphenaandenrign: Sijthoff and Noordhoff, 1978).

access to justice movement.[29] The first wave responds to *economic obstacles*, which prevent people from accessing either information or adequate legal representation. The second wave is a response to the problem of *organizational poverty*, which refers to the inability of individuals to vindicate rights effectively where the interests at stake are both collective and diffuse. The third wave is a response to *procedural obstacles* to access to justice, which recognizes that, in some cases, traditional contentious litigation through the courts might not be the best way to provide effective vindication of rights.

Some of the issues facing developing countries in ensuring access to justice are similar to those faced by developed countries, albeit more acute. There are, however, additional factors present in many developing countries which present complications in addition to the obstacles identified by Cappelletti and which need to be considered in designing programs to address deficits in access to justice. Anderson notes first that in many countries, the poor are reluctant to become involved with the legal system. He identifies several reasons for this. First, there is in some cultures a social stigma attached to involvement with the law; litigation can be seen as making trouble while in any run-in with the criminal law, however minor, communities may judge people to be guilty until proven innocent.[30] Second, such reluctance is a rational response to the opportunities and risks people face if they become involved with the legal system. Anderson discusses for example the plight of people living and working "in illegality". As a result of rapid urbanization and inadequate urban housing, people are often forced to build their homes either on illegally occupied land or in violation of local planning regulations. In rural areas, the poor may require access to resources such as water and firewood which may only be available illegally, for example, from privately-owned land. Similarly, in many countries, the poor are predominantly engaged in forms of self-employment which are outlawed under colonial laws.[31] Like squatter housing, employment is often conducted on roads, abandoned lots, and other public areas, rendering the poor vulnerable to laws prohibiting public nuisance or vagrancy. Given that their lives are entrenched in illegality, Anderson argues

---

[29]   Cappelletti continued to work within the framework of these three "waves" of the access to justice movement. See for example Mauro Cappelletti, "Alternative Dispute Resolution Processes within the Framework of the World-Wide Access-to-Justice Movement" (1993) 56:3 *The Modern Law Review* 282.

[30]   Michael R. Anderson, *Access to Justice and Legal Process: Making Legal Institutions Responsive to Poor People in LDCs* (Washington, DC: World Bank, Paper for Discussion at WDR Meeting, August 16–17, 1999) at 20.

[31]   Anderson refers to a survey of laws in Zambia which found that most self-employment among the urban poor – including vegetable sellers, builders, tailors, and traders – was outlawed under colonial legislation. Anderson, *supra* note 30 at 20.

that the poor are unlikely to draw attention to this fact by voluntarily seeking out contact with the legal system.[32]

Second, Anderson finds that laws are often expressed in a language that is incomprehensible to the poor. In some cases this is because colonial languages are the official language of the law, even where the majority of the population are not fluent in such languages. For example, English is the official language of the law in India, Kenya, and the Solomon Islands, even though only a small proportion of the population in these countries speaks English. Similarly, the official language is French in Niger and Portuguese in Mozambique. Those who do not speak the official language of the legal system will inevitably experience difficulties in accessing justice, even where the laws are protective of their rights. Further, Anderson argues that even where the law is written in local languages, many of its fundamental concepts are at odds with the frame of reference used by local communities.

Third, Anderson finds that in many developing countries, the legal profession has a monopoly on legal representation which prevents private citizens from presenting their own cases in court. However, in many cases, there are not enough lawyers to represent the poor as those who are in practice tend to focus on more lucrative commercial or government work.

D. Delivering Access to Justice

While it is internationally agreed that all persons ought to have access to justice, there are no universally applicable guidelines for how this can be achieved in practice. While recognizing the importance of finding solutions that are relevant to local political, economic, social, and cultural circumstances – which vary significantly between countries – it is also helpful to look for best practices and experiences in countries that have dealt with these issues. Here we use Cappelletti's 'waves' framework and discuss commonly used models of improving access to justice.

(i) Overcoming economic obstacles through legal aid

Legal aid is the primary means used to overcome economic obstacles to access to justice. Legal aid can be delivered in various ways and many jurisdictions use a mix of delivery methods. The various methods may broadly be described as follows. The first is a *staff model* where legal services are provided by a staff lawyer employed by the legal aid plan or by a contracted community clinic. The staff model may permit realization of scale and specialization efficiencies, espe-

---

[32]   Anderson, *supra* note 30 at 20.

cially in more routine matters.[33] Staff model legal aid clinics may also develop more insight into specific community needs. Community-based governance mechanisms may enhance this capacity and provide a basis for an expanded policy advocacy role on behalf of clinic constituents.[34] Community legal aid clinics can often also integrate different services, such as social workers and community legal workers, into one center, extending the work beyond traditional legal representation and creating awareness of legal issues in the community that may help avoid formal legal proceedings.[35] Potential disadvantages of a staff model include quality decline. The concern is that neither the client nor the legal aid authority will be in a position to easily assess the quality of the work done in any given case, and that lawyers may be prone to "burn-out" if they are burdened with excessive case-loads or high-volume, routine, professionally unchallenging work. This is a real risk in a model where the legal aid authority has a fiscal interest in getting as many cases processed as possible by staff lawyers.[36]

In criminal matters, a *public defender* system may be used where clients have little or no choice of lawyer. The public defender system has been criticized on a number of fronts, including that "under-resourced, inexperienced and over-loaded lawyers participate in factory-line justice, and poor and minority defendants suffer accordingly."[37] The system has also been criticized for a perceived lack of independence. Lefstein cites a British defence counsel's response to the establishment of a public defenders' office in the UK: "There emerges ... the sinister figure of the state salaried defender, paid, selected and controlled by the state. That fine warrior is to be sent to do battle on the field of liberty and human rights, with his opposite number, his local colleague at arms, the salaried state prosecutor – an all-state contest ... . Instead of the interests of justice being paramount, the culture of negotiated justice will prevail ... plea bargaining be-hind closed doors, pressures to abort trials, cosy relationships between prosecution and defence to maintain the conviction count and the volume of cases and to minimize the cost."[38]

Despite such concerns, studies have shown that the introduction of a public defenders' office alongside other delivery mechanisms can be a helpful addition

---

[33]   *Ibid.* at 105.

[34]   *Ibid.* at 105.

[35]   *Ibid.* at 114–15.

[36]   John D. McCamus (Chair) (ed.), *Report of the Ontario Legal Aid Review: A Blueprint for Publicly Funded Legal Services* (Toronto: Queen's Printer, 1996).

[37]   Kate Akester, *Public Defenders: Learning from the US Experience* (London: JUSTICE, International Commission of Jurists, 2001) at 5.

[38]   Norman Lefstein, "In Search of Gideon's Promise: Lessons from England and the Need for Federal Help" (2004) 55 *Hastings Law Journal* 835 at 888. Citing 595 Parl. Deb, H.L. (5th ser.) 1998 1149.

to ensuring access to justice.[39] A recent study of the US experience finds that there are some positive aspects of such a system which would be difficult, if not impossible, to replicate in private practice. These include the ability to provide a central administrative and technological support base, freeing lawyers for their core function of representing and assisting clients; the ability to offer specialized services such as those for youth offenders; the ability to research, lobby, and litigate on systemic problems in the criminal justice system; and the ability to promote innovation.[40] The report finds that the most critical success factor for a public defender system is an accountability structure, it suggesting that the most effective and respected public defender systems were those where there was an independent body, such as a Commission, mediating between the government and the service. Without such a body, even good systems are exposed to political pressure and change and more likely to be subject to cuts and uncertainties. Other key success factors were noted as being provision of adequate resources and funding; protection against case overload; and effective quality control.[41]

A second model of legal aid delivery is known as *judicare* and involves the distribution of a certificate or voucher to clients who may choose their own lawyer or select from a pool of lawyers in private practice who participate in the system. Lawyers are paid either by the hour or by the case at a rate established by regulation. The *judicare* model has the advantage of a decentralized bar offering clients the opportunity to choose their own representation. It also ensures independence and that the principal loyalty of the lawyer in a case is to the client.[42] However, this model also has some practical disadvantages. The tariff rate will have a significant effect on the quality and experience level of counsel who accept legal aid certificates. Where tariff rates are low, legal aid clients may only have a limited choice if more experienced counsel refuse to participate in legal aid. Another disadvantage is that the *judicare* model is based on the notion that legal aid clients need the same type of lawyer and legal service as non legal-aid clients. However, this is often not the case, with more creative responses often required in legal aid cases. Further, for many legal-aid clients,

---

[39] See for example Susan Charendoff, March Leach and Tamara Levy, "Legal Aid Delivery Models," in McCamus, *supra* note 36 at 573. The authors discuss an experimental Public Defender Project conducted in the province of British Columbia in 1981.

[40] Akester, *supra* note 37 at 8. Akester notes as an example of innovation a scheme in Dade County, Florida where work is done with health professionals, social workers, and other experts to develop diversion and sentencing options, encourage restorative justice approaches, and change attitudes to offending.

[41] Akester, *supra* note 37 at 7.

[42] *Ibid.* at 105.

visiting a "traditional lawyer in a traditional lawyer's office" can be a daunting experience and in itself can present a barrier to the client's access to the legal service provided.[43]

A third means of providing legal aid is through a *contracting* system, which may be either competitive or non-competitive. In a competitive system, an individual lawyer or firm bids to provide legal aid services to a particular constituency. The winning bidder, ideally chosen according to both price and quality, is paid according to negotiated terms.[44]

One of the above-mentioned three models tends to be used as the dominant model by many jurisdictions. There are, however, a number of other means of delivery. *Pro bono* legal services are relied upon to a varying extent in different jurisdictions to address unmet legal needs. *Pro bono* services involve work undertaken free of charge, as a public service. It is a long-standing tradition in Anglo-American legal systems, going back to practices in medieval ecclesiastical courts and to a 1496 English civil law statute. There are enormous difficulties in relying upon *pro bono* work to fill unmet legal needs, as evidenced in the United States where there has been found to be a wide gap between the rhetoric and the realities of *pro bono* commitments.[45] In that country, debate over whether to make *pro bono* commitments compulsory has engendered significant opposition from the legal community. The US experience suggests that while ways should be explored to increase the amount of *pro bono* work undertaken, it should not be relied upon extensively to ensure access to justice.

(ii) Overcoming organizational obstacles: protecting collective rights

A number of options are available to governments to protect collective or "social" rights in cases where the individual alone is incapable of effectively vindicating those rights. One approach is the so-called *relator action*, where a government office such as the Attorney General is charged with representing the public interest. Cappelletti refers to the English experience in this regard, noting a key weakness as being that the Attorney General maintains full discretion on whether to authorize an action and can withdraw authorization at any

---

[43] Susan Charendoff *et al.*, *supra* note 39 at 569.

[44] For more on the various delivery models of legal aid, see: Daniels and Trebilcock, *supra* note 2, Robert J. Rhudy, "Expanding Access to Justice: Legal Aid Models for Latin America," in Christina Biebesheimer and Francisco Mejía (eds), *Justice Beyond our Borders: Judicial Reforms for Latin America and the Caribbean* (Washington, DC: Interamerican Development Bank, 2000) and David Crerar, "A Cross-Jurisdictional Study of Legal Aid: Governance, Coverage, Eligibility, Financing, and Delivery in Canada, England and Wales, New Zealand, and the United States," in McCamus, *supra* note 36 at 1071.

[45] Deborah L. Rhode, "*Pro Bono* in Principle and in Practice" (2003) 53:3 *Journal of Legal Education* 413 at 424.

time. Another approach is to give *locus standi* to specialized governmental agencies such as a Consumer Ombudsman to bring actions in the public interest. Advantages of this approach include agency expertise in the relevant area. However, shortcomings include the risk of the agency being captured by the interests it was designed to control.

Other solutions include the *class action* suit. While a prominent feature of the US legal system, there are also examples of this approach being taken in civil law systems. For example, in Brazil, a system of class action suits was introduced as a means of improving access to justice following a period of military dictatorship and political repression.[46] When the class action was first instituted in the US in 1938, its main purpose was to provide compensation for large numbers of relatively small harms or injuries by opening access to justice to groups of people who were not able or inclined to seek redress individually. From the 1960s, however, a second purpose became apparent, that is, to enforce new collective and general values, and to achieve or provoke changes in standards of practice and regulation.[47]

In Europe, a number of governments have instituted the *action collective* (or, in Germany and Austria, the *Verbandsklage*) where standing to sue is given to associations such as those established to protect consumers or the environment, leagues against racial abuse, leagues for the furtherance of the rights of women, and so on. The main advantage of this approach is that the associations are specialized in the area they represent. However, unlike government agencies, they are independent and therefore in a stronger position to protect the interests of those they represent. Unlike the class action solution, however, most countries require associations to be registered in order to bring an action and states often impose quite rigid requirements that limit the range of groups that can bring actions. In class actions, on the other hand, any citizen can act as the representative for an entire class.[48] Moreover, the purpose of the European schemes tends not to be to provide for redress of individual harms, but to provide for legislative change.[49]

(iii)   Overcoming procedural obstacles through alternatives to litigation

Cappelletti argues that in some areas of concern, traditional contentious litigation in court might not be the best way to provide effective vindication of rights.

---

[46]   Antonio Gidi, *Class Actions in Brazil: A Model for Civil Law Countries* (Houston: University of Houston Law Center Public Law and Legal Theory Series No. 2006-A-11, 2006) at 330.

[47]   Michele Taruffo, "Some Remarks on Groups Litigation in Comparative Perspective" (2001) 11 *Duke Journal of Comparative and International Law* 405 at 409.

[48]   Cappelletti, *supra* note 29 at 286.

[49]   Taruffo, supra note 47 at 410.

In such cases, governments should identify alternatives to the ordinary courts and the usual litigation procedure.[50] Such alternatives can be classified under the heading "alternative dispute resolution" (ADR), with possibilities including negotiation, arbitration, mediation, conciliation, various community-based forms of dispute resolution, and a range of simplified procedures as well as small claims courts.[51] Common themes include a conciliatory, non-contentious approach, as well as special courts, often staffed with lay judges.[52] Although most often used in civil cases, ADR has also been used to a limited extent in criminal proceedings.[53] For example, *Gacaca* courts, based on traditional justice, have been established in Rwanda to prosecute perpetrators of the 1994 genocide, because formal courts could not cope with the number of accused persons.[54] ADR is also often used in the family law setting, where amicable resolution of disputes can be particularly important.

Cappelletti identifies a number of difficult questions to which governments must pay attention in designing and promoting alternative dispute resolution. First, they must consider what would be the best kinds of approaches and institutions to promote. Second, which are the best kinds of persons to staff such institutions? These may include lay persons and persons involved with and personally aware of the same kinds of interests and problems as the parties in the case.[55] Third, they must consider the minimum standards and guarantees to be maintained in the alternative institutions and procedures. There is a risk that the alternative will provide only second class justice if the adjudicators in the alternative courts and procedures lack adequate independence and training. As well, the procedures might lack formal guarantees of procedural fairness which are typical of ordinary litigation.[56]

The access-to-justice movement has found compelling reasons to move in the "third wave" direction, that is, to promote the use of alternative dispute resolution mechanisms. First, there are situations in which conciliatory justice is able to produce results that are better than the results of contentious litigation. For example, such a procedure is likely to be more accessible, more rapid, less formal, less expensive, and the adjudicators might be better aware of the envi-

---

[50]   Cappelletti, *supra* note 29 at 282.
[51]   See generally Joanne Goss, "An Introduction to Alternative Dispute Resolution" (1995) 34 *Alberta Law Review*.
[52]   Cappelletti, *supra* note 29 at 287.
[53]   John Linarelli and Carolyn Herzog, "Model Practices in Judicial Reform: A report on Experiences Outside the Region," in Biebesheimer and Mejíasupra, *supra* note 44 at 3.
[54]   Eugenia Zorbas, "Reconciliation in Post-Genocide Rwanda" (2004) 1 *African Journal of Legal Studies* 1 at 36–7.
[55]   Cappelletti, *supra* note 29 at 288.
[56]   *Ibid.*

ronment in which the dispute has arisen and more capable of understanding the parties' plight.[57] Second, alternative dispute resolution may assist in opening the judicial process to a broader segment of the population.[58] However, Economides argues that current trends towards alternative dispute resolution in Western countries should all be seen as attempts to divert, reduce, or spread the costs of expensive legal cases by experimenting with novel means of dispute processing, management and funding, with any subsequent enhancement of citizen access a positive but secondary side-effect.[59] She also finds that there is a danger in such experiments that citizens may be offered peaceful solutions that, while they may satisfy people, provide something less than they would receive if they were to enforce their rights through the official legal system.[60]

(iv) Overcoming lack of knowledge

Finally, there is one crucial obstacle which Cappelletti does not explicitly include in his framework, namely, lack of knowledge. If they are to benefit from legal aid and other initiatives to promote access to justice, it is critical in the first instance that citizens be aware of their legal rights (and obligations). To this end, it is important that information is disseminated to help people understand their rights and how they can seek to obtain redress. The UNDP suggests that key actors in such an endeavour include government departments responsible for justice and for education, schools and universities, legal aid providers, quasi-judicial bodies, labour unions and NGOs.[61]

E. Independence and Accountability

Chapter 1 noted the critical importance of ensuring that a society's legal institutions exhibit both independence and accountability. The key institutions implicated by the foregoing discussion of access to justice include the judiciary and other alternative dispute resolution institutions, as well as the organization that manages a country's legal aid system. We discussed independence and accountability of the judiciary in Chapter 2. Accordingly, the discussion here focuses on the institution that governs a society's legal aid scheme.

Legal aid schemes should be, and be seen to be, independent of government. This is critical because legal aid tends to fund a predominance of cases in which the government is the opposing party, such as the prosecutor in a criminal case or the opposing party in poverty law cases where people are seeking publicly-

---

57 *Ibid.* at 289.
58 *Ibid.* at 287.
59 Economides, *supra* note 28 at 10.
60 *Ibid.* at 12.
61 United Nations Development Program, 2004, No. 110 at 7.

funded services. Independence in these cases is critical because it would undermine the objective of securing access to justice if the government was involved in determining the nature and quality of services being provided to its adversaries in particular cases.[62]

It is equally important, however, that legal aid systems be held accountable to the government and to citizens for the efficient and effective use of public funds. Attention is required to design a system of accountability that will best permit the formulation of good policy objectives and also have the means of assessing whether they have been met.[63] As well, it has been suggested that because legal aid schemes compete with other priorities for government funding, a critical aspect of governance of legal aid schemes must be to ensure that those in charge act as credible and effective advocates for the fiscal needs of the system.

In terms of the governance models discussed, a *judicare* model managed by the legal profession ensures maximum independence from state interference or influence, particularly where the profession has powers of self-regulation. However, Friedland suggests that such a model may provide more than an optimal amount of independence for a body operating a large program involving the distribution of significant sums of public money.[64] His argument is that a law society or bar association, properly valuing its independence, may not want to accept a government's demands for accountability for the manner in which public funds are spent.[65] However, it may be difficult to control the tendency for supplier-induced demand, whereby lawyers act on an incentive to provide more services than are appropriate for the situation. Where a legal aid scheme is governed by the profession using a *judicare* model, lawyers may be able to persuade the relevant authority that a given case or class of cases should be funded. They are also able to control how much work they do in any given case. A staff model operated by the legal profession is likely to have similar drawbacks in terms of accountability and is also likely to be unpopular with members of the profession with a self-interest in the predominance of a *judicare* model. Such members are not likely to be inclined to experiment with alternative delivery models.[66]

Thus, the question of governance of legal aid schemes by the legal profession raises larger issues regarding independence and accountability. Friedland suggests that an optimal solution is for schemes to be governed by an independent

---

[62]   Martin L. Friedland, "Governance of Legal Aid Schemes," in McCamus, *supra* note 36 at 1018.

[63]   *Ibid.* at 1019.

[64]   *Ibid.* at 1044.

[65]   *Ibid.* at 1045.

[66]   *Ibid.* at 1024.

agency with multi-stakeholder representation which would have the advantage of being both independent of government, but more willing to accept strict accountability for its spending.[67]

F. Legitimacy

It is critical that legal aid schemes have the confidence of the public, the government, those delivering the services and users of those services. The question needs to be asked as to which system will attract the most confidence and enjoy the most legitimacy with these groups.[68] There has been debate over the respective merits of the two most common legal aid models, the *judicare* model, and the staff model. Evidence suggests that neither system is inherently more effective but that recognizing the strengths inherent in each model is likely to lead to the most effective delivery of services and acquire the greatest legitimacy among stakeholders.[69] Determining what is the best delivery mix for any given society requires an understanding of the needs of the relevant population.

Friedland refers to a number of characteristics that should be considered in thinking about governance of a legal aid scheme.[70] It is suggested here that legitimacy is in large part reliant upon the other governance characteristics noted by Friedland. In addition to independence and accountability, Friedland identifies first, the importance of choosing a system that is best at rationing and applying scarce resources to ensure both quality representation and coverage. Second, he stresses the importance of developing a system that will permit innovation and experimentation to determine the appropriate mix among the various types of existing and new legal aid delivery systems. He suggests that a key goal in this regard ought to be improving access to the law, not just access to court proceedings. Third, he discusses efficient governance, including the importance of attracting and retaining managerial talent and expertise. Fourth, he argues that whatever system of governance is chosen, it must ensure that the entire system is managed as a coordinated enterprise. Finally, he suggests that the level of government funding allocated to legal aid may be influenced by the credibility and legitimacy of the governance regime.

---

[67] *Ibid.* at 1048.
[68] *Ibid.* at 1019.
[69] *Ibid.* at 106–7.
[70] Friedland, *supra* note 62 at 1019.

II. EXPERIENCE WITH ACCESS TO JUSTICE REFORMS IN DEVELOPING COUNTRIES

A. Latin America

Beginning in 2001, the Association of the Bar of the City of New York, the Colegio de Abogados de la Ciudad de Buenos Aires and the University of Palermo Law School, have sponsored annual conferences on *pro bono* legal services and access to justice in Latin America. Participants, who include NGOs and members of the private bar, canvass approaches to encouraging *pro bono* legal services and enhancing access to justice more broadly construed.[71] In 2005, the Strategy Summit for the Americas, which built upon the preceding conferences, brought together representatives from Argentina, Brazil, Chile, Colombia, Mexico and Peru, and produced documentation on mechanisms for access to justice in each of these countries.[72] A follow-up conference was planned for late 2006.

Legal aid reforms in Latin America have been heavily focused on the provision of adequate resources for and training of legal aid personnel, and the institutionalization of previously *ad hoc* forms of public defence.[73] In Bolivia, for instance, prior to reforms there were only 11 public defenders working on criminal cases in the entire country, rendering the constitutional right to counsel *de facto* illusory. Since the creation of the Office of Public Defence in the Ministry of Justice in 1995, the number of public defenders had increased to 200 as of 2002, and public defenders now provide representation to a majority of criminal defendants.[74] High caseloads and insufficient funding have, however, been reported in US government reviews.[75] In 2003, a new National Public De-

---

[71]   See, for example, Association of the Bar of New York City, Report by the Committee on Inter-American Affairs on the Buenos Aires Conference on *Pro Bono* and Access to Justice (September 13–14, 2001 and November 29–30, 2001, Buenos Aires, Argentina).

[72]   The Cyrus R. Vance Center for International Justice Initiatives, Summit Report (Strategy Summit for the Americas: A Profession Supportive of Democracy, New York, March 3–5, 2005). See also Country Reports, online at: http://www.abcny.org/Vance-Center/library/index.htm

[73]   Richard J. Wilson, "Growth of the Access to Justice Movement in Latin America: The Chilean Example" (Justice Initiatives newsletter, Open Society Institute, February 2004) at 31.

[74]   USAID Office of Democracy and Governance, "Achievements in Building and Maintaining the Rule of Law: MSI's Studies in LAC, E&E, AFR, and ANE" (Occasional Paper Series November 2002, PN-ACR-220) at 40. [hereinafter "Achievements"].

[75]   US General Accounting Office, "U.S. Democracy Programs in Six Latin American Countries Have Yielded Modest Results" (Report to Congress, March 2003).

fence Office was established under the auspices of the Ministry of the President, with 54 staff attorneys as of 2005.[76] The relationship between the two bodies is not clear. In Panama, USAID was involved in the establishment of an Institute for Public Defenders that previously did not exist. Institutional support has been mainly in the form of case management and training innovations, and while USAID counts among its advances "increased professionalism and esprit de corps" it acknowledges problems of limited staffing, heavy caseloads, and inadequate facilities.[77]

In Colombia, the public defence office was first established in 1991 and began receiving international support in the mid-1990s with a USAID project that "sought to teach basic skills and approaches to case analysis, planning strategies, and defense techniques to inexperienced lawyers who would be defending indigents in criminal prosecutions."[78] From 150 public defenders in the mid-1990s, the Colombian public defence grew to 1,125 by 2002, with each public defender receiving basic training in case analysis, planning strategies, and defence techniques. USAID argues, however, that the program remains under-funded and under-staffed. Hammergren notes in this respect that the placement of public defence under the Human Rights Ombudsman within the *Procuraduria General* was a design flaw. She contrasts this arrangement with that in Costa Rica, where the public defence is installed within the judiciary.[79] Because the judiciary is guaranteed 6% of the national budget, public defence is well funded, public defenders are well paid, and the career is held in high esteem by lawyers. Hammergren blames this aspect of the Colombian system for low salaries and a lack of job security, which in turn force public defenders to take outside work. A similar effect can be observed in El Salvador, where the public defence body was also placed within the *Procuraduria General*, and serious funding problems have ensued.[80] Local officials have been reluctant to pay public defender salaries, leaving USAID to fill this role. When USAID funding has ended, salaries have sometimes not been paid.[81] Moreover, hiring and promotion practices became disassociated from

---

[76] US Department of State, "2005 Country Reports on Human Rights Practices: Bolivia" (March 8, 2006). Justice Studies Center of the Americas, Report of Justice 2nd edn, Bolivia, Public Defenders Office, online at: http://www.cejamericas.org/reporte/muestra_pais.php?idioma=ingles&pais=BOLIVIA&tipreport=REPORTE2&seccion=DEFPUBLI.

[77] *Ibid.* at 83.

[78] *Ibid.* at 50.

[79] Linn Hammergren, *Institutional Strengthening and Justice Reform* (USAID PN-ACD-020) at 17. Hammergren recognizes a potential conflict of interest but notes that in Costa Rica in particular, it has worked well.

[80] *Ibid.* at 25.

[81] Luis Salas, "From Law and Development to Rule of Law: New and Old Issues in Justice Reform in Latin America," in Pilar Domingo and Rachel Sieder (eds), *Rule of*

performance, and linked more to personal ties to the Procurador.[82] As Hammergren emphasizes, however, it is not the formal organizational placement of the public defence that is ultimately important but rather that "wherever located, the entity has sufficient funding and autonomy to meet its immediate needs."[83]

Another popular method of enhancing access to justice, exemplifying some of the key advantages of the staff model of legal aid, is the *Casa de Justicia*, or House of Justice. *Casas de Justicia*, located in poor and marginalized neighborhoods throughout Latin America, deal with "everyday problems, such as child support/custody issues, domestic violence, property disputes, misdemeanors, personal injuries, and administrative matters."[84] The Casas are not simply legal clinics, but incorporate local prosecutors, public defence lawyers, legal aid officers, police units, even social workers, counselors, and psychologists. As such, they are described as "one-stop legal shops."[85] The Casas are also closely linked to alternative dispute resolution, as they encourage innovative solutions to legal problems and try to channel cases away from the formal court system where appropriate. In the Colombian context, USAID argues in favour of these Casas that despite years of war, most crime affecting everyday people arises from a general lack of respect for the law and a sense of lawlessness. The "paramount failure of the law and public security in Colombia is (that) the formal justice system has had little presence, authority, or relevance to everyday life."[86] In other words, whereas previously, "'justice' to these communities meant 'more police,'" the "presence and operation of the *casas de justicia* reinforce the rule of law"[87] and embed legal culture at a grassroots level. Centers have also been set up in El Salvador, Costa Rica, Guatemala, and Argentina.[88] In 1994, the government of Ecuador assigned five of its *comisarias*, or local legal clinics, to specialize in matters of domestic violence. Initially, drastic under-funding and the fact that domestic violence was not illegal at the time in Ecuador made the specialized *comisarias* largely ineffective. Since then, the passing of anti-domestic violence legislation, funding by foreign donors, and partnerships with NGOs have increased the efficacy and accessibility of the specialized *comisarias* and the number of *comisarias* increased to 31 by 2002.[89]

Law in Latin America: The International Promotion of Judicial Reform (London: Institute of Latin American Studies, 2001) at 27.

82   Hammergren, *supra* note 79 at 22.
83   *Ibid.* at 28.
84   "Achievements," *supra* note 74 at 49.
85   *Ibid.*
86   *Ibid.*
87   *Ibid.* at 50.
88   *Casas de Justicia: Argentina* (prepared for "Summit of the Americas," New York, March 3–5, 2005).
89   "Achievements," *supra* note 74 at 63.

A hodgepodge of other programs has been developed across the region by NGOs and other private actors, many of which replicate to some extent the *Casa de Justicia* model of legal aid. The Community Legal Support Center, founded in 2004 in Moreno, Argentina, offers free legal representation on matters relating to public services, such as "transportation, drinking water, electricity, gas [or] sewage."[90] The Center coordinates legal resources across the community in order to arrange *pro bono* representation for each issue, and trains law students and other members of the community in "community advocacy."[91] In Brazil, the *Balcao de Directos*, established in 1996 in Rio, provides free legal representation to poor residents, sponsors legal education in the form of workshops and seminars, and trains mediators. In 2004, 15,979 consultations were undertaken.[92] In Colombia, the Non-remunerated Legal Services program offers legal assistance to non-profit organizations.[93]

Cappelletti's "second wave" of access to justice reform – responding to the inability of individuals to vindicate rights effectively where the interests at stake are both collective and diffuse – has been evident in Latin America. For example, in Costa Rica, reforms in 1989 led to the creation of the fourth Chamber of the Supreme Court, the Sala IV, with a strong mandate for constitutional review, giving Costa Ricans greater access to the Supreme Court and a new avenue to challenge government action. Prior to the reforms, the process for challenging national laws and action was highly devolved and citizens could appeal to members of the legislative assembly, the president, the cabinet, or to the courts; but this latter avenue was unpopular.[94] Sala IV has embarked on a publicity campaign to educate Costa Ricans about the Constitution and the justice system and the court has adopted user-friendly procedures for filing cases. Sala IV accepts cases of *amparos* (appeals to protect personal rights) and habeas corpus, "from anyone, of any citizenship, in any language, written on anything, without the need for legal counsel, legal knowledge, or filing fees. Thus, access to the judicial system was thrown wide open."[95] Since the creation of Sala IV, the Costa Rican Supreme Court has experienced a dramatic increase in its caseload and has been a significant and positive force in increasing access to justice in Costa Rica.

---

[90] Community Legal Support Center: Argentina (prepared for "Summit of the Americas," New York, March 3–5 2005) at 2.

[91] *Ibid.*

[92] *Balcao de Directos*: Brazil (prepared for "Summit of the Americas," New York, March 3–5, 2005) at 4.

[93] Non-Remunerated Legal Services: Colombia (prepared for "Summit of the Americas", New York, March 3–5, 2005).

[94] Bruce M. Wilson, Juan Carlos Rogríguez Cordero and Roger Handberg, "The Best Laid Schemes … Gang Aft A-gley: Judicial Reform in Latin America – Evidence from Costa Rica" (2004) 36 *Journal of Latin American Studies* at 518.

[95] *Ibid.* at 524.

Alternative Dispute Resolution (ADR) has also been popular in Latin America. In Argentina, for instance, mediation was, according to USAID, "virtually unknown"[96] until the 1990s. When legal service centers were established in Buenos Aires in 1991, they included the training of 30 mediators. These mediators were found to have "resolved many of the cases brought to the centers,"[97] and the Ministry of Justice was persuaded to launch a pilot program under which USAID trained Argentinean mediators. In 1995, with mediators resolving 75% of its cases, a law was enacted making mediation mandatory for all commercial cases.

In Guatemala, the Mediation and Conciliation Centre of the Judiciary was created in 1998 out of the 1997 Peace Accords. Through 2001, the Centre was staffed with four full-time and 17 part-time, well-trained conciliators, participation in the program was voluntary, and services were offered free of charge. In the first six months of operation, the Centre handled 300 cases, mostly family law matters, 141 of which were resolved. As a voluntary forum, the Centre does not have coercive powers of enforcement; however, staff at the Centre, who are responsible for monitoring compliance, argue that parties to a voluntary agreement are more likely to abide by its terms.[98] At the Universidad de San Carlos, law students participate in a mediation clinic at which, after receiving 16 hours of training, they mediate cases under the supervision of lawyers. By 2001, 150 cases, mostly minor penal matters, had been handled, half of which were resolved. Reparation in these proceedings is limited to compensation or apologies, and traditional punishments are not imposed.

In Ecuador in 2001 the World Bank launched a Judicial Reform Project, which, among other goals, sought to solidify and institutionalize ADR in the court system. ADR was to be a tool for judges, allowing them to refer a case to mediation when it seemed appropriate. Pursuant to this goal, the Bank trained professional mediators and judges, and "information … was disseminated to the general public and to legal professionals."[99] Though the ADR project now appears to be on a sound trajectory, World Bank project staff identifies resistance from judges and staff. Due to misperceptions about the nature of ADR "many within the Judiciary see ADR as a competitor to the courts."[100] Among other

---

[96]   "Achievements," *supra* note 74 at 35.

[97]   *Ibid.*

[98]   Martha A. Field and William W. Fisher III, *Legal Reform in Central America: Dispute Resolution and Property Systems* (Cambridge, MA: Harvard University Press, 2001) at 147–9.

[99]   World Bank, "Ecuador Judicial Reform Project Implementation Completion Report" (Document No. 26259) at 2, online at: http://www-wds.worldbank.org/servlet/WDSServlet?pcont=details&eid=000012009_20030708152143.

[100]   *Ibid.* at 20.

strategies, inclusion of law students in the ADR process is seen as an important way to develop next-generation support.

ADR programs for legal reform throughout Latin America have been criticized for underestimating the apathy or opposition to such programs and failing to ask why ADR, even though permitted by many of the civil codes in Latin America, was not heavily utilized in the past. "Donors have failed to gauge the legal culture ... . [and] have overestimated the degree of local support for the reform."[101] In addition to fears of lawyers and judges – the former of losing fees and the latter of losing control over cases – some ADR programs have met additional problems from ill-considered design. For example, in El Salvador the use of ADR in cases of juvenile delinquency has been heavily criticized for allowing mediation regardless of the seriousness of the offence, resulting in accusations of threats by gangs or criminal associates of the accused to compel the victim to accept conciliation.[102] Conversely, mediation and other forms of ADR also play a valuable role where judicial corruption is prevalent. Evidence has shown that, in circumventing the court system, ADR not only reduces corruption in its own right, but more specifically that it can enhance access to justice for poor populations who cannot afford to bribe judicial officials.[103]

Other NGOs have also undertaken projects aimed at public legal education. Street Law, a Washington, DC-based organization, has initiated programs in Haiti, Bolivia, Ecuador, Panama, and Chile, all partially funded by USAID.[104] The organization has held legal information seminars in Bolivia at prisons, women's community centers and other locations with a concentration of marginalized groups, radio demonstrations of legal issues by law students in Ecuador, and training of women community leaders and law students to lead workshops on legal and human rights for women in Panama.[105] In collaboration with Street Law, Human Rights Education Associates has assembled their "Manual on Street Law-type Teaching Clinics at Law Faculties" which "draws heavily from experiences in Central and Eastern Europe and the former Soviet Union in providing practical suggestions for setting up a teaching clinic at law schools, where law students teach everyday law to the public."[106]

---

[101] Salas, *supra* note 81 at 28.

[102] *Ibid.*

[103] Thomas J. Moyer, "Mediation as a Catalyst for Judicial Reform in Latin America" (2003) 18 *Ohio State Journal on Dispute Resolution* 619 at 650.

[104] Street Law website, Latin America and the Caribbean, http://www.streetlaw. org/latincaribbean.html.

[105] *Ibid.*

[106] Human Rights Education Associates, "Manual on Street Law-type Clinics," now available online, http://www.hrea.org/streetlaw.html.

B.   Central and Eastern Europe

The Communist-era legal aid system was incorporated into the machinery of the state. Citizens requiring free legal services applied to an attorney at their local advocacy center,[107] who in turn requested a decision from his or her supervisor. While Bárd and Terzieva argue that the Communist system created positive financial incentives for lawyers to accept legal aid cases, they do not address the question of whether the relationship between the advocacy centers and the Party tended to politicize legal aid decisions.[108] Moreover, the post-Communist legal aid systems in many Central and Eastern European countries have been characterized as narrow and *ad hoc*, due to both low levels of funding and inadequate procedures, such as a lack of objective criteria for determining eligibility for assistance.[109] One commentator has tied these contemporary problems to the Soviet legal aid philosophy of mandatory defence, which assigned counsel automatically for a limited number of serious offences, presumably on the theory that non-mandatory cases are relegated to second-order importance.[110]

In the Czech Republic, the 1993 Constitution and Charter of Fundamental Rights and Freedoms guaranteed the right to legal representation, but the guarantee has faced opposition in several forms. For instance, from 1990 to 1996, laws regulating attorney fees prohibited lawyers from offering legal aid services

---

[107]   By the description, advocacy centers appear to be analogous to (or perhaps another term for) the Soviet college of lawyers; see the section on Bar Associations, *infra*.

[108]   Károly Bárd and Vessela Terzieva, "Access to Legal Aid for Indigent Criminal Defendants in Central and Eastern Europe" (1998) 5 *Parker School Journal of East European Law* 209.

[109]   "There is no clear procedural requirement for granting legal aid outside mandatory defence in criminal cases. Appointment of a counsel in the non-mandatory cases is very rare, which results from the lack of procedural rules on how to handle such requests and lack of awareness … In some countries there is no "means test" and no uniform standards concerning when and how to appoint *ex officio* counsel … The appointment procedure for counsel is not transparent."*Access to Justice In Central and Eastern Europe: Forum Report* (European Forum on Access to Justice, December 5–7, 2002, Budapest, Hungary) at 13. In 2002, the World Bank found in Yugoslavia that "[d]espite all the good will and great dedication on the part of lawyers working for NGOs and lawyers in private practice, the assistance remains insufficient and on an *ad hoc* basis, and suffers from a lack of objective criteria for the provision of legal aid." (World Bank, Legal Department, *Federal Republic of Yugoslavia Legal and Judicial Diagnostic* (2002) at 35.) See also Second European Forum on Access to Justice (February 24–6, 2005, Budapest, Hungary) at 5–6.

[110]   Vessela Terzieva, "Access to Justice in Central and Eastern Europe: Comparative Report" (Columbia University Law School Public Interest Law Initiative) (PILI) 2003) at 1.

without the consent of the Czech Bar Association. This may be related to the post-Communist power struggle within the organized bar, in which traditional colleges (or advocacy centers) fought to retain their customary control of advocacy functions. With new market entrants in the form of private firms looming, tight control of free legal services would have been consistent with an attempt to institute price controls on the market. Moreover, until amendments to the Code of Criminal Procedure in 2001, the right to state-sponsored legal aid was limited to mandatory defence cases (pursuant to Article 39 of the Criminal Procedure Code). Beyond the scope of mandatory defence in criminal matters, and in civil, administrative and constitutional cases, free legal representation could be obtained only through a request of the Czech Bar. While the Bar did have certain procedures governing such requests and did in fact supply a significant number of parties with free representation, the arrangement is "not explicitly linked to the [legal] right to free legal aid."[111] In other words, representation is not ensured by government nor does it flow from the constitutionally-protected right; rather it is a privately administered solution, and "a makeshift response to the need to implement a constitutional right."[112] The 2001 amendments entrenched legal aid as a formal legal right in all criminal cases, where the defendant "proves that he or she does not have sufficient financial means to cover the costs of his or her defence." However, no administrative structure has yet been created for making the insufficient means determination; rather it is decided by the courts on a case-by-case basis, and by one account, has been unevenly applied.[113]

The implementation of guaranteed legal assistance has also been resisted by police, in the context of pre-trial access to counsel. A frequently used method of police interrogation has been the "explanation," an interrogation process taking place before the investigation officially opens, allowing police to justify denial of the constitutional right to legal counsel.[114] In 1996, a ruling from the Constitutional Court held that the right to legal aid encompassed explanations; the directive was ignored, and police continued to question suspects under the guise of the explanation until a 2001 procedural amendment explicitly required it.[115] Accused persons are informed of their rights at the time of arrest by way

---

[111]   Barbora Bukovská, "Access to Justice Country Report: Czech Republic" (paper presented at the European Forum on Access to Justice, Budapest, 5–7 December 2002) at 6, online at: http://www.pili.org/library/access/CEE%20Conference_CountryReports/PDF/CzechRepublic.pdf.

[112]   *Ibid.* at 2.

[113]   Barbora Buskovská, "Access to Justice Country Report: Czech Republic" (presented at the Second European Forum on Access to Justice, Budapest, Hungary, February 24–6, 2005).

[114]   *Ibid.* at 6.

[115]   *Ibid.*

of a statement essentially consisting of "direct quotations from the CCP [Code of Criminal Procedure]."[116]

Following a similar pattern, Article 24 of the 1991 Romanian Constitution guarantees the right to a defence.[117] The Code of Criminal Procedure states that a defendant "has the right to be informed of the charge 'as soon as possible' and 'in a language he understands', in the presence of a lawyer. From the moment the accused or defendant is charged, he must have legal assistance when questioned by police or prosecutors, or where confrontation takes place, and in general, during any investigative activity which requires his presence."[118] With the sole exception of extradition proceedings, however, where the rights and requirements with respect to legal aid are well established, the institutional structure of a legal aid system is mostly lacking. Further, local civil rights lawyer Monica Macovei argues that "the low quality of the services provided within the legal aid system makes this right meaningless."[119] She paints a harsh picture of the quality of legal aid lawyering:

> [L]awyers confine their role to signing written depositions, without having first discussed a defence strategy with their clients, and in most cases, without even having studied the evidence gathered by the police or prosecutor. Moreover, lawyers would often allow their clients, when questioned by police and prosecutors, to admit crimes with which they are not charged. Visits to clients are not a common practice. On the contrary, it is common that lawyers meet their clients only in the courtroom, and even at this point they don't have a serious talk about a defense strategy. They might not talk at all. In practice, most of the assigned lawyers do nothing but show up in the courtroom and plea for indulgence.[120]

A similar situation is described in Estonia, where court-appointed defence counsel are ill-prepared and unfamiliar with their clients, and in some cases in defence of their client state simply that "I leave this decision to the court."[121] Frank Emmert suggests that systemic problems are responsible, including the disparity in pay between private practice and appointed defence counsel, where

---

[116]   Mark Thieroff and Miroslav Krutina, "Country Report: Czech Republic" (1998) 5 *Parker School Journal of East European Law* 111 at 130; see also Bukovská, *supra* note 111 at 17.

[117]   Cozmin Obancia, Marinela Cioroaba and Andrei Savescu, "Access to Justice Country Report: Romania" (paper presented at the European Forum on Access to Justice, Budapest, December 5–7, 2002) at 3, online at: http://www.pili.org/library/access/CEE%20Conference_CountryReports/PDF/Romania.pdf.

[118]   Monica Macovei, "Country Report: Romania" (1998) 5 *Parker School Journal East European Law* 185 at 196.

[119]   *Ibid.* at 203.

[120]   *Ibid.*

[121]   Frank Emmert, "Administrative and Court Reform in Central and Eastern Europe" (2003) 9 *European Law Journal* 294.

partners in law firms bill 250 euros an hour compared to approximately 12 euros an hour for public defence counsel.[122]

Several Central and Eastern European countries have begun to implement ADR as part of judicial reform programs. For instance, before its dissolution in 2003, the Federal Republic of Yugoslavia had ratified all the major conventions on international arbitration, and was considering a law that would modernize its arbitral legislation based on the United Nations Commission on International Trade Law (UNCITRAL) model. However, despite the progressive legislation, the World Bank found resistance within the legal profession to ADR and a preference amongst judges and lawyers for resolving disputes in court.[123]

Private entities have also been involved in access to justice. The Rural Development Institute (RDI) is a US-based "organization of attorneys helping the rural poor in developing countries obtain legal rights to land."[124] Finding that an important reason for slow progress in the privatization of land rights in Russia had been the "rural population's lack of knowledge about their rights,"[125] RDI initiated a program offering legal support to Russian landowners. The Center for Land Reform Support in Vladimir Oblast (province) was established in 1996, followed by a similar center in 1998 in Samara Oblast, each staffed by two to three experienced lawyers and an accountant. The centers enhance public knowledge of legal rights through publication of articles and other written materials, posting notices, and holding public meetings to make presentations and answer questions; they represent clients in disputes with owners of large land collectives and advise them in their attempts to start private farms; and they advise local officials who themselves may be ignorant of legal rights held by local citizens. Other organizations have initiated similar programs in other substantive areas of law. For instance, USAID has assisted in the creation of public interest law centers throughout Russia that advise citizens on employment-related disputes, and the Union of Jurists of Karelia, a partially USAID-funded institution, provides legal advice on housing, pensions and alimony.[126] The role of private legal aid in former Soviet bloc

---

[122] *Ibid.*

[123] World Bank, Legal Department, *Federal Republic of Yugoslavia Legal and Judicial Diagnostic* (2002), at 37–8.

[124] RDI homepage, http://www.rdiland.org/HOME/HomeOne.html.

[125] Leonard Rolfes Jr. and Gregory Mohrman, "Legal Aid Centers in Rural Russia: Helping People Improve Their Lives" (RDI Reports on Foreign Aid and Development, No. 102, February 2000) at 1, online at: http://www.rdiland.org/PDF/PDF_Reports/RDI_102.pdf.

[126] "Achievements," *supra* note 74 at 18. See also First Legal Aid, a Russian organization of volunteer law students answering legal questions from fellow students with respect to issues such as army service, consumer law, and landlord/tenant disputes, as

countries is an important one, given potential resistance to state-funded legal defence. As the Constitutional and Legal Policy Institute (COLPI – now reconstituted as the Justice Initiative under the Open Society Institute (OSI)) and the Bulgarian Helsinki Committee noted in 1998, "defendants would never accept the services of lawyers employed by the state and would regard them as spies of the investigation agencies."[127]

C. Africa

In South Africa, the right to legal representation for criminal charges is constitutionally protected. The main state mechanism through which representation is provided is the Legal Aid Board, established under the Legal Aid Act of 1969. Initially, the Legal Aid Board provided representation primarily through a *judicare* system. Since 1990, however, the Board has increasingly provided legal aid through salaried public defenders. For instance, in 1993, the Attorney's Act was amended in order to allow prospective lawyers to complete their articling requirements through community service in legal clinics. By 1999, the Legal Aid Board had provided funding for 24 legal clinics, which are able to process cases at nearly half the average cost per case of the *judicare* system.[128]

Despite increases in government funding to the Legal Aid Board, however, the existing scheme is still unable to provide representation to all those who require it. Other methods of reducing the burden on the state have therefore been explored. For example, the Legal Aid Board has proposed the introduction of a 24-hour telephone service, available to all detained or arrested persons, providing information regarding their rights and legal advice.[129] The caller would be able to consult with a Board lawyer over the phone or arrange to meet with the lawyer in prison or any other detention facility.[130] Another example is the implementation of small claims courts in 1985. The small claims courts are authorized to hear claims for amounts up to R10,000[131] and deal with matters

---

another example of a form of private, *ad hoc* legal aid: http://www.nsu.ru/community/fla/.

[127]   Bárd and Terzieva, *supra* note 108 at 240.

[128]   David McQuoid-Mason, "Access to Justice in South Africa" (1999) 17 *Windsor Yearbook of Access to Justice* 230 at 238 and 241–2. See also David McQuoid-Mason, "The Delivery of Civil Legal Aid Services in South Africa" (2000) 24 *Fordham International Law Journal* 111.

[129]   The home page of the South African Legal Aid Board prominently displayed, as of August 2006, a phone number for those seeking legal aid. This may reflect the implementation of the telephone aid proposal (http://www.legal-aid.co.za/).

[130]   McQuoid-Mason, *supra* note 128 at 243.

[131]   As of July 2006: http://www.legal-aid.co.za/services/c_small.php.

such as disputes over wills, divorce and defamation. The courts are designed to enhance accessibility, for instance by holding evening hearings and prohibiting legal representation. In 1994–95, 25,746 trials were heard in small claims courts.[132]

The Nigerian Constitution provides that a right to state-provided legal representation exists where the arrest or detention is a "substantial" infringement of personal liberty and the "need for financial or legal aid is real."[133] Legal aid in Nigeria is delivered through the Legal Aid Council, but the resources made available to the Council are even more limited – and significantly so – than in South Africa.[134] Like South Africa, Nigeria uses a combination of methods to deliver legal aid, including salaried lawyers stationed in state legal aid offices.[135] The number of salaried lawyers has been criticized as seriously inadequate relative to the need for services, and in 2000 the Council began a drive to increase recruitment.[136] One commentator has suggested that Nigeria adopt a public defender system modelled on that of South Africa, creating public defender officers within each state legal aid office staffed by recent law school graduates and overseen by a senior lawyer.[137]

Legal assistance is also provided through non-governmental entities. The Legal Resources Centre in South Africa, first established in 1979, is a non-profit legal organization funded by donations from both local and foreign sources. During apartheid, the organization focused on defending the rights of disadvantaged individuals; after the 1994 elections, the Centre shifted its focus to constitutional litigation, legal reform and development-related legal work.[138] The centers, which now operate across five South African cities,[139] aim to enhance respect for constitutional and international human rights principles, combat gender and racial discrimination, enable the marginalized to assert their rights, and build respect for the rule of law.[140] A cross-section of past annual reports reveals a dedication to a broad array of substantive goals employing a varied assortment of methodologies. LRC has advocated,

---

[132]   McQuoid-Mason, *supra* note 128 at 244–5.

[133]   David McQuoid-Mason, "Legal Aid in Nigeria: Using National Youth Service Corps Public Defenders to Expand the Services of the Legal Aid Council" (2003) 47:1 *Journal of African Law* 107 at 111.

[134]   The funding allocated to the legal aid scheme as a per capita amount per year is lower in Nigeria (US$0.0017) than in South Africa (US$1.00).

[135]   McQuoid-Mason, *supra* note 133 at 112.

[136]   *Ibid.* at 113.

[137]   *Ibid.* at 114–16.

[138]   McQuoid-Mason, *supra* note 132 at 245–6.

[139]   As of July 2006, Johannesburg, Cape Town, Grahamstown, Durban and Pretoria. See LRC website at http://www.lrc.co.za/About/contact.asp.

[140]   "Mission Statement," LRC Annual Report, 2003–04 at 2.

among other things, for environmental safety,[141] social security rights,[142] the right to education,[143] the right to housing,[144] land reform[145] and women's rights,[146] through direct representation for individuals and communities, amicus briefs and public legal education.[147]

The Federation of Women Lawyers Kenya (FIDA Kenya) is an NGO devoted to increasing access to and participation in the legal system by women. Funded by donations from NGOs and corporations, the organization has been in existence since 1985 and runs four main programs. The Legal Aid Services programs runs legal aid clinics in Kisumu and Nairobi with the goals of providing representation to economically disadvantaged women and establishing legal precedents that further women's rights. The Women's Rights Monitoring and Advocacy Program performs an oversight function. For instance, it produces annual reports on the status of women's rights in Kenya with reference to international human rights documents. Through the Gender and Legal Rights Awareness Program, law enforcement agents are trained to be more sensitive to issues that they encounter which have a specific or disparate impact on women, such as domestic violence. FIDA's Public Relations and Fundraising program is principally directed at increasing the prominence of the organization and its objectives in Kenyan society.[148]

Institutional design reform has taken place in numerous African states. In Mozambique and Zimbabwe, village and community courts have been tried as a method of dispute resolution, usually in rural environments. These legal structures do not generally require legal representation for the accused, and involve the community in the dispute resolution process. In South Africa, similar structures have been popular for settling family and labour law disputes, particularly in rural areas. However, concern has been voiced about whether these mechanisms conform with human rights provisions under the Constitution.[149]

Other institutional design reforms have sought to redress a perceived gender bias in access to justice. In South Africa, USAID has sponsored a pilot family

---

[141]   LRC Annual Report, 2003–04 at 7–10.
[142]   LRC Annual Report, 2003–04 at 12–13; LRC Annual Report, 2001–02 at 13–15.
[143]   LRC Annual Report, 2003–04 at 14–15.
[144]   LRC Annual Report, 2003–04 at 18–19.
[145]   LRC Annual Report, 2000–01, at 5–8, 13–17.
[146]   LRC Annual Report, 2003–04 at 24; LRC Annual Report, 2001–02 at 18–21.
[147]   See LRC Annual Report, 1998–99 at 3–8 for a broad summary of the LRC's post-apartheid approach. The organization has a separate field which it terms "access to justice," but it would seem that most of its work, though framed in substantive terms, is concerned ultimately with enhancing access to the law.
[148]   FIDA Kenya, online: http://www.fidakenya.org.
[149]   McQuoid-Mason, *supra* note 132 at 245.

law project "which involved the setting up of specialist institutions … such as domestic violence, divorce and child maintenance courts and the office of the family advocate" within the existing court structures in five centers.[150] In Rwanda, USAID has provided financial assistance towards the establishment of a legal service for women and children called the Haguruka. The organization operates as a pyramid structure: local disputes can be taken to paralegals, who can refer cases to *juristes* operating at the regional level, who can refer cases to the head office in Kigali, where the dispute is considered for litigation in court. According to an evaluation of the program by USAID, it has had some success meeting its proposed goals.[151] The report notes that the culturally-condoned marginalization and passivity of women might make it more difficult for women to come forward with legal claims, which leads to the suggestion that perhaps the Haguruka should "adopt a more pro-active and investigative role" with respect to possible legal claims.[152]

In Sierra Leone, informal and traditional mechanisms of dispute resolution have been driven by the inaccessibility of the formal system, due to high legal fees and a dearth of lawyers in rural areas. However, many customary laws and procedures do not accord with either the Constitution or international human rights treaties to which Sierra Leone is a signatory. Discrimination on the basis of gender or social status, for example, is common. In conjunction with the National Forum for Human Rights in Sierra Leone, the Justice Initiative has established a program where selected individuals from five rural communities are trained to offer legal advice. Where formal courts remain inaccessible to disputing parties, these individuals will promote interpretations of customary laws and procedures that are respectful of the rights embodied in the Constitution and international treaties. Funds are also directed at creating and distributing a manual that describes aspects of law relevant to the daily lives of citizens such as family law and landlord and tenant law.[153]

Street Law has been active in Africa since 1986, when it began a public education program in South Africa under the auspices of the Centre for Socio-Legal Studies. The program, which now operates in 16 universities countrywide, provides for activities ranging from a National Youth Parliament to curriculum

---

[150] "Achievements," *supra* note 74 at 144.

[151] *Final Report: Legal Assistance and Human Rights Program*, 2002. USAID Grant No. 696-00-G-00003 at 9.

[152] *Ibid.* at 8.

[153] Vivek Maru, "The Challenges of African Legal Dualism: an Experiment in Sierra Leone," Justice Initiatives (Open Society Institute Justice Initiative, February 2005) 18–22. See also Paul James Allen, "Accessing Justice in Rural Sierra Leone – A Civil Society Response," Justice Initiatives (Open Society Institute Justice Initiative, February 2004) 57–9.

development and covers substantive legal areas such as family law and labour law.[154] It has been described as a "preventative legal education programme which provides students [at all levels of education] with an understanding of how the legal system works and how it may be utilized to safeguard the interests of people 'on the street.'"[155]

In conjunction with the Ford Foundation, Street Law also assisted in establishing the East African Public Legal Education (PLE) Network. The goal of the Network is to facilitate the sharing of expertise and resources amongst public legal education programs in Kenya, Tanzania and Uganda. The PLE Network contemplates two phases: the development of public legal education programs in East Africa and coordination between the different programs. An example of a project under the second phase is the East Africa/South Africa Internship program, where interns from participating East African countries are placed with Street Law's program in South Africa in order to gain expertise that they will be able to apply to public education programs in their home countries.[156] Other public education programs include the Centre for Advice, Research and Education on Rights (CARER) in Malawi, funded in part by USAID. At the local level, 'community-based educators' employed and trained by CARER provide education regarding legal remedies and rights under the law; more complex cases are referred to paralegals at the district level that are also employed and trained by CARER. Empirical evidence indicates that there is "not only a great need [for the services provided by CARER] ... but also that CARER has been able to expand rapidly."[157]

D.   Asia

In 2000, China had a population of over 1.2 billion and only 101,220 lawyers, a ratio of one lawyer for every 11,855 people.[158] In the past several years, this ratio has improved significantly with the rapid growth of the profession. However, average citizens still face significant problems in accessing the formal justice system. An insufficient number of lawyers, a rise in crime rates, and legal fees beyond the reach of the poor have been cited as factors contributing to the

---

[154]   Centre for Socio-Legal Studies, Street Law Program, online: http://www.csls. org.za/slintro.

[155]   McQuoid-Mason, *supra* note 132 at 248–9.

[156]   Street Law, online: http://www.streetlaw.org/eafricaple.html.

[157]   "Achievements," *supra* note 74 at 134–5.

[158]   In the United States, by comparison, there is one lawyer for every 269 people. Charles Ogletree, "Access to Justice: The Social Responsibility of Lawyers: The Challenge of Providing Legal Representation in the United States, South Africa, and China" (2001) 7 *Washington University Journal of Law and Policy* 47 at 48.

inaccessibility of justice.[159] This problem has been particularly pronounced in the countryside, where – because most lawyers have been drawn to urban centers – the number of lawyers remains extremely limited.[160]

Legal aid initiatives have mushroomed since the early 1990s. Before the introduction of the legal aid system in 1994, government supported legal aid was virtually non-existent.[161] In 1996, China adopted the Lawyers Law, providing legal aid in both civil and criminal cases for those unable to afford representation, and furthermore, requiring lawyers to provide *pro bono* legal services.[162] Whereas previous laws had prohibited lawyers from refusing legal aid cases, in this case the law imposed a positive obligation to engage in legal aid work.[163]

During the mid-1990s, the government also began to sponsor legal aid centers in every province, with the majority of cases handled by local and municipal legal aid centers.[164] In December 1996, the central government established the Ministry of Justice's Legal Aid Center to oversee the nationwide development of legal aid centers.[165] In 2002, the government made "establishing legal aid" a priority in its *Blueprint of the 10th Five-Year Plan of National Economic and Social Development*.[166] In 2003, the State Council Regulation on Legal Aid enacted legislation requiring all sub-national governments to establish legal aid centers and to stipulate eligibility requirements for receipt of legal aid. Non-governmental organizations, women's groups, and universities have also taken on the responsibility of providing legal services.[167] By 2003, more than 2,700

---

[159]   Ogletree, *supra* note 158 at 55.

[160]   Randall Peerenboom, *China's Long March Toward Rule of Law* (Cambridge: Cambridge University Press, 2002) at 362.

[161]   Charles Chao Liu, "China's Lawyer System: Drawing Upon the World Through a Tortuous Process" (2002) 23 *Whittier Law Review* 1037 at 1084.

[162]   "Supporting Legal Aid in China," The Asia Foundation (2001) available at http://www.asiafoundation.org/Locations/china_publications.html.

[163]   Ogletree, *supra* note 158 at 55.

[164]   "Legal Reform in China," The Asia Foundation (2003) available at http://www.asiafoundation.org/Locations/china_publications.html.

[165]   Benjamin Liebman, "Legal Aid and Public Interest Law in China" (1999) 34 *Texas International Law Journal* 211 at 222.

[166]   Vincent Cheng Tang, "Judicial and Legal Training in China: Current Status of Professional Development and Topics of Human Rights" (China-OHCHR National Workshop for Lawyers and Judges, 2002, citing "Chinese Legal Aid System Basically Formed, 600,000 People Aided in 5 years," China News Net, September 29, 2002.

[167]   Organizations including the Ford Foundation, The Asia Foundation, the Canadian International Development Agency (CIDA) and the United Nations Development Program (UNDP) have been involved, such as in the founding of the Center for the Protection of the Rights of the Socially Vulnerable at Wuhan University (Wuhan Center). Aubrey McCutcheon, "Contributing to the Legal Reform in China," in Stephan Golub and Mary McClymont (eds), *Many Roads to Justice: The Law Related Work of Ford Foundation*

legal aid centers nationwide – mostly at the county level – provided legal services to over 300,000 people.[168]

These legal aid centers have operated in different ways. The Guangzhou Legal Aid Center, first opened in 1995, is responsible for managing and overseeing the development of legal aid work by Guangzhou law firms. Other cities have created alternative models, providing service to the poor through the assistance of centers staffed by local lawyers or by assigning cases to local law firms.[169] In Beijing, the legal aid center coordinates legal aid work performed by law firms. The center has two distinctive characteristics: first, the city compensates lawyers for legal aid work through a legal aid fund, and second, local firms may opt out of the program by making payments to the legal aid fund.[170]

China has also addressed its paucity of lawyers through alternative mechanisms. Beginning in the 1980s, the government developed a network of para-professionals known as Basic Level Legal Workers.[171] These Basic Level Legal Workers are not lawyers, but have received some legal training and are licensed by the provincial justice bureau. They are permitted to represent parties in civil and administrative cases, but are not permitted to represent criminal defendants. There are approximately 100,000 such workers in China today. A 2004 report finds that the total number of litigation and non-litigation matters handled by Basic Level Legal Workers is 50% greater than the number handled by lawyers.[172]

However, the status of Basic Level Legal Workers is currently in flux. Originally designed to address legal needs in rural areas, many of these workers have moved to the cities to earn more money. Moreover, lawyers are increasingly complaining about the lower cost competition. Many argue that the system should be abolished or at the very least restricted, as the Basic Level Legal Workers are often ill-trained and lack ethical standards. Finally, what these workers do is technically illegal under the 1996 Lawyers Law, which states that only lawyers may represent clients for profit.[173]

Despite significant progress, several obstacles remain. First, legal aid centers have not been supported with sufficient funding, and have been concentrated

---

Grantees Around the World 170 (2000), available at http://www.fordfound.or/publications/recent _articles/docs/manyroads.pdf.

[168]   Legal Aid in China 2004, online: http://www.asiafoundation.org/pdf/ChinaLegalReform.pdf.

[169]   Liu, *supra* note 161 at 56.

[170]   *Ibid.*

[171]   Benjamin Liebman, "Access to Justice in China," Congressional-Executive Commission on China Roundtable on "Access to Justice in China," July 12, 2004, Columbia Law School [hereinafter Liebman].

[172]   *Ibid.*

[173]   *Ibid.*

in urban centres and the wealthier eastern provinces.[174] Second, critics complain that the quality of representation is low, with firms assigning their most junior lawyers to handle *pro bono* cases.[175] Third, local authorities generally determine which cases are eligible for state-supported legal aid. As a result, the centers overwhelmingly focus on cases that do not bring litigants into conflict with local authorities or locally-powerful enterprises. This problem is compounded by the fact that until recently, lawyers were officially government workers. A fourth problem is that the recent rise in the rate of crime has overshadowed the expansion of the legal aid service.[176] Finally, many legal aid centers have been reluctant to focus their limited resources on criminal cases. Guidelines issued in 1997 by the Ministry of Justice stated that legal aid should be provided to foreigners, juveniles, the disabled and those facing a death sentence.[177]

India is home to the largest number of poor people in the world.[178] Many have no access to courts, and may lack even basic knowledge about the operation of the legal system. According to former Chief Justice V.N. Khare, "the legal problems faced by the poor and downtrodden [are] compounded by their lack of awareness of whom to approach for redress of grievances." [179] When poor people are able to secure legal representation, it is often of low quality. Their lawyers may be poor themselves, and may have inadequate legal education, insufficient resources (such as a working library), and inadequate transportation facilities.[180] Furthermore, according to Justice Rajendra Babu of the Indian Supreme Court, courts are often biased against the poor. As a result, many of them "have chosen to avoid courts and other legal systems rather than face intimidation, cost and time-loss in legal proceedings."[181]

In 1978, the Legal Services Authorities Act established government entities "to provide free and competent legal services to the weaker sectors of the society to ensure that opportunities for securing justice are not denied to any citizen by

---

[174] *Ibid.*
[175] *Ibid.*
[176] Liu, *supra* note 161 at 58.
[177] Liebman, *supra* note 171.
[178] World Bank, "India at a Glance" (June 2006), online at: http://devdata.worldbank.org/AAG/ind_aag.pdf; Dhananjaya Chandrachud, "Poverty, Access to Justice, and Implementation of Human Rights" (New Delhi: November 2002, First South Asian Regional Colloquium on Access to Justice).
[179] "Make Sure the Poor Get Justice Says Khare," *The Hindu*, February 9, 2004, available at http://www.thehindu.com/2004/02/09/stories/2004020911110400.htm [hereinafter "Khare"].
[180] Chandrachud, *supra* note 178 at 4.
[181] *Ibid.*

reason of economic or other disabilities."[182] Moreover, courts have required that the exercise of the right to legal aid be facilitated by the state.[183] Nevertheless, it remains the case that Indians avail themselves of the courts only rarely.[184]

As in China, institutional design reform has helped deliver access to justice to a substantial element of the population excluded from the formal system. In an early attempt in the late 1950s, *panchayats* – traditional, indigenous fora of dispute resolution – were established with jurisdiction over specific categories of petty cases.[185] The *panchayat* was an attempt to "appeal to the virtues of the indigenous system."[186] However, the *panchayats* were different from the traditional institution in numerous respects, including the law applied and the appointment process, which proceeded by popular election rather than appointment from "leading men of the caste."[187] As Galanter and Krishnan summarize, these quasi-indigenous bodies represented an attempt "to recreate an idealized version of traditional society that emphasized democratic fellowship and ignored the caste basis of that society and its justice institutions."[188] In consequence, they failed to attract significant support from villagers, and caseloads rapidly declined.[189]

Following the decline of the *panchayat*, support for informal delivery of justice remained strong, and led eventually to the creation of *Lok Adalats*, which translates literally as "people's courts."[190] *Lok Adalats* take different forms, and indeed, in addition to "General" *Lok Adalats*, there are specialized *Lok Adalats* in fields as diverse as government pensions, utilities and women's rights.[191] Members of *Lok Adalat* panels are generally current or former members of the judiciary, may include lawyers or social workers, and in most cases are culled from "district" judges and "local" advocates, rather than "eminent … and prominent" jurists.[192] While there is a significant number of motor vehicle claims within the *Lok Adalat* docket, the tribunals hear a wide variety of petty disputes, including both civil and criminal cases. Unlike the *panchayats*, *Lok Adalats* are

---

[182]   R.K. Abichandani, " Obstacles to Justice and the Suffering Humanity" (New Delhi, November 2004, First South Asian Regional Judicial Colloquium on Access to Justice) at 10.

[183]   *Suk Das v. Union Territory of Arunachal Pradesh* (1986) 2 SCC 401.

[184]   Marc Galanter and Jayanth Krishnan, "'Bread for the Poor': Access to Justice and the Rights of the Needy in India" (2004) 55 *Hastings Law Journal* 789 at 789.

[185]   Galanter and Krishnan, *supra* note 184 at 792.

[186]   *Ibid.*

[187]   *Ibid.*

[188]   *Ibid.*

[189]   *Ibid.*

[190]   *Ibid.* at 791.

[191]   *Ibid.* at 810.

[192]   *Ibid.* at 800.

not empowered to render decisions, but rather are intended to lead to a settlement,[193] and thus appear to be a form of institutionalized ADR.

Lok Adalats have developed into a significant mode of dispute resolution in India. For instance, from 1982, when the first *Lok Adalat* was held, until March 1996, 13,061 *Lok Adalats* had been organized nationwide and 5,738,000 cases had been resolved by them.[194] The reason for this growth appears to be linked to the simplicity and expeditiousness of its approach, resolving cases in a fraction of the time of the formal court system.[195] Consequently, some tout *Lok Adalats* as a key approach to enhancing access to justice, pointing particularly to the low costs involved and prohibition on appeals from decisions of *Lok Adalats*.[196] Others, however, cite at least two reasons why the characterization of *Lok Adalat* as an instrument for access to justice is illusory: first, most cases at *Lok Adalats* are diversions from the regular court system, and do not involve disputes that would otherwise go unresolved; and second, the informal nature of the proceedings raise the concern as to whether weaker parties are coerced by stronger parties into unfavourable settlements.[197] These critics suggest that resources invested in *Lok Adalats* could more effectively be directed towards enhancements of the formal court system. As Galanter and Krishnan argue, to the extent that *Lok Adalats* represent a form of access to justice, it is "not that they deliver a superior form of justice, but that they represent deliverance from the agony of litigation in a system conceded to be terrible."[198]

Access to justice is a fundamental right enshrined in the constitution of Bangladesh.[199] In furtherance of this right, state-sponsored legal aid cells have been established across the country. Numerous NGOs, including, among others, the Bangladesh Legal Aid and Services Trust (BLAST), Ain-O-Salish Kendro (ASK) and the Bangladesh Environment Lawyers Association (BELA) have also helped provide access to Bangladeshi courts through direct representation.[200] However, in a pattern similar to India, a variety of factors, including delay, corruption, gender discrimination and complicated procedures, render the courts inaccessi-

---

[193]   *Ibid.* at 805.

[194]   *Ibid.* at 799.

[195]   *Ibid.* at 808.

[196]   "Khare," *supra* note 179.

[197]   Galanter and Krishnan, *supra* note 184 at 807.

[198]   *Ibid.* at 808; see also Marc Galanter and Jayanth Krishnan, "Debased Informalism: *Lok Adalats* and Legal Rights in Modern India," in Erik G. Jensen and Thomas C. Heller (eds), *Beyond Common Knowledge: Empirical Approaches to the Rule of Law* (Stanford University Press, 2003).

[199]   Shah Abu Nayeen Mominur Rahman, "Poverty and Access to Justice and the Role of the Higher Judiciary in Bangladesh" (New Delhi: November 2002, First South Asian Regional Judicial Colloquium on Access to Justice).

[200]   *Ibid.* at 2–3.

ble to many Bangladeshis.[201] With funding from the Ford Foundation, TAF and USAID,[202] local NGOs have therefore attempted to use *shalish*, traditional forms of dispute resolution, as alternative fora. Conventional *shalish*, like the courts, suffer from bias, [203] legal ignorance and patronage ties with community leaders.[204] NGOs have therefore supported adapted forms of *shalish*, more sensitive to the participation of women and other marginalized groups.[205]

Golub describes *shalish* as a "community-based, largely informal ... process through which small panels of influential local figures help resolve community members' disputes and/or impose of sanctions on them."[206] *Shalish* can take the form of arbitration, mediation or some hybrid thereof, but can be chaotic:

> The actual shalish is often a loud and passionate event in which disputants, relatives, [*shalish* panel] members and even uninvited community members congregate to express their thoughts and feelings. Additional observers – adults and children alike – gather in the room's doorway and outside ... Calm discussions explode into bursts of shouting and even laughter or tears. All of this typically takes place in a crowded school room or other public space ... The number of participants and observers may range from a few dozen to well over one hundred.[207]

Traditional *shalish* are run by village elders, who encourage compliance by virtue of their stature in the community. However, it is also by virtue of this exercise of community authority that *shalish* decisions tend to marginalize weaker parties,

---

[201]   Stephen Golub, "From the Village to the University: Legal Activism in Bangladesh," in Golub and Mary McClymont, *supra* note 167. Moreover, many among Bangladesh's perceive that they are not treated fairly by the courts. (USAID, *Strategic Objective 3 Close-Out Report* (February 2003)). See also USAID, "Alternative Dispute Resolution Practitioners Guide" (Document No. PN-ACP-335, March 1998) at 75. See also Dina M. Siddiqi, "Paving the Way to Justice: The Experience of Nagorik Uddyog" (One World, One Action), cited in Brynna Connoly, "Non-State Justice Systems and the State: Proposals for a Recognition Typology" (2006) 28 *Connecticut Law Review* 239 at 262.

[202]   Sixty per cent of MLAA's total budget comes from the Ford Foundation, with just under 33% coming from TAF and USAID. *Ibid.*

[203]   In its more extreme forms, as documented by Amnesty International in 1993 and 1994 reports, *shalish* have imposed brutal and even lethal punishment on women. Golub, *supra* note 201. See also USAID, "Alternative Dispute Resolution Practitioners Guide" (Document No. PN-ACP-335, March 1998) at 75.

[204]   See "Non-State Justice and Security Systems" (DFID Briefing, May 2004) at 4, citing Stephen Golub, "Non-state Justice Systems in Bangladesh and the Philippines" (Background Paper Prepared for the DFID Workshop on Non State Justice and Security Systems, March 2003), for a brief description of traditional Bangladeshi village power structures and the role of *Shalish* therein.

[205]   *Ibid.*

[206]   Golub, *supra* note 204 at 3.

[207]   Golub, *supra* note 201 at 137–8.

where decisions are used to further the vested interests of community leadership.[208] Moreover, the gender bias inherent in the shalish process, frequently noted by commentators, seems manifest, as women are often excluded from participation, even where their direct interests are involved. Punishments in criminal matters can also be harsh, particularly those imposed on women.[209]

NGO adaptations have been directed at these troubling elements of *shalish*. For instance, *Nagorik Uddyog* (NU), the women's access to justice program of London-based NGO One World, One Action, has two basic functions in adapted *shalish*. First, it establishes *shalish* in villages across the country, monitoring selection processes and ensuring that one-third of panel members are women. Second, *shalish* panel members undergo workshop training, in an attempt to make *shalish* decisions more consistent with state law.[210] These activities develop against the background of other more overtly political activities intended to enhance the utility and legitimacy of adapted *shalish*. For instance, NU begins each attempt to create a new *shalish* with a series of meetings with higher-level community leaders, in an effort to ensure political support. While NU counts this as an essential first step in the success of the *shalish*, there is surprisingly little discussion as to whether opposition is felt from community elite who benefit from traditional *shalish* structures.[211] Finding that a pro-active stance is required for women to overcome "cultural expectations of female passivity," NU has also embedded the *shalish* in a broader context of women's support initiatives.[212] For instance, NU organizes group meetings for women independent of the *shalish* process, offering a forum for discussion and education on legal rights, among other things. Similarly, Banchte Shekha, a local women's support organization, integrates *shalish* as an element of its broader gender equity approach.[213] In a survey of anecdotal evidence in 2003, Golub found strong support for NGO-adapted *shalish*, from both commentators and surveys of participants themselves. At the same time, however, Golub sees the need for confirmation of these findings through more formal quantitative analysis.[214]

The relationship between *shalish* and the formal court system is unclear. On the one hand, *shalish* yield to litigation where mediation has failed or more

---

[208] Sumaiya Khair *et al.*, *Access to Justice: Best Practices Under the Democracy Partnership* (Dhaka: The Asia Foundation, April 2002) at 8–9, and Taj Hashmi, *Women and Islam in Bangladesh: Beyond Subjection and Tyranny* (London: Macmillan, 2000) at 137, both cited in Golub, *supra* note 206 at 5–7.

[209] Golub, *supra* note 206 at 5–6.

[210] Sidiqqi, *supra* note 201 at 13.

[211] Sidiqqi, *supra* note 201 at 16.

[212] *Ibid.*

[213] Golub, *supra* note 206 at 10. See *ibid.* for a general summary of the activities of NGOs in relation to the adapted *shalish*.

[214] Golub, *supra* note 206 at 10–12.

technical legal knowledge is required.[215] NU reports that in some cases, it will refer cases to the formal system.[216] Decisions of NGO-adapted *shalish* are also more easily enforced in court, due in part to the advent of record-keeping, unknown in traditional *shalish*.[217] The Bangladeshi government has attempted to create a more formal link by creating a third kind of *shalish*, known alternately as government-administered *shalish*, village court or *grameen*.[218] In 1998, before village courts were well-established, USAID warned of a risk that absent broader reforms in the justice system, a government-administered *shalish* would adopt many of the traits which the NGO adaptations sought to avoid.[219] In 2003, Golub expressed the view that "often the reality of village courts does not differ substantially from that presented by the traditional process," particularly in terms of the politicized decision-making process.[220] He does, however, note that *grameen* have not imposed the severe punishments typical of traditional *shalish*, and that the participation of women in *grameen* has somewhat improved.[221]

In the Philippines, support for access to justice initiatives has come in a variety of forms. Traditional legal aid efforts have been supported through governmental agencies, the Integrated Bar of the Philippines (IBP), court-appointed lawyers, non-government organizations and several law schools.[222] In one prominent example during the Marcos period, the Task Force on Detainees in the Philippines provided legal counsel to political detainees. Due to the limited availability of skilled legal staff, however, legal aid has been restricted to relatively few cases.[223]

---

[215]   USAID, "Alternative Dispute Resolution Practitioners Guide" (Document Number PN-ACP-335, March 1998) at 72.

[216]   Sidiqqi, *supra* note 201 at 15.

[217]   Golub, *supra* note 206 at 10–12.

[218]   Golub refers to this entity as a government-administered *shalish*, or village court, established under the authority of the 1976 "Village Court Ordinance." In 1998, USAID described early discussions to create a local court known as a *grameen*. (ADR Guide, *supra* note 215 at 77). UNDP documentation refers to efforts to establish a "Grameen Court, or village court … fulfilling the 1976 Grameen Court Ordinance that mandated establishment of such councils." (Abul Hansat Monjurul Kabir, *Initiative to Establish a National Human Rights Commission in Bangladesh* (UNDP, Asia-Pacific Rights and Justice Initiative, July 2003) at 4. These all appear to be references to the same body.

[219]   ADR Guide, *supra* note 215 at 77.

[220]   Golub, *supra* note 206 at 8.

[221]   *Ibid.* at 9.

[222]   Supreme Court of the Philippines, Department of Justice and United Nations Development Programme, "The Other Pillars of Justice Through Reforms in the Department of Justice: Diagnostic Report IX" (2003), available at http://www.apjr-sc-phil.org/pub-reports.

[223]   Harry Blair and Gary Hansen, "Weighing in on the Scales of Justice: Strategic Approaches for Donor-Supported Rule of Law Programs," USAID Program and Opera-

A second strategy has been to encourage lawyers in private practice to take cases *pro bono*. However, representation rendered *pro bono* is often of low quality. In some cases, for instance, lawyers may fail to make contact with their clients prior to the first hearing. *Pro bono* representation may also aggravate delays in the system, with unprepared lawyers asking for multiple postponements.[224]

The third and most prevalent strategy entails support of alternative law groups (ALGs), domestic NGOs that champion the rights of disadvantaged populations such as women, labour, the urban poor, farm workers and fishermen through a combination of direct services, impact litigation and advocacy. The first ALGs were founded in the early 1980s and began receiving support from TAF and the Ford Foundation in 1986. The Foundations together covered the bulk of ALG staff salaries and expenses throughout the first half of the 1990s.[225]

ALGs are "alternative" in the sense that their goals and operations differ from that of traditional legal aid in the Philippines: in addition to providing legal services, ALGs seek to empower communities to develop their own legal and political strategies.[226] For instance, ALGs train community members in paralegal skills and facilitate direct citizen participation in local government through non-formal legal education. Paralegal development is the ALGs' most important strategy. After consulting with communities to identify the legal issues that most concern them, ALGs lead a series of paralegal training sessions. Saligan, Kaisahan and BMFI, three local ALGs, have trained almost 500 paralegals to guide farmers through Department of Agrarian Reform processes. The paralegals gather data, assemble applications and, if necessary, represent farmers at quasi-judicial hearings. The paralegals handle most applications themselves, but ALG attorneys provide legal representation if disputes reach court.[227] Some ALGs provide non-formal legal education to increase citizen participation in government, promote accountability and encourage enactment and implementation of progressive laws. The Local Government Code grants NGOs and people's organizations (POs) seats on local government councils. With funding from the Ford Foundation's local governance program, ALGs help to familiarize Filipinos with their rights and responsibilities under the Local Government Code, increasing their input into local government and legislative processes.[228]

---

tions Assessment Report No. 7 (1994), available at http://www.usaid.gov/our_work/democracy_and_governance/publications/pdfs/pnaax280.pdf.

[224] Cristina E. Torres *et al.*, "A Survey of Private Legal Practitioners to Monitor Access to Justice by the Disadvantaged" (2003), available at http://www.apjr-sc-phil.org/pub-reports at 3–4 [hereinafter UNDP Survey 2003].

[225] Stephan Golub, "Participatory Justice in the Philippines" in Golub and McClymont, *supra* note 167 at 204–05 [hereinafter Golub ("Philippines")].

[226] UNDP Survey 2003, *supra* note 224 at 46.

[227] Golub ("Philippines"), *supra* note 225 at 213.

[228] *Ibid.* at 215.

Another recent reform is the launch of the "mobile court." The "Justice on Wheels" program consists of equipping buses with the features necessary to render them functional courts, and then driving them to areas and regions that lack courthouses. The claimed benefits of this program are twofold. First, it creates a court presence where it was previously lacking, thereby increasing popular awareness of the court and legal system. The second benefit is premised on the assumption that the regions in which there are no courthouses are likely to be the poorest regions of the country, where people lack the resources to travel to larger centres that have courthouses. Bringing the court to these regions will therefore remove a significant barrier in the ability of the nation's poorest people to access the formal legal system.[229]

III. CONCLUSION

There has been much dispute about how access to justice programs can assist in development and what form such programs should take. It has been argued that many access to justice programs, however well intended, have been too formalistic and prescriptive, based on notions of development popular in the 1960s that have since been largely discredited. In particular, it has been argued that greater court access will not mitigate poverty in countries where law entrenches social, political, and economic exclusion.[230] This is not to suggest that there is no room for access to justice reforms. To the contrary, such reforms are critical to advancing the rule of law. However, they must be undertaken only after a careful assessment of their feasibility and ability to address wealth redistribution, social justice, and human development.[231]

In terms of Cappelletti's three "waves" of reform which respond to economic, organizational, and procedural obstacles respectively, consideration must be given not only to which obstacles are the most serious but also whether they are susceptible to being overcome. It is arguable that all three waves are important in a development context. As the South African case has shown, individualized rights such as property rights may be critical to ensuring economic stability.

---

[229] Remarks by Mr Joachim von Amsberg, World Bank Philippines Country Director, during the launch of the Supreme Court of the Philippines' Mobile Court (Manila, Philippines, December 20, 2004), online at: http://www.worldbank.org.ph/WBSITE/EXTERNAL/COUNTRIES/EASTASIAPACIFICEXT/PHILIPPINESEXTN/0,,contentMDK:20297244~menuPK:333001~pagePK:141137~piPK:141127~theSitePK:332982,00.html.

[230] Jeremy Perelman, "The Way Ahead? Access-to-Justice, Public Interest Lawyering, and the Right to Legal Aid in South Africa: The Nkuzi Case" (2005) 41 *Stanford International Law Journal* 357 at 18.

[231] *Ibid.*

Collective rights are also critical, particularly with respect to human rights issues. Finally, procedural issues are key in countries where alternative methods of dispute resolution may be more effective and appropriate from a cultural standpoint.

In terms of overcoming economic obstacles through provision of legal aid, a critical factor (but certainly not only the only factor) is ensuring provision of adequate economic and human capital resources. To this end, foreign financial aid has often been a key success factor for a number of innovative access to justice reforms, for example, the establishment of *Casas de Justicia* across Latin America, and Alternative Law Groups (ALGs) in the Philippines. Also crucial is determining the most appropriate approach for organization and delivery of resources. The most common approach to overcoming economic obstacles is provision of legal aid, which itself may be delivered using different models, most commonly the staff or *judicare* models. Staff models, where legal services are provided by a staff lawyer employed by the legal aid plan or by a contracted community clinic, may permit realization of scale and specialization efficiencies. However, such models may result in staff being burdened with high caseloads and low salaries. *Judicare* models are attractive by virtue of their independence from the state but, depending on levels of remuneration, may experience difficulty attracting legal representation of adequate quality.

Other constraints besides lack of economic resources also impact upon efforts to overcome economic obstacles, as well as to implement access to justice reforms that involve the second wave (overcoming organizational obstacles to collective justice) and third wave (overcoming procedural obstacles through alternatives to litigation).

Social and cultural practices may impede access to justice for reasons totally unrelated to access to resources. Formal, standardized and centralized court proceedings – one element of judicial reform – may simply not accord with local or indigenous conceptions of justice. Lengthy court procedures and biases against the poor may exclude that portion of the population from effective access to justice, even where qualified representation is provided. On the other hand, social and cultural practices within traditional methods of dispute resolution may impede access to justice for groups within those populations, such as women. In these cases, reformers have sought to create institutional structures such as judicial *panchayats* or *Lok Adalats*, marrying indigenous methods with liberal international norms such as equality before the law. In these cases, reformers have struggled to navigate the difficult compromise between two, sometimes conflicting, models of dispute resolution.

The political economy of barriers to access to justice appears to play a relatively limited role, at least in comparison with other institutions such as the judiciary and police, where it is often of central importance. To be sure, stronger and wealthier litigating parties gain an advantage over weaker ones in an adversarial context, which can be exacerbated where legal aid mechanisms are not in place. But in our case studies, we have identified few specific instances in which reform efforts have been thwarted by entrenched interest groups. Examples of this include the Czech Republic (where for some years, the organized bar held close control over legal aid appointments and opposed attempts at more universal, institutionalized forms of access to justice), and Ecuador (where judges have resisted innovations in ADR, viewing alternative models as direct competitors to courts). One important respect in which political economy and resource constraints intersect is that many countries lack a significant political constituency favouring the allocation of more social resources to access to justice reforms, particularly where this primarily entails providing legal representation to criminal defendants, most especially in contexts where high and rising crime rates are a major social concern that fuel demands for a crackdown on crime through tough law and order policies (suggesting the importance of conceiving access to justice reform more broadly in order to engage the support of a diverse range of constituencies).

8. Legal education

I. NORMATIVE BENCHMARKS

A. The Role of Legal Education in Developing Countries

Legal education is a tool of social and economic development in every jurisdiction.[1] It performs a number of functions which may contribute to development. One well-established view of legal education sees its primary function as being to prepare individuals to practice as legal practitioners.[2] To the extent that this is seen as the primary function of legal education, it is key to development in a number of respects. Trained legal practitioners are necessary to ensure access to justice[3] and to further rule of law reform. As Carothers argues, successful rule of law reform requires a community with a "will to change" their legal institutions.[4] A trained group of professionals executes those changes and represents the interests of the community within those institutions. Legal professionals therefore have an enormous influence on rule of law development. Their level of competence, set of values and conceptions of the law directly affect the success or failure of rule of law reform. As Burridge argues, legal education is one of the most influential sites for development of conceptions of justice and fairness.[5]

In addition to training practitioners, legal education also performs a number of critical broader functions related to development. Burridge suggests that these include defining and upholding democratic and legal accountability; describing and maintaining the function of the legal system and the administration of justice; monitoring and evaluating the use of state power, the regulatory role, and the discharge of statutory duties and fulfilment of civic responsibilities.[6]

Reform of legal education in developing countries was a key aspect of the Law and Development movement (LDM) which had its beginnings in the 1950s

---

[1]   Roger Burridge, "Six Propositions for Legal Education in Local and Global Development" (2005) 55:4 *Journal of Legal Education* 488 at 492.
[2]   *Ibid.* at 488.
[3]   See discussion of access to justice in Chapter 7.
[4]   Thomas Carothers, "The Rule of Law Revival" (1998) 77 *Foreign Affairs* 95.
[5]   Burridge, *supra* note 1 at 489.
[6]   *Ibid.*

in the US. The expectation was that reforming legal education would result in greater freedom, equality and participation in the legal systems of developing countries.[7] Legal education was considered to be the solution to the gap between a country's body of laws and the practical application of those laws.[8] The overall objective was to turn lawyers into legal activists, vested in the promotion of the rule of law and ready and able to assist in that process. At the height of the LDM movement in the mid-1960s and early 1970s, large numbers of American legal academics were consulting in developing countries, with funding provided by organizations such as the Ford Foundation and the United States Agency for International Development (USAID).

By the mid-1970s, the LDM movement had became subject to strong criticism and was in a state of "crisis."[9] In the area of legal education, challenges were raised against the ethnocentric assumption that making legal institutions in developing countries more like those in the US would result in desired social change.[10] Lowenstein argues that efforts to promote legal education were based on nothing more than "'hopeful speculation that education could overcome values instilled by family, class, religion, and other social forces."[11] Examples of failures of the LDM movement were abundant, for example, law school reforms in Latin America based upon US methods were criticized for their focus on a "liberal American model alien to local legal culture."[12] Not only were the assumptions ethnocentric, but US models were simply not appropriate in foreign contexts.

---

[7]   David M. Trubek and Marc Galanter, "Scholars in Self-Estrangement: Some Reflections on the Crisis in Law and Development Studies in the United States" (1974) *Wisconsin Law Review* 1062 at 1063.

[8]   Elliot M. Burg, "Law and Development: A Review of the Literature and a Critique of 'Scholars in Self-Estrangement'" (1977) 25 *American Journal of Comparative Law* 492–530.

[9]   For a discussion of the failures of law and development scholars in thinking about the role of legal education in development, see Trubek and Galanter, *supra* note 7 at 1076.

[10]   Peggy Maisel, "International Cross-Cultural Collaboration in Clinical Education: The Role of US Clinicians in Developing Countries" (paper presented to the 6th International Clinical Conference, October 2005).

[11]   Steven Lowenstein, *Lawyers, Legal Education and Development: An Examination of the Process of Reform in Chile* (New York: International Legal Center, 1970). Cited in Richard E. Messick, "Judicial Reform and Economic Development: A Survey of the Issues" (1999) 14:1 *The World Bank Research Observer* 117 at 126.

[12]   Burridge, *supra* note 1 at 493. Burridge cites Hugo Fruhling, "From Dictatorship to Democracy, Law and Social Change in the Andean Region and the Southern Cone of South America", as cited in Mary McClymont and Stephen Golub, *Many Roads to Justice: The Law-Related Work of Ford Foundation Grantees Around the World* (New York: Ford Foundation, 2000) at 56.

With the demise of the LDM movement, many US legal academics withdrew from projects in developing countries. However, the 1990s heralded a "new" LDM movement, which has included a focus on legal education.[13] In particular, there has been a growing trend to promote the use of clinical legal education in developing countries and US legal academics have played a key role in developing clinical legal education in these countries.[14] In addition to these efforts, international organizations have continued to emphasize legal education as an essential ingredient of rule of law development. Today, the United Nations calls for "governments, professional associations of lawyers and educational institutions [to] ensure that lawyers have appropriate education and training and be made aware of the ideals and ethical duties of the lawyer and of human rights and fundamental freedoms recognized by national and international law."[15] The American Bar Association's Central European and Eurasian Law Initiative (CEELI) makes law school reform a top priority, "because changing the mindset of future members of the legal profession is one of the surest ways to usher in lasting legal reforms."[16] The World Bank states on its website that it invests in legal education to "ensure that legal and judicial reforms contribute to changing the attitudes and behaviors of lawyers and citizens."[17]

Around the world, legal professionals are required to attend a legal training program before entering into practice. In many jurisdictions, legal education is divided into academic and vocational stages, with law schools focusing on training students to be critical thinkers and legal scholars, with bar associations and law societies overseeing the practical training for law school graduates and administer-

---

[13] See Carol V. Rose, "The 'New' Law and Development Movement in the Post-Cold War Era: A Vietnam Case Study" (1998) 32 *Law and Society Review* 93.

[14] Maisel, *supra* note 10.

[15] Office of the United Nations High Commissioner for Human Rights, Basic Principles on the Role of Lawyers, adopted 27 August–7 September, 1990. Accessed on July 10, 2006, http://www.ohchr.org/english/law/lawyers.html.

[16] American Bar Association The Central European and Eurasian Law Initiative (CEELI), Mission. http://www.abanet.org/ceeli/about/mission.html. Accessed on July 15, 2006.

[17] The World Bank, Law and Justice Institutions, online at http://web.worldbank.org (date accessed: December 8, 2006). The statement continues, "For this reason, legal training should be an integral part of legal and judicial reform strategies that are anchored on the rule of law and reflect a country's societal values. Legal education strengthens professionalism, builds public confidence, and facilitates consensus and momentum for further reforms. Legal education also improves the performance of legal professionals, enhances service quality and stimulates public respect. As a result, training programs should be designed not only to enhance performance but also to instil the values of impartiality, professionalism, competency, efficiency and public service." The World Bank Group, Legal and Judicial Reform: Legal Education, 2002 http://www4.worldbank.org/legal/leglr/legalreform_le.html. Accessed on July 23, 2006.

ing licensing examinations.[18] Universities have a key role to play in legal education, with many jurisdictions requiring lawyers to have studied law at university to degree level or equivalent in order to qualify for accreditation. Burridge suggests that the importance of a university legal education – as opposed to work-based training – lies in the opportunities for understanding the law's significance and its role in society as gained through reflection, analysis and critique in organized programs.[19] In some jurisdictions, a law degree granted by a university or other legal program is not a prerequisite for entering into practice. For example, in China, a lawyer may qualify by passing the National Bar Examination, which does not require a law degree as a prerequisite.[20] Whether it be a university degree or a program in another institution, these programs are critical as they begin the process of shaping a lawyer's understanding of the legal system. As Law Professor and US Supreme Court Justice, Felix Frankfurter, wrote: "the law is what lawyers are. And the law and the lawyers are what the law schools make them."[21]

Key to any discussion of the desirable attributes of legal education is the recognition that such education must be capable of serving local interests in a global environment. As Burridge notes in an article setting out a number of propositions for legal education in the context of development, the roles of a legal practitioner require a particular set of skills, knowledge, know-how, and social responsibility. Accordingly, it is critical that legal education provides such competencies, and that they be relevant to the varied social, economic, development, and constitutional needs of a given society.[22]

A 1983 report on legal education in Canada found that since the 1960s, law schools in that country had taken to offering a legal education that was both "humane and professional," rather than focusing narrowly on vocational skills. In other words, law schools were seeking to combine three elements: learning legal rules, learning legal skills, and developing a "humane perspective on law, and a deeper understanding of law as a social phenomenon and an intellectual discipline."[23] The report found the problem with this approach to be that law

---

[18] However, as discussed in Chapter 9, in many countries, professional bodies are too weak to fulfil this aspect of the legal educational mandate. In these countries, the role of law schools may need to be broadened to include more opportunities for practical instruction.

[19] Burridge, *supra* note 1 at 489.

[20] Cheng Han Tan, *et al.*, "Legal Education in Asia" (2006) 1:1 *Asian Journal of Comparative Law* 1 at 7.

[21] Letter from Felix Frankfurter, Professor, Harvard Law School, to Mr Rosenwald (May 13, 1927), quoted in Harry T. Edwards, "The Growing Disjunction Between Legal Education and the Legal Profession" (1992) *Michigan Law Review* 91:34 at 34.

[22] Burridge, *supra* note 1 at 489.

[23] Social Sciences and Humanities Research Council of Canada, *Law and Learning: Report to the Social Sciences and Humanities Research Council of Canada by the Con-*

schools had not adopted a sufficiently structured approach and were failing to provide an education that was either effectively professional or sufficiently broad and humane.

Achieving an appropriate balance between the theoretical and the practical is an ongoing challenge for legal education institutions. As Edwards argues:

> It is undoubtedly valuable for law students to learn economics or moral theory, whether they do so in "pure theory" classes or as part of the more traditional curriculum. It is also crucial for law students to understand and apply theoretical frameworks and philosophical concepts so that they will have a capacity to think beyond the mundane in assessing the work of the legal profession. But law students must also receive a doctrinal education. They must acquire a fluency with legal texts and concepts. This fluency is an integral skill for the practicing lawyer, just as a knowledge of anatomy, physiology, or pharmacology is integral for the practicing physician.

Different institutions and jurisdictions take varying approaches to balancing theoretical instruction with the teaching of practical skills. It has been argued in the US that many law schools – especially the elite ones – have swung too far in the direction of focusing on abstract theory while abandoning practical scholarship and pedagogy.[24] On the other hand, law schools in some developing countries tend to swing too far in the other direction, providing an education that emphasizes rote-learning and, as Tan argues, falling short in developing essential qualities such as a healthy scepticism, intellectual curiosity, and creativeness.[25]

Different schools and jurisdictions also take varying approaches towards teaching methodology and student assessment. In many developing countries, law schools use the traditional method of teaching where law teachers conduct their classes by giving formal lectures and there is little or no participation by students. For example, in India, students traditionally learned law through rote memorization of black-letter rules and the lecture remains the most commonly used method of teaching.[26] This also remains the case in much of Latin America.[27] It has been suggested that part of the reason for this is because law teachers traditionally saw themselves as "gurus" whose role was to simply impart knowledge to their students. In many Western countries, however, classes tend to be more participative, with conventional wisdom holding that this contributes

---

sultative Group on Research and Education in Law (Chair: Harry W. Arthurs) (Ottawa, 1983) at 47.

[24] Edwards, *supra* note 21 at 34.

[25] Tan, *supra* note 20 at 17.

[26] *Ibid.* at 18–19.

[27] See Joseph Thome, "Heading South But Looking North: Globalization and Law Reform in Latin America" (2000) *Wisconsin Law Review* 691.

positively to the learning experience and to students' ability to analyze and critique the law.

Across the world, law schools are adopting innovative teaching techniques. A notable recent innovation which began in the US but as noted above has spread to developing countries is that of clinical legal education, where students work with real facts developed from the perspective of the client, not theories of law, statutes, or decided cases. Clinics can be based in law school facilities or students may undertake externships, working in a firm under the supervision of a practising lawyer. If undertaken within a law school, a clinical program may be based on either real or hypothetical cases. Clinical courses utilize simulations and other role-playing techniques, exposing students to legal practice in a controlled environment. In some clinical courses, students engage in direct client representation, while in others they provide services in the community such as education on law and rights to students or vulnerable groups, such as prisoners. Other clinics provide transactional legal services in the sale of land, the writing of wills, or the creation of a small business or non-profit NGO.[28]

Wortham argues that interactions between teachers and students with clinic clients may assist in the development of relevant curriculum content. He bases this argument on the theory that because clinical education works from the particular problem that a client brings to the clinic, this helps to avoid what LDM critics saw as its flawed mission of imposing a US vision of desirable laws and legal institutions. As he argues, "each local law teacher, student and foreign consultant probably holds at least fragments of a theory of the relation of law to society and the role lawyers should play, although they may not think about this very consciously. But a poor client's case defines a point of view on the society, which may well be a different vantage point than that which a law teacher or student otherwise would have taken."[29]

On the other hand, clinics have sometimes been accused of failing to encourage critical analysis of prevailing norms. As Mosher explains:

> Clinical legal education, so history reveals, neither necessarily nor naturally facilitates transformative practice. In practice, clinical legal education has often been (and continues to be) permeated by the same vision of law and lawyering that informs classroom instruction. Indeed, many authors have critiqued law school clinics for

---

[28] Description of clinical legal education taken from the Open Society Justice Initiative website: http://www.justiceinitiative.org/activities/lcd/cle (date accessed: December 24, 2006).

[29] Leah Wortham, "Aiding Clinical Legal Education Abroad: What Can Be Gained and the Learning Curve on How to do so Effectively" (2006) 12 *Clinical Law Review* 615 at 668.

their failure to reflect critically about justice or about practice norms, and for the control and manipulation to which they routinely subject clients.[30]

According to Mosher, clinics often neither offer the kinds of critical thinking skills necessary for effective participation in legal reform, nor do they adequately protect the communities they service.[31] To meet these concerns, legal clinics must, at a minimum, employ sufficient numbers of well-trained staff who can both teach the students to critically analyze their experience and ensure that they represent their clients competently.

A key aspect of legal education is availability and inclusiveness. In many countries, the cost of a legal education is prohibitive to large numbers of potential students. To this end, programs that travel to more isolated students or communities may increase the availability of legal education to members of economically disenfranchised groups. For example, a recent initiative in Canada saw the Faculty of Law at the University of Victoria partner with the Nunavut Arctic College to establish the Akitsiraq Law School to provide an opportunity for Inuit students to receive a legal education in Nunavut. The initiative sought to fulfil a need identified for Inuit lawyers in both public and private practice in the Canadian territory of Nunavut, and thus to contribute to the development of Nunavut. The initiative enabled students from Nunavut to receive a legal education who otherwise would not have been in a position to do so, not only by providing education in Nunavut itself, but by providing funding assistance to support students throughout the program.

B. Independence and Accountability

The case for independence and accountability of legal education institutions is closely connected to the case for independence and accountability in universities more generally. Independence refers to the notion that academic institutions have the right to self-governance and should control most aspects of their management, including recruitment of staff, admission and grading of students, and

---

[30] Janet Mosher, "Legal Education: Nemesis or Ally of Social Movements?" (1997) 35:3 *Osgoode Hall Law Journal* 613 at 634.

[31] Mosher's concerns are echoed by a number of other commentators. See for example, Robert J. Condlin, "'Tastes Great Less Filling': The Law School Clinic and Political Critique" (1986) 36 *Journal of Legal Education* 36; Carrie Menkel-Meadow, "Two Contradictory Criticisms of Clinical Education: Dilemmas and Directions in Lawyering Education" (1986) 4 *Antioch Law Journal* 287; Minna J. Kotkin, "Creating True Believers: Putting Macro Theory into Practice" (1998) 5 *Clinical Law Review* 95; and Robert J. Condlin, "Learning from Colleagues: A Case Study in the Relationship Between 'Academic' and 'Ecological' Clinical Legal Education" (1997) 3 *Clinical Law Review* 337.

determination of degree requirements and the curriculum.[32] Accountability refers to the demand by those who fund higher education – governments, the public, and tuition-paying students – to know how monies are used, to determine how funds should be spent, and to monitor the effectiveness of programs.[33]

There are a number of arguments traditionally espoused for the independence of universities.[34] First, it is argued that tasks including the creation of new knowledge through scholarship and research and the development of students' capacity for critical and independent judgment are conducted best in environments which are free from direct government and bureaucratic controls, or political domination or influence. This argument has particular force in the case of law schools, given that lawyers are often called on to represent clients with interests adverse to the government.

A second argument is that higher education provides, through its staff and students, one of the important checks and balances in a democratic society through the freedom to critique and challenge ideas and policies. This role requires independence from interference by government or governmental agencies. However, it is important to note that academic freedom does not depend on institutional independence alone, but also on factors within the institutions.

Law schools themselves can also make a further claim for independence if they are to fulfil the expectations demanded by a law and development approach to legal education. There are arguments to be made for maintaining some degree of independence not only from the government, but also from the central university administration itself, the judiciary, bar associations, and bar examination boards.[35] As Arthurs notes, legal education is contested terrain, with both the higher education sector and the legal profession having a stake in its planning and implementation. He argues that the profession – the governing body, the major law firms, the bar association, the alumni – may pressure law schools to increase the number, length or content of "core" courses deemed necessary for the practice of law and to reduce the number of theoretical and interdisciplinary seminars and support for social activism.[36]

Independence – of both universities generally and law schools more specifically – may be limited not just by the laws under which such institutions operate but also by the fact that in many countries, universities depend on public fund-

---

[32]   Grant Harman, "The Erosion of University Independence: Recent Australian Experience" (1983) 12 *Higher Education Perspectives* 510 at 503.

[33]   *Ibid.*

[34]   *Ibid.* at 505–7.

[35]   James P. White, "Legal Education in the Era of Change: Law School Autonomy" (1987) 2 *Duke Law Journal* 292 at 293.

[36]   H.W. Arthurs, "The Political Economy of Canadian Legal Education" (1998) 25:1 *Journal of Law and Society* 14 at 22.

ing.[37] This is also where tension arises between independence and accountability – governments have a legitimate interest in exercising some control over how universities carry out their mandate; as Harman argues, they have an obligation to ensure that public funds are spent in a prudent manner and that universities are meeting the broad needs and interests of society.[38]

Monitoring of legal education institutions may be effectively carried out by private bodies. For example, the American Bar Association (ABA) publishes accreditation guidelines that form the basis for most law school curriculum design in the United States. ABA employees also conduct follow-up visits to assess all accredited programs. One prerequisite for writing most state bar exams is a Juris Doctor (JD) from an ABA accredited law school. Here again, tensions arise between independence and accountability as professional organizations, while creating accountability, can threaten the independence of legal educational institutions, for instance by attempting to prescribe curricula to mirror the skills and subjects tested in bar examinations, which in turn are likely to reflect the legal status quo (however socially inadequate this may be).

Maintaining an appropriate balance between institutional independence and accountability to government and the public remains one of the most important challenges facing universities generally and law schools specifically in both developed and developing countries. Such a balance may be found through means such as decentralized governance structures to ensure that legal education institutions are removed from direct state control.

In the case of developing countries, many have turned to direct foreign funding to augment national resources available for higher education. However, foreign funding for legal education may compromise institutional independence if it comes tied to particular ideologies. For example, American funding of legal education in India during the first wave of LDM funding led, over time, to American dominance over Indian legal scholarship.[39] This left little room for legal scholars trained in India to provide contextual analyses of their own legal system. It also stifled the development of an Indian approach to legal scholarship. Foreign funding can also be unreliable. As certain projects become unfashionable, funding dries up and communities are left stranded, unable to continue financing their law programs.[40]

---

[37] Harman, *supra* note 32 at 506.

[38] *Ibid.*

[39] Rajeev Dhavan, "Borrowed Ideas: On the Impact of American Scholarship on Indian Law" (1985) 33:3 *American Journal of Comparative Law* 505.

[40] James C. Paul, "American Law Teachers and Africa: Some Historical Observations" (1988) 31:1&2 *Journal of African Law* 31.

C. Legitimacy

Legitimacy of legal educational institutions is closely connected to issues of independence and accountability. Institutions that are too closely connected with or controlled by government bodies are likely to suffer from a lack of public legitimacy. Citizens, often rightly, see the graduates of government-run facilities as proponents of government ideologies. A particularly apt example is the former Soviet Union, where law students were required to engage in studies of "Scientific Communism" and "Fundamentals of Scientific Atheism."[41] While legitimacy is achieved through some measure of independence, it also requires that the educational institution address the specific needs of its community. Ethnocentric reform programs imported from abroad that do not reflect these needs will suffer from a lack of legitimacy.

As noted above, the LDM education reform efforts of the 1960s and 1970s exported an American-style education model to developing countries. Projects designed American institutions in foreign communities and exported American textbooks to be taught in foreign classrooms.[42] Gordon argues that the lawyers in charge of the LDM reform projects assumed that the institutions and text-books "automatically carried with … [them] … the benignly liberal-reformist social consequences of its US origins, where it had been the method of progressive social-democratic reformers."[43] It was an attempt to release students from what Gordon calls "reactionary formalism" and train them in reform-oriented problem-solving that incorporated policy concerns as well as a framework of rules. However, the break from formalist traditions did not guarantee liberal political consequences. In fact, in Latin America, many lawyers trained in the American curriculum used their skills instrumentally to revamp the legal landscape for the repressive authoritarian state. The student radicals who resisted these regimes often called for a return to the formalist system.

Rather than exporting one country's education system, legal education reform must take account of the specific context of the community in question. First, the programs offered must relate to jobs that are relevant to and needed in the community. This may mean training paralegals for smaller community projects

---

41   See the discussion of Eastern European law reforms below.

42   Varda Hussain, "Sustaining Judicial Rescues: The Role of Outreach and Capacity-Building Efforts in War Crimes Tribunals" (2005) 45:2 *Virginia Journal of International Law* 554 at 555.

43   Robert W. Gordon, "Modes of Legal Education and the Social Conditions that Sustain Them", paper delivered at the 2003 SELA conference at Universidad de Palermo in Buenos Aires, Argentina. Available online at http://islandia.law.yale.edu/sela/gordone.pdf.

instead of formal degree programs. Second, the curriculum must reflect the culture and economic situation of the population as a whole. Preparing lawyers for employment in large multinational corporations without also training community-oriented professionals will fail to address many legal needs and render the legal system irrelevant to many segments of the population (or alternatively alienate them from it).[44] In the pursuit of a commitment to law as an intellectual discipline, there must also be a movement to developing legal education institutions that teach law in a social context.[45]

Clinical legal education may also enhance the legitimacy not only of the legal education system, but of the rule of law as a whole. Clinics provide financially marginalized citizens with access to legal services, thereby contributing to the integration of the rule of law into the lives of the general population. As well, as noted above, exposure to the community affected by the legal system has potential to help evolve a curriculum with a local and critical focus and understanding, and in so doing may achieve greater public legitimacy.

II. EXPERIENCE WITH LEGAL EDUCATION REFORMS IN DEVELOPING COUNTRIES

A. Latin America

Overall, it has been found that the academic level of law schools throughout Latin America leaves much to be desired.[46] There is significant variation in standards. Pinto notes, for example, that "very expensive and exquisite teaching is provided by institutions like the Universidad de Lima, the Universidad Diego Portales, and the Universidad Torcuato Di Tella. They have not, however, attained the requisite number of graduates needed to exert considerable influence in society."[47] Thome, in a recent review of law reform in Latin America, notes that: "Notable exceptions apart, the five to six year formation and training by law students lacks the broadening enrichment of critical debate; and instead instruction is authoritarian in style, anchored in traditional pedagogy based mostly on foreign legal sources, and encyclopedist with an emphasis on memo-

---

[44]   *Ibid.*
[45]   William Twining, *Law in Context: Enlarging a Discipline* (Oxford: Clarendon Press, 1997).
[46]   See Robert M. Kossick Jr., "The Rule of Law and Development in Mexico" (PhD Thesis, Tulane University, April 2004).
[47]   Monica Pinto, "Developments in Latin American Legal Education" (2001) 21:1 *Pennsylvania State International Law Review* 61 at 61.

rization. Legal scholarship and education to this day, despite growing critiques and some notable exceptions, continues largely unchanged."[48]

Twenty-five years ago, Chile had 6,000 lawyers serving a population of 12 million.[49] Today there are roughly 20,000 lawyers,[50] a jump that is largely due to a proliferation in legal education institutions. Prior to 1981, the Chilean government strictly regulated legal education, providing public funding and monitoring through the Consejo de Rectores (the Consejo), a national agency. Admission and curriculum design in both fully funded public universities[51] and partially funded private universities were strictly controlled by the Consejo. In 1981, the government opened the doors to private education outside of the control of the Consejo. Private law schools spend eight to ten years under the supervision of a government education agency and are then granted permission to operate with complete autonomy. In the period between 1980 and 1996, public funding for law schools dropped from 100% to 55% of total operating costs.[52] Some public law schools, like the prestigious University of Chile Law School, have raised tuition fees in light of decreasing government contributions and now redirect almost half of their tuition dollars to the maintenance of other departments in the university. Because of this, there is little variation in public and private tuition fees.[53] Today, 20 law schools fall under the supervision of the Consejo. More private law schools have been established since 1981.

Students enter law school directly out of high school. Admission is based solely on their high school grade average and placement test score. The Consejo admission process does not include any affirmative action measures except for a few reserved places in each class for physically disabled students. Many of the best students choose to attend a Consejo school, leaving the less qualified candidates to apply to the plethora of private law schools.[54] The law program in Chile, unlike the three-year JD in the United States and Canada, extends over five years, and most students take six to seven years to complete the full curricu-

---

48 Thome, *supra* note 27.

49 Antonio Bascuñán Valdes, "Legal Education in Chile" (2002) 43 *South Texas Law Review* 683.

50 Advocates International, Latin America: Chile 2005, available online at: http://www.advocatesinternational.org/pages/global/latinAmerica/chile.php.

51 These public universities are not free, like many European and other Latin American institutions. Instead students pay a reduced fee.

52 Richard J. Wilson, "Three Law School Clinics in Chile, 1970–2000: Innovation, Resistance and Conformity in the Global South" (2002) 8 *Clinical Law Review* 515 at 533.

53 In 2000, the tuition at the University of Chile Law School was 1,500,000 pesos. At the private Diego Portales it was 1,900,000 pesos. Wilson, *ibid.*

54 Wilson, *supra* note 52 at 532.

lum.[55] Even the largest public universities have moderately sized law faculties. The University of Chile Law School, the largest in the country, has 350–400 students in its first-year class. However, there are few full-time law professors in Chile and most teachers are professionals with full-time practices and limited time for academic pursuits.[56]

This may be the reason that curriculum reform has seen little progress in Chile. The traditional Chilean curriculum is focused on,

> the *class magistral* [the lecture class] in which the professor systematically presents information. There is not, in an [sic] significant sense, study or analysis of cases or jurisprudence. The case method is virtually nonexistent. There is a predominance of the expository, central and authoritarian role of the professor. Debate in class is replaced by questions from the students on the presentation by the professor.[57]

Similarly, the role of the student had been limited to "regurgitating ingested information on examinations" and "memorization of secondary doctrinal sources."[58] While there have been some attempts at curriculum reform in the past ten years,[59] Stephen Meili argues that professors have vested interests "in maintaining their control over courses and their important role in the overall law school curriculum" which encourages them to "insulate the curriculum from fundamental change."[60] As well, a full-time practitioner faces significant time constraints when teaching a course. This leaves little time to devote to curriculum reform or developing new courses.

Reforms have occurred in the area of clinical legal education in Chile. Though clinics are not a mandatory component of legal education, many law schools offer some clinical opportunities.[61] Chile has adopted a strict legislative scheme governing the limits of student involvement in court proceedings. Only fourth,

---

[55]   Antonio Bascuñán Valdes, "Legal Education in Chile" 43 (2001–2002) *South Texas Law Review* 683 at 686.

[56]   Stephen Meili, "Legal Education in Argentina and Chile," in Louise G. Trubek, *Educating for Justice Around the World: Legal Education, Legal Practice and the Community* (Aldershot: Ashgate/Dartmouth, 1999) 138–57 at 142.

[57]   Wilson, *supra* note 52 at 557.

[58]   Meili, *supra* note 56 at 140.

[59]   At the Law School of the Catholic University of Chile, a curriculum reform review in 1997 proposed that in five courses some class time be taught by practitioners and instruction be included on treaties, cases and institutional structures. Recommendations were adopted by the University, but after three years had been implemented for only one class because "[n]o other faculty member … was willing to take on this task." *Ibid.*

[60]   *Ibid.* at 153.

[61]   The Catholic University Law School has recently added clinical education as a mandatory course in the fifth year. Wilson, *supra* note 52 at 546.

fifth and sixth-year students from an authorized university are permitted to appear in legal matters and each student must be supervised by a licensed practitioner. Students are prohibited from appearing alone in more serious matters.[62] Some clinic programs are well established, like that at the University of Chile Law School, started in 1975. Others are products of a 1995 clinic education project funded by the Ford Foundation.[63] The private law school, Diego Portales, received a Ford grant to establish an inter-university network with seven other law schools in Chile, Argentina and Peru. The grant supports public-interest legal clinics at all participating schools as well as an academic journal on clinical legal education, run from Diego Portales. The law schools meet twice a year to discuss ongoing challenges in clinical education and methods of support and advancement of practical legal education. In Chile, clinic participation is often the only exposure to practical legal skills a law student will receive.[64]

Argentina's legal education institutions are beginning to incorporate clinical programs. Traditionally, practical skills and training in professional ethics were largely excluded from curricula and legal scholarship.[65] The inter-university public interest action program has worked to change this trend, establishing three public interest clinics at the University of Buenos Aires, the University of Palermo and the University of Comahue. All three of these clinic programs aim to increase legal services to poorer communities while improving the practical skills of Argentina's law students. These three clinics are highly successful and have remained features of their respective programs for over ten years. However, a 2002 study by the University of Palermo law school revealed a general aversion to clinical education throughout Argentina. It identified inflexible and highly regulated curricula, lack of capacity for practical legal training, political conservatism, institutional obstacles and resistance from the profession as the five main factors impeding the growth of clinical programs.

Argentine law schools are divided between public and private institutions. Prior to 1958, all law schools were publicly funded and controlled with almost no tuition costs for students. In 1958, the government opened the doors to private legal education. Presently, there are 17 public law schools in Argentina and a large number of private law schools. Private schools include religiously affiliated confessional institutions and, beginning in the early 1990s, American-style law

---

[62]   *Ibid.* at 537.

[63]   *Ibid.* at 539.

[64]   Over the course of five years only two to three courses are elective, of the electives offered, rarely more than one or two have practical content.

[65]   Pepe Clarke, Education Coordinator, Environmental Defender's Office (NSW), "International Developments in Clinical Legal Education: Clinical legal Education in Argentina, Challenges and Opportunities" (July 10, 2003), online at: http://www.cedha.org.ar/docs/doc135-eng.htm (accessed on July 16, 2006).

programs.[66] One more recent example of private legal education is the Universidad Torcuato Di Tella Law School (UTDT). Established in 1996, the curriculum embraces an interdisciplinary approach to legal education. The mandatory course of study includes programs in law and economics, philosophical bases of law and elections and democracy.[67] In contrast with the traditional Latin American approach to legal education and its focus on memorizing laws, the UTDT graduate is trained in oral and written expression and reasoned argumentation. UTDT typically limits enrolment to a total of 300 students while public programs, like the University of Buenos Aries Law School, have upwards of 30,000 students at any one time.[68]

The quality of legal education in Argentina varies considerably due to resource constraints in large public law school programs[69] and lack of accountability for private law school programs.[70] Despite the fact that law students begin their studies directly out of high school, the length of law programs in the country varies from one year to five years. As well, many students opt to complete their law degree on a part-time basis, which takes much longer than the standard full-time degree program.

Despite the variation between programs in Chile and Argentina, there is much cooperation among Latin American law schools. Some of this alignment in structure and curriculum is due to the MERCOSUR Regulations which establish a common market in South America. Part of that agreement, added in 1998, is an understanding that high school and first university degrees will be accepted throughout the region, irrespective of the originating nation. For this reason, legal education in Brazil, the largest country in South America, is very closely aligned with that of Chile and Argentina. There, too, private law schools have filled in the gap left by tightly controlled public institutions. Like Argentina, the quality of private instruction varies, while public universities struggle with high enrolment and resource constraints. Unlike Argentina and Chile, Brazil's law

---

[66]   Monica Pinto, "Legal Education in Argentina and Other South Latin American Countries" (Association of American Law Schools, 2000). Available online at: http://www.aals.org/2000international/english/argentina.htm (accessed on June 24, 2006).

[67]   Universidad Torcuato di Tella, Escuela de Derecho, online at: http://www.utdt.edu/departamentos/derecho/grado/orientacion.htm (accessed on July 12, 2006).

[68]   Thomas Lehrman, "Linkage: There was Argentina" (2002) 1:2 *Yale Law School Linkage*. Available online at http://72.14.207.104/search?q=cache:eMrWDP-cOOsJ:islandia.law.yale.edu/linkage/newsletters/july02.pdf+%22legal+education%22+argentina+resources&hl=en&gl=ca&ct=clnk&cd=14 (date accessed: January 18, 2007).

[69]   *Ibid.*

[70]   Gustavio E. Fischman, "Globalization Consumers, citizens, and the 'Private School Advantage' in Argentina (1985–1999)" (August 25, 2001) 9:31 *Education Policy Analysis Archives*. Available at http://epaa.asu.edu/epaa/v9n31.html.

curriculum is still controlled by the Ministry of Education, leading to a uniform five-year program for public and private law school students.[71]

B.   Central and Eastern Europe

The key problem faced by legal education institutions in Central and Eastern Europe is expressed succinctly by the Dean of the School of Law at Vytautas Magnus University in Lithuania: "It is axiomatic that Soviet law did not serve the same purpose as law in states recognizing the rule of law … institutions of Eastern Europe providing legal education needed to reform subsequent to the changes of the late 1980s; it is clear that, for example, contracts in a state with no free market are very different from contracts in a free market economy, and that hence the teaching of contracts must be reformed."[72] Yet this is not an easy task, given that the individuals teaching law have remained the same, even while the environment changed around them. Klimas cites a law professor in the Czech Republic who stated in 2000 that:

> Against expectations, the old, unqualified, and xenophobic professors did not die out. They reproduced themselves through inbreeding, selecting future teachers from among their students according to the criteria of loyalty and lack of intellectual chal- lenge to the current incompetent professoriate.[73]

Legal education in the USSR was heavily controlled by the Soviet govern- ment. The rector of each state-run university was appointed by the executive and was responsible for hiring, admissions, and "the ideological posture of the university."[74] USSR ministries, "and especially the USSR Procuracy,[75] deter- mined most aspects of legal education policy."[76] Soviet students were told that "the nature of legal education is explicitly political because the legal profession is by its very nature political. Therefore, ideological education is a key part of Soviet legal education."[77] Since the collapse of the Soviet Union, law degrees have gained in popularity. This has driven the proliferation of "substandard law

---

[71]   Nadia de Araujo, "Status of Brazilian Legal Education" (2000). Accessed on July 12, 2006. http://www.aals.org/2000international/english/brazilian.htm.

[72]   Tadas Klimas, "Legal Education in the New Europe and the USA: Shall the Twain Ever Meet?" (2004) 5:3 *German Law Journal* 321 at 322.

[73]   Tucker Aviczer, "Reproducing Incompetence: The Constitution of Czech Higher Education" (2000) 9:3 *East European Constitutional Review* 94 at 95.

[74]   George E. Glos, "Soviet Law and Soviet Legal Education in an Historical Con- text: An Interpretation" (1989) 15 *Review of Socialist Law* 227 at 257.

[75]   See the section on Prosecutorial Reforms for a detailed discussion.

[76]   Susan Finder, "Legal Education in the Soviet Union" (1989) 15 *Review of Social- ist Law* 197 at 207.

[77]   *Ibid.*

schools that are widely known to be 'diploma mills.'"[78] As well, widespread corruption in the law school admissions process and student grading has further undermined the legitimacy of legal education programs.

Nevertheless, the region has undergone significant legal education reforms. For those countries associated with the European Union, the European Community Action Scheme for the Mobility of University Students (ERASMUS) program has enhanced the level of cooperation between law schools and developed a transnational legal curriculum. Countries that fall outside of the ERASMUS program have received funding and support for clinical legal education from the Central and East European Initiative (CEELI).

ERASMUS implements its reforms to higher education in stages. The thrust of the first stage is student exchange. Law students may spend three months to a full academic year studying at another ERASMUS member school. The exchange aims to encourage a European perspective amongst all member law students as well as fostering the development of a second language of study. The second stage of ERASMUS reforms includes teaching exchanges, transnational curriculum development, international intensive programs at the host institution, and inter-regional cooperation programs that connect private and public institutions.[79] Currently, law schools in Estonia, Hungary, Slovenia, Poland, the Czech Republic, Latvia, Lithuania, Slovenia, Bulgaria and Romania participate in the ERASMUS program.[80] Funding for the program's reforms is available annually from the European Union.

The CEELI has directed its efforts to the development of practical legal education. Fifteen years ago, student clinics, moot court exercises and mock trials were "virtually unknown in most host countries."[81] By the mid-1990s Russia and the Ukraine had established student legal clinics. The University of Pristina in Kosovo founded a clinic program in 2004. Bulgaria, Moldova, Uzbekistan, Kyrgyzstan and Armenia are in the process of creating minimum clinical legal education standards. The CEELI has established a Center for Methodological Support of Clinics in Kyrgyzstan and Eurasia-wide "Clinical Alliance." Bosnia was chosen to host the CEELI Moot Court Competition and CEELI funding sent teams from Belarus, Kazakhstan, Kyrgyzstan, Moldova, Russia, Tajikistan

---

[78]   CEELI, "CEELI Focal Area: Legal Education Reform," available online at: http://www.abanet.org/ceeli/areas/legaled.html (accessed on July 10, 2006).

[79]   European Commission: Education and Training, "ERASMUS and the University," http://ec.europa.eu/education/programmes/socrates/erasmus/university_en.html (accessed July 10, 2006).

[80]   Associate Dean Louis F. Del. Duca, "Cooperation in Internationalizing Legal Education in Europe – Emerging New Players" (2001) 20:1 *Penn State International Law Review* 9.

[81]   CEELI, *supra* note 78.

and Uzbekistan to the 2005 Philip C. Jessup International Law Moot Court Competition.[82] In the past 15 years the CEELI has introduced practical education to much of Central and Eastern Europe.

Law schools in the Federal Republic of Yugoslavia suffer from chronic underfunding, lack of institutional independence, and an antiquated curriculum that is common to post-Communist countries. The Milosevic government introduced the Law on Universities in 1998, dismissing professors and replacing them with regime supporters. Recently, with the assistance of the CEELI, several law schools have managed to introduce interactive teaching styles and curriculum redesign. The University of Montenegro has been at the forefront of legal education reform and is working in direct cooperation with the University of Nebraska to review and improve its curriculum. The Faculty is also seeking to improve access to legal information through electronic databases and internet access, to develop legal clinics and mooting programs, and include non-governmental organizations, for example the Centre for Human Rights, on campus.[83]

Under Soviet rule, the Republic of Georgia had only one law school, the Tbilisi State University. Graduates were subject to a Soviet Communist curriculum and began professional practice under a tightly controlled government scheme. After 1991, the number of law schools grew and graduated a larger number of students into what was already a "saturated system."[84] Lawyers established under the old Soviet system effectively resisted a new bar examination until 2003, before which any graduate of a law program was licensed to practice. The Justice Initiative, a United States-based NGO, has directed significant development funds into Georgia's legal education system. In 2002, the Sokhumi State University in partnership with the Justice Initiative established a legal clinic and began the groundwork for a street law initiative aimed at bringing legal information regarding basic rights to high school students.[85]

In some former Soviet countries there has been resistance to change from older professors with entrenched ideas and vested interests in the status quo. To avoid this problem in higher education institutions in Albania, professors were removed from their positions due to "their political ideas or their perceived ideas. As a result, Albania now suffers from a large number of young, inexperi-

---

[82] *Ibid.*

[83] World Bank, Legal Department, *Federal Republic of Yugoslavia Legal and Judicial Diagnostic* (2002) 40.

[84] Joseph A. Dailing, "Lessons from the Caucasus: Legal Aid, Nation Building and Civil Rights in the Republic of Georgia," available online at Technology Information for the Poverty Law Community at: http://lstech.org (accessed on June 12, 2006).

[85] Open Society Justice Initiative, "National Criminal Justice Reform, Georgia: Policing", available online at: http://www.justiceinitiative.org/regions/cafsu/georgia (accessed on July 10, 2006).

enced staff without a tradition of scholarship or experienced staff to provide assistance in developing appropriate courses."[86] The CEELI Sister Law School Program in Belarus, Croatia, Kazakhstan, and other countries works to remedy this problem. An East European professor who is conducting research, or attempting to develop new programs, courses, or curricula, has the option of working directly with a professor in the same field at an American university.

C. Africa

In British colonial Africa, the only way to achieve a legal education was to travel to London, join an Inn of Court or acquire a British LL B.[87] Local legal education was actively discouraged by the colonial powers.[88] Africans had little interaction with colonial common law courts and settled most internal disputes in local "customary courts." Formal court procedures were only initiated in the case of serious crimes.[89] It was not until 1961, when the Committee on Legal Education for Students from Africa, chaired by Lord Denning, recommended that African countries require local training after the British LL B before allowing graduates to practice, that the movement for African legal education programs began.

In light of strict colonial control over legal education in Africa's history, all former British colonies on the continent, with the exception of Lesotho, Liberia and South Africa, have directly adopted the British model of a three-year undergraduate law degree model. The curriculum and teaching style, however, is more formal than in current British law schools. Although former British colonies in Africa operate in the common law tradition, students are confined, for the most part, to memorizing rules and spotting inconsistencies with regard to the application of these rules. In some cases, British textbooks are used with little local content added. Incorporating local material into the curriculum is difficult as local law reports and academic legal articles are often not available or do not exist. Muna Ndula, Director of the Institute for African Development at Cornell Law School, points out that African countries are presently in a state of constant economic and social change. This makes a rule-based law curriculum particularly dangerous as the specific knowledge generated will likely not apply, or not apply in the same way, in the near future.[90] Efforts are under way in some

---

[86] Edi Spaho, "Dire Straits: Albanian Legal Education" (2000) 9:3 *East European Constitutional Review* 90 at 91–2.

[87] Manu Ndulo, "Legal Education in Africa in the Era of Globalization and Structural Adjustment" (2002) 20:3 *Pennsylvania State International Law Review* 489.

[88] *Ibid.*

[89] *Ibid.*

[90] *Ibid.* at 493.

countries to change this state of affairs. In Botswana, for example, efforts have been made to ensure a comprehensive law curriculum that goes beyond the traditional core courses and deals with areas of law that reflect the country's development needs, such as law and health care, gender and the law, HIV/AIDS awareness courses, law and the media, international trade and investment, intellectual property, human rights, and environmental law.[91]

The present situation in South Africa's legal education institutions is still marked by the legacy of the Apartheid education program. Until 1994, black law students were restricted to historically black universities unless they could prove that their particular program of study was only available at a white institution. By the 1980s, bantulands, rural areas designated for black housing, established their own universities to service the needs of black students. These universities were, and still are, chronically under-funded and under-staffed.[92]

Between 1994 and 1999, after the fall of Apartheid, the Ministry of Justice and the Law Society of South Africa established Justice Vision 2000, an action plan aimed at designing a new LL B curriculum and degree, incorporating practical experience as part of the new LL B, vocational training for legal community services and the establishment of bar admission exams. Out of this plan emerged the present, four-year LL B which serves as the necessary qualification step for all legal practitioners in South Africa, including both Advocates and Attorneys. [93]

There are currently 21 law faculties in South Africa. The University of South Africa offers a correspondence law degree. The other schools require attendance in class in order to complete the program. Of the 20 law faculties that do require attendance, nine cater primarily to black students and 11 cater primarily to white students.[94] However, 80% of South Africa's population is black.[95] In comparison with white faculties, these nine historically black universities (HBUs) generally have higher student–faculty ratios, fewer available library resources, insufficient or non-existent support and insufficient administrative support. HBUs produce fewer than half of the law graduates in South Africa every year.[96]

---

[91]   Emmanuel Kwabena Quansah, "Educating Lawyers for Transnational Challenges: Perspectives of a Developing Country – Botswana" (2005) 55:4 *Journal of Legal Education* 528 at 533.

[92]   Philip F. Iya, "From Lecture Room to Practice: Addressing the Challenges of Reconstructing and Regulating Legal Education and Legal Practice in the New South Africa" (2002–3) *Third World Legal Studies* 144.

[93]   *Ibid.* at 151.

[94]   John B. Kaburise, "The Structure of Legal Education in South Africa" (2001) 51 *Journal of Legal Education* 365.

[95]   *Ibid.*

[96]   *Ibid.*

Despite these discrepancies between black and primarily white faculties, curriculum standards in each school are uniform. Education qualifications are governed by the South African Qualifications Authority Act of 1995 which establishes Standards Generating Boards. Though the Board for legal education in particular was not established until June 2006,[97] the curriculum at most South African law schools has adhered closely to the guidelines set out for the new LL B program.

Curriculum reform in South Africa has made significant changes to the kind of law that students are exposed to throughout their legal studies. Students enter the law program directly out of high school and, under the new LL B system, may choose between a number of full-time, part-time and distance learning options. Over four years, they study constitutional, administrative, family, criminal, property law amongst other core courses. There is also core material on an introduction to law/legal method, an introduction to legal systems, writing skills, African customary law and elective options including jurisprudence, dispute resolution, private and public international law and comparative law courses.[98] Practical legal education is also stressed. Most of the country's law schools have run independently-funded law clinics for at least 20 years. The University of Natal (Durban), a school that almost equally serves white and black students, established a legal clinic as early as 1973. Recently, clinics associated with law faculties have joined with South African Legal Aid and an NGO network of paralegals to create "justice centers:" clinics that offer a range of legal services at a single location.[99] This emphasis on practical education in the law school is reinforced by bar admission guidelines. Students hoping to enter the Attorney's bar must produce a certificate showing two years of practical training facilitated by a "school of legal practice."[100]

Initiatives are under way to increase the number of African legal clinics. In June 2003, the Justice Initiative NGO with the South African Association of University Legal Aid Institutions and the University of Natal held an All-Africa Colloquium on Clinical Legal Education. Twenty-two African countries sent delegates and the colloquium generated a program to assist the development of clinics in West Africa, a ten-day intensive training course for African clinical professors at the University of Natal in 2004, and the development of a databank

---

[97] South African Qualifications Authority (SAQA), No. 505 (2 June 2006) Government Gazette No. 28891, available online at: http://www.info.gov.za/gazette/notices/2006/28891c.pdf (accessed on July 10, 2006).

[98] Iya, *supra* note 92 at 368.

[99] Open Society Justice Initiative, Activities: Clinical Legal Education in Africa, available online at: http://www.justiceinitiative.org/activities/lcd/cle/cle_africa (accessed on July 10, 2006).

[100] Iya, *supra* note 92 at 369.

of resource materials regarding the establishment of university-based clinics in Africa.[101] The Justice Initiative has also helped establish a clinic program at the Law Faculty of Eduardo Mondlane University in Mozambique. This clinic was developed through a staff exchange with South Africa's clinic at the University of Natal. The Open Society Institute with students from Yale Law School established a legal clinic at Fourah Bay College in Sierra Leone in 2000. This program entails the publication of a quarterly newspaper, internship placement in human rights organizations for students, a research and documentation project that investigates current human rights abuses in the area and generates recommendations for the government, as well as legal representation for the community.

Overall, legal education in Africa continues to suffer from under-funding and lack of institutional support. As Ndula observes, "in most African law schools one gets the distinct impression that the aims of legal education have not been given serious attention."[102]

D.   Asia

A recent survey of legal education in Asia noted that it is in a state of "ferment," with widespread recognition among law professors of the need to improve the current state of legal education.[103] Tan *et al.* suggest that priorities across Asia must be to improve the physical infrastructure of law schools, noting that many classrooms are not well designed for interactive teaching and learning. As they note: "many faculty in law schools in Asia … do not have their own offices within the law school, and this affects research and teaching productivity as well as the collegiality that is essential to all academic institutions of higher learning. Better libraries are also essential and law schools in Asia have a long way to go in this area."[104] Overall, they conclude that while Asia has a number of very good law schools (including, for example, the National University of Singapore, Hong Kong University and the National Law School of India in Bangalore), there are many that have a great deal of work to do in order to provide a legal education that conforms to international best practices.

In 1978, China had only two partially functioning law faculties and about 60 qualified law professors in the whole country. No national qualifying exam for lawyers existed before 1986 and the concept of lawyers as independent professionals was not recognized until the early 1990s.[105] As a result, China's more

---

[101]   Kaburise, *supra* note 94.
[102]   World Bank, Legal Department, *supra* note 83 at 502.
[103]   Tan *et al.*, *supra* note 20 at 21.
[104]   *Ibid.*
[105]   Mei-Ying Hung, "China's WTO Commitment on Independent Review: An Opportunity for Political Reform" (Carnegie Endowment for International Peace, Working

than 150,000 lawyers vary widely in educational and occupational background.[106] Today, China has the largest array of legal education opportunities in the world, composed of over 2,000 law schools,[107] specialized colleges and centers for the training of judges, prosecutors and lawyers, and junior colleges for administrative clerks and judicial support staff.[108] In March 2002, over 360,000 people took part in a two-day State Judicial Exam. No other country has ever held a law exam of this size.[109] Nevertheless, there is still only one lawyer for every 9,000 citizens.

The Chinese government now claims that the "vast majority" of the judges have received at least college-level training in law.[110] While legal education has indeed improved, the professional status and quality of the Chinese judiciary are still relatively low. Of the 360,000 people who took the 2002 State Judicial Exam, only 7% passed. Moreover, it is still a "recognized fact"[111] that the overall professional quality of Chinese judges and prosecutors is lower than that of private attorneys: while approximately 70% of Chinese practising lawyers have university degrees, only about 30% of Chinese judges do. Some multi-member courts do not have a single judge with a university-level law degree.[112]

The Ford Foundation, between 1983 and 1995, worked to strengthen the faculties of seven universities by facilitating bilateral exchanges of legal scholars, enabling more than 250 Chinese law students and professors to pursue foreign legal education and research.[113] Although over 68% of participants who went abroad with the Ford Foundation program returned to China, only 49% took up legal teaching or research positions as the program had originally envisaged. Professor Randle Edwards of Columbia Law School, the first American

---

Paper No. 5, 2002), citing Zhongguo Tongxun She, "Beijing to Introduce Re-education-Through-Labour Law This Year", February 19, 2001.

[106] Leah Fasten, "Why China?" (2006) *Harvard Law Bulletin*.

[107] Estimate according to Li Xiaoming, Managing Partner at White and Case's Beijing office. Frances Presma, "Duke Law in China" (2005) 23:2 *Duke Law Magazine*.

[108] Vincent Cheng Tang, "Judicial and Legal Training in China: Current Status of Professional Development and Topics of Human Rights" (China-OHCHR National Workshop for Lawyers and Judges, 2002), citing "Chinese Legal Aid System Basically Formed, 600,000 People Aided in 5 Years," *China News Net*, September 29, 2002.

[109] *Ibid.*, citing "Why is the SJE so Hot?," *Legal Daily*, February 17, 2002, at 1.

[110] Li Zhenghui and Wang Zhenmin, "The Developing Human Rights and Rule of Law," in "Legal Philosophy and in Political Practice in China, 1978–2000", available at http://dex1.tsd.unifi.it/jg/en/index.htm?surveys/rol/wang.htm, citing "Strike Hard to Reform for Fairness and Efficiency – An Interview with SPC President Xiao Yang," *Legal Daily*, March 10, 2002, available at http://www.court.gov.cn/channel7/xinwen_40.htm.

[111] *Ibid.*

[112] *Ibid.*, citing "Many Judges Fell in SJE," *South Weekend*, July 11, 2002.

[113] *Ibid.*

co-chairperson of the program, attributes the low rate of return to the increased marketability of Chinese lawyers with postgraduate degrees in the private sector. In addition, Peter Geithner, the Ford Foundation's first representative in China, points out the relevance of the political climate in China. Following the Tiananmen Square tragedy, for example, some students remained abroad until prospects for contributing to China's development by going home improved.[114] Some participants who returned to China, but declined to rejoin law faculties, spurred rule of law reform in other, unanticipated ways as partners in important law firms, government officials, members of NGOs and judges.[115]

Today, foreign involvement in Chinese legal education revolves around skill-building through clinical work. Traditional Chinese legal education emphasizes theory and has no practical component apart from an apprenticeship served immediately before formal admission to practice.[116] In 2000, the Ford Foundation supported the implementation of practical curriculum reform at ten Chinese universities, including Wuhan University, Peking University, Zhongshan University, Fudan University and Sichuan University. University-based clinics are beginning to develop a range of areas of expertise, such as legislative aid (Northwest University of Political Science and Law) and criminal justice (Sichuan University).[117]

Since 1992, the Ford Foundation has supported clinical legal education for law students at Bangladesh's three major law schools at Chittagong, Dhaka, and Rajshahi Universities. While legal clinics initially focused on classroom-based training, students were later given the opportunity to work with local NGOs. By constructing a "pipeline"[118] that would channel motivated law students into public interest work on a full-time, part-time or *pro bono* basis, the Ford Foundation believed it could help form a constituency for long-term systemic reform of the country's judicial system.[119] In the past, students and professors thought derisively of "well-paid NGO types all driving Pajeros [expensive, four-wheel-drive vehicles]."[120] Today, students and professors better understand and respect the work of NGOs. Interaction between the two communities also helped address NGOs' fears that working with students would "drag their or-

---

114   *Ibid.*

115   Stephanie Wang, "Funding The Rule of Law and Civil Society" (Human Rights in China, Issue Paper No. 3, 2003), available online at: http://iso.hrichina.org/download_repository/ 2/HRIC_issues_paper3.2003.pdf.

116   *Ibid.*

117   *Ibid.*

118   Stephen Golub, "From the Village to the University: Legal Activism in Bangladesh," in Golub and McClymont, *supra* note 12 at 127.

119   *Ibid.*

120   *Ibid.*

ganizations into [the] bitterly partisan politics" [121] associated with some student groups. Participants in Ford-sponsored workshops report that student internships at NGOs have helped break down these stereotypes.[122]

Curriculum reform in Asia has met with less success than has clinical education. In Bangladesh, for example, Azam finds in a recent study that the legal education system is said to have resisted change of any sort. Traditionally, legal education in Bangladesh was considered to be nothing more than a means of enabling graduates to become juniors to "senior" lawyers.[123] In 1992, then Vice Chairman of the Bangladesh Bar Council, Barrister M. Amirul Islam, outlined the broad objectives of legal education in Bangladesh as including to "create an environment and ability for reshaping the structure of the society for the purpose of achieving more national goals."[124] However, 15 years later, Azam finds that the curriculum followed in the country's public universities and law colleges is too traditional, archaic, and to a certain extent obsolete. While noting that the curricula at the top universities incorporate some innovative and practical skills he finds a need for many more modern subjects in order to make the curriculum responsive to socio-economic development and social change.[125] Further, he finds that the majority of law graduates in Bangladesh are unfamiliar with important aspects of the lawyer–client relationship and do not have the requisite skills such as interviewing, investigation, fact and case analysis, negotiating, writing and advocating.[126]

In 1992, the government of Indonesia and USAID sponsored the Economic Law Institutional and Professional Strengthening (ELIPS) project to assist Indonesia in strengthening its economic legal framework. The law reform project was unique in that it contained a significant legal education component. The majority of law reform projects assume that "there are enough experts to carry out the new designs."[127] ELIPS set out an intensive three-part plan to ensure expert assistance for development. First, ELIPS focused on the use of knowledgeable and effective teachers. Second, there was an emphasis on the preparation of written resources for students to reinforce curriculum content. Third, ELIPS provided for intensive and in-depth educational opportunities as well as shorter introductory training programs.[128] ELIPS also provided scholar-

---

[121]   *Ibid.*

[122]   *Ibid.*

[123]   *Ibid.*

[124]   Cited in Mohammad Monirul Azam, "Reforming Legal Education in Bangladesh" (2005) 55 *Journal of Legal Education* 560 at 561.

[125]   *Ibid.* at 564.

[126]   *Ibid.* at 567.

[127]   Golub, *supra* note 118.

[128]   *Ibid.*

ships for over a dozen students to receive a Masters degree in law at an American university. Though many of those sent abroad returned, the project revamped its strategy to encourage a higher return rate. In 2002, ELIPS II was established to improve on the work begun in 1992.[129]

Legal education reforms have not traditionally provoked interest among the Korean public. While there have been numerous debates over changes to Korean legal education, the reformist agenda, formulated and debated solely by legal scholars, failed to attract the attention of the public or the government. In 1995, a new momentum for reform arose during the Kim Young Sam administration when the Presidential Commission on the Promotion of Globalization announced a plan to combat corruption and make the infrastructure of Korean society globally compatible.[130] The plan for reforming legal education created intense controversy. The proposal envisioned a Korean legal education system very similar to that in the United States. Current undergraduate legal studies would be replaced with a three-year graduate course, the judicial examination would be made similar to the bar examinations administered in the United States, and the Judicial Research and Training Institute, dedicated to continuing legal education, would be abolished.[131] The reformers argued that undergraduate legal studies provided insufficient grounding to deal with complex legal problems, and moreover that the current system was deficient at producing specialists such as patent attorneys and international lawyers.

The proposals were opposed by most of the Korean legal profession. The Association of Korean Law Professors argued that a legal education system such as the one being proposed would be inappropriate for a civil law jurisdiction like Korea. Law professors who had been educated in Korea worried that the introduction of the new US-style education system might relegate them to second-class status.[132]

III. CONCLUSION

Evidence suggests that the international community is not mistaken in the emphasis it has placed on legal education reform in developing countries. As Azam notes, it is in the classrooms of the law faculties that future lawyers, judges, legislators, human rights activists, and social reformers are nurtured and groomed. Accordingly, "what is taught in the law classes, who are taught, how they are

---

[129]   *Ibid.*
[130]   Jan Won Kim, "The Ideal and the Reality of the Korean Legal Profession" (2001) 2 *Asian-Pacific Law and Policy Journal* 45 at 64.
[131]   *Ibid.* at 65.
[132]   *Ibid.* at 67.

taught, and what goals and visions are set before them, are paramount questions for the society."[133] The curriculum and teaching methods adopted are critical, in order to avoid turning out legal practitioners with a mechanical knowledge of black-letter law and lack of impetus and desire to effect reform.[134]

In each of the regions explored in this chapter, legal education reform has had some successes in increasing accessibility of legal institutions and contributed to the creation of competent professionals able to represent community interests in those institutions. International aid efforts in this area have focused on the establishment of clinical legal education and curriculum development that equip graduates for practice in both local and international arenas.

The law curriculum in Latin America remains focused on rote learning and regurgitation. Some law schools suffer from over-population, while other, smaller private programs are not sufficiently monitored to ensure adequate training for enrolled students. The large variation in program length may suggest an attempt at flexible legal education structures that respond to the needs of local communities, but this variation is more likely to be the product of lack of accountability in the design of legal curricula in the region. Legal educational institutions in Central and Eastern Europe are more tightly controlled than similar programs in Latin America. This has provided a standardized and inflexible legal curriculum. However, under-funding and lack of institutional support still creates variation in the quality of legal instruction. This region suffers greatly from resistance from vested professionals accustomed to the Soviet regime. Weak governmental support for education reforms leads to little accountability by legal educational institutions. Given this, it is not surprising that corruption and sub-standard degree programs are common.

Legal education in Africa is extremely varied with respect to institutional support, funding and curriculum development. South Africa, a relatively rich nation on the continent, has considerable legal education infrastructure, but suffers from continued *de facto* segregation and under-funding of historically black institutions. Other African countries are just beginning to establish functioning legal education institutions with the support of international aid organizations. In Asia, there are a large number of legal education institutions, with the greatest numbers found in India, China, and Indonesia. Overall, the quality of education varies enormously, from internationally recognized law schools to those that fall dramatically short of meeting international best practices in legal education.

In all four regions, students are generally admitted to legal education programs directly out of high school. This places increased pressure on legal

---

[133]   Azam, *supra* note 124.
[134]   *Ibid.*

curricula to provide the theoretical groundwork necessary for critical analysis of the role of the legal system in their countries.

Resource constraints are a significant impediment to successful legal education reform. In some countries, such as those in Central and Eastern Europe, government funding results in a lack of independence, although such a result is not inevitable. Private funding requires tuition fees that are too high for most students in developing countries. Most institutions compromise, requiring some tuition fees while operating with inadequate public resources for the delivery of a serious legal education program.

Social/cultural/historical practices and beliefs influence the design of legal education programs in the regions discussed. The pervasive nature of a formalist curriculum design may be explained by cultural factors. Classroom education with an emphasis on rote learning and regurgitation exists in many legal education institutions. There has been limited movement in any region towards creating an interactive classroom environment where critical dialogue between students and their professor is encouraged. Some commentators explain this phenomena in the classroom as the understanding that "education is a process that transmits dogma, producing conformists and followers."[135]

Political economy impediments to legal education reform are common in each region examined in this chapter. Latin American countries' emphasis on rote learning can be attributed to the vested interests of professors (and existing practitioners) who seek to insulate the curriculum from fundamental change, which would entail the depreciation of their existing human capital and require investments in new human capital. In the former Soviet Union, changing legal education from a tightly controlled and highly formalized system to a more pluralistic legal curriculum pursued in legal education institutions with a substantial degree of autonomy threatens to render much of the current profession's education obsolete. Reforms in Africa and Asia have both provoked similar resistance from professional elites. Lawyers who are trained and practice in a socially dysfunctional legal system regime and make substantial investments of human capital in learning how to function in such a system, are often not a progressive force for legal reform.

---

[135]   Mariano Grondona, "A Cultural Typology of Economic Development," in Lawrence E. Harrison and Samuel P. Huntington (eds), *Culture Matters* (New York: Basic Books, 2000).

9. Professional regulation

I. NORMATIVE BENCHMARKS

A. The Role of Professional Regulation in Developing Countries

Through regulation, governments have power to articulate norms to which legal professionals must adhere and to establish mechanisms to ensure such adherence. In so doing, however, governments limit the freedom of both individuals and organizations. Thus, regulation must be justified on principled grounds. The most important justification for regulatory intervention with respect to the legal profession is to correct market failure arising from the information asymmetries between legal professionals and their clients. While some clients such as large business will often have few information problems, an imbalance exists in many other cases due to the specialized knowledge required on the part of the professional.[1] Given this knowledge imbalance, legal professionals generally act as agents for their clients, acting on their behalf in making informed decisions about the purchase of services.[2] Such a relationship can be problematic because lawyers will often have a financial interest in advising their clients to purchase services from them or members of their firm. The knowledge imbalance also makes it difficult for clients to judge the value of legal services offered and supplied.[3]

Trebilcock, Tuohy and Wolfson find that informational problems in the legal market may be serious, and in the absence of a well-functioning professional agency relationship, market failure may result. They therefore find a *prima facie* case for regulatory intervention to the extent necessary to establish, maintain and monitor such agency relationships.[4]

Another, although less commonly cited, ground for regulatory intervention arises from externalities imposed upon individuals or groups who are not party

---

[1] Michael Trebilcock, "Regulating Legal Competence" (2001) 34 *Canadian Business Law Journal* 444 at 447.

[2] M.J. Trebilcock, C.J. Tuohy and A.D. Wolfson, *Professional Regulation: A Staff Study of Accountancy, Engineering and Law in Ontario: Prepared for the Professional Organization Committee* (Ontario: Professional Organizations Committee, 1979) at 51.

[3] *Ibid.*

[4] *Ibid.* at 56.

to the transaction between lawyer and client, for example, a beneficiary adversely affected by a poorly drafted will or children suffering unnecessarily in divorce or custody proceedings or a poorly conceived legal precedent resulting from low-quality advocacy.[5]

Professional regulation in the context of the legal market is largely concerned with quantity, quality, and price. Regarding *quantity*, the key issue to be addressed is the potential for legal professionals to generate demand for their services resulting in excessive utilization of those services. This requires regulation to ensure that practitioners do not take advantage of clients by exploiting the discretionary power inherent in the professional agency relationship.[6] Professionals should not generate a demand for their own services greater than that which fully informed consumers would demand if they had perfect information.[7] Regarding *quality*, the inability of clients to evaluate fully the quality of services received leads to a risk of unscrupulous or negligent practitioners delivering services of poor quality without being detected. As such, "supply side" regulation is required to ensure the quality of services.[8] Regarding *price*, market imperfections which undermine the effectiveness of competitive pressures may result in prices that are unnecessarily high and thus may require regulation.[9]

Service *quality* encompasses two main aspects. First, in many cases, clients do not have sufficient information to adequately judge what levels (and price) of services they require to promote a desired outcome.[10] Second, consumers are often unable to evaluate the nature of services received, even if they know what service they need. Thus, high quality services are those which are appropriate in terms of client needs and which are well-performed.[11] These two dimensions of quality can be regulated either in terms of the services produced or the producers of the service. That is, government or a delegated agency can regulate either the *inputs* in professional markets, focusing on who is entitled to provide services, or the *outputs*, focusing on the quality of services provided.[12]

There are two main options for implementing *output* regulation. First, civil liability is a mechanism for addressing quality of both services and their outcomes. The injured client is given a private right of action against a provider

---

5   Michael Trebilcock, *supra* note 1 at 446.
6   *Ibid.* at 61.
7   *Ibid.* at 52.
8   *Ibid.* at 62.
9   *Ibid.* at 63.
10 *Ibid.* at 65.
11 *Ibid.* at 66.
12 *Ibid.* Citing D. Wittman, "Prior Regulation Versus Post Liability: The Choice Between Input and Output Monitoring" (1977) 6 *Journal of Legal Studies* 193.

guilty of negligence in the provision of legal services.[13] The second option involves establishing standards of performance and monitoring or reviewing the activities of professionals to ensure that their practices conform to those standards.[14] Unlike civil liability, enforcement of standards through disciplinary procedures is administered by the professional's peers.[15]

On the *input* side, the goal is to ensure production of quality services by regulating the producers of the services, rather than the services themselves. Two main modes of regulation fall under the heading of input regulation. *Licensure* gives a profession a monopoly on the activity regulated. This may be done through legislation where licensed practitioners gain an exclusive right to deliver certain services. A less restrictive option is *certification*, which involves giving recognition to designations of individuals who have met predetermined qualifications set by a regulatory agency or professional body. Non-certified individuals may still offer services but they may not use the term "certified" or the designated title. The most common method of regulation for the legal profession is licensure.

It should be noted that professional regulation may also operate to protect the profession itself. For example, by controlling entry to the profession along with the role of cognate professionals or para-professionals, or prohibiting true competition, self-regulatory bodies are able to protect themselves from competition to the detriment of consumers, hence underscoring the importance of appropriate constraints on self-regulation.

A number of approaches may be taken to designing a regulatory regime and they may be seen as occupying a continuum, with pure forms of government regulation and self-regulation at opposite ends.[16] Where there is direct state control over regulation of the legal profession (classic "command and control" regulation), the state is responsible for all aspects of regulation and administration. Combinations of government and self-regulation are possible where a profession has authority to govern itself but relies on a state agency to carry out certain functions such as investigation and adjudication of complaints. Such regimes would fall in the middle of the continuum. Self-regulation describes a situation where most members of the governing entity are members of the profession itself. The governing entity is responsible for all decisions relating to

---

[13] Trebilcock *et al.*, *supra* note 2 at 67.

[14] *Ibid.* at 70.

[15] See M.J. Trebilcock, "Regulating Service Quality in Professional Markets," in D.N. Dewees (ed.), *The Regulation of Quality: Products, Services, Workplaces and the Environment* (Toronto: Butterworths, 1983) at 90–91; and Trebilcock *et al.*, *supra* note 2 at 71.

[16] Neil Gunningham and Joseph Rees, "Industry Self-Regulation: An Institutional Perspective" (1997) 19:4 *Law and Policy* 363 at 366.

admission requirements, accreditation of legal education institutions, codes of ethical and professional conduct, continuing education, and disciplinary matters.

The international community has long recognized the importance of regulating the legal profession. In 1947, representatives of 34 national bar associations met and created the International Bar Association (IBA). Today, 192 countries are represented in the IBA.[17] As will be discussed below, the IBA promotes establishment of independent, self-governing associations of lawyers. The IBA articulates the functions of lawyers' associations in its 1990 Standards for the Independence of the Legal Profession. These Standards state that such associations have, *inter alia*, "a vital role to uphold professional standards and ethics, to protect their members from improper restrictions and infringements, to provide legal services to all in need of them, and to co-operate with governmental and other institutions in furthering the ends of justice."

Another international effort to articulate regulatory goals for the legal profession is represented by the Legal Profession Reform Index (LPRI). The LPRI was prepared by the Central European and Eurasian Law Initiative (CEELI). CEELI is a public service project of the American Bar Association (ABA) that supports legal reform processes in Central and Eastern Europe, Eurasia, and the Middle East. CEELI created the LPRI to enable it to assess the role of lawyers and the legal environment in which they operate. The LPRI is based on a series of 24 factors drawn from internationally recognized standards for the legal profession developed by the United Nations and the Council of Europe.[18]

The LPRI and the IBA Standards for the Independence of the Legal Profession provide a guide to the functions of a regulatory regime in respect of the legal profession. The suggested functions of a regulatory regime fall within both the categories of input and output regulation. On the *input* side, the key function is to promote a high standard of legal education as a prerequisite for entry into the profession. On the *output* side, functions include: to maintain the competence, ethics, and standards of conduct of the profession; adopt and enforce a code of professional conduct of lawyers; provide continuing education for lawyers; and participate in their country's law reform process.[19]

In terms of entry prerequisites, the LPRI recognizes the importance of input regulation in its requirement for bar admission to be based on "passing a fair,

---

[17]   The International Bar Association, http://www.ibanet.org/aboutiba/overview.cfm (accessed on July 31, 2006).

[18]   The Central European and Eurasian Law Initiative, The Legal Profession Reform Index Factors, June 2003. http://www.abanet.org/ceeli/areas/lpri_factors.html (accessed on July 31, 2006).

[19]   *Ibid.* at Factors 21 to 24.

rigorous, and transparent examination … ."[20] Licensing examinations are particularly important in developing countries with weak legal education institutions, where students may bribe their way through law school or simply receive inadequate instruction.[21] The legal regulatory body, in this context, operates as a gatekeeper for the profession. However, in doing so, it must ensure that, "admission to the profession of lawyer is not denied for reasons of race, sex, sexual orientation, colour, religion, political or other opinion, ethnic or social origin, membership in a national minority, property, birth, or physical disabilities."[22]

The content of licensing examinations varies significantly across countries. For example, the American National Conference of Bar Examiners requires legal licensing examinations to test the applicant's ability to analyze legal problems, his/her understanding of the local law and his/her ability to apply that knowledge in a reasonable fashion to a complex fact pattern under time constraints.[23] Other members of the US legal community contend that the licensing process would be more successful in weeding out incompetent practitioners if it tested practical skills such as counselling, interviewing clients, directing the work of others, organizing the flow of work, interviewing witnesses and negotiating.[24] While most bar examinations test knowledge of local law, the International Law Association's Committee on Teaching International Law has called for the inclusion of public and private international law in any bar examination, arguing that such subjects are necessary for competent lawyering in a globalized world.[25] Some legal educators argue that bar examinations unfairly impede the independence of legal education institutions, forcing them to teach to an examination set by a professional body.[26] However, recognition of the need for some sort of licensing exam is clearly universal.

In terms of *output* regulation, the LPRI identifies disciplinary proceedings as essential, noting that lawyers must be "subject to disciplinary proceedings and sanctions for violating standards and rules of the profession."[27] This requires some mechanism for reviewing and sanctioning the behaviour of member pro-

---

[20] *Supra* note 18, Factor 9.

[21] See discussion in Chapter 8, "Legal Education", pp. 281–2.

[22] *Supra* note 18, Factor 11.

[23] Daniel R. Hansen, "Do We Need the Bar Exam? A Critical Evaluation of the Justifications for the Bar Examination and Proposed Alternatives" (1995) 45 *Case Western Reserve Law Review* 1191 at 1204.

[24] Leonard L. Baird, "A Survey of the Relevance of Legal Training to Law School Graduates" (1978) 29 *Journal of Legal Education* at 264.

[25] Available at http://www.ila-hq.org/html/layout_committee.htm.

[26] Joan Howarth, "Teaching in the Shadow of the Bar" (1997) 31 *USF Law Review* 927.

[27] *Supra* note 18, Factor 17.

fessionals as well as responding to client complaints. In order to effectively monitor member compliance with professional regulations, a regulatory body must be granted powers of investigation, including the right to seize records and review the past conduct of a practitioner.[28]

Another aspect of output regulation emphasized by the LPRI is continuing legal education (CLE). This is considered critical to ensuring that lawyers maintain and strengthen the skills and knowledge required by the profession of law.[29] This follows the approach taken in the US where the ABA's 1992 Mac-Crate Report on the state of legal education and post-graduation training of members of the bar argued that CLE is necessary for the maintenance of competence in practice.[30] The MacCrate Report argues that CLE can only be truly effective if it is mandatory.[31] However, others suggest that professionals maintain their competence in many idiosyncratic ways and that targeted CLE requirements for those practitioners who demonstrate a need for increased competence in certain areas would be more efficient.[32] If the regulatory body does choose to make CLE mandatory, it becomes more analogous to a legal education institution, and must become sensitive to issues such as access and quality.[33]

CLE can be particularly important for building the capacity of legal professionals who have graduated from weak legal education institutions. It also strengthens the skills of those professionals who were licensed by the regulatory body before legal reforms were instituted and do not possess the necessary education for competent practice. It must be noted, however, that CLE can be prohibitively costly for legal professionals in developing countries.

In terms of substantive standards to be promoted and enforced by regulatory regimes, the LPRI's factors articulate a number of standards that fall within the scope of output regulation. The IBA's International Code of Ethics also provides guidelines. Standards include that legal professionals must, *inter alia*:

- Avoid conflict of interest situations;
- Perform their work competently;

---

[28]   William A. Williams, "The Whole is Greater than the Sum of the Parts: The Discipline of Benjamin J. Eicher, Attorney at Law" (2003–4) 49 *South Dakota Law Review* 389.

[29]   *Supra* note 18, Factor 14.

[30]   American Bar Association, MacCrate Report, "Legal Education and Professional Development: Report of the Task Force on Law Schools and the Profession: Narrowing the Gap" (July 1992). Available at http://www.abanet.org/legaled/publications/on-linepubs/maccrate.html (accessed on July 4, 2006).

[31]   *Ibid.*

[32]   Trebilcock, *supra* note 1 at 452.

[33]   See Chapter 8, Legal Education.

- Represent all clients fully, irrespective of the monetary reward for such services;
- Abide by the law and remain candid with the court at all times; and
- Operate a fiscally responsible practice.

A particularly critical norm is avoidance by lawyers of conflict of interest situations. The IBA's International Code of Ethics mandates that lawyers "shall preserve independence in the discharge of their professional duty. Lawyers practising on their own account or in partnership where permissible, shall not engage in any other business or occupation if by doing so they may cease to be independent."[34]

Conflict of interest issues can be divided into four sub-categories: (i) former client conflicts, where a lawyer's previous client is invested in a negative outcome for the present client; (ii) migrating lawyer conflicts, where a lawyer's previous firm was retained by a client whose interests conflict with that of the present firm's client; (iii) concurrent client conflicts, where a lawyer is retained by two clients who hold opposing interests in the same matter at the same time; and (iv) corporate affiliate conflicts, where a lawyer's private interests conflict with the interests of his client in the present case.[35] Negotiating this range of relationships is further complicated by the widely accepted norm that when one lawyer in a firm is disqualified, the other members of that firm are also disqualified.[36]

The IBA International Code of Ethics also mandates that lawyers "shall at all times give clients a candid opinion on any case. They shall render assistance with scrupulous care and diligence. This applies also if they are assigned as counsel for an indigent person."[37] This regulation requires lawyers to act competently, an important element in any set of legal regulations, and to do so regardless of financial compensation.[38]

Legal professionals, unlike many other businesses, often hold money for their clients, either following commercial transactions or to guarantee payment for

---

[34] International Bar Association, *International Code of Ethics*, 1988, Rule 3, http://www.swisslawyers.com/ge/04_sav/02_Statuten_Richtlinien/02_International/IBA_e.pdf (accessed on July 30, 2006).

[35] Dan S. Boyd, "Current Trends in Conflict of Interest Law" (2001) 53:1 *Baylor Law Review* 2.

[36] American Bar Association, Model Rules of Professional Conduct, Rule 1.10(a) (1983). As law firms and clients move to transnational business models, the question of what constitutes a conflict of interest becomes more complicated.

[37] *Supra* note 36, Rule 10.

[38] The IBA continues, stating that, "For this reason it is improper for lawyers to accept a case unless they can handle it promptly and with due competence, without undue interference by the pressure of other work." *Ibid.* See also Chapter 7, Access to Justice.

future services. The IBA's International Code of Ethics states that in pecuniary matters, lawyers "shall be most punctual and diligent. They should never mingle funds of others with their own and they should at all times be able to refund money they hold for others."[39] To enforce such a regulation, any professional regulatory body must have powers of investigation, including the power to audit its members.

Lawyers must in some sense also be independent from their own clients, and remain faithful to the service of the profession. As the IBA's International Code of Ethics warns, "the loyal defence of a client's case may never cause advocates to be other than perfectly candid, subject to any right or privilege to the contrary which clients choose them to exercise, or knowingly to go against the law."[40] The standard code identifies a lawyer as a "'neutral partisan' for his or her client: 'neutral' in that he does not let his moral values affect his actions on behalf of his client; 'partisan' in that she does whatever she can within the limits of the law to advance her client's stated interests."[41] However, this boundary is not an easy one to police. As Glendon observes, in the US, there is an "amazing shrinking concept of the lawyer as independent counsellor" given the financial rewards that can come from successful proceedings.[42] Legal regulatory bodies must therefore be aware of the economic, social and political pressures that can cause legal professionals to cross the line between zealous representation and illegal conduct.

It is arguable that to effectively carry out their functions on both the input and output side, regulatory bodies require mandatory membership. It is extremely difficult if not impossible to regulate the profession effectively if individual practitioners have the ability to opt out of the requirements set by the governing body. Mandatory membership is important in two other respects. First, it increases the dues-paying base of the regulatory body and hence its financial ability to undertake effective regulation. Second, it increases the legal regulatory body's ability to represent the profession. When the entire profession

---

[39] *Supra* note 36, Rule 15.

[40] As Anthony Kronman puts it, "Law is an essential condition for the existence of a market, and those who make the law, those who build the house of law, which provides the necessary stability for any market system, cannot be acting in the same self-centered way that Adam Smith's tradesmen do. They must have an eye out for the good of the whole. They must be directly concerned with the structure of law that frames the market and cannot rely on the invisible hand to produce or sustain it." (Anthony T. Kronman, "Legal Professionalism" (1999–2000) 5 *Florida State Law Review* 5.)

[41] Thomas G. Bost, "The Lawyer as Truth-Teller: Lessons from Enron" (2005) 32 *Pepperdine Law Review* 505.

[42] Mary Ann Glendon, *A Nation of Lawyers: How the Crisis in the Legal Profession is Transforming American Society* (Cambridge, MA: Harvard University Press, 1994) at 79.

is involved in decision-making within a regulatory body, that body can speak for the profession as a whole which gives it greater influence with the government and the general public. It should be noted that the role of professional regulatory bodies will be of particular importance in those developing countries where corruption is prevalent among public officials.[43] In such countries, professional regulatory bodies have a role to play in monitoring not only private practitioners, but also public defenders and prosecutors. Where governments are reluctant to enforce laws that prohibit corrupt practices such as bribery, an independent professional regulatory body has the potential to assume an enhanced role in the enforcement of ethical behaviour. For instance, a public complaints process within the regulatory body can help citizens hold public legal personnel accountable.

B. Independence and Accountability

It is critical that the legal profession be granted sufficient independence to operate without undue influence from third parties, including government. In many cases, lawyers represent clients who are involved in disputes with government or government agencies. In such cases it is critical that lawyers are able to act independently from government so as to ensure no conflict of interest or compromising of their clients' interests. However, as discussed below, independence must be tempered with adequate accountability mechanisms.[44]

The IBA has recognized the importance of having an independent legal profession in various resolutions and documents. In the Preamble to the 1990 Standards for the Independence of the Legal Profession, it notes that "the independence of the legal profession constitutes an essential guarantee for the promotion and protection of human rights and is necessary for effective and adequate access to legal services." It also states that the independence of lawyers in the discharge of their professional duties without any improper restrictions, pressures or interference, direct or indirect, is imperative for the establishment and maintenance of the rule of law. To promote independence, the IBA advocates establishment of associations of lawyers that are self-governing, democratic and independent from state authorities. The 1990 Standards require that lawyers' associations act to defend the role of lawyers in society and pre-

---

[43]   In these contexts, public officials become harder to monitor through traditional mechanisms. Brian C. Harms, "Holding Public Officials Accountable in the International Realm: A New Multi-Layered Strategy to Combat Corruption" (2000) 33 *Cornell International Law Journal* n. 11.

[44]   "Licensing: Admission to the profession of lawyer is administered by an impartial body, and is subject to review by an independent and impartial judicial authority." *Supra* note 18, Factor 10.

serve the independence of the profession.[45] In its 1998 Resolution on Deregulating the Legal Profession, the IBA resolved that "the preservation of an independent legal profession is vital and indispensable for guaranteeing human rights, access to justice, the rule of law and a free and democratic society."

Independence of the legal profession is particularly important in authoritarian administrations, where legal professionals who speak out about rights transgressions risk harassment and potential sanctions from government for their actions.[46] To this end, the IBA International Code of Ethics requires that, "Lawyers shall without fear defend the interests of their clients and without regard to any unpleasant consequences to themselves or to any other person." [47] In countries where harassment is a problem, the IBA advocates that any independent professional regulatory body must acknowledge and attempt to assist in addressing these concerns. This may include lobbying government institutions for more effective law enforcement, lobbying international organizations for assistance in combating repressive regime policies or funding private security solutions for individual members.

The composition of a professional regulatory body directly affects its independence. As noted earlier, regulatory regimes occupy a continuum from self-regulated to government-controlled. From a perspective that acknowledges the importance of the independence of the legal profession, self-regulatory regimes are optimal, given the risk that state regulation may hamper attempts to protect citizens from arbitrary or oppressive government action. Self-regulatory bodies may also be preferred because they tend to have a greater degree of expertise and technical knowledge of practices in their profession than government agencies. As well, such systems generate peer pressure which arguably helps to ensure that professionals adhere to the standards set by their profession.[48] On the other hand, serious accountability concerns arise with self-regulatory regimes. Accountability is a critical aspect of any regulatory regime and this may be compromised, or be seen to be compromised, by a self-regulatory regime. There are a number of reasons why accountability is a critical factor for legal professional regulatory bodies. From a public perspective, key concerns include, first, that the legal profession may have a tendency to engage in protectionist behaviour that generates rents from lack of competition; and second, that the

---

[45]   Article 18(c).

[46]   For example, in Chile, during Pinochet's rule, lawyers faced harassment and violence when their legal practice brought them before the courts with claims against the regime. See http://www.memoriayjusticia.cl/english/en_law.html.

[47]   *Supra* note 34, Rule 6.

[48]   Margot Priest, "The Privatization of Regulation: Five Models of Self-Regulation" (1997) 29 *Ottawa Law Review* 233 at 270.

profession is incapable of effectively ensuring professional competence and protecting clients' interests.[49]

Priest argues that self-regulation is the ultimate form of regulatory agency capture and is incapable of being impartial and fair. She describes it as tantamount to "putting the fox to guard the henhouse."[50] Self-interest may result in "under-regulation" due to lack of enthusiasm on the part of members of the group for promoting and enforcing self-denying constraints on inappropriate professional conduct.

Given these accountability concerns, even when a legal profession is self-regulated, the regime will usually, at some level, acknowledge a higher governmental authority. Priest argues that self-regulation works best when it operates "in the shadow" of government intervention, receiving its impetus from the prospect of government action.[51] Similarly, Gunningham and Rees suggest that self-regulatory mechanisms underpinned by some form of state intervention are more resilient and effective than self-regulation in isolation.[52] Government accountability may reside in part in the power to approve regulations or by-laws established by the body. However, government review in some developing countries may facilitate political influence that would be detrimental to the profession's regulatory independence. Accountability may also be enhanced by representation of specified non-lawyer stakeholder constituencies in the governing body and committees, requiring that disciplinary hearings be public, and that a right of external appeal be provided to both professionals and complainants.[53]

C. Legitimacy

In order to promote public confidence, it is important that the legal profession displays both independence and accountability. In many developing countries, the appearance of independence is likely to be particularly critical given histories of weak legal institutions and intrusive government control.[54] Thus, the profes-

---

[49] Trebilcock *et al.*, *supra* note 2.

[50] Priest, *supra* note 48 at 271. Citing M.G. Cochrane, "Buyer Beware: The New Regulatory Reality in Canada," *Law Times* (September 1996).

[51] *Ibid.* at 238.

[52] Gunningham and Rees, *supra* note 16 at 366.

[53] Priest, *supra* note 48 at 252.

[54] As Richard Abel points out, in many developing countries lawyers have no public legitimacy and have a "visible dependence on the State" for institutional and financial support. (R. Abel, "The Underdevelopment of Legal Professions: A Review Article on Third World Lawyers" (1982) 7:3 *American Bar Foundation Research Journal* 871 at 873, 891.) David B. Wilkins asserts that a state-controlled system of legal regulation "endanger[s] individual liberties, flout[s] the separation of powers and retard[s] the de-

sional regulatory body must not only adopt regulations governing the conduct of its members, but must effectively enforce those regulations.

Another crucial aspect of legitimacy is minimizing opportunities for allegations that the legal profession is elitist and out of touch with the needs of ordinary people. This is particularly important in developing countries where in many cases, people may perceive the legal profession as only relevant to the wealthy and the business community. Thus, it is desirable to ensure that as many lawyers as possible are exposed to problems and issues facing all sectors of society, not just the elite. Professional regulatory bodies have a key role to play in this regard, for example, by fostering the establishment of community legal clinics, and by organizing compulsory CLE that addresses the full range of problems that citizens face, as well as international perspectives such as human rights. Also, regulatory bodies have a role to play in encouraging use of alternative dispute resolution techniques including those based on informal, customary law. These types of steps are all important to ensuring that the legal profession is relevant to citizens. Unfortunately, the legal profession often tends to be a conservative force with respect to these types of innovations. In many cases, lawyers have learned to work within the existing system and do not support changes which may diminish the value of their existing human capital.

II. EXPERIENCE WITH PROFESSIONAL REGULATION REFORMS IN DEVELOPING COUNTRIES

A. Latin America

Rule of law reform in Mexico has focused on judicial independence and competence since 1987, attempting to modernize its legal system in line with its neighbours to the North.[55] In 1994, the Zedillo administration presented a comprehensive package intended to strengthen the federal judiciary. However, despite a dramatic increase in law school graduates – from 1,006 in 1970 to 17,124 in 2001[56] – these reforms have ignored the legal profession and its lack of regulation and organization. As José de Jesús Gudino Pelayo observes, ignoring reforms in the legal profession leads to inadequate implementation of all

---

velopment of a legal doctrine." David B. Wilkins, "Who Should Regulate the Lawyers" (February 1992) 105:4 *Harvard Law Review* 799–887 at 813.

[55] Robert Kossick, "The Rule of Law and Development in Mexico" (2004) 21:3 *Arizona Journal of International and Comparative Law* at 726.

[56] *Ibid.* at 733.

judicial reforms. The lawyer is responsible for presenting his or her case adequately, thereby supporting the judge in his or her structures.[57]

Mexican attorneys are licensed by the Direccion General de Profesiones. The only requirement imposed by the state in order to permit an individual to advocate for a client is a law school degree. A recent proliferation of law schools within the country has made the quality of these degrees difficult to monitor or assess. According to Robert Kossick's analysis of Mexican legal developments, even with these minimal restrictions, a number of students bribe their way out of the thesis requirement for graduation or pose as attorneys despite lacking the necessary qualifications.[58] There are associations of legal practitioners within the country, the largest of which is the Barra Mexicana Colegio Abogados. However, membership is optional. As of 2004, only 2,000 of Mexico's 40,000 lawyers were members of this association.[59] Judges provide the only recourse for malpractice amongst the profession as a whole. They are empowered by the Federal Code for Civil Procedures to impose disciplinary sanctions or reprimand lawyers who are guilty of misconduct or gross incompetence while appearing before them during proceedings.[60]

At the same time, public defenders are subject to a number of controls that do not extend to private legal practitioners. They must guard against conflicts of interest, are audited periodically and are evaluated with regard to their professional performance. In order to operate as a public defender a law school graduate must have "(i) at least three years professional work experience in relevant matters, (ii) a good reputation and trustworthiness, (iii) admission exams and successful public examinations for the position, and (iv) never have been condemned for a fraudulent crime that carries a prison term of more than one year."[61] With government-implemented quality control comes a sacrifice in independence. As Oropeza observes, "the executive continues to very much control criminal procedure in the country."[62] The executive controls prosecutorial officers who indict all felons in Mexico. It also appoints the Attorney General, directly responsible for all public defenders, who may, at any time, be removed by the President, creating a criminal process that is vulnerable to state influence.[63] This, though similar to

---

[57]   José de Jesús Gudino Pelayo, "Pending Issues in the Mexican Justice System" (July–December 2004) 2 *Mexican Law Review* at 3.

[58]   *Supra* note 55 at 740.

[59]   *Ibid.* at 741.

[60]   Articles 54–7, 41, 89, 390 and 391 of Federal Code for Criminal Procedures.

[61]   Pelayo, *supra* note 57.

[62]   Manuel Gonzalex Oropeza "Recent Developments on the Rule of Law in Mexico" (2005) 40 *Texas International Law Journal* 577 at 581.

[63]   *Ibid.*

the organization of many Western nations, has been used to unduly influence the criminal process in Mexico.[64]

A further concern regarding criminal proceedings stems from the strength of narcotics organizations. Bergman and Kossick observe that many lawyers involved in criminal proceedings are particularly vulnerable to the high levels of violence and corruption in the drug industry.[65] Because of the absence of a reliable system of security, threats of violence adversely impact the ability of some lawyers to carry out their professional functions.

There have been some progressive reforms in Mexico. The Barra Mexicana imposes continuing legal education requirements upon its members. Those that do not belong to the Barra Mexicana have access to a number of university-run lectures on emerging legal issues and practical ethics. Still, the cost of attending these lectures is often prohibitively high for those lawyers not associated with the government or a large firm.

With no mandatory membership requirement, Mexico's independent bar has no mechanism to enforce its regulations. The problems inherent in optional membership are compounded by problems in the education system and the lack of gateway exams or assessments for licensing.

Mexico's experience is not unlike that of other Latin American countries. In Chile, for example, the Colegio de Abogados was established in 1928 with the goal of enhancing access to justice. Membership of the bar was made mandatory[66] but throughout the 1970s its authority was limited by the military regime of General Pinochet. In 1981, Pinochet significantly weakened the association when he removed its authority to review and sanction professional ethics and allowed non-members to practice law.[67] Today there are a handful of non-mandatory associations in Chile.[68] These formations are sometimes more effective than those in Mexico, though limited enrolment leads to inconsistent results.

---

[64]   In 2004 the Mayor of Mexico City was indicted for cooperating with a corporation charged with criminal activity. It is widely believed that the indictment, an abnormal legal procedure in Mexico, was pursued for political reasons relating to the approaching election. That same year former President Luis Echeverria was indicted for the beating of 26 students during a police confrontation in 1971. This indictment clearly falls outside of the statute of limitations. Again, it is thought that this indictment was motivated by political jockeying for advantage in the 2006 elections. *Supra* note 61.

[65]   Robert M. Kossick Jr. and Marcelo Bergman, "The Enforcement of Local Judgments in Mexico: An Analysis of the Quantitative and Qualitative Perceptions of the Judiciary and Legal Profession" (2003) 34:3 *Inter-American Law Review* at 460.

[66]   It is not clear when mandatory membership began.

[67]   Richard J. Wilson, "Three Law School Clinics in Chile, 1970–2000: Innovation, Resistance and Conformity in the Global South" (2002) 8 *Clinical Law Review* 515 at 526.

[68]   See IABA website, http://www.iaba.org.

There are over 70 bar associations in Argentina and legal professionals can choose to belong to more than one association. Each bar association is free to adopt its own ethical guidelines and hold disciplinary tribunals for its members. However, by far the largest concentration of lawyers is in Buenos Aires, making the Colegio de Abogados de la Ciudad de Buenos Aires one of the most influential legal professional organizations in the country.[69] The Colegio promotes judicial independence and the support of alternative dispute resolution, professional ethics, and the rights of the lawyer. It acts as a lobby group as well as a loose association. The Asociación de Abogados de Buenos Aires, a second, smaller, bar association within Buenos Aires, has established a legal service center that provides free civil and commercial representation for clients without means.[70]

In other countries, such as Peru, Ecuador and Brazil, bar associations are more closely akin to those in North America, where only members of the bar may practice law. However, Dakolias argues that in countries where bar association membership is mandatory, and associations therefore have the opportunity to regulate lawyer quality, disciplinary mechanisms are often inadequate in practice. For instance, "punishments may be so minimal that enforcement does not deter unethical behaviour by lawyers. In Ecuador, sanctions for violation of the ethics code range from warnings to small fines, depending on the nature of the violation. Only recently did the Peruvian bar acquire the power to expel a member."[71]

B. Central and Eastern Europe

In Eastern European countries under Soviet rule, the bar was composed of a series of regionally focused colleges of approximately 150 lawyers. These colleges then divided into bureaus, placing approximately 20 lawyers in every town. In this way, access to justice and even distribution was ensured.[72] Despite a 1939 Statute ostensibly establishing an organized bar, in practice the colleges "exercised significant control over the life of each *advokat*, regulating admission, discipline, and the activities of its constituent legal consultation bureaus."[73]

---

[69] The Cyrus R. Vance Center for International Justice Initiatives, "Country Report: Argentina," http://72.14.207.104/search?q=cache:OSvbmavrv0AJ:www.abcny.org/VanceCenter/library/PDF/strategysummit/countryreports/Argentina_Eng_abridged.pdf+argentina+bar+association+reform&hl=en&gl=ca&ct=clnk&cd=11 (accessed on July 29, 2006).

[70] *Supra* note 69.

[71] A Strategy for Judicial Reform: The Experience in Latin America, at 224.

[72] Gordon B. Smith, *Reforming the Russian Legal System* (New York: Cambridge University Press, 1996) at 150.

[73] William D. Meyer, "Facing the Post-Communist Reality: Lawyers in Private Practice in Central and Eastern Europe and the Republics of the Former Soviet Union," (1995) 26 *Law and Policy International Business* 1019 at 1037.

Elections to the ruling organs of the colleges were controlled by state interests. The colleges were run by a small ruling elite and, by the late 1950s, about 70% of the bar were Communist Party members.[74] The Ministry of Justice held veto power over policy decisions of the ruling organs of the bar,[75] and placed tight restrictions on lawyer fees that encouraged bribe taking and corruption.[76]

With the fall of the Soviet Union, the college structure was left lacking funding and institutional support. It quickly lost its relevance in the daily practice of most lawyers.[77] Legal professionals trained in a Communist economy were largely ignorant about the fundamentals of an independent bar association. They were left with little guidance or governance.

CEELI has been a critical driver of change throughout the region, emphasizing bar examinations, ethics, and mandatory membership of professional associations. Its legal reform program involves it in working to develop "effective and sustainable bar associations capable of providing a core set of services that are crucial to the advancement of the legal profession."[78] For example, to promote bar association development in Bulgaria, CEELI contributed to bar examination reforms that made the exam more demanding and comprehensive. In Armenia, CEELI facilitated the creation of a unified bar association in January 2005, convening a meeting at which Armenian lawyers adopted a charter, passed a code of ethics and elected officers for the new organization.

In Russia, CEELI has implemented a "development of the legal profession" program aimed at "improving the competence, integrity and institutional capacity of the Russian Bar Association."[79] To date, CEELI has spearheaded a series of CLE courses and provided literature regarding the disciplinary process to all local divisions of the Russian Bar. Some CLE has taken place through international partnerships with the US, specifically surrounding the development of an adversarial system, jury trials and plea bargaining, all new elements of the Russian legal system. Over 400 lawyers have participated in this exchange program.[80] CEELI, along with the Ford Foundation and the Russian bar Association, is working to generate guidelines aimed at reducing sex discrimination within the Russian legal profession. An assessment of the rights of women in

---

[74]   Stephen C. Thaman, "Reform of the Procuracy and the Bar," (1996) 3 *Parker School Journal of East European Law* 1 at 21.

[75]   *Ibid.*

[76]   *Ibid.*; Smith, *supra* note 72 at 150.

[77]   *Supra* note 74 at 1052.

[78]   The Central European and Eurasian Law Initiative, http://www.abanet.org/ceeli/ areas/legalprof.html (accessed on July 30, 2006).

[79]   USAID, http://russia.usaid.gov/en/main/documents/index.shtml?lang=en&id=791 (accessed on July 31, 2006).

[80]   *Ibid.*

the legal profession was completed in 2005. The Russian bar is working now to comply with the United Nations convention prohibiting discrimination against women (CEDAW).[81]

In Kyrgyzstan, bar development began in 1994 with meetings between CEELI and groups of lawyers in the Bishkek region. In early 1995, CEELI launched a lecture series on topics including client interaction and practising in an adversarial system. The meetings became a weekly event with an average attendance of 50 lawyers. This small group formed the basis for a new bar association. In July of that year, the Association of Attorneys of Kyrgyzstan (AAK) was established, with 40 founding members, a board of directors, and a controlling charter. The AAK continued to attract members by offering more CLE programs. In 1997, it expanded its focus beyond Bishkek to the southern city of Osh. The project in Osh was undertaken in much the same way as that in Bishkek, working at a grassroots level by contacting individual lawyers, sponsoring roundtables, and conducting training seminars in Kyrgyz law.[82] In the following years, efforts to increase membership of the bar were furthered by close contact with law students, sponsoring law student participation in international mooting competitions. In February 1997 the first edition of the Commercial Newsletter was published, enhancing the dissemination of information and creating a forum for discussion. In undertaking this effort, the AAK took advantage of the successes of the Kazakhstani bar in this area by initiating cross-country exchanges with groups of lawyers from Kazakhstan.[83] Other publications have also been released such as the October 1998 police manual on human rights and a 1999 *Advocates Handbook*.[84]

In 1995 the Kyrgyz bar secured temporary funding from CEELI to support its operations, but its financial situation remained difficult.[85] In 2000, direct financing from CEELI was terminated, but the AAK managed to establish its own budget by courting larger law firms for membership and concomitant financial support. Through 1995 and 1996, drafts of a law on professional advocacy were circulated, and in mid-1996 a Ministry of Justice draft destined for Parliament in the fall was submitted to CEELI and the AAK for comments. The draft included mandatory membership in the bar but with full discretion regarding admission vested in the Ministry. Further, the AAK undertook an examination of the ABA Model Code of Professional Conduct and held a series of seminars

---

[81]   *Ibid.*

[82]   American Bar Association, "Kyrgyzstan" (1998) 8:1 CEELI Update 25.

[83]   American Bar Association, "Kyrgyzstan" (1997) 7:1 CEELI Update 21.

[84]   American Bar Association, "Kyrgyzstan" (1998) 8:4 CEELI Update 23.

[85]   For instance, in 1997 the organization received a grant from a local organization that allowed it to facilitate the distribution of information by purchasing a photocopy machine: American Bar Association, "Kyrgyzstan" (1997) 7:4 CEELI Update 27.

with its members in an effort to develop a code of ethics. A code was adopted in 1997.

A similar grassroots strategy was adopted in Kazakhstan in 1994. The Kazakhstani National Bar Association was formed, and its leaders along with CEELI attempted to encourage development of the institution by traveling to three key regional cities and holding seminars on criminal procedure and contract law. In 1995, the Practising Lawyers Association of Almaty was formed. CEELI continued to sponsor a series of CLE seminars that included the discussion of various draft laws and codes, including the ABA Model Rules of Professional Conduct, and a draft law on professional advocacy then being debated in the Kyrgyz Parliament. Through 1998 and 1999, efforts continued to focus on increasing membership in the bar and improving lawyers' knowledge of the law through a series of roundtables, seminars, public meetings with politicians, and programs aimed at law students. In particular, smaller niche associations were established to appeal to a wider audience of lawyers, such as the Kazakhstan Association of Young Lawyers and the Women Lawyers' Association of Kazakhstan.[86]

Following three years of consultations between CEELI and the Bulgarian Bar Association and Supreme Bar Council, Bulgaria has recently passed the new Law on Attorneys, which establishes a national bar exam, a new Code of Ethics, mandatory continuing legal education, and a requirement to maintain professional liability insurance.[87] The first sitting of the Bulgarian bar exam was held in December 2004.

C. Africa

South Africa maintains the strongest bar association on the continent, including a number of local associations that bolster the activities of the national bar. However, with only 12,000 practising lawyers to serve over 40 million citizens, legal services are scarce.[88] Membership in the Law Society of South Africa is mandatory for all practitioners, and regional associations control the adherence of all legal professionals in their area to the national standards. They may also impose further obligations upon their members. This leads to some discrepancy between the practical requirements in richer provinces, like the Western Cape, and poorer, rural areas in the north.

---

[86]   See, for instance, American Bar Association, "Kazakhstan" (1999–2000) 9:4 CEELI Update 21.

[87]   American Bar Association, "Bulgaria Passes New Attorneys Act and Holds First-Ever Bar Exam" (winter 2005) 15:1 CEELI Update.

[88]   David J. McQuoid-Mason, "The Delivery of Civil Legal Aid Services in South Africa" (2000) 24 *Fordham International Law Journal* 111.

All legal professionals must complete a four-year LL B degree before being considered for admission to the Law Society.[89] However, practical requirements vary depending on which bar one chooses to join. South Africa maintains a "split bar," dividing the profession between Attorneys and Advocates. Attorneys are legal generalists with whom clients first make contact. They must article for two years before sitting the examination for admission. Advocates have specialized expertise in various areas of the law, particularly in appearing in court. They may either serve as a pupil for one year and write an examination for admission to the Organised Bar or enter the Criminal Bar directly after the completion of their LL B degree.[90] Only the High Court has jurisdiction to admit or remove both Attorneys and Advocates from the bar.[91] Under pressure from the National Bar, the Minister of Justice is considering an amalgamation of the split bar, requiring the same standard of admission for all practitioners.[92]

Rule of law reform in South Africa has been a national project since 1994. The dismantling of the Apartheid system required a complete overhaul of existing legislation. Laws were and are still in the process of being redrafted in accordance with international standards.[93] In South Africa, legal professional associations are an important part of this development process.

Continuing legal education is not mandatory, though it is reported that voluntary seminars are often oversubscribed.[94] There are a number of high quality law schools that produce professionals with a capacity for further learning and a good grasp of legal concepts. However, some universities, specifically historically black universities, struggle with low quality instruction and a lack of resources.[95]

There is marked room for improvement in regulation of the South African legal profession. The old Apartheid divisions still mar the composition of the legal profession. As of 2002, 20% lawyers in South Africa are of colour, leaving 80% of white lawyers to serve a population that is overwhelmingly black.[96] This discrepancy negatively impacts the availability of legal resources to the majority of South African citizens.

---

[89] This was changed in 1998 in order to promote the merging of South Africa's split bar (explained later in this section).

[90] *Supra* note 88.

[91] *Ibid.*

[92] *Ibid.*

[93] http://www.soros.org/resources/articles_publications/publications/sajustice_20060223.

[94] *Supra* note 93.

[95] P.F. Tya, "Maintaining Quality in Legal Education" (2000) 2 *Stellenbosch Law Review* at 244.

[96] USAID Office of Democracy and Governance, *Achievements in Building and Maintaining the Rule of Law: MSI's Studies in LAC, E&E, AFR, and ANE* (Occasional Paper Series November 2002, PN-ACR-220) at 144.

The implementation of regulation is also inadequate in South Africa. Attorneys are audited annually, but the rest of the profession is loosely monitored. Taswell Papier, President of the Cape Law Society, observes that the capacity to investigate and enforce professional standards at a national level is lacking. This leads to little accountability on behalf of the profession to the citizens it serves.

Outside of South Africa, professional regulation is of variable quality, with many countries in sub-Saharan Africa suffering from a lack of effective regulation. In Kenya, all practising lawyers must join the Law Society of Kenya. The Law Society was formed by an Act of Parliament.[97] At present, the Society publishes a magazine called *The Advocate* and has in place the following three programs: the Economic Reform Program, the Constitutional Reform Program and the Public Interest Litigation Program.[98] The agenda of the Economic Reform Program is to link changes in the areas of constitutional and human rights law to economic prosperity. According to the Law Society, legal practitioners and government officials in the past have neglected to consider the impact of constitutional reform on economic conditions in the country; in addition, they have failed to include key stakeholder sectors such as industry and agriculture in the constitutional reform process.[99] The Law Society of Kenya has joined with the Canadian International Development Agency (CIDA) and the Canadian Bar Association to implement a two-year pilot project for providing continuing legal education.[100]

The American Bar Association (ABA) has formed partnerships with the Algerian Bar and the Algerian Judges' Association. The partnership with the Judges' Association has already resulted in the development of a Code of Ethics for judges and an analysis of the Defamation Code of Algeria.[101]

Alongside internationally-led reform initiatives, many African countries have participated in continental partnerships. The South African Development Community, formed in August 1999, serves as a regional association aimed at the harmonization of legal systems and the resolution of conflicts between countries in the region.[102] The African Bar Association, which claims to represent conti-

---

[97]   Law Society of Kenya, online: http://www.lawafrica.com/lsk/profile/index.html. With respect to connections to the government, the Law Society website states that it had a significant role in bringing about the termination of one-party rule and has an ongoing role in constitutional reform in Kenya.

[98]   Online: http://www.lawafrica.com/lsk/programmes.

[99]   Online: http://www.lawafrica.com/lsk/programmes/economic.html.

[100]   Available at http://www.lsk.or.ke/lskprofile.asp?categoryid=6.

[101]   ABA-Africa Law Initiative Council, online: http://www.abanet.org/aba-africa. See Projects link.

[102]   Online: http://www.lssa.org.za. See SADC link, then Info link.

nental interests as well, has been in existence since 1992. According to Ato Getachew Kitaw, President of the Ethiopian Bar Association, the African Bar Association is inadequate as a continental association because it no longer plays a prominent role in continental legal affairs and is comprised only of Anglophone African countries.[103] In 2002, the Pan-African Lawyers' Union (PALU) was created with the objective of harmonizing legal systems across language barriers, including English, French and Arabic communities.

D. Asia

Like many bar associations in Asia, the Chinese bar is at an early stage of its development. In 1956, China began a brief experiment with a Soviet-style bar association, but it was terminated only three years after its inception because of political opposition.[104] The government took over regulating professionals, leaving legal practitioners at the mercy of the state. Unlike many bar associations, which act as institutions of self-regulation for lawyers, Chinese bar associations were organized to supplement government regulation of the legal profession. The responsibility of bar associations in China, defined under the Lawyers Law of 1996,[105] is limited to organizing continuing legal education, educating attorneys about their ethical responsibilities, conducting exchanges with foreign bar associations and mediating disputes arising from the practice of law.[106] The Ministry of Justice has regulatory responsibility for the legal profession. The Chinese Communist Party's opposition to autonomous organizations and professions has inhibited the growth of an independent Chinese bar.

The experience of the Shanghai Bar Association (SBA) illustrates the tension between the Chinese bar associations' aspirations for autonomy and the associations' need to ally themselves with the government. The Shanghai Bureau of Justice (SBOJ), as a government agency, has the status to take actions, which the SBA does not. The SBA, in response, maintains a close relationship with the SBOJ, requiring cooperation to achieve effective disciplinary measures and receive adequate funding. However, behind this cooperation is a steady effort on the part of the SBA to expand its independence. The main point of contention between the SBA and the SBOJ is control over the attorney approval process

---

[103] "Addis Ababa Chosen as Seat for PALU" (2002) *The Ethiopian Reporter*. Online: http://www.ethiopianreporter.com/eng_newspaper/Htm/No270/r270new2.htm.

[104] Stanley Lubman, "Bird in a Cage: Chinese Law Reform After Twenty Years" (2000) 20 *Northwestern Journal of International Law and Business* 383 at 388.

[105] David Lee, "Legal Reform in China: A Role for Non-Governmental Organizations" (2000) 25 *Yale Journal of International Law* 363 at 400.

[106] *Ibid.*

and disciplinary oversight. Currently, these are under the control of the SBOJ. The SBA is currently pushing for greater control over these areas. The SBOJ's current policy is to consult with the SBA before deciding on whether to censure, suspend, or disbar an attorney.[107] However, the SBOJ has the final authority in such matters.

There has been disagreement between the SBOJ and the SBA regarding the chairmanship of the SBA. Although the SBA formally elects its own chairman, the person elected is nominated by the SBOJ.[108] While there is usually agreement between the two parties, occasionally conflicts have arisen. In 1998, the members of the SBA disapproved of the nominee because they felt he was not sufficiently sympathetic to attorney interests. It is unclear what prompted the SBOJ to change their decision, but they withdrew the nominee and instead nominated someone more palatable to the SBA.

The SBOJ has the power to protect the SBA from government encroachment. However, the SBA's reliance on the SBOJ reinforces the SBOJ's control over the Shanghai legal profession. This control may be particularly problematic because the SBOJ personnel in charge of overseeing the Shanghai bar are not members of the legal profession. Thus, although Shanghai lawyers appear to be self-regulated, the close control of the SBOJ indicates that government-appointed officials exercise more control over legal regulation than the members of the profession.[109]

In Malaysia, achieving truly independent legal regulation has also been a challenge. Lawyers are regulated by the Legal Profession Act 1976, which established an independent Malaysian Bar Council (MBC). The mandate of the MBC is to "uphold the cause of justice without regard to its own interests or that of its members, uninfluenced by fear or favour."[110] However, there is continuing tension between Malaysian lawyers and the government regarding the ability of professionals to practice with sufficient independence from government influence. In January 2000, the government charged lawyer Kaupal Singh with sedition for stating, during the defence of his client then charged with murder, "I suspect that people in high places are responsible for the situation."[111] This charge was in direct violation of the guarantee that lawyers are granted civil and penal immunity for statements made in good faith before a court.

East Timor experienced a slow collapse of a formal legal system with Indonesia's violent take-over in 1975. Fighting between Timorese rebels and the

---

107   *Ibid.*
108   *Ibid.*
109   *Supra* note 104 at 403.
110   Malaysia – Attacks on Justice 2000, International Commission of Jurists, available at http://www.icj.org/news.php3?id_article=2580&lang=en&print=true.
111   *Ibid.*

Indonesian armed forces continued until 1999, when the United Nations intervened in support of East Timor's independence. The United Nations' control over East Timor's transition came with high hopes for rule of law reform in the country. The United Nations Transitional Administration took over the exercise of the administration of justice and began rebuilding the judicial and law enforcement system.[112] Independence has done little to quell the violence, however, and, in the face of internal armed conflict, rule of law reform has been all but impossible.

To compound the challenges facing the East Timorese bar, in 2006 the government proposed importing the Portuguese legal system to replace the Indonesian system in which current professionals were trained. This has required a shift in language instruction as well as education relating to legal precedents and institutions for the country's 100 practising lawyers.[113] The United Nations has worked to train and organize judges and police officers, but has done little to promote organizations for practising lawyers. Instead, Avocats Sans Frontières[114] has spearheaded efforts to increase the capacity of the country's legal professionals.

East Timor has one formal bar association, the Asociasaun Advogado Timor Lorosa'e (AATL). Formed in January 2003, membership is not mandatory and the association focuses its efforts on private practising lawyers. To date, 85 private practitioners comprise the entire membership of the AATL, a reflection of both the small numbers of lawyers in the country in general (almost all legal professionals must travel to Indonesia to receive any form of legal training) and the recent genesis of the Association.[115] The AATL is the site for new governance initiatives regarding professional regulation. Despite its small size, members are in the process of creating minimum standards for private legal practice to present to the Ministry of Justice.

Even if the AATL grew substantially in the next few years, the level of capacity building necessary in the region would be too great for a local organization with voluntary membership. A number of projects are under way to bring legal professionals in contact with each other and the traumatized population just beginning to return to their home areas. Given the small numbers of formally trained legal professionals, Avocats Sans Frontières (ASF) has begun a com-

---

[112] Avocats Sans Frontières, Activity Report (January 2004), available at http://www.asf.be/EN/ENfield/timor/report_training_aatl_aug02_jan04.pdf.

[113] Australian Community Legal Centres: East Timor Support Project, http://www.naclc.org.au/activist/etclcproj.html (accessed on July 31, 2006).

[114] Avocats Sans Frontières is an NGO created in 1992 to promote, strengthen, and protect civil, social, political and cultural human rights of individuals.

[115] AATL website, available at http://aatl.minihub.org/about/aatl_Chronology%20_English.pdf.

munity legal liaison training program aimed at creating a pocket of paralegals in rural communities to facilitate citizen access to formal justice procedures. These liaisons also run community workshops on legal process and human rights. Private lawyers are trained in separate workshops designed to encourage practical skills such as running a law firm and working with interpreters. In 2005, ASF introduced educational opportunities surrounding professional ethics, gender issues, human rights, juvenile justice and a number of other areas relevant to common legal proceedings. Finally, ASF has placed mentors in a number of private legal offices around the country to assist with case management, office technology, budgeting and financial management. In 2006, Portuguese language classes will be run out of the Portuguese Embassy to prepare for the transfer to that country's legal system.[116]

III.   CONCLUSION

Professional regulation is critical in ensuring that legal professionals do not take advantage of clients by generating unnecessary demand for their services, ensuring quality of legal services, and helping to keep prices at appropriate levels. Key to professional regulation in Western countries is the presence of independent, self-governing professional bodies or bar associations that play a key role in establishing and enforcing professional and ethical standards. Guidance for developing countries engaged in establishing such regulatory bodies and standards can be found in a number of international best practices such as those promulgated by the International Bar Association.

Professional regulatory reform efforts in the countries and regions surveyed have focused on creating accountable and independent institutions with mandatory membership and effective enforcement mechanisms. However, to date, resource constraints have impeded the establishment and operation of such bodies in many developing countries. Requiring mandatory membership of a central regulatory body would in general be a desirable development. At present, many developing countries have very fragmented professions, with numerous bar associations, often having optional membership. This poses a significant hurdle to both the content and enforcement of regulation. It is impossible to regulate the legal profession if individual practitioners have the ability to opt out of the requirements set by the governing body. Mandatory membership of a central body would increase the governing body's ability to represent the profession both by allowing the profession to speak as a whole and by providing a greater revenue base from membership dues to finance more effective regulation.

---

[116]   *Supra* note 110.

In some cases, where the legal profession is highly fragmented, creation of a multi-stakeholder governing body may be a desirable interim strategy, with members of various professional groups electing representatives to this body, supplemented by representatives of cognate professions, demand-side interests and perhaps a minority of government appointees.

Social/cultural/historical practices and beliefs have also impeded the development of effective legal professional regulation. In some countries, including those in Eastern Europe, and in China, there is entrenched ideological resistance to the separation of legal professionals from state control. This resistance may be attributed to a long history in the region of government involvement in all aspects of the legal system.

Political economy factors also explain why governments or incumbent political elites in many developing countries favour a weak, fragmented, disorganized legal profession, or alternatively a profession rendered subservient by strong direct government control, so that in both cases arbitrary or oppressive government actions are less likely to face effective legal challenges.

10. Rethinking rule of law reform strategies

I. INTRODUCTION

In this book we have made two parallel and mutually reinforcing claims. First, we have proceeded on the premise that, on a sufficiently parsimonious definition, the rule of law is a universal good tied inextricably to development. In making this claim, we have not supposed any particular form of political organization, economic philosophy, or even legal culture. Rather than engaging in the details of substantive law, we have therefore focused on the institutional structures responsible for administering the rule of law. At the same time, however, we have declined to accept the view that obedience to a given set of rules – the rule of rules or rule by law – is a normatively defensible conception of the rule of law. In order to infuse a normative basis into our institutional approach to the rule of law, we have elaborated a set of *procedural values* central to any effective, institutional approach to the rule of law. Broadly, these values encompass process values (transparency, predictability, enforceability, stability), institutional values (independence, accountability), and legitimacy values. We have then identified a set of institutions which constitute essential elements of the rule of law. Drawing wherever possible on international consensus we have, in the context of each institution, elaborated a set of structural conditions reflective of these core procedural values, although we freely acknowledge that particular institutional entailments or instantiations of the rule of law will be shaped by normative considerations particular to given social, historical, cultural and legal contexts (as is true also of developed countries).

Second, observing that states have had difficulty implementing even this baseline institutional structure, we have hypothesized that three classes of impediments – resource constraints, social/cultural/historical values, and political economy – are responsible for the relative failure of many rule of law reform initiatives to date. The boundaries between these three classes are not always sharp, and indeed in some circumstances, seemingly unitary factors can be cast in terms of two, or even all three, categories. Nevertheless, this typology is useful for two reasons. First, our empirical research has established beyond doubt, across institutional structures and geographic regions, that each of these three classes of impediment to reform has some role to play. Second, as we attempt to elaborate in greater detail below, we believe that conceiving of impediments to rule of law reform in this manner can help focus the international reform community, in terms of both the goals of rule of law reform and the methods appropriate to achieving those goals.

II. REVIEW OF EMPIRICAL EVIDENCE

Resource constraints may in some sense be the most pervasive category of obstacle, in that there are few reform efforts in respect of which more resources would not be preferable to less. Across every institution, individual actors in many developing countries have been underpaid and undertrained. Underpaid staff tend to be more vulnerable to corrupt behaviour, a phenomenon observed particularly in the judiciary, police, prosecution, corrections and tax administration. Low salaries render recruitment more difficult in every institution, making it harder to hire qualified staff and, in some circumstances, such as the judiciary or public defence – or sometimes even the bar more broadly – causing the profession to be held in low esteem. Expertise in a variety of fields, such as budgeting or information technology, is lacking in multiple contexts, including tax administration and court operations. Poor physical infrastructure is also widespread, reflected most noticeably in correctional institutions, but also in inadequate courthouses. Finally, resource shortfalls in one institution may have ramifications for others, for instance where slow court processes exacerbate overcrowding in correctional facilities.

However, reformers should avoid an overemphasis on increasing resource flows as a panacea to flawed reform efforts. While some obstacles, such as the need for courthouses or prisons, are truly resource-driven, many others are bound up with more complicated processes better expressed in terms of cultural values or entrenched interests. For instance, corruption and incompetence across nearly every institution considered throughout this book can be linked to resource constraints, in the sense that low salaries make job positions less attractive and encourage corruption. However, while increasing salaries may, in some cases, reduce incentives for corruption, in many other circumstances increased resources can have limited, or even regressive, effects. By conceptualizing these obstacles in terms of their more structural, underlying elements – cultures of corruption, undervalued professional positions, incentives and capabilities to misuse public funds – a broader and more effective field of reform strategies can be brought to bear.

Cultural, social and historical values can impact the success or failure of rule of law reform in many ways. These values might be held by specialized actors instrumental to the reform process itself, or they might be held by the public at large, affecting the popular legitimacy of the institutions targeted. Judges may decline to apply alternatives to imprisonment or delay implementation of streamlined court procedures by adhering to entrenched practices. Law professors and law school administrators in Latin America have at times been reluctant to incorporate elements such as clinical education or theoretical or interdisciplinary perspectives into legal curricula, adhering instead to a traditional vision of legal education as rule learning by rote.

Public perceptions, which may be more deep-seated, play a role in nearly all reform efforts and are relevant across every institution. Public calls for law and order approaches to criminal justice, especially in contexts of high or rising crime rates, can encourage vigilante police justice and impede the development of civilian police forces attentive to human rights norms. Similar domestic pressures can devastate penal reform efforts, both by making alternatives to imprisonment politically untenable and by counteracting reductions in prison populations (particularly in pre-trial detention centers) with increases in new detainees. Public scepticism of rule of law institutions is rampant in many developing countries. Citizens may perceive judges, prosecutors, public defenders, and the bar as a whole as tools of the state, and choose non-state or informal methods of dispute resolution. This perception becomes stronger where historical connections between legal institutions and the state are lengthier and more profound, manifested most clearly in former Soviet bloc states, where nearly every legal institution was bound up intimately with the role and ideology of the Communist Party. Citizens may also be extremely distrustful of police forces, particularly where police have been historically tied to military governments, a phenomenon especially prevalent in Latin American states, but also evident in Africa and Asia.

Locally held cultural values are most problematic for rule of law reform when they are directly inimical to core rule of law values. This issue has arisen particularly where reformers have sought to enhance the legitimacy, efficacy and fairness of legal processes by establishing or reinforcing forms of informal or community-based dispute resolution combining traditional and cosmopolitan values. In these cases, reformers have tried a variety of arrangements in an attempt to achieve an appropriate balance. At the borders, however, a direct conflict sometimes seems inevitable.

The political economy of rule of law reform is the third key class of obstacle, and, broadly, can be manifested in three ways: as power struggles waged by a hegemonic political leadership; as more subtle, entrenched interests held by key actors in state agencies or legal institutions; and as corrupt behaviour on the part of individual actors interacting more directly with citizens who in turn in many cases may derive substantial perquisites from corrupt behaviour by agents of the state. In the latter two cases, political leadership may be aligned with corrupt legal actors for political or economic purposes, or conversely may be seeking to further reform efforts.

Individual and low level corruption is endemic in all eight institutions surveyed. Law students may bribe their way to a degree, police may extract payments through harassment, tax officials may be bribed by large, wealthy taxpayers and judges and court officials may be bribed by litigating parties. This form of political economy is highly diffuse, and in that sense less systemic than other varieties. It is also behaviour that, while an impediment to both the rule of law and economic development, is not unique to developing countries, and can sometimes be found in the legal institutions of the most advanced Western industrialized states.

The entrenched interests of actors in pre-reform legal institutions or of state agencies represent perhaps the subtlest, most context-specific variant of the political economy impediment, and for that reason the most difficult about which to generalize. In post-Communist states, judicial institutions face constant encroachments on institutional independence due to their high resource dependence on local government or private agencies. This dependence flows directly from Communist political structures, combined with more recent failures to exert central governmental authority. In Latin American court systems, judges and prosecutors resist movement away from inquisitorial forms of criminal procedure in an effort to maintain the centrality of their role and authority in court proceedings. Shifts toward more clinical or analytical approaches to legal education have engendered opposition from law professors and the bar more generally, both of whom fear the depreciation of their investments in human capital under existing regimes. Military-run police forces have resisted the re-conceptualization of police officers as civil servants and the incorporation of police forces within public accountability regimes. The organized bar has occasionally felt threatened by attempts to institutionalize legal aid mechanisms, fearing both loss of control over free representation and the dilution of the market for legal services and in turn is often seen as a threat to abuses of office by public authorities. Judicial councils have faced opposition from higher court judges and executive and legislative branches of government where their duties have included functions previously exercised by those bodies.

Many of the fiercest battles evident in the reform literature develop between entrenched political leadership and rule of law reformers seeking to constrain political authority. Dramatic political battles have unfolded in the context of judicial reform, which tends to challenge political authority most directly. Judiciaries and judicial councils in Latin American and former Soviet bloc states have been subject to purges, claims of bias and corruption and outright battles with the executive or other judicial branches for public legitimacy. Several Asian governments, including those in China and Laos, have maintained impenetrable control over correctional institutions, leaving them all but closed to monitoring by domestic and international civil society. The Chinese government has impeded the development of independent bar associations, retaining substantial influence over the legal system through its control over the admission and regulation of legal professionals.

It is difficult – and probably of not much practical value – to assess in the abstract which of these classes of impediments is the most important for rule of law reform. As our empirical evidence has demonstrated, each institution has its own systemic tendencies, and each country its own embedded values, power structures and resource capabilities. However, from the perspective of the international community and its role in rule of law promotion, it is our view that a focus on the political economy of rule of law reform will be the most fruitful approach. As we have already observed, resource constraints rarely operate independently as a barrier to rule of law reform. Where higher level political authorities are ambivalent to, or even complicit in corruption, increasing resources to government or its agencies is unlikely to be of assistance and may exacerbate the underlying problems. While we acknowledge the important role of the international community in providing non-monetary forms of resources, such as legal and technical skills training, we are wary of a strictly *ad hoc*, technocratic approach to rule of law reform. As other commentators have observed,[1] and as our empirical evidence has shown, no element of rule of law reform operates in isolation either from other institutional complements or from the broader political environment. Where adequate investment in training or technical capabilities is lacking, there are often more systemic factors at play.

We also acknowledge the role of sociocultural values as a critical success factor in rule of law reform. Throughout the history of the law and development movement, foreign-funded reforms have foundered on their insensitivity to the needs and contexts of target states by espousing top-down, one-size-fits-all reform blueprints.[2] However, our review of institutional approaches to rule of law reform suggests that there is seldom popular opposition to institutional structures of the rule of law *per se*: independent and effective mechanisms of dispute reso-

---

[1]   See, for example, Thomas Carothers, "The Rule of Law Revival" (1998) 77 *Foreign Affairs* 95; Rachel Kleinfeld, "Competing Definitions of the Rule of Law" (Carnegie Paper No. 55, Carnegie Endowment, Washington, DC, 2005); Stephen Golub, "A House Without Foundation" and "The Legal Empowerment Alternative," in Thomas Carothers (ed.), *Promoting the Rule of Law Abroad: In Search of Knowledge* (Washington, DC: Carnegie Endowment for International Peace, 2006); Wade Channell, "Lessons Not Learned About Legal Reform," in Carothers, *op. cit.*; José María Maravall and Adam Przeworski, Introduction; and Stephen Holmes, "Lineages of the Rule of Law," in Jose Maria Maravall and Adam Przeworski (eds), *Democracy and the Rule of Law* (New York: Cambridge University Press, 2003).

[2]   See contributions in David Trubek and Alvaro Santos (eds), *The New Law and Development: A Critical Appraisal* (New York: Cambridge University Press, 2006); Golub, *supra* note 1.

lution, civilian police forces, independent prosecutorial bodies or state-funded access to justice mechanisms. Rather, popular sentiment may hold a perception of legal institutions as tools of the state, or may be wary of some particular institutional form. In the former case, we can see no better alternative than to ensure that institutions do in fact operate independently – in other words, to adequately address the factors we have grouped under the heading of political economy. In the latter case, we doubt that it will be foreign states or international organizations that will be best placed to evaluate the nature and role of local values. It is for this reason that forging partnerships with local, reform-minded NGOs or community organizations or Alternative Law Groups have been perhaps the most consistently successful approach to reform.[3]

More generally, given the wide variety of institutional arrangements observable even in developed countries that seek to vindicate or instantiate rule of law values, it would be both presumptuous and counterproductive for the international community to attempt to proselytize, let alone impose, some external blueprint of the rule of law paradigm – even a relatively parsimonious, procedurally-oriented conception of the rule of law such as we have espoused – on developing countries, each with their distinctive, social, historical, cultural and legal traditions and norms. Thus, the international community, before seeking to promote specific or concrete rule of law reform initiatives in developing countries, needs to seek firm evidence of domestic "ownership" of such initiatives reflecting the support of a broadly representative range of domestic constituencies, even though often not constituting, for various reasons canvassed below, a winning or decisive political coalition.[4] However, we would emphasize that sensitivity to particularities of context should not be elided with a radical relativism, nihilism or the naturalistic fallacy wherein the "is" becomes the "ought" and hence an excuse for policy paralysis. A major advantage of the relatively thin conception of the rule of law that we have adopted is that it would seem to be a necessary albeit not sufficient basis for any of a range of substantive conceptions of the rule of law or justice more broadly, and hence compatible with substantial forms of legal pluralism. Moreover, in our review of each of the major classes of legal institutions in this book, we have sought, wherever possible, to invoke as our normative benchmarks precepts endorsed in international covenants, codes, agreements and guidelines that have attracted broad consensus from many countries, developed and developing, hence seeking to minimize concerns that the benchmarks we employ reflect an externally imposed, ethnocentric conception of the rule of law.

---

[3]   See Golub, *supra* note 1.
[4]   See Channell, *supra* note 1.

Here we note a number of thoughtful process lessons drawn from past US experience in promoting law reform in post-Communist states by Jacques Delisle in an extensive review of this experience.[5]

The first lesson drawn by the author is that US programs to provide legal assistance and efforts to propagate US legal models seem to fare better when they respond to what relevant groups in recipient countries see as their needs and when they work reasonably closely with key institutions and elites in recipient countries.

The second and in practice closely related process lesson is that US programs to provide legal assistance and other efforts to export US legal models are more likely to have an impact when they involve relatively sustained commitments by advice providers and export promoters.

A third (related) process lesson is that US programs to provide legal assistance and efforts to export US legal models are more likely to be effective if providers are familiar with the language, culture, laws and other conditions and traditions of recipient countries ("local knowledge").

A fourth and final process lesson teaches that US legal assistance programs and efforts to export US legal models are more likely to succeed if they eschew detailed, distinctively US-derived prescriptions in favour of presenting advice or exemplars in terms of more general standards, international norms, universal principles, and some context-specific solutions that are not peculiarly American. Advice and models that mandate only general goals or principles are relatively agnostic about detailed rules, and thus give recipients greater room to find and to choose the least disruptive and most easily implemented specific options among those that are consistent with the general standard. The author notes also that there is a seemingly banal but important lesson of "parallelism": US legal models are more likely to be emulated and US providers' legal advice is more likely to be followed when the substance of the US prescriptions or American templates is relatively compatible with the recipient nations' pre-existing system or its agenda for legal reform.

We would add a fifth and related process lesson: it will often be appropriate for developing countries contemplating rule of law reforms to look for reference points not to developed countries primarily but to other developing countries with substantial affinities to the country in question who have achieved significant successes in the relevant domain (like Costa Rica and Uruguay in Latin America; Botswana and South Africa in Africa; Hong Kong and Singapore in Asia.)

---

[5]   Jacques Delisle, "Lex Americana? United States Legal Assistance, American Legal Models, and Legal Change in the Post-Communist World and Beyond" (1999) 20 *University of Pennsylvania Journal of International Economic Law* 179.

With these caveats, we believe that the most important area of focus for the international community is in the sphere of political economy. Unlike deeply held local values, the international community may be well-placed to pressure equivocal political administrations, or to help support local, grassroots reform. Unlike resource constraints, our empirical evidence suggests that various forms of power structures often represent root-cause impediments to the rule of law.

III. STYLIZED POLITICAL FORMATIONS

Given our emphasis on political economy as a key element in the success or failure of rule of law reform, we believe that a tailored approach, overtly attentive to the domestic political context of the target state, will necessarily enhance the likelihood of success. If, as many have argued, the rule of law is ultimately a political phenomenon, we think that such political attention only makes sense. We begin this politically-oriented discussion by introducing a set of hypothetical political formations with varying degrees of support for rule of law reform. These paradigmatic formations, each of which can be related to real-life examples, will necessarily pose different kinds of challenges for rule of law reformers, and create different openings and opportunities for an international role. Thus, the relative salience of each of the three obstacles to reform discussed above will vary as between these different formations (and almost infinite variations on them) – and with them, the role of the international community.

The first stylized formation is characterized by an environment of broad political support for the rule of law. The state we envision has progressive-minded political leadership at the highest levels, strong administrative support from within the ruling party and broad popular support for legal reform. The archetype administration is that of Nelson Mandela in South Africa, particularly in the early days after his election in 1994. Not only did Mandela himself have a strong mandate, but support for legal reform was widespread as well. Another perhaps more contentious example is Lee Kuan Yew, Prime Minister of Singapore from 1959 to 1990, and senior government minister thereafter, who was strongly committed to a highly competent, meritocratic non-corrupt public administration throughout his lengthy term as Prime Minister, although the independence of the judiciary in some contexts has been more problematic. Yet further examples include several countries in Central Europe following the collapse of the Soviet Union.

The second stylized formation is more ambiguous in its support for rule of law reform. This administration is marked by a strong desire for rule of law reform at the highest political levels, but more systematic opposition from a variety of complex economic and social relationships operating below the political surface. This kind of opposition might be rooted, for instance, in an entrenched ideological orientation inconsistent with the rule of law, or in powerful public or private interests with a stake in a general state of lawlessness. These administrations will often be identifiable by the rise of a charismatic or prominent leader in a time of general political or economic turmoil. Somewhat ironic examples include Mikhail Gorbachev, Boris Yeltsin and Vladimir Putin. In their early days, these leaders brought tremendous promise of reform, despite, among other problems, the meteoric rise of an oligarchic class of extraordinarily powerful organized criminals, rampant corruption, and the pervasive influence of Communist ideology including, not least, a not insignificant degree of popular support for it.

The third stylized formation is marked by a highly corrupt political leadership with strong incentives for maintaining the status quo and no predisposition to reform. In such states there may be varying degrees of organized popular opposition in the form of NGO or other civil society activity, and there may be some degree of opposition from, or some tendency towards, or pockets of reform within, the leadership of some governing factions or government agencies. However, where the political leadership establishes any sort of lasting foothold, it will almost invariably have complex webs of support in military, administrative or judicial branches of government, and often among some segments of the public. There are myriad examples of authoritarian and kleptocratic administrations to pick from, including the long-standing regime of Robert Mugabe as Prime Minister, and then President of Zimbabwe, President Mobutu in Zaire, the Duvaliers in Haiti, or the stranglehold of the late Saparmurat Niyazov, self-anointed "leader of the Turkmens," as President of Turkmenistan. While these states will very often be undemocratic or authoritarian, we emphasize that it is not an absence of democracy *per se*, but rather hostility to the rule of law that will place an administration in this category. Governments with nominal election procedures in an otherwise repressive context may be very hostile to rule of law reform – indeed, Mugabe is an example *par excellence*. More legitimate, popular elections may also produce governments hostile to many of the characteristics of the rule of law, as with the popular election of Yasser Arafat's Palestinian Authority in 1996.

There are several ways in which this trichotomy should be viewed as merely suggestive rather than exhaustive or definitive. First, the lines between these three categories are not strict demarcating boundaries. States may slide in and out of each category, as governments change policy and character over time. Moreover, ruling parties in any given state may have differing interests across different institutions, and therefore support reform efforts in some institutions, and in some respects, but not in others. Second, there may be substantially different political formations within each of these categories, with significant implications for rule of law reform prescriptions. As we have already noted, our categories do not follow the markings of democracy but rather those of the rule of law. Consequently, within each category there are likely to be widely differing political contexts, to which reformers will have to be sensitive in selecting appropriate strategies for reform. For instance, in states with authoritarian governments – even those generally in favour of reform – it may be more difficult to pursue legal remedies against the state or its representatives in court proceedings (Singapore may be an example).

Nevertheless, there remain key commonalities among states within each group that are relevant to the potential of the international community as a supporter of reform. We turn now to a more detailed discussion of that role.

IV. OPTIONS FOR THE INTERNATIONAL COMMUNITY

The international community has numerous instruments at its disposal to help encourage the success of rule of law reform initiatives. These instruments vary along various dimensions: they may be exercised through state or non-state channels; their source may be bilateral, regional, or multilateral; and they may operate as a carrot, a stick, or some combination of both. Most importantly, they have manifested varying degrees of success in different political contexts and across different policy areas.

These approaches can be usefully classified into three groups of an increasingly coercive nature. First, reformers promote the rule of law by providing resources in the form of funds and expertise either to reform-oriented governments or their agencies or to reform-oriented local NGOs or community organizations generally carrying out circumscribed mandates in a specific legal field in a particular location. There are numerous examples of this latter approach scattered throughout our review of the empirical evidence, including, for instance Alternative Law Groups (ALGs) in the Philippines and elsewhere.[6] A variant on this approach is where international NGOs with highly specific expertise in a given field establish a direct presence in target communities – in other words, they "think globally, act locally." Examples in our survey of the literature include Penal Reform International (PRI), Street Law, or One World, One Action, which operates the *Nagorik Uddyog* program in Bangladesh. These organizations are often funded, in turn, by developed states or larger NGOs, and may themselves partner with yet smaller, local NGOs. There are two essential characteristics of this approach. First, it may circumvent the state entirely, interacting with local communities in a grassroots fashion. Second, it is entirely non-coercive.

The second broad category encompasses a wide range of "conditionalities:" policy conditions imposed by states or supranational organizations in exchange for some desired benefit. Conditionalities can occur in trade policies, either in the process of World Trade Organization (WTO) accession, the WTO system of

---

[6] See Golub, *supra* note 1.

preferences, or in bilateral trade agreements; as a part of accession to regional political organizations, such as the EU or the African Union; or in exchange for aid or debt relief. This mechanism operates in the traditional state system, through agreements between state parties or intergovernmental organizations. Most conditionalities are somewhat ambiguous in their character as carrot or stick. Conditionalities constitute a promised benefit in exchange for some policy choice, rather than a punishment for some perceived failure. In practice, however, conditionalities are imposed in long-term, ongoing relationships in which benefits begin to flow before policy conditions are satisfied. Conditionalities are therefore usually effectuated by taking away benefits, or threatening to do so, and in that sense, have a more coercive character. But while the threat to deny benefits remains the promisor's ultimate bargaining chip, parties may also seek to encourage compliance through the exercise of soft power, in the form of dialogue and negotiation. This practice, dubbed *positive* conditionality, is therefore on the less coercive end of the conditionality spectrum. Outright threats to end an existing relationship, termed *negative* conditionality, lie at the more coercive end.

Third, reform may be encouraged by imposing sanctions. Sanctions, which may also be imposed in different ways and in different contexts, necessarily involve punishment as a means to show disapproval. Therefore, they represent the most coercive of the three mechanisms.

We now turn to a more detailed discussion of the latter two mechanisms, conditionality and sanctions, with an emphasis on the likelihood of success or failure of each across varying circumstances.

A. Conditionality

1. Trade policy
In principle, there are three ways in which conditionalities encouraging the rule of law can be incorporated into trade policy: the WTO accession process, the WTO Generalized System of Preferences (GSP), and Bilateral and Intra-Regional Trade Agreements.

WTO accession negotiations provide only a limited opportunity to induce rule of law reform in developing countries. Article XII of the WTO Agreement states that accession to the WTO will be "on terms to be agreed" between the acceding government and the WTO. Accession to the WTO is therefore a process of negotiation, but one which tends to focus strictly on economic considerations.[7] In China, an important test case, the Protocol of Accession does set out three requirements relating to the legal system: uniform administration, transpar-

---

[7]   WTO accessions follow procedures laid out in a note by the Secretariat WT/ACC/1 on March 24, 1995.

ency, and judicial review. However, these requirements are fairly vague and provide little detail of what is actually required in practice. Moreover, these conditionalities are limited to matters relating to trade and investment, and do not touch the broader legal system. As Matthew Stephenson argues,[8] it may be unrealistic to expect significant spill-over effects.

The WTO Generalized System of Preferences embeds in WTO rules an exception to the GATT most-favoured-nation (MFN) requirement by permitting member states to offer preferential market access to exports from developing countries.[9] The GSP is an important potential avenue for influence, because it carries important implications for developing states.[10] The EU and the US have both employed conditionalities in this context, although these conditionalities tend to be more substantive – such as environmental protection, good governance and human rights – and impact the rule of law only indirectly.[11] However, the potential for WTO member states to use conditionality in the GSP context is uncertain, given the claim from some critics that the GSP does not permit member states to differentiate between developing countries. A 2004 WTO Appellate Body ruling held that differential treatment as between developing countries will be consistent with WTO obligations of non-discrimination where the rules governing those distinctions are objective and transparent, and where all "similarly situated" countries are treated equally.[12] The precise implications of the ruling are not clear; but WTO obligations may be met, as Howse argues, "when the

---

[8] Matthew Stephenson, "A Trojan Horse in China," in Carothers, *supra* note 1.

[9] There are currently 13 national GSP schemes notified to the UNCTAD secretariat – Australia, Belarus, Bulgaria, Canada, Estonia, the European Community, Japan, New Zealand, Norway, the Russian Federation, Switzerland, Turkey and the US. See http://www.unctad.org/Templates/Page.asp?intItemID=2309&lang=1; see also Michael J. Trebilcock and Robert Howse, *Regulation of International Trade*, 3rd edn (New York: Routledge, 2005) at 472. The key rules are found in the *Differential and More Favourable Treatment Reciprocity and Fuller Participation of Developing Countries*, November 28, 1979, GATT BISD (26th Supp) 203 (1980).

[10] Amy M. Mason, "The Degeneralization of the Generalized System of Preferences (GSP): Questioning the Legitimacy of the US GSP" (2004) 54 *Duke Law Journal* 513 at 524.

[11] European Commission, "Generalised System of Preferences: EU 'GSP+' Granted to an Additional 15 developing Countries," online, European Commission: http://europa.eu.int/comm/trade/issues/global/gsp/pr211205_en.htm. Office of the United States Trade Representative, Executive Office of the President, *US Generalized System of Preferences Guidebook* (Washington, DC, November 2005).

[12] *European Communities – Conditions for the Granting of Preferences to Developing Countries* (2004), WTO Doc. WT/DS246/AB/R (Appellate Body Report), at para. 155. For further commentary, see Robert Howse, "Appellate Body Ruling Saves the GSP, at Least for Now" (2004) 8:2 *Bridges Monthly Review* 5 and Gene M. Grossman and Alan O. Sykes, "A Preference for Development: The Law and Economics of GSP" (2005) 4:1 *World Trade Review* 41.

same level of tariff preferences is accorded to all developing countries, but they have to fulfill certain minimum conditions – objective, origin-neutral, transparent – in order to receive that general level of preferences."[13]

Bilateral and intra-regional trade agreements may offer the greatest promise for rule of law conditionality, perhaps because they are unburdened by the strictures of multilateral rules. The EU has been the global leader in this respect, embedding a variety of law-related conditionalities in its trade agreements. For instance, several documents signed in the context of the Euro-Mediterranean Partnership (EMP), the general framework for political, economic, and social relations between the EU and 10 countries in the south-east Mediterranean area, incorporate respect for human rights and democracy as essential elements of the partnership, although these requirements are often vaguely defined.[14] Technical and financial assistance provided pursuant to the EMP is based, *inter alia*, on "respect for democratic principles and the rule of law;"[15] programs have included strengthening of institutions which guarantee the independence and effectiveness of the judicial system, the training of national security services and civil protection.[16] Principles of democracy and fundamental human rights were also included as conditions precedent to an October 2000 free trade agreement between the EU and Mexico.

The successes of these efforts have been mixed. Youngs argues that in practice, in the context of the EMP, the EU has focused principally on economic reform and other goals, applying little coercive pressure for political change or democracy.[17] In the context of the Mexico–EU agreement, Syzmanski and Smith are more optimistic. They argue that the Mexican government accepted the conditions because, among other reasons, of domestic political and economic changes, and the relevance of the clause to its aspirations to membership in the group of "first world" democracies.[18] Similarly, they expect the agreement to

---

[13]   Howse, *supra* note 12.

[14]   See, for example, Barcelona Declaration, adopted at the Euro-Mediterranean Conference, November 27–8, 1995; Euro-Mediterranean Agreement between the European Communities and their Member States and Tunisia, Official Journal of the European Communities (L92/2, March 30, 1998).

[15]   Article 16 MEDA regulation amended by Council Regulation No. 780/1998.

[16]   Article 2 MEDA regulation.

[17]   Richard Youngs, *Laying the Foundations: European Strategies in the 1990s* (Washington, DC: Carnegie Endowment for International Peace, 2004) at 4. Vania Scalambrieri, *Democratic Conditionality Within the Framework of the Euro-Mediterranean Partnership* (Italy: Jean Monnet Centre EuroMed, Working Papers in Comparative and International Politics, University of Catania, 2004) at 32.

[18]   Marcela Syzmanski and Michael E. Smith, "Coherence and Conditionality in European Foreign Policy: Negotiating the EU-Mexico Global Agreement" (2005) 43:1 *Journal of Common Market Studies* 171 at 172.

make the Mexican government more sensitive to its international reputation in general, and its protection of human rights and civil society in particular.[19]

2. Regional political organizations

Membership in regional political organizations has been another context for the application of conditionalities relating to the rule of law. The most prominent example is again the EU, where accession mechanisms have existed in various forms for decades. In the late 1980s and early 1990s, during the post-Communist European democratic euphoria, democracy and its typical accoutrements became increasingly prominent in EU accession discourse. A set of bilateral agreements signed beginning in 1991, called "Europe Agreements", included conditions based, *inter alia*, on the rule of law.[20] In 1993, the Copenhagen European Council established a more formal framework, including criteria relating to democracy, the rule of law, human rights and protection of minorities.[21] Agreements with individual candidate states have included similar references. In Turkey, for instance, among the steps required prior to accession are, in addition to specific protection for various standards of human rights, improvements in the functioning and efficiency of the judiciary.[22]

While these instruments could perhaps all be characterized as 'conditionalities' of one sort or another, standards for accession have been applied in different ways and with different levels of success. For instance, in the early 1990s, the Copenhagen criteria were applied in a more positive than negative sense, proceeding principally by dialogue and soft power, rather than threats of coercion.[23] By the late 1990s, with the realization that not all candidate states could achieve accession at the same time, the Copenhagen conditions became more formalized and applied in a more negative fashion, with the EU refusing negotiations with countries which failed to meet the criteria.[24] Grabbe finds that positive conditions have generally been more effective in EU accession negotiations than negative condi-

---

[19] Syzmanski and Smith note that since the Global Agreement entered into effect in October 2000, the results have been very encouraging. As well as increased trade between the EU and Mexico, there have been various cooperation activities including an EU–Mexico civil society forum in November 2002. *Ibid.* at 187.

[20] Karen E. Smith, *The Making of EU Foreign Policy* (New York: St Martin's Press, Inc., 1999) at 93.

[21] See online at: The European Commission, http://www.europa.eu.int/comm/enlargement/intro/criteria.htm#Accession%20criteria; http://www.europa.eu.int/.

[22] Council Decision of 8 March 2001, on the principles, priorities, intermediate objectives and conditions contained in the Accession Partnership with the Republic of Turkey (2001/235/EC), *Official Journal of the European Communities* L85/13.

[23] Smith, *supra* note 20 at 124.

[24] Gunter Verheugen, "The Enlargement of the European Union" (2000) 5:4 *European Foreign Affairs Review* 439 at 441. Smith, *supra* note 20 at 129.

tionalities for a variety of reasons, including the fact that negotiations can be halted only in accordance with significant procedural requirements, reducing its impact as a threat mechanism;[25] that conditions are often vague and general, and not directly tied to punitive measures for non-compliance; and that accession goals are generally long-term, encouraging governments to delay implementation of reforms until a point further along in the process.[26] Consequently, Grabbe finds, EU accession has not proven successful as "a scalpel to sculpt institutions and policies during the accession process; rather, it is a mallet that can be used only at certain points in the process to enforce a few conditions at a time."[27] Pridham casts similar conclusions in different terms, finding the EU accession mechanism to be most valuable insofar as it "provides a consistent and direct pressure for the introduction and elaboration of democratic rules and procedures."[28]

Case studies examining attempts to use EU accession conditionality to transform policies have also found diverse results across varying political circumstances. Not surprisingly, where high-level political will has been broadly predisposed to reform, conditionalities have been significantly more successful. For instance, attempts to effect broad political change in Slovakia in the mid-1990s were largely ineffective in the face of the authoritarian tendencies of the government of Vladimir Mečiar. A series of warnings between 1994 and 1997, culminating in the exclusion of Slovakia from formal accession talks in December 1997, prompted little in the way of democratization.[29] With Mečiar's removal in 1998 elections came swift reform of the institutional encroachments of his administration, and with that, EU membership in 2004. While Krause attributes little of this overall progress to the EU – he doubts the power of accession to make democracy more attractive to leaders who have decided it is not otherwise in their best interest – he notes also that once the new government took power, the rewards of membership became more palpable and the influence of the EU more important.[30] Grabbe, similarly, cites Slovakia as an example of the relative impotence of negative conditionality in this context.[31]

---

[25] Geoffrey Pridham, "EU Enlargement and Consolidating Democracy in Post-Communist States – Formality and Reality" (2002) 40:5 *Journal of Common Market Studies* 953 at 958.

[26] Heather Grabbe, "How Does Europeanization Affect CEE Governance? Conditionality, Diffusion and Diversity" (2001) 8:6 *Journal of European Public Policy* 1013 at 1020.

[27] *Ibid.* at 1026.

[28] Pridham, *supra* note 25 at 959.

[29] Kevin Deegan Krause, "The Ambivalent Influence of the European Union on Democratization in Slovakia," in P.J. Kubicek (ed.), *The European Union and Democratization* (London: Routledge, 2003) 56 at 60.

[30] Krause, *supra* note 29 at 81. See also Pridham, *supra* note 25.

[31] Grabbe, *supra* note 26 at 1021.

Given the approach to the rule of law in this book, it is worth noting here that where the EU has encouraged rule of law reform as part of the accession mechanism, it has not done so in a strictly institutionalist manner – though this has been part of the approach – but as part of a highly politicized drive towards democratic governance. While we do not link democracy inextricably to the rule of law, we acknowledge that there are close affinities between the two concepts – and more specifically, that the EU approach to democracy is highly consistent with, if only one manifestation of, our vision of the rule of law. Moreover, as Grabbe has observed, among the reasons for the diffuse influence of the accession process is the fact that EU demands are not simply a set of conditions for receiving defined benefits, but an evolving process that is highly politicized on both sides. We would expect that the EU's approach, by embedding its demands in a comprehensive democratic framework, encourages more resistance of this sort than might be experienced by a more focused, institutional, and more politically pluralistic approach. At the same time, recognizing, as we have, the highly political nature of any worthwhile attempt at rule of law reform, we expect the long-term effectiveness of the EU approach to be stronger than one premised upon a purely technocratic conception of rule of law reform.

Other regional organizations have some, more limited potential to exert similar influence through accession mechanisms, and have been less successful. NATO has embedded the rule of law in the preamble of its constitutive document, the Treaty of Washington, and made reference to the "positive developments" in Eastern Europe toward the rule of law in its 1997 Madrid Declaration (although again little effort is made to define the constituent elements of the rule of law).[32] However, citing past failures to reprimand member states experiencing periods of non-democratic rule, Reiter argues that NATO has not and will not advance the rule of law or democratization in Europe.[33] Similarly, the African Union (AU) incorporates numerous broad references to the rule of law in its public documentation (but again with little attempt at definition).[34] Article 30 of the Constitutive Act permits suspension of member states whose governments have "come to power through unconstitutional means."[35] While this provision seems limited in scope – and inapplicable to more subtle institutional reform within administrations – Magliveras and Naldi argue that "its proper and consistent application … should … give to the Union the op-

---

[32] Madrid Declaration on Euro-Atlantic Security and Cooperation, July 1997.

[33] Dan Reiter, "Why NATO Enlargement Does Not Spread Democracy" (2001) 25:4 *International Security* 41 at 46, 57.

[34] Constitutive Act of the African Union (adopted at Lomé, Togo, July 11, 2000), preamble, Article 4.

[35] Konstantinos D. Magliveras and Gino J. Naldi, "The African Union: A New Dawn for Africa?" (2002) 51 *International and Comparative Law Quarterly* at 423.

portunity to promote democratic principles and the rule of law among Member States."[36] On the whole, however, the membership standards seem vague, have not, as yet, been operationalized through institutional structures, and have not been applied in key test cases, such as Zimbabwe.[37]

3. Aid and debt relief

Conditional aid has been highly contentious, as scores of critics have assailed, among other things, its ineffectiveness and its anti-democratic character. Burnside and Dollar, for instance, find that the link between aid and good policy has often been tenuous and that, in general, donors have not effectively tailored their assistance to the specific country and phase of the reform process.[38] Indeed, better policies and improving performance often lead to decreasing levels of development aid, reducing incentives to reform.[39] Burnside and Dollar conclude that political considerations remain important in determining aid flows, especially for large donors and multilateral institutions. Other studies have found that conditionalities are often unenforced, in the sense that lending agencies continue to disburse funds in the face of failures by borrower states to fulfil conditions. This phenomenon has been blamed on the strong incentives on lending agencies to maintain borrower accounts as a means of self-perpetuation.[40] Finally, because money is fungible, aid funds become difficult to monitor.[41]

The importance of domestic political support has also become widely recognized. The World Bank has concluded that foreign aid cannot take the lead in promoting reform if there is little domestic movement in that direction.[42] Similarly, where popular opposition to the policies of aid conditionality is manifested, aid conditionality can undermine democratic processes by supplanting domestic public policy-making. Santiso argues that high levels of aid dependency can

---

[36]   *Ibid.* at 424.

[37]   Tiyanjana Maluwa, "The Constitutive Act of the African Union and Institution-Building in Postcolonial Africa" (2003) 16 *Leiden Journal of International Law* 165–6.

[38]   Craig Burnside and David Dollar, *Aid, Policies, and Growth* (Washington, DC: Policy Research Working Paper 1777, World Bank, 1997). See also William Easterly, *The White Man's Burden: Why the West's Efforts to Aid the Rest Have Done So Much and So Little Good* (New York: The Penguin Press, 2006).

[39]   Paul Collier and David Dollar, *Development Effectiveness: Have We Learnt?* (Washington, DC: The World Bank, 2001).

[40]   P. Mosley, J. Harrigan and J. Toye, *Aid and Power* (London: Routledge, 1995); The World Bank, *Attacking Poverty* (New York: Oxford University Press (for the World Bank), 2000) at 193. See also Easterly, *supra* note 38.

[41]   The World Bank 2000, *supra* note 40 at 199.

[42]   The World Bank, *Assessing Aid: What Works, What Doesn't, and Why* (New York: Oxford University Press (for the World Bank), 1998) at 48.

weaken democratic governance when the imperatives of aid management supersede the requirements of domestic decision-making and lead to perverse patterns of "reverse accountability."[43] Given the importance of sociocultural values and other domestic factors for the success of rule of law reform, as emphasized throughout our review of the empirical evidence, we find this point to be of particular relevance in this context. Where there is domestic support, however, including within the recipient country's government, it has been suggested that aid conditionality may have an important role to play.[44] First, governments truly committed to reform may agree to aid conditions that bind them to a policy and protect them from internal special interests. Such a conditional loan is a type of self-commitment mechanism that helps government resist the temptation to deviate from good policy in the pursuit of short-run interests. Second, conditional aid can be useful as a signalling device to indicate to private investors (domestic and foreign) that the government is serious about reform and that the new policy regime is likely to remain in place.[45]

There are a number of factors that may enhance the effectiveness of aid conditionality where political support for rule of law reform is tenuous.[46] First, any threat to withdraw aid by reason of a violation of a certain condition must be credible. Second, a donor government or agency may have a better chance of forcing change if the recipient government is in a weak political position domestically. Third, it can be helpful if the recipient government is able to use external intervention to strengthen its domestic position against vested interests opposed to reforms. Fourth, the level of dependency on the aid involved will play a part, as will the importance to the recipient state of the relationship with the donor country or agency. Fifth, likelihood of success will be greater if the donor country's action is likely to provoke an international snowball effect. Finally, international coordination is likely to be more effective than unilateral efforts.

Rule of law aid conditionality has also been used by the EU, through the Cotonou Agreement, and before that, the Lomé Convention, both of which have included multiple references to the rule of law. Article 4 of the Lomé Convention offered a description of the rule of law, including a "means of recourse enabling individual citizens to enforce their rights," an independent

---

[43] Carlos Santiso, "Responding to Democratic Decay and Crises of Governance: The European Union and the Convention of Cotonou" (2003) 10:3 *Democratization* 148 at 156.

[44] The World Bank 1998, *supra* note 42 at 58.

[45] *Ibid.* Daniel Farber, "Rights as Signals" (2002) 31 *Journal of Legal Studies* 83.

[46] Olav Stokke, "Aid and Political Conditionality: Core Issues and State of the Art," in Olav Stokke (ed.), *Aid and Political Conditionality* (London: Frank Cass, 1995) at 42.

judiciary, equality before the law, a "prison system respecting the human person," and a "police force at the service of the law."[47] The June 2000 Cotonou Agreement contains similar terms, and in Articles 96 and 97 establishes procedures for violations of those terms. These procedures, which combine consultative processes with, ultimately, suspension from the Cotonou Agreement should consultations fail, have been used in varying ways on 12 occasions. Santiso finds that the EU's approach has most often emphasized positive measures of support and inducement, reflecting a strategy of constructive engagement.[48] This approach, argues Santiso, is based on a set of assumptions that conceptualize democratization as a gradual process of political and institutional change.

B. Sanctions

Whereas conditionalities tend to be imposed *ex ante*, sanctions are typically a reactive mechanism instituted *ex post*. Sanctions include any "denial of customary interactions intended to promote social, political, or economic change in a target state."[49] On this broad definition, sanctions may be imposed by state or non-state actors, and may take diplomatic, economic or military form. *Diplomatic* sanctions may include action such as withholding recognition or refusing normal diplomatic relations, denying extradition or air landing rights, restricting foreign assistance or investment, freezing assets, denying credit, or refusing most-favoured-nation trading status.[50] They may also include multi-lateral political actions, such as suspension or expulsion from an international organization. *Economic* sanctions may include trade restrictions (e.g., import or export bans, quotas, licensing requirements, tariffs and conditions on government procurement),[51] as well as cessation of economic relations including full economic embargoes. *Military* sanctions may include assaults, invasion, or occupation (or "siege").[52] We assume that it will be the first two kinds of sanc-

---

[47] Commission Communication to the Council and Parliament – Democratisation, the Rule of Law, Respect for Human Rights and Good Governance: The Challenges of the Partnership between the European Union and the ACP States (Brussels, COM (98) 146, March 12, 1998).

[48] Santiso, *supra* note 43 at 151.

[49] See Neta C. Crawford, "Trump Card or Theater?," in Neta C. Crawford and Audi Klotz (eds), *How Sanctions Work: Lessons from South Africa* (London and New York: MacMillan and St Martin's Press, 1999).

[50] Sarah H. Cleveland, "Human Rights Sanctions and International Trade: A Theory of Compatibility" (2002) 5:1 *Journal of International Economic Law* 133 at 135–6.

[51] *Ibid.* at 135.

[52] See H.G. Askari *et al.*, *Economic Sanctions: Examining Their Philosophy and Efficacy* (Westport, CT: Praeger, 2003) at 18.

tion, diplomatic and economic, that are likely to be most relevant for rule of law reform.

The success of sanctions as a tool to effect policy change is at best uncertain. In one study of sanctions in the twentieth century, Hufbauer *et al.* conclude that, on average, sanctions have been successful in about 34% of cases.[53] The success rate varies depending on the type of policy or governmental change sought. Cases involving modest policy changes were found to be successful more frequently than sanctions designed to procure destabilization of the target country government or entire regime change.[54]

The literature identifies several factors tending toward successful use of sanctions:

- *An existing relationship with the targeted state* will likely enhance the effect of sanctions, perhaps because of a desire on the part of the targeted state to maintain the integrity of the overall relationship.[55]
- *Effective monitoring* mechanisms can enhance compliance in a variety of ways, for instance by "naming and shaming" violators, or by improving dialogue between the relevant parties.[56]
- *Targeted sanctions*, meaning application of pressure on specific decision-making elites and the companies or entities they control,[57] or against specific products or activities that are vital to the conduct of an objectionable policy,[58] may also help induce compliance. In addition to their focus on key pressure points, these targeted sanctions, when properly implemented, may minimize the effect on civilian populations.

---

[53] Hufbauer *et al.* rank the success of sanctions on a numerical scale, looking at two key aspects: the extent to which the policy outcome sought by the sanctioning country was in fact achieved, and the contribution made by the sanctions (as opposed to other factors, such as military action) to a positive outcome. G.C. Hufbauer, J.J. Schott and K.A. Elliot, *Economic Sanctions Reconsidered* (Washington, DC: Institute for International Economics, 1990) at 41 and 93.

[54] *Ibid.* at 93.

[55] *Ibid.* at 100.

[56] See David Cortright and George A. Lopez, *Sanctions and the Search for Security: Challenges to UN Action* (Boulder, CO: L. Rienner Publishers, 2002) for a detailed discussion of the role of the Security Council in monitoring and enforcing sanctions relating to Angolan rebel activity in 1999 and 2000.

[57] For instance, sanctions levied directly against the Taliban leadership in 1999 and 2000 (Security Council Resolutions 1267 (1999) and 1333 (2000)) or against leaders of the Sierra Leone AFRC military junta (Security Council Resolution 1132).

[58] For instance, Security Council Resolution 1306, adopted on July 5, 2000, targeted a vital sector in Sierra Leone when it imposed a ban on the import of diamonds from that country unless they were controlled by the government through a Certificate of Origin program.

- *Long-term sanctions* have been linked to compliance in ending Apartheid in South Africa on the basis that they encouraged the expectation that there were more sanctions yet to come.[59]
- *Multilateral sanctions* have tended to be more effective than unilateral sanctions, because sanctions from only one state will in most cases have only a partial effect on some limited portion of the target state economy, and will leave the target state free to trade with other non-sanctioning states.[60] These effects were both observed, for instance, in the US–Cuba and US–Iran trade embargoes.[61] The disadvantage of multilateralism, of course, is the difficulty in generating consensus.[62]

V.   REFORM STRATEGIES IN POLITICAL CONTEXT

Given the relative strengths of these various forms of political pressure, we offer a tentative range of conclusions about the role of the international community in rule of law reform. As we move along the spectrum from Type I states to Type III states, top-down, state-centric reform strategies become less feasible, and bottom-up, community-based reform strategies become a more promising option.[63]

Type I states   In these states, where broad political and popular support for rule of law reform exists, the role of the international community should be focused most heavily on alleviating resource constraints. While sociocultural factors and various forms of vested interests may still act as important barriers to reform, in these states it will be domestic governments, rather than the international community, who will be best placed to address these concerns. We think this point is self-evident with regard to sociocultural values, but it should apply equally to lower level corruption.

---

[59]   Ivan Eland, "Economic Sanctions as Tools of Foreign Policy," in D. Cortright and G. Lopez (eds), *Economic Sanctions: Panacea or Peacebuilding in a Post-Cold War World?* (Boulder, CO: Westview Press, 1995) at 38.

[60]   Chien-Pin Li, "The Effectiveness of Sanction Linkages: Issues and Actors" (1993) 3 *International Studies Quarterly* at 353.

[61]   Ernest H. Preeg, *Feeling Good or Doing Good with Sanctions: Unilateral Economic Sanctions and the US National Interest* (Washington, DC: Center for Strategic and International Studies, 1999).

[62]   See Jennifer Davis, "Sanctions and Apartheid: The Economic Challenge to Discrimination," in Cortright and Lopez, *supra* note 59 at 176, for a discussion of obstacles in generating support among Security Council members in respect of South Africa throughout the 1970s. See Geoff Simons, *Imposing Economic Sanctions* (London: Pluto Press, 1999) at 92, for a similar discussion of Libya through the 1990s.

[63]   See Golub, *supra* note 1.

The preferred method of intervention in the most favourable cases (admittedly rare) should be unconditional aid, leaving to the domestic government concerned choice of reform priorities and strategies and sources of technical advice unless for credible commitment and signalling purposes the recipient government requests conditionality. Domestic political support for rule of law reforms, by assumption strong in Type I states, is perhaps the most important success factor of unconditional or conditional aid. The "mallet"-like political pressure of accession mechanisms will play little fruitful role, because the state is already generally politically aligned with the viewpoint of reformers. Similarly, because trade policy does not direct new resources to rule of law initiatives, it will be irrelevant in these circumstances. Due to their punitive nature, sanctions would be entirely misplaced.

While making the case for conditional aid in more equivocal cases, however, it is important to emphasize again that government policy may be fluid, and that strongly pro-reform administrations can shift policies quickly, particularly where they come to power in a period of transition or during a key "constitutional moment." Donors must therefore be vigilant in monitoring the trajectory of Type I governments – and enforcing conditions where appropriate – an historical weakness of development agencies. Lessons can be drawn, for instance, from the experience of the World Bank with the government of Alberto Fujimori of Peru in the mid-1990s, discussed in greater detail in Chapter 2 (judicial reform).

Funding of non-state drivers of rule of law reform such as local NGOs can also play a role in these states, as they can in almost any situation. However, in these cases, NGOs that cooperate with, rather than oppose government policies, are likely to be more effective.

Type II states In states with generally reform-minded political leadership but with a less secure political base and widespread opposition from vested interests within state agencies, including legal institutions and perhaps private sector parties who benefit from dysfunctional public institutions, a more diverse set of strategies will be necessary. In these cases, resources may still be scarce, but international agencies or external donors cannot responsibly commit to unconditional aid. Even where high-level political leadership supports reform, increased aid flows to antagonistic public or legal institutions can be misdirected and wasted or used for regressive purposes. With respect to conditional aid, as we noted above governments truly committed to reform may agree to conditional aid that binds them to a policy and protects them from internal special interests. A case can be made for conditionality through accession or trade preferences on similar grounds. Also, there may be a good case for non-state-led reforms through local NGOs or Alternative Law Groups operating more independently from the state in institutional contexts where independence of legal institutions is likely to be problematic.

Type III states   Our discussion of international policy mechanisms suggests
that governments unequivocally opposed to rule of law reform will rarely be
sensitive to state-level pressure mechanisms, a point made both in the context
of sanctions and all forms of conditionality. As Preeg argues in respect of US
sanctions (e.g. denial of MFN trading status) against China, "the basic reason
why these unilateral economic sanctions are ineffective is that the foreign
policy objective is to change the oppressive behaviour of an authoritarian or
totalitarian government, which constitutes a direct threat to its control if not
survival."[64] While China is not our test case – US sanctions in this case were
intended to stimulate democracy more than the rule of law – the point remains
the same.

In these cases, the role of non-state actors should become a central aspect of
rule of law reform efforts, with a particular focus on those local and international
NGOs developing reforms independent of state agencies and the provision of
financial and technical assistance to them. In China and Laos, NGOs have
played an important role as *de facto* monitoring mechanisms for correctional
institutions where the state has denied access to formal state-level monitoring
channels. Properly designed and implemented non-state dispute resolution
mechanisms, often based on traditional forms of community-based dispute settlement, can also be a vital element of access to justice in circumstances where
courts suffer from chronic backlog, corruption or bias and hence a lack of
legitimacy.

It will be obvious that over time states may evolve either negatively or positively from one stylized type to another in our foregoing typology, requiring the
international community continuously to reassess its rule of law reform promotion strategies and to readjust its menu of strategies accordingly. However, even
acknowledging this, and acknowledging further that all desirable rule of law
reforms cannot be realistically embarked upon simultaneously, if only because
of resource constraints and pressing demands on those resources, even in the
most favourable (Type I) political environments issues of prioritization and sequencing will invariably arise. While these must largely be resolved by domestic
constituencies committed to rule of law reform, as must the particular forms of
institutional vindication or instantiation of rule of law values, nurturing an increasingly robust domestic constituency for the rule of law over time requires
that a broadly representative range of social, economic and political interests
come to see their interests and values as aligned with the promotion and preservation of the rule of law. In this respect, we question (along with others) the
aptness of the relatively high priority often accorded to formal judicial reform
by the international community in the rule of law reform initiatives that it has

---

[64]   Preeg, *supra* note 61 at 21.

promoted in developing countries in recent years[65] and the relative lack of attention to reforms that are more likely to affect the day-to-day interactions of the citizenry with the legal system – police, prosecutors, specialized law enforcement and administrative agencies (such as tax administration), access to justice initiatives such as informal community-based dispute resolution mechanisms (often reflecting adaptations to and elaborations of traditional dispute settlement mechanisms), and Alternative Law Groups, where more visible and immediate material benefits from successful institutional reform are likely to be experienced by a wide cross-section of the citizenry.

We, of course, acknowledge that the success of institutional reforms in one context ultimately often depends, to an important extent, on complementary institutional reforms in other contexts,[66] although this does not, in practical terms, mean that everything can be pursued at once. Judicial reforms (and, we should probably acknowledge, reforms to legal education) are likely to have longer-term and less visible social pay-offs to the citizenry at large and hence are less likely to engage their interest and support, given the many more pressing and immediate survival challenges they often face. Thus, both domestic and international proponents of rule of law reform in developing countries face a hitherto under-acknowledged challenge of rendering rule of law reform politically salient to most citizens of these countries. Strategic choices on sequencing are important in addressing this challenge.

---

[65] See Carothers, *supra* note 1; Golub, *supra* note 1; Bryant Garth, "Building Strong and Independent Judiciaries for the New Law and Development: Beyond the Paradox of Consensus Programs and Perpetually Disappointing Results" (2003) 52 *DePaul Law Review* 383.

[66] See Kleinfeld, *supra* note 1.

Index

Abramkin, Valery 178
academic institutions, *see* legal
    education; universities
access to justice
    accountability 245, 249–51
    Africa 262–6
    Asia 266–76
    Europe 247, 258–62
    human rights law 240–41
    independence 249–51
    Latin America 252–7, 277
    legitimacy 251
    models of provision 243–9
    obstacles to 241–3, 276–8
    and the police 259–60
    role of 236–40
    see also justice
accession to regional organizations
    345–8, 353
accountability
    access to justice 245, 249–51
    correctional institutions 171–2, 187–8,
        194–5
    and independence 64, 153–5
    judiciary 32, 59–61, 63–5, 104–6
    legal education 32, 285–7
    police 115–18, 129–30
    professional regulation 32, 315–17
    prosecution 32, 145–6, 147, 151–3
    rule of law 7, 30–31, 32–3, 34
    tax administration 210–11, 235
accusational procedure 146–7, 152, 155,
        156, 165–6, 168, 169, 236–7
action collective (*Verbandsklage*) 247
Action Program for Judicial Reform
    (APJR), Philippines 101
adversarial procedure 146–7, 152, 155,
        156, 165–6, 168, 169, 236–7
Afghanistan 46, 48
Africa
    access to justice 262–6

correctional institutions 181–92
judiciary 88–94, 106
legal education 297–300, 305
police 130–35
professional regulation 324–7
prosecution 164–5
tax administration 203, 222–5
African Bar Association 326–7
African Commission on Human and
    People's Rights 182, 240
African Union 342, 347–8
Airey v. Ireland (1979) 241
Albania 45, 48, 56, 296–7
Algeria 48, 56, 326
alternative dispute resolution (ADR)
    mechanisms 100, 248, 256–7, 261,
        270–74, 355
Alternative Law Groups (ALGs) 100,
        275, 277, 341, 353, 355
Ambos, K. 149
American Bar Association (ABA) 287,
        310, 312, 323, 324, 326
American Convention on Human Rights
        240
American National Conference of Bar
        Examiners 311
Amirul Islam, M. 303
Amnesty International 126, 189, 195–6
Anderson, Michael 242–3
Andorra 46, 48
Angola 43, 48, 57
Anti-Corruption Initiative for
    Asia-Pacific 167–8
Antigua and Barbuda 48
arbitration 247–9
Argentina 42, 48, 56
    access to justice 252, 254, 255, 256
    judiciary 67–70, 76–7, 106
    legal education 292–3
    police 112, 119–20
    professional regulation 321

tax administration 216
Armenia 44, 48, 55, 295, 322
Arthurs, H.W. 286
Asia 45–6
    access to justice 266–76
    correctional institutions 192–6
    judiciary 94–104
    legal education 300–304, 305
    police 135–42
    professional regulation 327–30
    prosecution 165–8
    tax administration 225–34
Asia Foundation, The (TAF) 100, 167, 272, 275
Asociación de Abogados de Buenos Aires, Argentina 321
Asociasaun Advogado Timor Lorosa'e (AATL), East Timor 329
Association of Attorneys of Kyrgyzstan (AAK) 323
Australia 46, 48, 53, 142
Austria 46, 48, 53
authoritarian regimes 217, 294–5, 316
Avery, John 113
Avocats Sans Frontières 329–30
Azam, Mohammad Monirul 303, 304
Azerbaijan 44, 48, 57, 222

Babu, Rajendra 269
Baer, Katherine 206, 221–2
Bagchi, Amaresh 204, 206
Bahamas 48
Bahrain 48, 54
Bangladesh 46, 48, 57, 271–4, 302–3, 341
bar associations (professional regulation)
    accountability 32, 315–17
    Africa 324–7
    Asia 327–30
    Europe 321–4, 331
    independence 31, 314, 315–17
    Latin America 318–21
    and legal education 281, 287, 299, 310
    legitimacy 317–18
    role of 307–15, 330–31, 333, 334, 335
Barbados 48, 54
Bárd, Károly 258
Bardhan, Pranah 5–6
Barra Mexicana Colegio Abogados 319
Barry, Brian 17, 18–19

Bayley, David 111, 112, 115
Beatty, David 19
behavioural accountability 64–5, 104
Beijing Principles 61, 62–3
Belarus 44, 48, 55, 82–3, 106, 295, 297
Belgium 46, 48, 54
Belize 48, 55
Benin 43, 48, 55
Bergman, Marcelo 320
Berkowitz, Daniel 35
Bhutan 46, 48
bilateral trade agreements 344–5
Bird, Richard 201, 204, 205, 206, 211, 212
Blocglinger, Karen 104
Bolivia 9, 42, 48, 56
    access to justice 252–3, 257
    judiciary 71–2, 105, 106
    tax administration 215, 216
Brogden, Mike 124
Bosnia-Herzegovina 45, 48, 55, 88, 127–30, 295
Botswana 38, 43, 48, 54, 88, 93, 192, 298
Brazil 42, 48, 55
    access to justice 247, 252
    correctional institutions 175, 176
    legal education 293–4
    police 112, 124
    professional regulation 321
    tax administration 213
bribery 138–9, 142, 168, 199, 207
Britain, *see* United Kingdom (UK)
Brody, Reed 122
Brooks, Rosa Ehrenreich 24–5, 34–5
Brunei 45, 48
Bulgaria 45, 48, 55, 161–2, 221, 295, 322, 324
Burkina Faso 43, 48
Burnside, Craig 348
Burridge, Roger 279, 282
Burundi 43, 48
Business Against Crime (BAC), South Africa 164–5

Call, Chuck 121, 122
Cambodia 45, 48, 102, 141–2
Cameroon 43, 48, 57, 88, 224–5
Canada 46, 48, 53, 118, 149, 282–3, 285, 326

Canadian International Development
Agency (CIDA) 97, 326
Cangman County v. Long Gang Rubber
(1999) 95–6
capability 25–7
Cape Verde 38, 43, 48
capital investment 5–6
Cappelletti, Mauro 241, 243, 246, 247,
248, 249, 255, 276
Carothers, Thomas 1, 3–4, 35, 197, 279
Casa de Justicia (House of Justice)
254–5, 277
Casanegra, Milka 201
Center of Judicial Studies (CEJURA),
Argentina 68
Central African Republic 43, 48
Central Europe
access to justice 258–62
correctional institutions 177–81
judiciary 77–88
legal education 294–7, 305, 306
police 124–30
professional regulation 321–4
prosecution 158–63
tax administration 217–22
Central European and Eurasian Law
Initiative (CEELI) 281, 295–7, 310,
322–4
centrally planned economies 217, 294–5,
316
Centre for Advice, Research and
Education on Rights (CARER),
Malawi 266
Centre for Human Rights and Rehabilita-
tion (CHRR) 184
Centre for Human Rights and Rehabilita-
tion (CHRR), Malawi 182
Centre for the Study of Violence and
Reconciliation (CSVR), South
Africa 186–7
certification 309
Chad 43, 48, 57
Channell, Wade 87–8
Charter of the Organization of American
States 241
Chavez, Hugo 121
Chevigny, Paul 109, 111, 112
children 186, 191–2, 265
Chile 37, 42, 48, 54
access to justice 252, 257

correctional institutions 176
judiciary 77
legal education 290–92
professional regulation 320
prosecution 157–8
China 4–5, 13, 45, 48, 55
access to justice 266–9
correctional institutions 192–4, 199
judiciary 94–8, 105
legal education 282, 300–302, 305
police 135–7
professional regulation 327–8, 331
prosecution 165–6
rule of law reform 335–6, 342–3, 354
tax administration 225–6
Chirwa, Vera 182–3, 184, 188, 189, 190,
197
Choksy, Nairman 227
citizens' role 7, 103
civil law 146–7, 240, 304
civil liability 308–9
civilian oversight 116–18
class action suits 247
clinical legal education 281, 284–5, 289,
291–2, 295–6, 299–300, 302–3
coercion 127
Colegio de Abogados de la Ciudad de
Buenos Aires 321
collective rights 246–7
Colombia 42, 49, 55, 216, 252, 253, 255
common law 146–7, 148–50, 236–7, 297
Commonwealth Human Rights Initiative
(CHRI) 195
community justice 185–6, 274, 334, 354
community policing programs 124,
134–5
community service 173, 184, 186
Comoros 43, 49
complexity, of tax administration 206–7
compliance 208, 225–6, 227, 229, 232–3
computerized systems 212–13, 215,
220–21, 225, 229–31, 233, 234
conciliation 247–9
conditional aid 353
conditionalities of reform 341–50
conflicts of interest 312–13
Congo, Democratic Republic of the
(Congo-Kinshasa) 43, 49, 57
Congo, Republic of (Congo-Brazzaville)
43, 49, 56

Consejo de Rectores, Chile 290–92
Constitutional and Legal Policy Institute
    (COLPI) 262
constitutions 15, 94–5, 99, 101–2, 103–4,
    263
continuing legal education (CLE) 312,
    318, 322, 323, 324
contracting system, of legal aid 246
correctional institutions
    accountability 187–8, 194–5
    Africa 181–92
    alternatives to 180, 184
    Asia 192–6
    Europe 177–81
    Latin America 175–7
    reform 196–9, 333
    staff training 174, 176, 178, 180, 189
    standards 170–75
Corrections Portfolio Committee, South
    Africa 187, 188
corruption 7, 334–5
    access to justice 257
    correctional institutions 199
    corruption perceptions index 53–7
    judiciary 95–6, 335
    legal education 305, 335
    police 114–15, 124–35, 138–9, 142,
        335
    prosecution 157, 158
    tax administration 222–4, 227, 335
Costa Rica 8, 37, 42, 49, 54
    access to justice 253, 255
    correctional institutions 176
    judiciary 66, 74–5
Costiniu, Viorica 162
costs 207
Côte d'Ivoire 43, 49, 57
Cotonou Agreement 349–50
courts 76–7, 83–7, 90–91, 156–7,
    164–5
Craig, Paul 18
criminal justice system 176, 183–4,
    185–6, 190–91, 192–4, 199
criminal law 239
Criminal Procedure Law (CPL), China
    165–6
Croatia 45, 49, 55, 297
Cuba 49, 55, 352
cultural values
    access to justice 270–71, 277

correctional institutions 184, 185–6,
    192–4, 197–8
    judiciary 105
    legal education 280, 304, 306
    police 143–4
    professional regulation 331
    prosecution 169
    and rule of law reform 39, 332, 333–4,
        338, 349, 352
    tax administration 235
customs departments, and tax 217
Cyprus 46, 49, 54
Czech Republic 45, 49, 55, 258–60, 278,
    295

Dakolias, Maria 83, 321
Dankwa, E.V.O. 188
Danner, Allison Marston 33
Das-Gupta, Aridnam 204, 206, 212
debt relief 348–50
decisional accountability 64, 65, 104
Delisle, Jacques 338
democracy 16–20, 344, 345, 347
democratic policing 110–12
Denmark 46, 49, 53
developing countries 2–4, 37–8
development 1–12, 201–4, 279–85,
    332–3
Dezalay, Yves 1
Di Federico, G. 154
Dicey, Albert Venn 15
dignity 236–7
diplomatic sanctions 350
disciplinary action 174, 192–4, 311–12
discretion, of the police 113
dispute resolution mechanisms 100, 248,
    256–7, 261, 270–74, 355
Djibouti 49
D.K. Basu v. State of West Bengal (1997)
    140
Dollar, David 348
Dominica 49
Dominican Republic 42, 49, 55, 76
Draft Inter-American Declaration
    Governing the Rights and the Care
    of Persons Deprived of Liberty
    172–5
drugs 320
Duce, Maurice 151, 152
Dudziak, Mary 89

Duhalde, Eduardo 69–70
Dworkin, Ronald 19
Dyzenhaus, David 237, 239

East African Public Legal Education
    (PLE) Network 266
East Timor 46, 49, 328–30
Easterly, William 143
Eastern Europe 45
    access to justice 258–62
    correctional institutions 177–81
    judiciary 77–88
    legal education 294–7, 305, 306
    police 124–30
    professional regulation 321–4
    prosecution 158–63
    tax administration 217–22
economic freedoms 27
Economic Law Institutional and
    Professional Strengthening
    (ELIPS) project, Indonesia 303–4
economic obstacles (access to justice)
    242, 243–6, 277
economic policy 5–6, 68–70
Economic Reform and Development
    Program (PRED), Mali 92–3
economic sanctions 350
Economides, Kim 249
Ecuador 42, 49, 56
    access to justice 254, 256, 257, 278
    correctional institutions 175–6
    professional regulation 321
education 3, 166–7; *see also* legal
    education; training
Edwards, Randle 283, 301–2
effectiveness, of tax administration
    204–15, 229–30
efficiency, of tax administration 204–15
Egypt 49, 55
El Salvador 42, 49, 55, 70–71, 121–3,
    158, 253–4, 257
election of the judiciary 66
emergency telephone systems 110, 122
Emmert, Frank 260–61
employment law 238
enforceability, as process value 30
enforcement 209–10, 215, 225–6, 228–9
England, *see* United Kingdom (UK)
equality 16–20, 139–40, 236–7
Equatorial Guinea 43, 49

equitable distribution 238
Eritrea 43, 49, 56
Estonia 45, 49, 54, 260–61, 295
ethics 312–14
Ethiopia 43, 49, 56, 91–2, 133–4
Euro-Mediterranean Partnership (EMP)
    344
Europe
    access to justice 247, 258–62
    correctional institutions 177–81
    judiciary 77–88
    legal education 294–7, 305, 306
    police 124–30
    professional regulation 321–4, 331
    prosecution 158–63
    tax administration 217–22
European Community Action Scheme for
    the Mobility of University Students
    (ERASMUS) 295
European Convention on Human Rights
    240
European Court of Human Rights 85,
    241
European Union (EU) 86, 218, 219–21,
    295
    conditionalities of reform 342, 343,
        344, 345–7, 349–50
Ewing, K.D. 59

Fagan, Hannes 186
fairness 20–23
family law 238, 239
Federation of Women Lawyers, Kenya
    (FIDA Kenya) 264
Fiji 45, 49
financial resources; *see* resource
    constraints
Finland 46, 49, 53
fiscal reform 202–3; *see also* tax
    administration
Fjeldstad, Odd-Helge 206, 224
Florence Access to Justice Project 241–2
Foglesong, Todd 78–9
Ford Foundation 97, 266, 272, 275, 280,
    292, 301–3, 322
foreign aid 2, 277, 287, 341, 348–50, 353
former Soviet Union, *see* country names;
    Soviet Union
Frampton, Dennis 204
France 46, 49, 54

Frankfurter, Felix 282
freedom 5, 25–7, 48–53
Friedland, Martin 62, 250, 251
Fujimori, Alberto 72–4, 353
Fukuyama, Francis 9, 10
Fuller, Lon L. 21

Gabon 43, 49, 55
Gacaca tribunals 185–6, 248
Galanter, Mark 34–5, 36, 270, 271
Gambia, Republic of The 43, 49, 56
Garth, Bryant 1, 67, 241
Geithner, Peter 302
gender equality 188
Generalized System of Preferences
    (GSP), WTO 343–4
genocide 92, 185–6
Georgia 44, 49, 57, 222, 296
Gerardi, Juan, Bishop 156–7
Germany 46, 49, 54, 155
Ghana 43, 49, 55, 222
Gillis, Malcolm 232, 233
Glendon, Mary Ann 314
Gnazzo, E. 204–5
Golub, Stephen 272, 273
Gordon, Richard 210
Gordon, Robert W. 288
governance 5–12, 250–51
government effectiveness 7
Grabbe, Heather 345–6, 347
grameen (village courts) 274
Grandcolas, Christophe 213
Greece 46, 49, 54
Grenada 49
Gryzlov, Boris 127
Guatemala 42, 49, 56, 105, 156–7, 216,
    254, 256
Guinea 43, 49
Guinea-Bissau 43, 49
Gunningham, Neil 317
Guyana 49

Haiti 49, 57, 257, 340
Hamilton, Alexander 59
Hammergren, Linn 60, 68, 74, 75–6,
    253–4
Harman, Grant 287
Hayek, Friedrich A. von 16
health 3, 173–4, 179, 195–6
Helsinki Committee 262

Henan Securities v. Shanghair KeJiao 96
Heyman, Philip B. 148
Hills, Alice 130–31, 132
Hinton, Mercedes 112
historical values 39, 332, 333–4, 349,
    352
    access to justice 277
    judiciary 77, 105
    legal education 297, 306
    police 143–4
    professional regulation 331
    prosecution 169
    tax administration 235
Hobbes, Thomas 14, 237
Holda, Zbigniew 180–81
Holmes, Stephen 37, 40–41, 161
Honduras 42, 50, 56, 77
Hong Kong 38, 45, 54, 300
House of Justice (*Casa de Justicia*)
    254–5, 277
Howse, Robert 343–4
Hufbauer, G.C. 351
Human Development Index (HDI) 2, 4
human rights
    conditionalities of reform 344, 345
    correctional institutions 188, 189
    international law 240–41
    and the police 110–12, 127–30, 132–3,
        136–7, 141, 142, 144
    prisoners 170–75, 181–2, 193–5
    and prosecution 151–2, 155
Human Rights Center, Russia 125
Human Rights Commission 187
Human Rights Watch (HRW) 82, 125,
    129
Hungary 45, 50, 54, 83–5, 105, 221, 295
Huntington, Samuel P. 34
Huskey, Eugene 77–8

Iceland 47, 50, 53
Iglesias, Elizabeth 147, 153
Ignatieff, Michael 26
Iliushenko, Aleksei 161
immigration 239
impartiality 118
income levels 3, 242–3, 285
independence
    access to justice 249–51
    accountability 64, 153–5
    correctional institutions 171–2

judiciary 31, 59–63, 89–90, 95, 104–6
  legal education 31–2, 285–7
  police 112–15
  professional regulation 314, 315–17
  prosecution 31, 145–6, 147, 148–51,
    153–5
  rule of law 30–32, 34, 335, 337
  tax administration 210–11, 234, 235
  see also state
India 46, 50, 56
  access to justice 238, 243, 269–71
  correctional institutions 194–5
  legal education 283, 287, 300, 305
  police 137–40
  tax administration 226–7
Indonesia 8, 45, 50, 57, 166–7, 231–4,
    305
information technology (IT) 212–13,
    215, 220–21, 225, 229–31, 233,
    234
inquisitorial procedure 146–7, 155, 156,
    159, 165–6, 169, 335
institutional values 30–33, 203, 206–7,
    332
institutions 7–12, 23–9, 30–32, 201–2,
    337
instrumental approach, to policing
    110–12
instrumental freedoms 27
Inter-American Court of Human Rights
    120
interest groups 106
international assistance, reform strategies
    341–52
International Bar Association (IBA) 310,
    312–14, 315–16, 330
International Bridges to Justice (IBJ)
    136
International Center for Prison Studies
    (ICPS) 178
International Centre for Criminal Law
    Reform and Criminal Justice Policy
    (ICCLR) 176, 192
International Centre for Prison Studies
    (ICPS) 176
International Commission of Jurists 145
International Committee of the Red
    Cross (ICRC) 194
International Covenant on Civil and
    Political Rights (ICCPR) 170, 240

International Criminal Investigative
    Training Assistance Program
    (ICITAP) 122
international financial assistance 2, 277,
    287, 341, 348–50, 353
international law 240–41
International Law Association 311
International Monetary Fund (IMF) 208
international organizations, diversity of
    approaches 337–9
International Police Task Force (IPTF)
    127–30
internet 225
intimidation 127
intra-regional trade agreements 344–5
Iran 50, 56, 352
Iraq 50, 57
Ireland 47, 50, 54
Israel 50, 54
Italy 47, 50, 54, 154

Jamaica 50, 55
Japan 47, 50, 54
Jordan 50, 54
Judges Law, China 94, 95, 97
judicaire system, of legal aid 245–6, 250,
    251, 262, 277
Judicial Branch Administrative Corpora-
    tion, Chile 77
judicial councils, Latin America 75–6
Judicial Qualification Committee (JQC),
    Russia 78, 79, 80
judiciary
  accountability 32, 59–61, 63–5, 104–6
  Africa 88–94, 106
  Asia 94–104
  diversity of approaches 58–9
  Europe 77–88
  independence 31, 59–63, 89–90, 95,
    104–6
  Latin America 62, 66–77
  and legal education 91–3, 96–8, 100
  legitimacy 65–6, 104–6
  and police 116
  priority of 354–5
  and prosecution 31, 145–6, 147,
    148–51, 153–5
  reform 333–4, 335, 353
justice 18–20, 23, 238; *see also* access to
  justice

Justice, Department of (DOJ), South
  Africa 164–5
justice centres 299
Justice College, South Africa 164
Justice Initiative 296, 299–300
Justice Studies Center of the Americas
  (JSCA) 67, 77
juveniles 186, 191–2, 265

Kalaydjieva, Zdravka 161
Kalinin, Yuri 177–9
*Kampala Declaration on Prison
  Conditions in Africa* 181
Kaufmann, Daniel 6–8
Kazakhstan 44, 50, 56, 179–80, 295, 297,
  323, 324
Kazannik, Aleksei 161
Kenya 43, 50, 57
  access to justice 243, 264, 266
  judiciary 88
  police 134
  professional regulation 326
  tax administration 222
KGB 124–5
Khare, V.N. 269
Khordorkovsky, Mikhail 79
Kiribati 45, 50
Kitaw, Ato Getachew 327
Kleinfeld, Rachel 13, 41–2
Klimas, Tadas 294
Klun, Maja 201, 207
knowledge 249
Korea 101–2, 168, 304; *see also* North
  Korea; South Korea
Kosovo 295
Kossick, Robert 319, 320
Kraay, Aart 6–8
Krajick, Kevin 177, 178
Krause, Kevin Deegan 346
Krishnan, Jayanth 270, 271
Kuwait 50, 54
Kyrgyzstan (Kyrgyz Republic) 44, 50,
  57, 295, 323–4

language 243, 338
Laos 45, 50, 195–6, 199, 335, 354
large taxpayer units (LTUs) 213–14,
  216–17, 221–2, 227–8
Larkins, Christopher 60–61
Latin America 42–3, 335

access to justice 252–7, 277
correctional institutions 175–7
judiciary 62, 66–77
legal education 280, 283, 288, 289–94,
  305, 306, 334
police 108, 111, 119–24
professional regulation 318–21
prosecution 146, 151, 152, 156–8, 169
tax administration 215–17
Latvia 45, 50, 55, 217–19, 222, 295
law, rule of, *see* rule of law
Law and Development movement (LDM)
  279–81, 284, 288
law enforcement, *see* police; prosecution
law schools, *see* legal education
Law Society of Kenya 326
Law Society of South Africa 324
lawyers 307, 312–14, 316, 320
Lawyers Law, China 327
Lebanon 50, 56
Lebedev, Platon 79
Lee Kuan Yew 339
Lefstein, Norman 244
legal aid 243–6, 249–51, 277, 335
  Africa 262–6
  Asia 267–9, 274–5
  Europe 258–62
  Latin America 252–5
  see also access to justice
legal education
  accountability 32, 285–7
  Africa 297–300, 305
  Asia 300–304, 305
  corruption 305, 335
  Europe 294–7, 305, 306
  independence 31–2, 285–7
  judiciary 91–3, 96–8, 100
  Latin America 280, 283, 288, 289–94,
    305, 306, 334
  legitimacy 288–9
  and professional regulation 281, 287,
    299, 310
  role of 279–85, 304–6
  see also education; training
Legal Profession Reform Index (LPRI)
  310, 311–12
Legal Resources Centre, South Africa
  263–4
legal system, desiderata 21
legislative role of the judiciary 59

legitimacy
  access to justice 251
  judiciary 65–6, 104–6
  legal education 288–9
  professional regulation 317–18
  prosecution 155–6, 160
  rule of law 33–7, 203–4, 332
  tax administration 201–2, 207, 210
legitimacy values 33–7, 203–4, 332
Lesotho 43, 50, 297
Lewis, Colleen 116–17
Liberia 43, 50, 90–91, 105, 297
liberty 16–20
Libya 50, 56
licensing examinations 311
licensure 309
Liechtenstein 47, 50
life expectancy 3
Lindholt, Lone 110
Lindseth, Peter L. 33–4
Lithuania 45, 50, 54, 295
litigation, alternatives to 247–9
local forums 93–4, 274, 334, 354
Locke, John 14
Lok Adalats 270–71, 277
Lomé Convention 349–50
Lowenstein, Steven 280
Lukashenko, Aleksandr 82–3
Lumet, Stephen 65
Luxembourg 47, 50, 54

Macao 45
MacCrate Report 312
Macedonia 45, 50, 56
Macovei, Monica 260
Madagascar 43, 50, 55
Magliveras, Konstantinos D. 347–8
Malawi 43, 50, 56, 91, 182–5, 198, 266
Malaysia 45, 50, 54, 328
Maldives 46, 50
Mali 43, 50, 55, 92–3
Malta 50, 54
mandatory membership of regulatory
    bodies 314–15, 330
mandatory prosecution 147
Mandela, Nelson 145, 339
Maneka Gandhi v. Union of India (1978)
    194–5
Mann, Arthur 223
Manning, Peter 110

Maravall, José María 40
Marshall Islands 45, 50
Marshall Jr., Donald, prosecution of 149,
    154
Martens, Jo Beth 228
Mauritania 44, 50
Mauritius 38, 44, 50, 55
McAdams, Richard 36
McCarten, William 216
mediation 247–9
Meili, Stephen 291
MERCOSUR (Southern Common
    Market) Regulations 293
Mexico 8, 42, 51, 55
  access to justice 252
  conditionalities of reform 344–5
  police 123–4
  professional regulation 318–20
  tax administration 215, 216
Micronesia 45, 51
military, role of the 108, 121–3, 130–35,
    156–7, 167, 334
military sanctions 350
militsiya 124–5
Miller, David 19
mobile courts 276
Model Court Development Project,
    World Bank 76–7
Moldova 44, 51, 56, 222, 295
Monaco 47, 51
money, lawyers' responsibilities 313–14
Mongolia 45, 51, 55
monitoring, of correctional institutions
    174–5, 176, 180, 181–2, 187–8,
    194–6, 199
monitoring, of tax administration 228
Monk, Richard 127
Montesquieu, Charles de Secondat, baron
    de 14
Mookherjee, Dilip 212
Morocco 51, 55
Moscow Center for Prison Reform
    (MCPR) 177
Mosher, Janet 284–5
Mozambique 44, 51, 56
  access to justice 243, 264
  correctional institutions 188–91, 197,
    198
  judiciary 92
  legal education 300

Mugabe, Robert 340
multilateral sanctions 352
Museveni, Yoweri 131
Myanmar (Burma) 45, 48, 57

Nabli, Mustapha K. 28
Nagorik Uddyog (NU) 273–4, 341
Naldi, Gino J. 347–8
Namibia 38, 44, 51, 55, 192
National Bureau of Investigation (NBI),
    Philippines 140–41
National Council of the Judiciary (NCJ),
    Peru 73–4, 81
National Council on Correctional
    Services (NCCS), South Africa
    187–8
National Human Rights Commission
    (NHRC), India 137–8, 140
NATO (North Atlantic Treaty Organiza-
    tion) 347
Nauru 46, 51
Ndula, Muna 297, 300
negative conditionality 342, 345–6
negotiation 247–9
neighbourhood forums 93–4
Nepal 46, 51, 56
Netherlands 47, 51, 53
Neumann, Michael 20, 22–3
neutrality, of lawyers 314
New Agenda for Penal Reform 171–2
New Institutional Economics (NIE) 4–5,
    27–9
New Zealand 47, 51, 53
Newburn, T. 114
Nicaragua 43, 51, 56
Nield, Rachel 108, 115, 116
Niger 44, 51, 57, 243
Nigeria 44, 51, 57, 132, 134–5, 150,
    191–2, 263
non-governmental organizations (NGOs)
    302–3, 341, 353, 354; *see also*
    organization names
North, Douglass 27
North Korea 45, 51; *see also* Korea
Norway 47, 51, 53
Nugent, Jeffrey B. 28
Nyalali, Francis 89–90, 106

Oldman, Oliver 212
Olson, Mancur 38

Oman 51, 54
ombudsman 247
One World, One Action 341
Open Society Institute (OSI) 81–2, 135,
    262, 300
operational accountability 63–4, 65, 104
oral courts 76–7, 156–7
Organization for Economic Cooperation
    and Development (OECD) 46–7,
    168, 204, 210, 211, 214, 219–20
Organization for Security and
    Co-operation in Europe (OSCE) 127
organizational poverty (access to justice)
    242, 246–7, 277
Orland, Leonard 126–7
Oropeza, Manuel González 319
*Ouagadougou Declaration on
    Accelerating Prison and Penal
    Reform in Africa* 181–2
outsourcing 215–16
overcrowding, of correctional institutions
    172–3
    Africa 182–3, 184–5, 186, 190
    Asia 196
    Europe 177–8, 179–81
    Latin America 175–6
    and rule of law reform 196–7

Pakistan 46, 51, 57
Palau 51
Palestinian Authority 56, 340
Pan-African Lawyers' Union (PALU)
    327
Panama 43, 51, 55, 123, 176, 253, 257
panchayats 270, 277
Pande, Rohini 11–12
Papier, Taswell 326
Papua New Guinea 46, 51, 56
Paraguay 43, 51, 57
Paralegal Advisory Service (PAS),
    Malawi 183–4
Paravicini, Luis 72
Pastukhov, Mikhail 83
pecuniary responsibilities 313–14
Pelayo, José de Jesús Gudino 318
Pellechio, Anthony 204
Penal Reforms International (PRI) 178,
    184, 186, 187, 191, 341
penal system, *see* correctional
    institutions

People's Law Enforcement Board
(PLEB), Philippines 141
Peru 43, 51, 55
  access to justice 252
  correctional institutions 175
  judiciary 72–4, 106, 353
  legal education 292
  professional regulation 321
  tax administration 216
Philippines 46, 51, 56
  access to justice 274–6, 277, 341
  judiciary 98–101, 105, 106
  police 140–41
  prosecution 167–8
Pinochet, Augusto (General) 320
Pinto, Monica 289
Pistor, Katharina 35
Poland 45, 51, 55, 81–2, 85–6, 180–81,
  219–21, 295
police
  and access to justice 259–60
  accountability 32, 115–18, 129–30
  Africa 130–35
  Asia 135–42
  Europe 124–30
  independence 31, 112–15
  and judiciary 116
  Latin America 108, 111, 119–24
  and professional regulation 323
  and prosecution 150–51
  reform 333, 334, 335, 355
  role of 107–12
  social values 143–4
Police Service Commission (PSC),
  Nigeria 135
Policía Nacional Civil (PNC), El
  Salvador 121–3
political economy
  access to justice 277–8
  correctional institutions 180–81, 194,
    197–9
  judiciary 61, 67–70, 71–4, 82–3,
    89–90, 94, 98–101, 105–6
  legal education 306
  police 108–9, 115, 119–20, 124–5,
    130–35, 137–40, 141–2, 144
  professional regulation 331
  and prosecution 158–61, 167, 169
  rule of law reform 39–41, 332,
    334–9

  tax administration 235
political formations 339–41, 352–5
political freedoms 27
Popkin, Margaret 70
Popov, Sergei 178
Portugal 47, 51, 54
positive conditionality 342, 345–6
Posmakov, Pyotr 180
Posner, Richard 15
poverty 3, 242–3, 285
predictability 28–9, 30
Preeg, Ernest H. 354
press coverage 137, 162, 180
Pridham, Geoffrey 346
Priest, Margot 317
prisoners' rights 177, 193–5
prisons 170–75, 180, 184, 196–9
  Africa 181–92
  Asia 192–6
  Europe 177–81
  Latin America 175–7
  staff training 174, 176, 178, 180,
    189
private legal practitioners 319–20
private prosecutions 167–8
pro bono legal services 246, 252, 267,
  269, 275
procedural obstacles (access to justice)
  242, 247–9, 277
process values 29–30, 203, 206–7,
  208–10, 332
Procuracy, Russia 158–61
professional regulation
  accountability 32, 315–17
  Africa 324–7
  Asia 327–30
  Europe 321–4, 331
  independence 31, 315–17
  Latin America 318–21
  legal education 281, 287, 299, 310
  legitimacy 317–18
  role of 307–15, 330–31, 333, 335
property rights 11–12, 27–9
prosecution
  accountability 32, 145–6, 147, 151–5
  Africa 164–5
  Asia 165–8
  Europe 158–63
  independence 31, 145–6, 147, 148–51,
    153–5

Latin America 146, 151, 152, 156–8, 169
legitimacy 155–6, 160
reform 333, 334, 355
role of 145–7
Przeworski, Adam 40
public defender system, of legal aid 244–5, 262, 263
public defenders 319–20, 334
publicity 137, 162, 180
publicity condition 237
Putin, Vladimir 79, 87, 125, 340

Qatar 51, 54
Quinn, Brian 103

R. v. Commissioner of Police of the Metropolis; Ex Parte Blackburn (1968) 112
Ramsey, Carolyn B. 152
Ratushny, Kim 80
Rawls, John 20, 22
Raz, Joseph 14, 17, 18, 20–21, 22
redistributive role of the justice system 238
Rees, Joseph 317
reform strategies 341–55
refugees 239
regime relativity 60–61
regional political organizations 345–8
regulation 7; *see also* professional regulation
Reiter, Dan 347
relator action 246–7
Resnick, Judith 63–4
resource constraints
access to justice 252–4, 260–61, 263, 266–9, 274, 277–8
bar associations 333
conditionalities of reform 348–50
correctional institutions 183, 188, 190, 196, 198, 333
as impediments to reform 38–9, 336
judiciary 63, 82, 83–5, 90–91, 96–8, 99–101, 105, 333
legal education 293, 298, 300, 305, 306
police 113–14, 120, 123, 133, 139, 141–2, 143, 333
professional regulation 323, 325, 329–31

prosecution 158, 167–8, 169, 333
reform strategies 341, 352–3
rule of law reform 332, 333
tax administration 202–3, 215, 222, 234–5, 333
"Restorative Justice" 171–2
Rethinking the Welfare State (Daniels and Trebilcock) 236
Revenue Department Consortium (RDC), Thailand 231
Richard, Jean-Francois 35
Rodrik, Dani 8, 11
Romania 45, 51, 56, 162–3, 260, 295
Rousseau, Jean Jacques 15
rule of law
access to justice 237–8
definitions 12–14
and development 1–12, 332–3
diversity of approaches 33, 337–9
impediments to reform 37–42
institutional values 30–33
and legal education 279–85
legitimacy values 33–7
measure of governance 7
police 107–12
political formations 339–41, 352–5
political philosophy 14–15
process values 29–30
reform obstacles 333–9
reform strategies 341–55
statistical analysis 9–12
and tax administration 203–4
"thick" conceptions 16–20
"thin" conceptions 20–23
"thinner" conceptions 23–9
World Bank indicators 42–7
Rural Development Institute (RDI) 261
Russia 44, 51, 56
access to justice 261–2
correctional institutions 198–9
judiciary 78–9, 86–7
legal education 295
police 124–7
professional regulation 322–3
prosecution 158–61, 169
Russian Prison Administration (GUIN) 177, 178
Rwanda 44, 51, 185–6, 222, 248, 265

Saint Kitts and Nevis 51

Saint Lucia 51
Saint Vincent and the Grenadines 51
Samoa 46, 51
San Marino 47, 51
sanctions 311–12, 342, 350–52, 353
Sandel, Michael 18–19
Santiso, Carlos 348–9
São Tomé and Príncipe 44, 52
Saudi Arabia 52, 55
security, of lawyers 316, 320
security services, privatization of 134–5
Seitner, Manfred 129
self-assessment 209, 233
self-regulation 309–10, 316–17
semi-autonomous revenue authorities
    (SARAs) 210–11, 216, 217–19,
    222–4
Sen, Amartya 4, 5, 25–7
Senegal 44, 52, 55
sentences 176, 180, 197
Serbia and Montenegro 52, 56
sexual assault 164
Seychelles 38, 44, 52, 54
Shanghai Bar Association (SBA) 327–8
Shanghai Bureau of Justice (SBOJ)
    327–8
Shelley, Louise 108
Shklar, Judith 17–18
Sierra Leone 44, 52, 56, 265, 300
Silvani, C. 206
simplicity, of tax administration 206–7,
    211, 215–16, 224–5, 227, 232, 235
Singapore 38, 46, 52, 53, 103–4, 229–30,
    300, 339
Singh, Kaupal 328
Singh, Veerinderjeet 203
skills development, *see* training
Slovakia (Slovak Republic) 45, 52, 55,
    346
Slovenia 8, 45, 52, 54, 295
Smith, Andrew 116–17
Smith, Gordon B. 160
Smith, Michael E. 344
Smith, Stephen 2–3
social coordination 22–3
social legitimacy 33
social rights 246–7
social values
    access to justice 257, 270–71, 277
    bar associations 334

judiciary 105, 333–4
legal education 280, 304, 306
and legitimacy 34–7
police 119–20, 121, 134–5, 137,
    143–4, 334
professional regulation 331
prosecution 158, 169, 334
rule of law reform 39, 332, 333–4,
    336–7, 349, 352
tax administration 225–6, 235
social welfare 238, 239
Solomon, Peter H. 78
Solomon Islands 46, 52, 243
Somalia 44, 52, 93–4
South Africa 8, 38, 44, 52, 54, 339, 352
    access to justice 241, 262, 263–6, 276
    correctional institutions 186–8, 192
    legal education 297, 298–9, 305
    professional regulation 324–6
    prosecution 155–6, 164–5
South Asia 46
South Korea 8, 9, 45, 52, 54, 228–9; *see
    also* Korea
Soviet Union 44, 334, 335
    access to justice 258
    judiciary 77–8, 86, 106
    legal education 288, 294–5, 306
    police 108, 124–5
    professional regulation 321–2
    prosecution 158–61
    see also names of independent states
Spain 8, 47, 52, 54, 155
Special Rapporteur on Prisons and
    Conditions of Detention in Africa
    182, 188–91, 196, 197, 199
specialized law enforcement, *see* tax
    administration
Sri Lanka 46, 52, 55, 213, 227–8
stability 7, 30
staff model, of legal aid 243–4, 251, 254,
    277
Standards for the Independence of the
    Legal Profession 310, 315–16
standards of professional regulation 309,
    310, 312–14, 315–16
state
    military governments 334
    and the police 108, 130–35, 137–40,
        141–2
    political formations 339–41, 352–5

professional regulation 307, 309, 317, 327–8
role of 5–6
rule of law reform 335, 341–52
tax administration 202–3, 210–11, 216, 222–4
see also independence; political economy
State Revenue Service (SRS), Latvia 217–19
status legislation 239
Stenning, Philip 117, 118
Stepankov, Valentin 159, 161
Stephenson, Matthew 13, 343
Street Law 257, 265–6, 341
Subramanian, Arvind 8, 11
sub-Saharan Africa 43–4
Sudan 44, 52, 57
Summers, Robert S. 23, 24
Sunstein, Cass 16–17, 19
Suriname 52, 54
Surrey, Stanley 201
Swaziland 44, 52
Sweden 47, 52, 53, 209
Switzerland 47, 52, 53
Syria 52, 55
Syzmanski, Marcela 344

Taiwan 46, 52, 54
Tajikistan 44, 52, 57, 222, 295
Takko, Adolfo Ismael v. Freddo S.S. s/ despido (2002) 69
Tamanaha, Brian 1–2, 13, 36
Tan, Chong Han 283, 300
Tanase, Joita 163
Tanzania 44, 52, 56, 89–90, 106, 222, 223–4, 266
Tanzi, Vito 204
tax administration
accountability 210–11, 235
Africa 203, 222–5
Asia 225–34
centrally planned economies 217
and development 201–4
effectiveness and efficiency criteria 204–15, 229–30
Europe 217–22
Latin America 215–17
legitimacy 201–2, 206, 210
reform 202–3, 224, 235, 333, 335, 355

role of 200–201, 234
tax evasion 225–6
tax policy 202–3
Terzieva, Vessela 258
Thailand 46, 52, 55, 196, 198, 230–31
"thick" conceptions of rule of law 16–20
"thin" conceptions of rule of law 20–23
"thinner" conceptions of rule of law 23–9
Thome, Joseph 66–7, 289–90
Tigray People's Liberation Front (TPLF) 133
Todaro, Michael 2–3
Togo 44, 52
Toharia, Jose Juan 33
Tonga 46, 52
torture 110, 111, 125–7, 141, 192–4, 196
trade agreements 344–5
trade policy 342–5, 353
training
access to justice 268
correctional institutions 174, 176, 178, 180, 189
judiciary 91–3, 96–8, 100
police 133, 134, 136–7, 142
prison staff 174, 176, 178, 180, 189
prosecution 158, 162–3, 164, 166–7
tax administration 214, 221, 227–8, 233, 234
see also education; legal education
transparency 29–30, 235
Transparency International 53–7
Trebbi, Francesco 8, 11
Trebilcock, M.J. 307
Trinidad and Tobago 52, 55
Trubek, David 34–5, 36
Tunisia 52, 54
Tuohy, C.J. 307
Turkey 45, 52, 55, 345
Turkmenistan 44, 52, 57, 340
Tuvalu 46, 52

Udry, Christopher 11–12
Uganda 44, 52, 56
access to justice 266
correctional institutions 192
police 132–3
tax administration 207, 222, 223–4
Ukraine 8, 44, 52, 57, 80, 222, 295
unconditional aid 353

Ungar, Mark 67, 72, 119, 120–21, 175,
177
United Arab Emirates 52, 54
United Kingdom (UK) 47, 52, 53
access to justice 244, 246–7
correctional institutions 176, 178
legal education 297
police 113, 117
prosecution 155
tax administration 209
United Nations (UN)
Basic Principles on the Independence
of the Judiciary 61, 62–3
Basic Principles on the Role of
Lawyers 241
Basic Principles on the Use of
Force and Firearms by Law
Enforcement Officials 107
Code of Conduct for Law Enforcement
107, 110
Committee on the Rights of the Child
191–2
Committee on Torture 192, 193
Convention on the Elimination of all
forms of Discrimination Against
Women (CEDAW) 323
Declaration of Human Rights 61
Guidelines on the Role of Prosecutors
147, 148, 151
International Covenant on Civil and
Political Rights (ICCPR) 170, 240
legal education 281
Office of the High Commissioner for
Human Rights (OHCHR) 136
police 129–30
professional regulation 329
Standard Minimum Rules for the
Treatment of Prisoners 170–75
Universal Declaration of Human
Rights 170
United Nations Commission on Human
Rights (UNCHR) 142
United Nations Commission on
International Trade Law
(UNCITRAL) 261
United Nations Development Program
(UNDP) 2, 4, 97, 102, 140, 236,
249
United Nations Economic Commission
for Africa (UNECA) 202–3

United Nations Latin American Institute
for the Prevention and the
Treatment of Offenders (ILUNAD)
176
United States (US)
access to justice 245, 246, 247, 252
correctional institutions 197–8
corruption perceptions index 54
freedom rating 52
judiciary 31, 61–2, 66
legal education 280–81, 284
police 31, 108, 114
professional regulation 310, 311, 312,
322
prosecution 31, 150–51, 152, 155
rule of law 36, 47, 338, 343, 354
tax administration 229
Universal Declaration of Human Rights
170
Universidad Torcuato Di Tella Law
School (UTDT), Argentina 293
universities 282, 285
Urban Coexistence Code 120
Uruguay 37, 43, 53, 54
USAID (United States Agency for
International Development)
access to justice 253, 256, 257, 261,
264–5, 272, 274
judiciary 67–8, 70, 71–2, 76, 77, 85,
90–93
legal education 280, 303–4
police 122–3, 124
prosecution 158, 164–5
tax administration 223
Uzbekistan 44, 53, 56, 295, 296

Vanuatu 46, 53
Venezuela 8, 43, 53, 56, 120–21, 176, 216
victims, and prosecution 155–6
Vietnam 46, 53, 56, 102–3
vigilante groups 135, 144
village courts 274
violence 139, 165, 254, 316, 320
voluntary tax compliance 208, 225–6,
227, 229, 232–3

Waldron, Jeremy 19–20
Waller, J. Michael 125
Walther, Susanne 151, 155
Wang Yunsheng 194

Washington Consensus 6
Westin, Susan 136
Whitford, William 21–2
Widner, Jennifer 89
Wilson, Bruce M. 75
Wolfensohn, James 4
Wolfson, A.D. 307
women 264–5, 273, 322–3
World Bank
    access to justice 256, 261
    foreign aid 348
    governance research 6–7
    judiciary 74, 101, 353
    legal education 281
    Model Court Development Project
        76–7
    rule of law 2, 42–7

tax administration 218, 223, 227,
    230–32
World Trade Organization (WTO) 341,
    342–4
Wortham, Leah 284

Xiao Yang 193, 194

Yeltsin, Boris 125, 161, 340
Yemen 53, 56
Youngs, Richard 344
Yugoslavia 45, 127–30, 261, 296

Zaire 340
Zambia 44, 53, 56, 134, 192, 222
Zimbabwe 44, 53, 56, 264, 340, 348
Zoido-Lobatón, Pablo 6–8